101 Ways to Promote Your Web Site

Sixth Edition

Filled with Proven Internet Marketing Tips, Tools, Techniques, and Resources to Increase Your Web Site Traffic

Susan Sweeney

MAXIMUM PRESS
605 Silverthorn Road
Gulf Breeze, FL 32561
(850) 934-0819
www.maxpress.com

Publisher: Jim Hoskins

Manager of Finance/Administration: Joyce Reedy

Production Manager: Gina Cooke

Cover Designer: Lauren Smith

Copyeditor: Ellen Falk

Proofreader: Jacquie Wallace

Indexer: Susan Olason

Printer: P.A. Hutchison

This publication is designed to provide accurate and authoritative information in regard to the subject matter covered. It is sold with the understanding that the publisher is not engaged in rendering professional services. If legal, accounting, medical, psychological, or any other expert assistance is required, the services of a competent professional person should be sought. ADAPTED FROM A DECLARATION OF PRINCIPLES OF A JOINT COMMITTEE OF THE AMERICAN BAR ASSOCIATION AND PUBLISHERS.

Library of Congress Cataloging-in-Publication Data

Sweeney, Susan, 1956-
101 ways to promote your web site : filled with proven Internet marketing tips, tools, techniques, and resources to increase your web site traffic / Susan Sweeney.— 6th ed.
p. cm.
Includes index.
ISBN 1-931644-46-2
1. Internet marketing. 2. Web sites—Marketing. I. Title: One hundred one ways to promote your web site. II. Title: One hundred and one ways to promote your web site. III. Title.
HF5415.1265.S93 2006
658.8'72—dc22
2006007368

Acknowledgements

Many, many, many thanks to my great team at Verb Interactive (*http://www.verbinteractive.com*)—Ed Dorey and Andy MacLellan who have been with me since their university days, and our whole team of Internet marketing experts.

Thanks to Roula el-Diri for all the help with this edition of *101 Ways to Promote Your Web Site*.

The Internet is a fascinating, vast, and publicly accessible resource from which we can learn a great deal. I'd like to thank all those people who share their information so freely on the Net through such sites as Wilson Web (*www.wilsonweb.com*) by Dr. Ralph Wilson, SearchEngineWatch by Danny Sullivan, and newsletters such as I-Search by Detlev Johnson.

Many thanks to my large network of experts whom I know I can always call to get the latest scoop on what's really happening. Joe Mauro of *inBox360.com* and Ken Teeter of *nTarget.com* are always extremely knowledgeable and helpful in terms of ever-changing world of private mail list marketing.

Thanks to Jim Hoskins, Gina Cooke, and Joyce Reedy at Maximum Press. This is our tenth book together. It's always a pleasure to work with you. One of these days we're going to have to meet face to face!

Special thanks to my absolutely wonderful husband Miles, who makes all things possible. I wouldn't be able to do what I do if not for you. Also thanks to our three amazing children—Kaitlyn, Kara, and Andrew—for their love, encouragement, and support. Love you more than the last number!

Special thanks to mom and dad, Olga and Leonard Dooley, for always being there and for instilling in me the confidence to know that I can do anything to which I set my mind. It's amazing what can be done when you "know you can."

Disclaimer

products mentioned in this book. The manufacturer's product documentation should always be consulted, as the specifications and capabilities of computer hardware and software products are subject to frequent modification. The reader is solely responsible for the choice of computer hardware and software. All configurations and applications of computer hardware and software should be reviewed with the manufacturer's representatives prior to choosing or using any computer hardware and software.

Trademarks

The words contained in this text which are believed to be trademarked, service marked, or otherwise to hold proprietary rights have been designated as such by use of initial capitalization. No attempt has been made to designate as trademarked or service marked any personal computer words or terms in which proprietary rights might exist. Inclusion, exclusion, or definition of a word or term is not intended to affect, or to express judgment upon, the validity of legal status of any proprietary right which may be claimed for a specific word or term.

Your "Members Only" Web Site

The Internet world changes every day. That's why there is a companion Web site associated with this book. On this site you will find updates to the book and other Web site promotion resources of interest. However, you have to be a member of the "101 Ways Insiders Club" to gain access to this site.

When you purchased this book, you automatically became a member (in fact, that's the only way to join), so you now have full privileges. To get into the "Members Only" section of the companion Web site, go to the Maximum Press Web site located at *www.maxpress.com* and follow the links to the "101 Ways" area. From there you will see a link to the "101 Ways Insiders Club" section. When you try to enter, you will be asked for a user ID and password. Type in the following:

- For your user ID, enter: *1016e*

- For your password, enter: *sat*

You will then be granted full access to the "Members Only" area. Visit the site often and enjoy the updates and resources with our compliments—and thanks again for buying the book. We ask that you not share the user ID and password for this site with anyone else.

Susan Sweeney's Internet Marketing Mail List

You are also invited to join Susan Sweeney's Internet Marketing Bi-weekly Internet Marketing Tips, Tools, Techniques, and Resources Newsletter at *www.susansweeney.com.*

Table of Contents

Chapter 1:
Planning Your Web Site   **1**

The Fundamentals—Objectives, Target Markets, and
Products and Services 2
Common Objectives 3
   Advertising Your Products or Services Online 3
   Selling Your Products or Services Online 4
   Providing Online Customer Service or Support 4
   Providing Product or Corporate Information 4
   Creating and Establishing Company Identity or
     Brand Awareness 5
   Other Primary Objectives 5
Other Things to Consider up Front 6
   Designing Your Site to Be Search Engine Friendly 6
   Including Repeat Traffic Generators on Your Site 7
   Getting Visitors to Recommend Your Site 7
   Leveraging Your Sales Force 8
   Using Permission Marketing 8
   Creating Loyalty Among Visitors 8
   Including "Stickiness" Elements 9
A Final Word on Objectives 9
Target Markets 10
Products and Services 13
The Fundamentals 14
Using Competitor Sites to Your Advantage 14
Storyboarding Your Web Site 16
Internet Resources for Chapter 1 19

Chapter 2:
Your Site—From Storyboarding to Programming   **20**

Detailed Web Site Planning 21
Content Notes 22
Text Notes 22

Color Notes 23
Navigation Notes 23
Graphics Notes 25
Visual Notes 26
Other Notes 27
Internet Resources for Chapter 2 27

Chapter 3:
Web Site Elements That Keep 'Em Coming Back   28

Rationale for Encouraging Repeat Visits 29
Use a What's New Page for Repeat Visits 30
Free Stuff—Everyone Loves It 30
Give a Taste of Your Product with Sample Giveaways 31
Everyone Wants the Best Price—Coupons and Discounts 31
Specials and Promotions 33
A Calendar of Events Keeps Visitors Informed 34
Luring Customers with Contests and Competitions 34
Using Employment Opportunities to Increase Visitors 37
Creating Useful Links from Your Site 37
Providing a Featured Product or Tip of the Day/Week to
    Encourage Repeat Visits 38
Ensuring Your Site Gets Bookmarked 40
World Interaction with Bulletin Boards, Forums, Discussion Groups 40
Inviting Visitors to Contribute with Surveys 41
Encourage Repeat Visits with Your Site of the Day 41
Keep Them Happy with Cartoons 42
Benefiting from Humor with Jokes and Trivia 42
Who Doesn't Love Games? 43
Keep Customers in Touch with Update Reminders 43
Special Events Reminder Services/Gift Registry 43
Establish Yourself as an Expert with Advice Columns 45
MP3s/Podcasts 45
Distribution through RSS Feeds and Autoresponders 46
Internet Resources for Chapter 3 46

Chapter 4:
Spreading the Word with Viral Marketing   47

Capitalizing on Viral Marketing Opportunities 48
    Word of Mouth *48*
    Pass-It-On Viral Marketing *51*

E-Books 52
Small Utility Programs 52
Fun Videos 53
Digital Games 53
Checklists 53
Podcasts, MP3 or Audiozine 53
Articles 53
Product- or Service-Based Viral Marketing 54
The Hotmail Example 54
Blue Mountain—Taking Viral Marketing to the
Next Level 54
Virtual Postcards 55
Internet Resources for Chapter 4 56

Chapter 5:
Permission Marketing   57

Permission Marketing Explained 57
Uses of Permission Marketing 59
Legislation Regarding Permission-Based Marketing 60
Privacy Concerns 61
Personalization 61
Sell the Benefits 62
Data Mining 63
Cooperative Permission Marketing 63
Incentive-Based Permission Marketing 64
A Closing Comment on Permission Marketing 64
Internet Resources for Chapter 5 64

Chapter 6:
Designing Your Site to Be Search Engine Friendly   65

Methodology to Make Your Site Search Engine Friendly 66
Understanding Search Engines 66
Decide Which Search Engines Are Important 68
Learn the Search Engine Ranking Criteria 69
Keywords Are Critical 71
*Brainstorming, Surveying, and Reviewing Promotional
Material* 72
Review Competing and Industry-Leading Web Sites 73
Assess Your Web Site Traffic Logs 75
Keyword Suggestion and Evaluation Tools 75

Fine-Tuning Your Keyword Phrases 79
Assign Specific Keywords to Specific Pages 85
Title Tags—Use Descriptive Page Titles 86
Keywords Meta-Tag 88
Description Meta-Tag 90
Alt Tags 91
Hypertext Links 91
Domain Name and File names 92
Body Text—Header Tags and Page Copy 92
Headings—<H1>Header Tags</H1> 93
Page Copy 93
Spamming 94
Quality Guidelines—Basic Principles 98
Quality Guidelines—Specific Recommendations 98
Other Important Design Factors 99
Frames 100
Robots.txt, Meta-Robots Tag 101
Clean Code Is King 102
Navigation Techniques 102
Revisit Meta-Tag 102
Cascading Style Sheets (CSS) 102
Dynamic Pages and Special Characters 103
Splash Pages and the Use of Rich Media 103
Use of Tables 104
Custom Error Pages 104
Image Maps 105
Optimization for Search Localization 105
Monitoring Results 107
Internet Resources for Chapter 6 110

Chapter 7:
Search Engine and Directory Submissions   112

Submission Process 112
A Closer Look at Search Engines and Directories 113
Submitting to the Search Engines 116
Free Submissions 117
Paid Inclusion 117
Is Your Page Already Indexed? 118
Submitting to the Directories 118
Preparing your Directory Submission 119
Pay Careful Attention to Titles and Descriptions 121

Pay Careful Attention to All Fields on the
Submission Form 121
More Directory Submission Tips 122
Keep a Record of your Submissions 123
Effective Use of Submission Tools and Services 124
Complete Your Site Before You Submit 125
Get Multiple Listings 126
Some Final Pointers 126
Internet Resources for Chapter 7 127

Chapter 8:
Developing Your Pay-to-Play Strategy   128

Generating Targeted Traffic Using PPC Advertising 129
Exploring Google AdWords 130
How AdWords Works *131*
Where Do Your Ads Appear? *132*
Extending Your Reach with Yahoo! Search Marketing 132
How Yahoo! Search Marketing Works *133*
Where Do Your Ads Appear? *134*
Maximize Exposure with Contextual Advertising 135
Geo-Targeting Your Campaigns 136
Dayparting 136
Maximizing Your Exposure 137
Maximizing Your Budget 138
Internet Resources for Chapter 8 139

Chapter 9:
Utilizing Signature Files to Increase Web Site Traffic   140

Presenting Your e-Business Card 140
How to Develop Your Signature File 141
The Do's and Dont's of Signature Files 142
Sig Files to Bring Traffic to Your Web Site 144
Internet Resources for Chapter 9 147

Chapter 10:
The E-mail Advantage   148

Making the Connection 149
E-mail Program versus Mail List Software 149
Effective E-mail Messages 150

The Importance of Your E-mail Subject Line *150*
E-mail "To" and "From" Headings Allow You to Personalize *151*
Blind Carbon Copy (BCC) *151*
Effective E-mail Message Formatting *152*
A Call to Action *153*
Appropriate E-mail Reply Tips *154*
HTML or Text? *154*
Always Use Your Signature Files *154*
Discerning Use of Attachments *155*
Expressing Yourself with Emoticons and Shorthand 156
E-mail Marketing Tips 158
Include a Brochure and Personal Note *158*
Gather a Library of Responses *159*
Following Formalities with E-mail Netiquette 159
Reply Promptly *159*
Internet Resources for Chapter 10 160

Chapter 11:
Autoresponders
161

What Are Autoresponders? 161
Why Use Autoresponders? 162
Types of Autoresponders 163
Autoresponder Features 164
Personalization *164*
Multiple Responses *164*
Size of Message *164*
Tracking *164*
HTML Messaging *164*
Successful Marketing through Autoresponders 165
Internet Resources for Chapter 11 165

Chapter 12:
Effective Promotional Use of Newsgroups
167

Newsgroups—What Are They? 168
The Changing Face of Newsgroups 168
The Benefits of Newsgroups 169
Thousands of Newsgroup Categories 169
Target Appropriate Newsgroups 171
Read the FAQ Files and Abide by the Rules 171
Lurking for Potential Customers 172

Tips on Posting Messages 172
Tips to Ensure That Your Messages Are Well Received 173
Keep to the Newsgroup Topic 173
Stay on the Thread 174
Make a Contribution 174
Don't Post Commercials or Advertisements 174
You Don't Have to Have the Last Word 174
Newsgroup Advertising Hints 174
Cross-Posting and Spamming 175
Earning Respect with Newsgroup Netiquette 175
Internet Resources for Chapter 12 176

Chapter 13:
Effective Promotion Through Publicly Accessible
Mailing Lists   177

Connecting with Your Target Audience 177
Types of Publicly Accessible Mailing Lists 178
Moderated Discussion Lists 178
Unmoderated Discussion Lists 178
Targeting Appropriate Discussion Mailing Lists 179
Finding the Right Mailing List 180
Subscribing to Your Target Mailing Lists 181
List Digests 181
Composing Effective Messages 181
Building Your Own Private Mailing Lists 183
Starting Your Own Publicly Accessible Mailing List 183
Internet Resources for Chapter 13 184

Chapter 14:
Establishing Your Private Mailing List   185

Why Have Your Own Mailing List? 186
Permission-Based Marketing 186
Benefits of Private Mail Lists 188
The Issue of Privacy 189
Where We Need To Be 190
The Right Mail List Technology 190
Using Your E-mail Program 191
Using Mail List Software 191
Outsourcing Your Mail List 194
Building Your Database or Mail List 195

Promoting Your Private Mail List 197
Your Communication with Your Mail List 197
Stay Under the Spam Radar 199
Recent Legislation 202
Measure, Measure, Measure 204
Where to Go from Here 204
Internet Resources for Chapter 14 204

Chapter 15:
Effective Promotion Through Direct Mail Lists   206

How Direct Mail List Companies Work 206
How to Select a Direct Mail Company 207
How to Work with a Direct Mail List Company 208
Costs Related to Direct Mail List Marketing 209
Make the Most of Your Direct Mail List Marketing 210
Internet Resources for Chapter 15 211

Chapter 16:
Developing a Dynamite Link Strategy   212

Links Have an Impact 213
Links Have Staying Power 213
A Quick Talk about Outbound Links 214
Strategies for Finding Appropriate Link Sites 215
Explore These URLs 216
Tools to Identify Your Competitors' Links 218
Other Potential Link Strategies 219
Winning Approval for Potential Links 220
Making Your Link the Place to Click 223
To Add or Not to Add with Free-for-All Links 224
Add Value with Affiliate Programs 224
Maintaining a Marketing Log 225
A Word of Caution with Link Trading 225
Internet Resources for Chapter 16 226

Chapter 17:
Affiliate Programs   227

Affiliate Programs: Increase Traffic to Your Web Site 228
   Commission-Based Affiliate Programs 228
   Flat-Fee Referral Programs 228

Click-Through Programs 230
Selecting an Affiliate Program That Is Right for You 230
How to Succeed with Your Affiliate Site 230
Benefits of Creating an Affiliate Program 231
Purchasing Affiliate Software 232
Internet Resources for Chapter 17 234

Chapter 18:
Maximizing Promotion with Meta-Indexes — 235

What Are Meta-Indexes? 235
How to Find Appropriate Meta-Indexes 237
Enlisting Meta-Indexes for Optimal Exposure 239
Internet Resources for Chapter 18 241

Chapter 19:
Winning Awards, Cool Sites, and More — 242

It's an Honor Just to Be Nominated 243
Choosing Your Awards and Submitting to Win 244
What's Hot and What's Not in the Name of Cool 245
Posting Your Awards on Your Site 246
Becoming the Host of Your Own Awards Gala 246
Internet Resources for Chapter 19 247

Chapter 20:
Productive Online Advertising — 248

Expanding Your Exposure through Internet Advertising 249
Maximize Advertising with Your Objectives in Mind 251
Online Advertising Terminology 251
Banner Ads 251
Click-Throughs 252
Hits 252
Impressions or Page Views 252
CPM 252
Keywords 252
Geo-targeting 253
Jump on the Banner Wagon 253
Exploring Your Banner Ad Options 254
Banner Ad Tips 256

Interesting Banner Ads 257
Location, Location, Location 260
   Search Engines 260
   Content Sites 260
Banner Ad Price Factors 260
Considerations When Purchasing Your Banner Ad 261
Make Sure Visitors Can See Your Banner 262
Making It Easy with Online Advertising Networks 262
Bartering for Mutual Benefits with Banner Trading 263
Tips for Succeeding with Classified Ads 264
Form Lasting Advertising with Sponsorships 264
Commercial Links 265
Sponsoring a Mailing List 266
Online and Offline Promotion 267
Internet Resources for Chapter 20 267

Chapter 21:
Maximizing Media Relations

268

Managing Effective Public Relations 269
Benefits of Publicity Versus Advertising 269
What Is a News Release? 270
   Writing a News Release 270
      Notice of Release 270
      Header 271
      Headline 271
      City and Date.. 271
      The Body 272
      The Close 272
Advantages of Interactive News Releases 273
Sending News Releases on Your Own versus Using a
   Distribution Service 273
Golden Tips for News Release Distribution 276
   News Release Timing and Deadlines 277
      Monthly Magazines 277
      Daily Newspapers 277
      TV and Radio 277
Formatting Your E-mail News Release 277
What Is Considered Newsworthy 278
What Isn't Considered Newsworthy 279
Developing an Online Media Center for Public Relations 280

Internet Resources for Chapter 21 282

Chapter 22:
Increasing Traffic Through Online Publications 283

Appealing to Magazine Subscribers on the Net 284
What Exactly Are E-zines? 284
Web-Based E-zines 285
E-mail E-zines 285
Using E-zines as Marketing Tools 286
Finding Appropriate E-zines for Your Marketing Effort 286
The Multiple Advantages of E-zine Advertising 287
Guidelines for Your Advertising 288
Providing Articles and News Releases to E-zines 290
Reasons You Might Start Your Own E-zine 291
Developing Your Own E-zine 292
Internet Resources for Chapter 22 294

Chapter 23:
Web Rings as a Promotion Tool 295

An Effective Alternative to Search Engines and Directories 296
What Are Web Rings? 296
How Do Web Rings Work? 298
How to Participate in Web Rings 298
Web Ring Participation Costs 299
The Benefits of Web Rings 299
Business Reluctance to Participate in Web Rings 300
Other Marketing Opportunities Provided by
    Web Rings 301
Internet Resources for Chapter 23 301

Chapter 24:
Landing Pages 302

What Is a Landing Page? 302
Considerations for Landing Page Content 304
Testing Your Landing Page 305
    Landing Page Content 306
    Landing Page Layout and Presentation 306
Internet Resources for Chapter 24 308

Chapter 25:
Really Simple Syndication
309

What Is RSS? 309
How Does RSS Work? 310
RSS Content Options 310
Benefits of RSS.. 313
How to Promote Your RSS Content 314
Getting the Most out of Your RSS 314
Internet Resources for Chapter 25 316

Chapter 26:
Blogs
317

What Is a Blog?.. 317
How Do I Put a Blog on My Site? 318
To Blog or Not to Blog?.. 319
    Pros and Cons of Blogging 319
Promote Your Blog 320
Resources for Chapter 26 321

Chapter 27:
Podcasting
322

What Is Podcasting? 322
Podcast Mechanics 323
Podcast Content... 324
Promoting Your Podcast 325
Internet Resources for Chapter 27 327

Chapter 28:
Mobile Marketing
328

What Is Mobile Marketing?.. 328
Benefits of Mobile Marketing 329
Internet Resources for Chapter 28 331

Chapter 29:
The Power of Partnering
332

Ideal Partner Sites 332

Partnering Opportunities 333
Internet Resources for Chapter 29 335

Chapter 30:
Grand Opening Tips for Your Web Site
Virtual Launch   336

Launching and Announcing Your Web Site 336
Your Web Site Virtual Launch 337
Internet Resources for Chapter 30 338

Chapter 31:
Effective Offline Promotion   339

Offline Promotion Objectives 339
URL Exposure through Corporate Literature and Material 340
URL Exposure through Promotional Items 341
URL Exposure through Clothing 343
URL Exposure on Novelty Items 344
Promotion with a Touch of Creativity 344
URL Exposure on Your Products 345
Internet Resources for Chapter 31 345

Chapter 32:
Web Traffic Analysis   346

Do You Know Who Is Visiting Your Web Site? 347
Using Log Files to Your Advantage 347
Analyzing Log Files with Web Traffic Analysis Software 348
Developing a Profile of Your Visitors 348
Which Pages Are Popular and Which Pages Are Not? 350
Find Out How Each Visitor Found Your Site 350
Identifying Your Target Market 353
Find Out What Forms of Online Promotion Work for Your Site ... 353
How Do You Get Web Traffic Analysis Software for Your Site? ... 353
Internet Resources for Chapter 32 354

Chapter 33:
Web Metrics   355

Measuring Your Online Success 356
What to Measure 357

Conversion Ratio (CR) 358
Sales per Visitor (SPV) 358
Cost per Visitor (CPV) 359
Cost per Sale (CPS) 359
Net Profit per Sale (NPPS) 359
Return on Investment (ROI) 360
Web Analytics—The Next Generation 360
Internet Resources for Chapter 33 361

About the Author 363

1

Planning Your Web Site

With millions of Web sites competing for viewers, how do you get the results you're looking for? When asked if they are marketing on the Internet, many people say, "Yes, we have a Web site." However, having a Web site and marketing on the Internet are two very different things. Yes, usually you need a Web site to market on the Internet. However, a Web site is simply a collection of documents, images, and other electronic files that are publicly accessible across the Internet. Your site should be designed to meet your online objectives and should be developed with your target market in mind. Internet marketing encompasses all the steps you take to reach your target market online, attract visitors to your Web site, encourage them to buy your products or services, and make them want to come back for more.

Having a Web site is great, but it is meaningless if nobody knows about it. Just as having a brilliantly designed product brochure does you little good if it sits in your sales manager's desk drawer, a Web site does you little good if your target market isn't visiting it. It is the goal of this book to help you take your Web site out of the desk drawer, into the spotlight, and into the hands of your target market. You will learn how to formulate an Internet marketing strategy in keeping with your objectives, your product or service, and your target market. This chapter provides you with an overview of this book and introduces the importance of:

- Defining your online objectives

- Defining your target market and developing your Web site and online marketing strategy with them in mind

- Developing the Internet marketing strategy that is appropriate for your product or service.

The Fundamentals—Objectives, Target Markets, and Products and Services

Things have changed dramatically over the past several years in terms of Web site design and development methodology. Back in the olden days—a couple of years ago in Internet years—it was quite acceptable, and the norm, for an organization to pack up all of its brochures, ads, direct-mail pieces, news releases, and other marketing materials in a box, drop it off at the Web developer's office, and after a short conversation ask when they might expect the Web site to be "done." The Web developer would then take the marketing materials and digitize some, scan some, and do some HTML programming to develop the site. By going through this process, organizations ended up with "brochureware." Brochureware is no longer acceptable on the Web if you want to be successful. Sites that are successful today are ones that are designed around the:

- Objectives of the organization

- Needs, wants, and expectations of the target markets

- Products and services that are being offered.

Everything related to Internet marketing revolves around these three things—objectives, target markets, and products or services. It is critically important to define these things appropriately and discuss them with your Web developer. It is your responsibility, not your Web developer's, to define these things. You know (or should know) what your objectives are more clearly than your Web developer. If you don't articulate these objectives and discuss them with your Web developer, it is impossible for him or her to build a site to achieve your objectives!

You know your target market better than your Web developer. You know what your buyers want, what they base their buying decisions on, and what their expectations are. You need to provide this information so that your Web developer can build a Web site that meets the needs, wants, and expectations of your target market.

Let's spend the remainder of the chapter on these fundamentals—objectives, target markets, and products and services—so you can be better prepared for the planning process for your Web site.

Common Objectives

Before you even start to create your Web site, you must clearly define your online objectives. What is the purpose of your site? Brainstorm with all parts of your organization, from the frontline clerks, to marketing and sales personnel, to customer support, to order fulfillment and administration. Generate a list of primary and secondary objectives. Every element of your site should relate back to your objectives. When you decide to update, add, or change any elements on your Web site, examine how these changes relate to the primary and secondary objectives you have identified. If there is not a clear match between your objectives and your intended changes, you might want to reconsider the changes. It's amazing how many Web sites have been developed without adequate planning or without ensuring that the Web site ties in with the corporate objectives.

Some of the most common primary objectives include:

- Advertising your product or service

- Selling your product or service

- Providing customer service and product support

- Providing product or corporate information

- Creating and establishing company identity or brand awareness.

Advertising Your Products or Services Online

The objective of some sites is simply to advertise but not directly sell an event, product, or service. A prime example of this is a movie studio that develops a Web site to promote a "soon-to-be-released" movie. The objective is to create awareness or a "buzz" about the movie, generate interest in the film, and, ultimately, have a large number of people attend the movie when it is released. This type of site might include multimedia clips of the movie, pictures and stories of the actors in the movie, viral marketing ("Tell a friend about this movie") elements to encourage word-of-mouth marketing, an intriguing story about the film, press releases for entertainment writers, and other elements to help them achieve their objective with their target market in mind.

Selling Your Products or Services Online

Selling products or services online is a common objective. The Internet provides a broad geographic reach and a huge demographic reach. Often businesses combine the objectives of advertising their products or services with trying to sell them through their Web site. This works well because visitors are not only given information about your products and services, but they are given the option of easily ordering and purchasing online. The easier you make it for people to make a purchase from your company, the more likely they are to buy. You will have to provide detailed information on your products and services, your return policies, guarantees and warranties, and shipping options. If you are planning to sell directly from the site, you also need to address security issues.

Providing Online Customer Service or Support

You might decide that the main reason for your business to have an online presence is to provide more comprehensive customer service and support. A great benefit of a Web site is that you can provide customer assistance 24 hours a day, 7 days a week, 365 days a year. If your company develops software, it is a good idea to include downloadable upgrades as well as an FAQ (Frequently Asked Questions) section where you can provide solutions to common problems. By providing an easy way for your customers to solve their problems, you increase customer loyalty. Include the appropriate contact information for customers who have more complicated problems and need to talk to a human. There are even companies that you can outsource this to if you are a single person operation. See *http://www.patlive.com/signup/ssc* for a great deal I have negotiated for my e-club members.

Providing Product or Corporate Information

Some organizations simply wish to provide information on their products or services to a particular target market. Others might want to provide corporate information to potential investors. Information-driven Web sites tend to be text-oriented, with graphics used only to accentuate the points being made and to provide visual examples. These types of sites usually have an FAQ section that provides useful and pertinent information on the company and its products or services. If the organization courts the media, it might include a Media Center, which can include all its press releases, corporate background, information on key company officials, articles that have been written about the company, and a gallery of relevant pictures that the media can use, as well as a direct link to the company's media person.

Creating and Establishing Company Identity or Brand Awareness

Another objective might be to create and establish company identity or brand awareness. To "brand" your product, a memorable name and an eye-appealing product logo are necessities. Also, the graphics developed for your Web site must be top-notch and reflect the colors associated with the product logo. A catchy slogan further promotes brand identity. The same branding techniques are also applicable to establishing corporate identity. If building and reinforcing corporate and brand identity is important to you, your Web site must have a consistent look and feel. Likewise, all offline promotional campaigns and materials must be consistent with your online presence.

Based on the success of companies such as America Online, Yahoo!, Travelocity, Amazon, and eBay, it is apparent that branding a company or product on the Web can occur swiftly. It is amazing how quickly these relative newcomers to the business world have achieved megabrand status. Although they all had significant financial resources, each company used a combination of online and offline advertising to meet its objectives. Each of the sites features a prominent logo, consistent imagery, and a consistent color scheme. Check out the sites of these upstarts that have become big online players if branding is your goal. There is a lot we can learn from them.

Other Primary Objectives

Brainstorm with all the stakeholders in your organization to come up with other primary objectives for the organization. This process is critical to the organization's online success. Everything else revolves around your objectives—the elements included on your site and the Internet marketing techniques you use. If you were building new office space, you would want to include the input of all people working in your office to ensure that their needs were taken into consideration and the office was designed appropriately. The same is true when building a Web site—everyone must be included in the brainstorming session.

As much time should be spent in the planning stage as in the construction phase. By going through this process, you will be able to develop the best blueprint for your proposed Web site.

Other Things to Consider up Front

Although setting your primary objectives is vital, it is just as important to identify your secondary objectives. By setting appropriate secondary objectives, you will be more prepared to achieve all of your online goals. Many companies identify only primary objectives for their Web site and completely neglect secondary objectives that can help them succeed online. If you're going to build a Web site, you might as well build it to achieve all of your objectives. Following are some common secondary objectives for online businesses to consider:

- The site should be designed to be search engine friendly.

- The site should be designed to encourage repeat traffic.

- The site should have viral marketing elements that encourage visitors to recommend your products or services to others.

- The site should include elements to leverage its sales force.

- The site should incorporate permission marketing, where visitors are encouraged to give you permission to send them e-mail on a regular basis.

- The site should be designed to encourage customer loyalty.

- The site should incorporate stickiness, encouraging visitors to stay a while and visit many areas of the site.

Designing Your Site to Be Search Engine Friendly

Creating a site that is search engine friendly should be an objective of every company that wants to do business on the Internet. Search engines are the most common way for Internet surfers to search for something on the Net. In fact, 85 percent of all people who use the Internet use search engines as their primary way to look for information. By using keywords relating to your company in appropriate places on your site, you can improve how search engines rank you. You want these chosen keywords in the domain name if possible, your page titles and page text, your Alt tags for graphics, and your page headers and keyword meta-tags as well as in each page's description meta-tag. Many search engines place a lot of emphasis on the number and quality of links to a site to determine its ranking. This means that the more Web sites you can get to link to your site, the higher your site is shown in search engine results. (See Chapter 6 for more information on designing your site for high search engine ranking.)

Including Repeat Traffic Generators on Your Site

Every Web site should be designed to entice its visitors to return again and again. No matter if the primary objective of your Web site is to sell your products and services or to create brand awareness, generating repeat traffic to your Web site helps you achieve these goals. Generating repeat traffic to your site is a key element of your online success and can be accomplished in numerous ways. Using contests and competitions, as well as games, advice columns, and many other techniques, can increase your Web traffic. Chapter 3 describes many of these repeat traffic generators in much more detail.

Getting Visitors to Recommend Your Site

The best exposure your Web site can get is to be recommended by a friend or unbiased third party. It is critical that you try to have elements of your Web site recommended as often as possible; therefore, you should have a way for people to quickly and easily tell someone about elements on your site. The best way to encourage people to recommend your site is to include viral marketing techniques such as a "Tell a Friend" button on your site. You might want to include some variations on this as well. Under articles or press releases, you can have an "E-mail this article to a friend" button for people to refer their friends and associates to your site. Virtual postcards are also a good way to get people to send more people to your Web site. There are many ways to encourage viral marketing. These are discussed in detail in Chapter 4.

Leveraging Your Sales Force

If your objectives include trying to sell your products, you might want to leverage your sales force by making use of an affiliate or associate program. Affiliate programs once again use the advantage of having your site recommended to create traffic to your site. The difference is that an affiliate program is more formal than just having your site recommended by site visitors. Most affiliate programs involve having a contractual agreement, having specific links placed on the affiliate's site to yours or in the affiliate's outbound marketing, and having software to track where your traffic is coming from so that you can compute and send referral fees to your affiliates as they are earned. The contract usually states the compensation you will pay to your affiliates for the sales they produce. This is one more way to have other people working to build traffic to your Web site. (See Chapter 17 for details on affiliate or associate programs.)

Using Permission Marketing

You always want your company to be seen as upholding the highest ethical standards and being in compliance with anti-spam legislation, so it is important not to send out unsolicited e-mail—known as spam—promoting your company or its products. This is why it's important to develop a mailing list of people who have given you permission to send them messages, including company news and promotions. When you're developing your Web site, an objective should be to get as many visitors to your site as possible to give you their e-mail address and permission to be included in your mailings. You can do this by having numerous ways for your visitors to sign up to join your e-club and to receive newsletters, notices of changes to your Web site, coupons, or new giveaways. Chapter 3 has many examples of ways to encourage visitors to request to be added to your e-mail list and Chapter 5 provides all the details on permission marketing.

Creating Loyalty among Visitors

The way to create loyalty among visitors is to provide them with some incentives for joining your online community and provide them with proof that you really appreciate their business. You can do this by having a members-only section of your Web site or an e-club that has special offers for them as well as discounts or freebies. When people sign up to join your e-club, you can ask for their e-mail address and permission to send them e-mails regarding company or product promotions and news. People like to do business with people who appreciate their business. We are seeing a real growth in loyalty programs online.

Including "Stickiness" Elements

To get your target market to visit your site often and have them visit a number of pages every time they visit, you need to provide interesting, interactive, and relevant content. You want to have your site visitors feel as if they are part of your online community and to want to make your site one of the sites they visit every day. You create "stickiness" by including many elements that keep your visitors' attention and adding new content on a regular basis. Your site can have a daily advice column, descriptions of your many products, a discussion forum with constantly changing interesting conversations relative to your products, a news section that is updated daily, as well as a weekly contest that site visitors can enter. The combination of these elements makes a site sticky. You want your site to be a resource people return to often and not a one-time event.

A Final Word on Objectives

Setting your Web site's objectives before you begin building your site is essential so that you can convey to your Web developer what you want your Web site to achieve. You obviously will have a number of different objectives for your site, but many of these objectives can work together to make your Web site complete.

Whatever your objectives might be, you must carefully consider how best to incorporate elements in your Web site and your Internet marketing strategy to help you achieve them. Successful marketing on the Web is not a simple undertaking. Before you begin to brainstorm over the objectives of your Web site, be certain you have read and studied all the information that is pertinent to the market you are attempting to enter. Read everything you can find, and examine the findings of industry experts.

Your Web site objectives form a critical element in your Web site design and development, as you will see in the next chapter on Web site design and development methodology.

Target Markets

It is important to define every one of your target markets. If you're going to build this Web site, you might as well build it for all of your target markets. For each and every one of your target markets, you need to determine:

- Their needs

- Their wants

- Their expectations.

For each and every one of your target markets, you should also try to determine an appropriate "WOW" factor. What can you provide for them on your Web site that will WOW them? Your objective should be to exceed the target market's expectations.

Your main target market might be your potential customer, but other target markets might include existing customers, or the media, or those who influence the buying decision for your potential customers, associates, or affiliates.

When you look at—really look at—potential customers versus existing customers, you realize that what these two groups want and need from your Web site are probably different. Someone who is an existing customer knows your company. Your products, your business practices, and the like, are not a priority for this person on your site. A potential customer needs these things before giving you that first order. "Customer" is such a huge target market; it needs to be broken down into segments. Every business is different. If you were a hotel, for example, your customer target market might be broken down further into:

- Business travelers

- Vacation travelers

- Family travelers

- Meeting planners

- Handicapped travelers

- Tour operators

- Groups.

You get the idea. You need to segment your customer target market and then, for each segment, you need to do an analysis of needs, wants, and expectations. If the media is part of your target market, make sure you plan to have a media center, or if you want to reach potential investors, make sure you have an investor relations page.

If you intend to market children's products, your Web site should be colorful and the text simple and easy to understand, in keeping with what appeals to your target market. Chances are, fun-looking graphics will be used extensively on your site to draw children further into it (see Figure 1.1). If you market financial services, your Web site requires a more professional approach. Your graphics must provide a clean appearance, and the text should be informative and written in a business-like fashion (see Figure 1.2). As this example demonstrates, the content and tone of your site must be tailored to your target market. After all, this is the best way to attract the attention of the people who are interested in purchasing your product or service.

Another aspect to consider when designing your Web site is your target market's propensity to utilize the latest technologies and the configuration they are likely to be using. An online business that markets custom, streaming multimedia presentations expects its clientele to be technically inclined. These clients are more likely to have the latest software, advanced Web browser technologies, and faster machines.

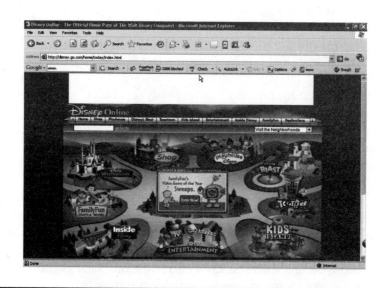

Figure 1.1. Web sites designed to appeal to children include fun, colorful images.

Figure 1.2. A business-oriented site incorporates informative text and a clean, magazine-style layout.

On the other hand, clients of a vendor that sells gardening supplies online might be less likely to have fully embraced the latest technologies. Most people looking for these products are connecting from home rather than from their workplace. They might still have a dial-up connection to the Internet, slower machines, and older software. They might still be using the Web browser that was originally installed on their system, simply because they are uncomfortable downloading the latest version of the browser, are unaware of the more recent version, or are uninterested in downloading a large file. If your target market includes this demographic, be careful with your use of Java, Flash, and large graphic files.

What does this mean for developing and designing your Web site? Well, streaming multimedia developers can design their Web sites with more graphics and dynamic multimedia effects because their clients expect to be impressed when they visit the developer's site. If vendors of gardening supplies designed their sites similarly, many of their clients might be alienated because the site would be too slow to load and might include elements inaccessible to them. They might take their business elsewhere. The gardening supplies site requires a more basic design with less concentration on large graphics and multimedia effects and more focus on presenting information.

Products and Services

It is important to define the products and services you want to promote online. Sometimes the products and services you offer offline in your physical store are the same as in your online store, but quite often there are differences.

Business owners that have a bricks-and-mortar location sometimes assume that their online storefront is an extension of their offline storefront and that they will provide exactly the same products and services online as offline. In some cases, fewer products are offered online than in the physical store. This is often the case if you are test marketing, but also if some of the products you sell in your physical location are not appropriate for online sales because of competitive pricing or shipping logistics.

In other cases, your online store might offer more products or services than the bricks-and-mortar location. For example, your offline bookstore might not offer shipping or gift wrapping. If your online bookstore does not offer these services, you will lose a lot of business to your online competition. When a site's product offerings include items that are appropriate for gift giving, it is essential to also offer wrapping, customized cards, shipping to multiple addresses, and shipping options. The consumer is "king" and is very demanding. You have to meet and beat your consumers' expectations online to garner market share. People shopping for gifts online are looking for convenience, and the site that provides the greatest convenience and the greatest products at the lowest prices will be the winner.

Web sites and Internet marketing strategies differ depending on the product or service being sold. A company that markets toys has to develop a fun and interactive Web site that is attractive to children. The Web site should also give children a way to tell their friends about the site as well as a reason to return to the site. The toy company might want to offer an electronic postcard service whereby children can send a colorful and musical message to their friends and tell them about the site.

Another idea is to provide a "wish list" service. Children can make a list of the toys they want, and this list is sent to their parents via e-mail. The parents can then make better-informed purchasing decisions and might become loyal to the toy company's site. Likewise, some toy companies offer reminder services that send an e-mail message to visitors who have registered and have completed the appropriate questionnaire to remind them of a child's birthday and to offer suggestions for gift ideas. Once again, this promotes sales and repeat traffic and increases customer loyalty.

As another example, a software development company might want to provide downloadable demo versions of its software products and allow people to review its products for a specified period of time before they make a purchasing decision.

A travel agency's Web site might include features such as an opt-in mailing list to send people information on weekly vacation specials or a page on the site detailing the latest specials. The travel agency's site might also want to include downloadable or streaming video tours of vacation resorts to entice visitors to buy resort vacation packages. Another idea is to have a system in place to help customers book vacations, rent cars, and check for available flights. The travel agency might also want to store customer profiles so they can track where particular customers like to sit on the plane, the type of hotel room they usually book, and their credit card information to make bookings more efficient for the customer and the agency.

If you are marketing a service online, it is difficult to visually depict what your service is all about. Visitors to your site need some reassurance that the service you are selling them is legitimate and valuable. Therefore, you might wish to include a page on your site that lists testimonials from well-known customers. This gives prospective customers more confidence about purchasing your service.

The Fundamentals

Once you have clearly defined your online objectives, your target markets, and the products or services you want to promote online, you are ready to move on to the next phase of planning your Web site—doing your competitive analysis.

Using Competitor Sites to Your Advantage

One of your Web site's objectives is to always meet and beat the competition in terms of search engine rankings and Web site content. To do so, you must understand exactly what it is your competition is doing. Take the time to research competitors and compare them on an element-by-element basis.

There are a number of ways you can identify your competition online. You can find your competition by conducting searches with the appropriate keywords, seeing which competing Web sites rank highly in the major search engines and directories. Similarly, there are many other online resources you can use to research your competition, including industry-specific Web portals and directories.

Once you have gathered a list of competing Web sites, analyze them element by element to determine which Web elements your competitors include on their sites and how their sites compare to one another. You want to look at what types of content they are providing to your target market. Other components you should analyze include the visual appeal of your competitors' sites, content, ease of navigation, search engine friendliness, interactivity, and Web site stickiness—or what they do to keep people on their site. This information can provide you with details on what you need to incorporate into your site to meet and beat the competition.

You have to realize that your online competition is different from your offline competition. Online, you are competing with all organizations that have an online presence and sell the same products and services you do. When doing your competitive analysis online, you want to select the "best of breed"—those fantastic Web sites of organizations selling the same products and services you do—no matter where they are physically located.

When we do a competitive analysis for clients, we reverse-engineer (or dissect) the competing Web site from a number of different perspectives. Generally, you will choose five or six of the absolute best competing Web sites. Then you start to build a database using Excel or a table in Word.

Start with the first competing Web site, and from your review start to add database elements to the first column. Note any types of content, target markets defined, repeat traffic techniques used, viral marketing techniques used, search engine friendliness features used (you'll get these in Chapter 6), download time for different types of Internet connections, cross-platform compatibility, cross-browser compatibility, innovative elements, etc. When you have dissected the first competing Web site and have noted appropriate database elements for comparative purposes, move on to the second competing Web site. Go through the same process, adding only different or new elements to what you already have in your database. Continue building the first column of your database by continuing through all the sites you want to include in your competitive analysis.

The next step is to develop a column for each of the sites you want to include in the competitive analysis. Then add two more columns—one for your existing Web site to see how your site stacks against the competition and the second for future planning purposes.

The next step is to go back and compare each site against the criteria for column 1, noting appropriate comments. For content information, you want to note whether the particular site has the specific content and how well it was presented. For download speeds, note specific minutes and seconds for each type of connection. A free tool to help you with this element can be found at:

- BizLand Download Time Checker *(http://www.bizland.com/product/sitedoctor.html)*

For each repeat traffic generator, you may choose to include details or just Yes/No. Continue with this process until you have completed the database, including your own existing site.

By this time, you should have a good feel for users' experiences when they visit your competitors' sites. Now you are ready to do your planning. In the last column of your database, review each of the elements in the first column, review your notes in your competitive analysis, and, where appropriate, complete the last column by categorizing each of the elements as one of the following:

- A—Need to have; essential, critical element; can't live without

- B—Nice to have if it doesn't cost too much

- C—Don't need; don't want at any price.

Now you have done your competitive analysis. Having completed identification of your objectives, target markets, products and services, and your competitive analysis, you are ready to develop your storyboard or architectural plan or blueprint for your site.

Storyboarding Your Web Site

Next you are ready to visualize and plan your Web site—integrate your objectives, your target market information, the findings of the competitive analysis, and your own ideas as well as those of others. This is done through the process of storyboarding. The storyboard is the foundation of your Web site. Consider it the architectural plan or blueprint of your site. It should show you, on paper, the first draft of the content and layout of your site. It gives you the chance to review the layout and make changes before development begins.

A Web site storyboard can be thought of much like a hierarchical organizational chart in a business. In a typical business structure, the executives sit on top, followed by their subordinates, and so on. Figures 1.3 and 1.4 are examples of two modified sections of a storyboard layout developed by our office for a client prior to building a Web site. Think of your Web site storyboard like this: You begin with your main page or home page at the top. Under the main page you have your central navigation bar. Each of the navigation options should

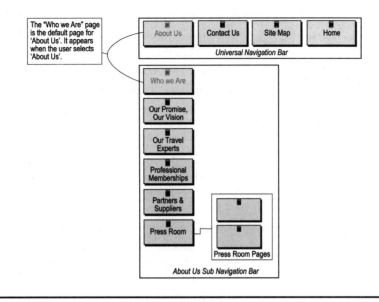

Figure 1.3. A sample layout of a home page and the main site components.

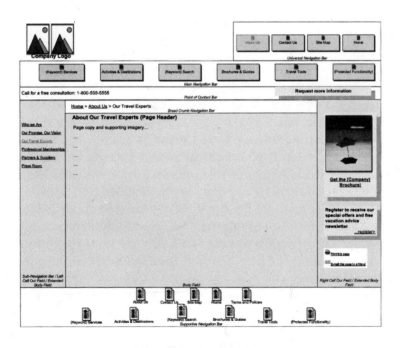

Figure 1.4. A sample layout of a subsection and the details included within.

be available on each page, regardless of where the user is on your site. Within each of the sections listed on your main navigation bar, you're going to have subsections, and so on.

The storyboard can be created with a software program like Microsoft Visio, with sheets of paper, or with any other mechanism. Quite often when we begin storyboarding a project for a client, we'll start with yellow sticky notes on a wall. Very low tech, but it works! It is very easy to get a visual of the navigation structure and easy to fill in the content pages (one per sticky note) in the appropriate places. It is also very easy to edit—simply move a sticky from one section to another or add another sticky note for a new page.

Once your first draft is done, you need to go back and review the proposed Web site against each and every one of your objectives, each and every one of your target markets (needs, wants, expectations, WOW factor), and each and every one of your products and services. You need to review the proposed Web site from the competitive analysis viewpoint. Have you included all the must-haves and left an opportunity for the elements that fit into the would-be-nice category? Will the proposed Web site beat the competition? Review the proposed site with your stakeholders and a few members of your target market. Get feedback from your various target markets and fine-tune the blueprint until you've got it right. It is easy (and cheap) at this stage to add new content and change the layout.

When developing your storyboard, remember to keep the layout of your site simple and logical, as this is how it will be laid out for users once the site is completed. Do not move forward with the Web development process until you have finalized the layout of the storyboard, ensuring that the site will be easy for your target audience to use and that it provides all the elements you need to achieve your objectives. Review your storyboard to ensure that all of the target markets have been addressed. If you want to address the media, be sure to include a Media Center. If you want to attract potential investors, be sure to include a comprehensive investor relations section. Give consideration to viral and permission marketing elements that can be included on your site and where they can best be positioned. We discuss these elements in depth in later chapters.

Once you have the completed and approved storyboard, it becomes the blueprint for construction of your site. You are now ready to move on to the actual construction. The next chapter discusses some of the content and design elements of your site.

Quite often these days, the Web development is done in two phases. The first phase is storyboard development. Only after the storyboard is developed is a Web developer really in a position to quote you a price on the Web development phase. Many people will pay a fee for the storyboard and then send the storyboard out to several reputable firms to request a proposal on development of their Web site.

Internet Resources for Chapter 1

I have developed a great library of online resources for you to check out regarding Web site design and development in the Resources section of my Web site at *http://www.susansweeney.com/resources.html*. There you can find additional tips, tools, techniques, and resources.

I have also developed a seminar on this topic which can be taken at any time over the Internet, can be taken live over the Internet at a scheduled time, or can be purchased as a seminar on CD. See *http://www.susansweeney.com/store.html*.

2

Your Site—From Storyboarding to Programming

Your storyboard is the blueprint for your site, but there are many steps to take before you can start construction. In Web development, the majority of the time should be spent in the planning. In this chapter we cover:

- Detailed planning of your site before a line of code is ever written

- Content guidelines

- Text guidelines

- Color guidelines

- Navigation guidelines

- Graphics guidelines

- Visual guidelines

- Other guidelines.

Detailed Web Site Planning

In the previous chapter you learned how to develop your storyboard. The storyboard is your blueprint for the site, but now you need to think about construction. For each page of your site, you need to develop the specific content—the specific text and the specific graphics for each page of your site.

Generally you (yes, you) will develop the first draft of the text for each page. You know your target market best—you know what makes them buy, you know what they want, you know the buzz words for your industry far better than your Web developer.

The next step is to have this text reviewed and edited by an online copywriter. Online copywriters usually have a background in advertising, where they learn to get the message across in as few words as possible. They know how to grab the reader's attention and get them to do what you want them to do. Internet users don't want to read pages and pages—they want to get what they're looking for quickly. The text should be short, to the point, and written so it can be easily scanned.

Once the online copywriter has done his or her magic, you will review and approve. You want to make sure that only the form—not the substance—has been changed.

The next step is to have the content reviewed and edited by an Internet marketer—someone who has expertise in search engines and their ranking criteria as well as repeat traffic generators and viral and permission marketing. The Internet marketer will review and edit the text and graphics—again, making sure that the keywords are used in the appropriate places for high search engine ranking. There is a real science to this. The keyword assigned to a particular page should be used appropriately in the page title, the text throughout the page, the meta-tags for keyword and description, the headers, the Alt tags, and the comments tags.

The Internet marketer usually develops the content for these tags, titles, and headers at this point. Sometimes the Internet marketing is handled by your Web developer's team and sometimes it is a separate outsourced activity. You'll learn more about designing your site to be search engine friendly in Chapter 6.

The Internet marketer also ensures that you have used the appropriate repeat traffic generators (see Chapter 3), appropriate permission marketing techniques (see Chapter 5), and appropriate viral marketing techniques (see Chapter 4). Again, you need to review and approve the changes to make sure your message is still presented appropriately for your target market.

The next step is graphic design. Sometimes the graphic designer is part of your Web development team and sometimes this activity is outsourced. The graphic designer develops the "look and feel" for your site—the navigation bar, the background, and the separator bars. The graphic designer knows that your online and offline corporate identity should be consistent. Again, you review and approve the graphic design.

Once all this is done, and everything has been reviewed and approved, you are ready for the programming to start.

Content Notes

Make your contact information readily available. Consider including contact information on every page. This includes your address, phone and fax numbers, and especially your e-mail address. Make it easy for people to get in touch with you.

Avoid "Under Construction" pages on your site; they are of no value to the visitor. When you have information, post it. Until then, don't mention it. "Under Construction" can actually hinder your search engine placement with some of the popular search engines and directories.

Include security information. Explain to your customers when transactions or exchanges of information on your Web site are secure. This is important if your site will be accepting credit card orders.

Include your privacy policy. Tell people how their personal information (e.g., their name, e-mail address, etc.) will and will not be used. This makes visitors more comfortable submitting inquiries to your site or joining your mail list.

Minimize use of background sounds and autoplay sounds. Some people surf the Web from their office at work and wish to discreetly go from one site to the next. Background sounds and sounds that load automatically can compromise their discreetness. Give your visitors the option of listening to a sound, but do not force it upon them.

Text Notes

The tone of your text and the design of your graphics conveys your intended image. When determining the text content of your site, be mindful of the fact that your own biases may preclude you from placing information on your site that is second nature to you, but important for your visitors. Review all text content on your site to ensure that you have not omitted anything crucial. Better yet, have your target market review and provide feedback—sometimes you are too close to the forest to see the trees.

Also, keep text brief. Almost 80 percent of Web users scan text online as opposed to actually reading it. Therefore, make your key points quickly and succinctly, and use lots of bulleted lists, headers, and horizontal rules to create visual breaks in the content. This keeps visitors interested enough to read the information on your site. If they are faced with huge blocks of text, most visitors are overwhelmed by the quantity of the information and are too intimidated to read your message. Write for scannability.

Don't set your text size too small, as this is too hard to read. But don't set it too large, as this looks like you are shouting. Also, avoid using ALL CAPS, WHICH ALSO COMES ACROSS AS SHOUTING.

Color Notes

Keep your online and offline images consistent. Be consistent with your use of logos, corporate colors, and other marketing collateral associated with your company.

Choose your background and font colors carefully. Using backgrounds that are too busy obscure your text and do not provide a pleasant viewing experience for your visitors. Only certain colors show up properly on certain backgrounds. A light background with dark text is easiest on the eyes. Most sites these days opt for a clear white background.

Use the default colors for links whenever possible. Blue text usually indicates an unvisited link. Purple, maroon, or darker blue usually represents a link you have visited, and red is the color of an active link. It should not be difficult for visitors to identify your links. If you decide not to use the default colors, your links should be emphasized in a consistent manner through font size, font style, or underlines.

Navigation Notes

Ease of navigation is very important to your site. In a consistent location on every page, provide a navigation bar that links to all of the major pages of your site. Make it easy to get from one page to any other. Search engines can index any page from your site, so your home page might not be the first page visitors come to. Never have dead ends where viewers scroll down a screen or two of information only to find that they must scroll all the way back to the top to move on (because you have no links at the bottom of the page). A consistent-looking and well-positioned navigation bar with functioning links is the key to efficient site navigation.

Your visitors should be able to get anywhere they want to go on your site in three clicks or fewer. Develop an effective navigation bar as previously described. For very large sites (i.e., sites consisting of more than eight to ten major sections), it is a good idea to include a site map that users can access from any page in your site. Site maps, as shown in Figures 2.1 and 2.2, are usually text-based lists that name all of the site's pages and their content. Site maps make it easy for users to access the information they are looking for without causing them much frustration. Include a link from your main navigation bar to the site map for the easiest possible reference. Site maps are great for submission to the search engines as they provide links to every page of your Web site, ensuring, as much as possible, that every page of your site gets included in the search engines' database.

An additional feature you might wish to include is an internal search tool. This allows users to enter their query and have all relevant matches returned, based on their query. This is a particularly useful feature if you sell many products directly on your Web site or if your site contains many pages of content. It

Figure 2.1. *LA Times's* site map.

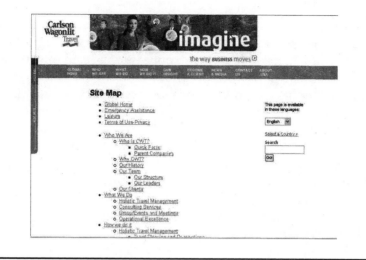

Figure 2.2. Carlson Wagonlit's site map.

allows the user to quickly search for the desired item or information using the product's name or a relevant keyword. Intel, the computer chip manufacturer, operates multiple sites and offers many products and services. To help users locate the information they're looking for, Intel has integrated a useful search tool. Keep the design of your site consistent. Font types, headers, footers, navigational bars, buttons, bullets, colors, and so on, should be consistent throughout the site to maintain a polished, professional look.

Graphics Notes

Graphics that take too much time to download can cause visitors to leave your site before they get a chance to see it. The combined size of the text and graphics on any Web page should not exceed 50 KB.

Some people turn graphics off in their browsers to save time, so you should provide all of your information in text as well as graphics. Use descriptive **Alt attributes** in your image tags. The Alt text will load in place of the images when the graphic does not display for any reason. Visitors who choose not to browse with graphics turned on will have an easier time navigating your site. Also, Alt text is spidered and indexed by many of the major search engines. Using keywords

Alt attributes
Descriptive text associated with respective images on a Web site.

in your Alt text in your image tags will improve your ranking in search engines and will provide a description of the images in the event that they are not loaded.

Use thumbnail graphics where applicable. When you have a page with a lot of large images (e.g., an online photo collection), create small "thumbnail" versions of each image and give visitors the option of clicking through to the larger versions. This is far superior to making your visitors wait for a series of large images to load.

You should be careful with your use of image maps as well. Image maps are large graphics with clickable "hot spots." Image maps typically are used for navigation and usually have text embedded in the graphic. Search engines cannot read text embedded in a graphic, so from the standpoint of search engine friendliness, if you use image maps always ensure that you provide your appropriate text and Alt tags for the search engine.

Very often, when a large graphic is used for an image map, visitors must wait for the entire image to load before it is apparent where they must click to begin navigating a site. Instead of using a large image map, break the image into smaller images so that visitors receive faster feedback from your site without having to wait for a huge graphic to load. Also, always provide an alternate text link navigation system to assist people who surf with their graphics turned off.

It amazes me how often I see Flash intros as the home page for a Web site. The Flash intros are basically videos and the search engines have a difficult time indexing them as there is no text on the page, no Alt tags, no meta-tags, no headers, nor any of the other elements in the search engine ranking formula.

Visual Notes

Check your site using different browsers. What viewers see when your site is downloaded depends on what browser they are using. Different browsers display the same Web site differently. Before you post your site online, check your site with the most popular browsers. You might want to check your Web traffic analysis to see what browsers your Web site visitors are using.

Also make sure that you review your site on both a Mac and a PC, as sometimes your Web site looks different depending on the platform.

Design your site for various screen widths. Try to accommodate visitors regardless of the screen resolution they use. Some Web users still run their systems at 640 pixels by 480 pixels; keep this in mind when designing your site. Use your Web traffic analysis software to determine the screen resolution preferences of your visitors. See Chapter 32 for more information on Web traffic analysis software and the reports you can access.

Your Web site should steer clear of scrolling marquee text. Scrolling marquees are difficult to read and are not compatible with all browsers. Simply post text directly on your pages if you have something important to say.

Other Notes

Your **home page** should be 50 KB or less and should be displayed on no more than one or two screens. Studies have shown that visitors rarely wait beyond 15 seconds to download a site. Test the download time of your site using different connection speeds to ensure that it is reasonable for all users.

Home Page
The main page of a Web site.

Also avoid dead links. These are links that don't go anywhere and the viewer usually receives a "404—File not Found" error message from the Web server after clicking on a dead link. Ideally you can designate your site map, if you have one, as the default page rather than a "404—File not Found" error message. Verify periodically that all your links are still active.

Internet Resources for Chapter 2

I have developed a great library of online resources for you to check out regarding Web site review in the Resources section of my Web site at *http://www.susansweeney.com/resources.html*. There you can find additional tips, tools, techniques, and resources.

I have also developed a seminar on this topic which can be taken at any time over the Internet, can be taken live over the Internet at a scheduled time, or can be purchased as a seminar on CD. See *http://www.susansweeney.com/store.html*.

3

Web Site Elements That Keep 'Em Coming Back

There are many little things that will spice up your Web site to "keep 'em coming back." Learn the tips, tools, and techniques to get visitors to return to your site again and again. In this chapter, we cover:

- Attractive Web site content

- How to have your own What's New page, Tip of the Day, and Awards page

- Ensuring that you are bookmarked

- Cartoons, contests, jokes, and trivia

- Calendar of events and reminder services

- Blogs, Podcasts, and RSS feeds

- Online chat sessions, workshops, forums, and discussion groups

- Special guests or celebrity appearances

- Giveaways, awards, and surveys

- Offline tactics for promotion.

Rationale for Encouraging Repeat Visits

Just as you would want customers to visit your place of business frequently, so too in cyberspace you want present and potential customers to visit often. The more often people visit your site, the more likely they are to purchase something. You want to ensure that the techniques you use to get repeat traffic are appropriate for your target market. For example, if you were having a contest on your site targeted toward children, you would not want to give away a bread-maker as the prize. That would be fine, however, if your target market is families or homemakers. You want to offer something of interest to the market you are targeting. If your target is business professionals, then something along the lines of the latest pocket PC that they could use in their everyday business would be appropriate. If your target market is skiers, then a weekend in Vail might work. You should always remember your objectives when doing any form of online marketing, because you don't want to do something inappropriate that might drive your target audience away from your site.

I am a big proponent of leveraging everything you do for maximum marketing results. Almost every repeat traffic generator provides an opportunity for permission marketing and also for viral marketing. Make sure you review the repeat traffic generators you use on your site and incorporate the appropriate permission and viral marketing elements.

The more often a person visits your site:

- The more your brand is reinforced

- The more your target markets feels a part of your community, and people do business with people they know and trust

- The more likely they are to give you permission to stay in touch

- The more likely they are to tell others about you

- The more likely you will be first in mind when they go to buy your types of products or services.

Use a What's New Page for Repeat Visits

A What's New page can mean different things to different sites. For some, this page updates users with summaries of the most recent product or service offerings. Your What's New page should be accessible from your home page so that when people visit your site they do not have to search through your entire site to find out what is new. If visitors repeatedly find interesting additions in the What's New section, they will come back to your site on a regular basis to check out what's new. Without this, they might visit and search through your site and find that nothing is new and they just wasted 20 minutes looking for anything new. Here you can leverage this repeat-traffic generator with permission marketing by asking if visitors would like to be notified via e-mail when you've added something to the What's New section. It's all about getting their permission to send them e-mail and therefore include them in your community.

Other approaches for the What's New page could be What's New in your industry, What's New on your site, What's New in your company, What's New in your location, or What's New in your product line. Whatever it is, you should always make sure that it is of interest to your target market. Again, you can ask your visitors if they would like to be notified when updates are made to this section of your Web site. This once again gives you permission to e-mail them and present them with new information that might make them want to come back to your site again.

Free Stuff—Everyone Loves It

Giving things away is a great way to increase traffic—everybody likes a freebie. If you give away something different (and valuable to your target market) each week, you are sure to have a steady stream of repeat traffic. When you have freebies or giveaways on your site, your pages can also be listed and linked from the many sites on the Internet that list places where people can receive free stuff. To find these listings of free stuff, simply go to a search engine and do a search on "Free Stuff Index" or "Free Stuff Links." You will be amazed at how many people are giving things away online.

You don't have to give something away to everyone. You could simply have a drawing every week. You could then ask entrants if they would like you to notify them of the winner, which again gives you permission to e-mail them.

If you want to bring only people from your target market to your site, then don't give away mainstream items as screen savers, shareware games, utilities, and so on. Try to give away something that only people interested in your industry would want. If you don't care what traffic comes your way, and any traffic is good traffic, then give away useful things that everybody needs. Try to have your logo and URL displayed on the item. For example, a neat screen saver can be made that displays your logo and URL. When this is made available as a download, there are no handling or shipping charges associated with it. If your freebie is something that has your URL on it and is something that is generally kept around a computer, it reminds and encourages people to visit your site. A mouse pad displaying your URL is a good example.

You should change your freebie often and let your site visitors know how often you do this. Something like "We change our free offer every single week! Keep checking back" or "Click here to be notified by e-mail when we update" also works well.

Freebies provide ideal viral marketing opportunities as well. Have a "Tell a friend about this" button near the freebie so site visitors can quickly and easily tell their friends.

Give a Taste of Your Product with Sample Giveaways

Use a traditional marketing approach and give away free samples of your product from your Web site. After giving away the samples, follow up with an e-mail. Ask the people who received a sample what they thought of it, if they had any problems, and if they have any questions. Direct the samplers back to your Web site for more information and discounts on purchasing the regular version of the product. If you have a number of products, you might consider alternating your free samples. Ask if visitors would like to be notified by e-mail when you change your free sample. This gives you permission to e-mail the visitors on a regular basis to remind them about the sample. You also get to update them with new information regarding your Web site, your products, or your company. This can entice them to visit your site again. Make sure you include your signature file in your e-mail message.

Free samples also provide a great viral marketing opportunity.

Everyone Wants the Best Price—Coupons and Discounts

Offer coupons and discount vouchers that can be printed from your site. You can change the coupon daily or weekly to encourage repeat visits. People will come back to your site again and again if they know they can find good deals there. This is a great strategy to use in conjunction with a free sample giveaway. If people liked the sample, give them a coupon to purchase the regular version at a discount. If they like the regular version, they may purchase it again at full price or recommend the product to a friend. You can also ask people if they want to be notified by e-mail when you update the coupons on your Web site. This once again gives you the opportunity to present them with new information about your business. Offering coupons is a great idea if you have a physical location as well as a Web site. These can be your loss leader to get customers to come into your store.

You can develop a coupon banner ad that links to your site, where the coupon can be printed. The banner ads should be placed on sites frequented by your target market. You can trade coupons with noncompeting sites that target the same market you do; your coupon on their site links to your site, and their coupon on your site links to their site.

By offering coupons from your Web site, you also cut down your overhead cost because people are printing the coupons on their own printers, thus not using your paper. Remember that you should have terms and conditions on the coupons that are available for printing. For example, you should have an expiration date. Someone could print a coupon, then visit your store in a year and try to use it. You should try to have the expiration date close to the release of the coupon. This will create some urgency, enticing the visitor to use the coupon more quickly and then come back for more coupons.

We are seeing an increase in the number of coupon-related sites that are appearing on the Internet. CoolSavings.com (*http://www. coolsavings.com*) is an online coupon network where businesses can advertise and place coupons for their products and services, as seen in Figure 3.1. Sites like this are a good way to promote your business, for they receive a high amount of traffic. Another benefit is that the traffic is already in a buying mood. CoolSavings.com has been a household name since it launched its national advertising campaign in the late 1990s. If you offer coupons from your site, it benefits you to be listed on these types of sites. If you are not aiming for a national appeal, you should search to find out if there are coupon networks in the geographic location that you are targeting. Other coupon sites are listed in the Internet Resources section at the end of this chapter. There are meta-indexes to sites with coupons or discounts from which you can be linked for greater exposure.

Coupons provide ideal viral marketing opportunities—for example, "Send this coupon to a friend."

Figure 3.1. CoolSavings.com offers coupons from businesses to people all over the USA.

Specials and Promotions

Everyone likes to get a deal. You might consider having a special promotions section on your Web site. You'll want to change your promotion fairly frequently and let your site visitors know: "We change our specials every week. Bookmark our site and keep checking back!"

You might employ permission marketing here as well: "We change our specials every week. Click here if you'd like to be notified when we update" or "Click here to join our e-club and receive our e-zine, advance notice of deals, member only e-specials, and other great stuff every week." If you send e-specials via e-mail, make sure you give viewers a reason to visit your site and provide the appropriate hypertext links in the e-mail.

Make it easy to have your site visitors tell their friends about your specials. Have a "Tell a friend about this special" button placed next to each one of your special promotions. You can leverage the viral marketing with an incentive: "Tell three friends about our special and be included in a drawing for [something appropriate for your target market]."

A Calendar of Events Keeps Visitors Informed

A comprehensive, current calendar of events related to your company or your industry can encourage repeat visits. Your calendar should always be kept up to date and be of value to your readers. A calendar of events for a band might show its scheduled appearances. A calendar of events of what is going on in your business community is very appropriate for a Chamber of Commerce or Board of Trade site. This can encourage a lot of repeat traffic as long as the calendar is kept current and complete. Calendars of events are also appropriate on community sites, because residents access these calendars often to stay current. Again, you can ask people if they'd like to be notified via e-mail when you update your calendar of events.

If you have a great calendar of events, you can encourage others to use it by providing a link to it from their Web site. This offer works well because it is win/win—you are providing them with great content that is kept current and they are providing you with traffic.

If you don't have the time or inclination to develop your own calendar of events but one would be great content for your site, you might provide a link from your Web site to a calendar you consider top-notch. If you do this, make sure your link opens a new browser window rather than taking the visitor from your site to the referred site.

Luring Customers with Contests and Competitions

Contests and competitions are great traffic builders. Some sites hold regular contests on a weekly or monthly basis to generate repeat visitors. Holding contests is also a great way to find out about your target market by requesting information on the entry form.

What type of contest you hold depends upon your Internet marketing objectives. If you want to attract as many people as possible to your site regardless of who they are, then offer items such as money, trips, cars, computers, and so on, as in Figures 3.2. If you want to attract potential customers from your target market, then give away something that relates to your products and industry.

You can simply request that people fill out an electronic ballot to enter the contest. If you want to find out something about the people entering, ask them to answer an appropriate question or two. If you want to do some market research, again, ask a question or two. Make it easy and unobtrusive. The more fields they have to fill out, the fewer people will enter your contest. Be selective with the questions you ask.

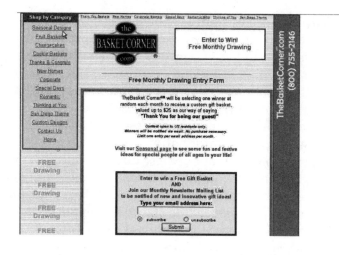

Figure 3.2.   Contests are a great way to encourage repeat traffic.

If the prize is one of your products, consider asking entrants to write a short note outlining why they would like to have the product you are giving away. You can award the winner(s) with the product and follow up with the other entrants. These people might be in a position to buy your products, and you will have gained some valuable knowledge from the notes submitted.

If your product is appropriate for a prize that would be of interest to many different types of people, consider finding contest sites that are willing to offer your product as the prize on their site. This can generate brand awareness for your product. You can have the site show a picture of your product with a link to your site. The contest site should be more than happy to do this because you are offering to give something for free that adds value to that site.

You can turn a contest into a competition. If your Web site relates to cooking or baking, ask entrants to submit their best recipe using your food product. People will visit your site to see the winning recipes, and you might get some ideas for future marketing efforts. Other competitions might include things such as best photo with product X, best short story about product X, best drawing of product X, and so on. This creates better brand awareness and reinforces sales of your product. The closer the contest relates to your product, the better. Instead of offering just one prize, offer a number of smaller prizes as well. This makes the odds look better and people feel they have a better chance of winning.

You might have contestants answer three questions relating to your product or service on the entry form. Of course, to find the answers to the questions, the visitor has to visit a number of pages on your site, and the three questions are marketing related.

You can have the contest one where you get information about your target market. When contestants enter the contest, have them rank what influences their buying decision. The information you request can also provide you with demographic or psychographic information.

Allow site visitors to enter your contest often. It boggles my mind when I see these contests that limit the number of times a visitor can enter their contest. The objective of the contest is to get visitors back to your site on a regular basis! I'd suggest that to accomplish this objective it might be more appropriate to tell your Web site visitors to "Enter today! Enter often!" "Bookmark this site—The more times you enter the more chances you have to win!"

You might consider changing the information on the contest Web page around the entry form on a regular basis. Create Web site stickiness by providing links to other areas of your site—perhaps to other repeat-traffic generators such as your coupons or your e-specials.

Whatever type of contest you determine best meets your marketing objectives, be sure you encourage permission marketing ("Click here to be notified when we have a new contest") and viral marketing ("Tell a friend about this great contest"). Leverage, leverage, leverage: "Tell five friends and receive an extra ballot for yourself."

Make your contest conditional: "Sign up to receive our weekly e-specials and be included in our drawing for [something of interest to your target market]."

Before you go ahead with holding any kind of contest, find out if any legal issues concern you. There may be restrictions that you are not aware of (e.g., you might be required to purchase a legal permit to hold lotteries). You should also remember to ask the entrants the e-mail address at which they want to be notified of the winner. This, again, grants you permission to e-mail them to tell them who the winner was, and also to inform them of the specials that you might have at your site that month.

You want to promote your contest through public and private mail list postings, newsgroup postings, your e-mail signature file, press releases, and links from contest sites. Some popular contest sites you might want to be listed on include:

- The Sweepstakes Wire *(http://www.sweepstakes.bz)*

- Contest Hound *(http://www.contesthound.com)*

- About Contests *(http://contests.about.com)*

- Contests and Sweepstakes Directory *(http://www.sweepstakes-contests.com)*

- Winning Ways Online Sweeps *(http://www.onlinesweeps.com)*.

It always amazes me when I see an online contest where the winner is announced only on the Web site. What a missed opportunity! If your product or service is part of the prize, the people who entered the contest have identified themselves as your target market interested in receiving your product or service. Don't let them get away! As much as contest owners might like to think that all the people who entered the contest are anxiously awaiting the date the contest ends (perhaps they have even put a reminder in their scheduler) and the winner is announced so that they can beat a path back to your site to see if they were the winner—it's not going to happen! To take full advantage of having the contest and achieving your objectives, you want to send an e-mail to all contest participants notifying them of the winner and, in the same e-mail, offer them the contest prize at a discount only available to the contest entrants for a limited time or for the first 20 respondents. In the same e-mail you want to also tell them about your new contest and provide a link back to the new contest entry form.

Using Employment Opportunities to Increase Visitors

People involved in a job search or interested in new job opportunities will revisit your site occasionally to see your list of available positions.

Creating Useful Links from Your Site

Provide visitors with links to other sites similar to yours or a meta-index of links that would be of interest to your target market (see Figure 3.3). Do not put outbound links on your home page. Place them down a level or two after the visitors have seen all the information you want them to see before you provide the links away from your site. Links can be incorporated in two ways. The first is where clicking the link loads the new page in the same browser

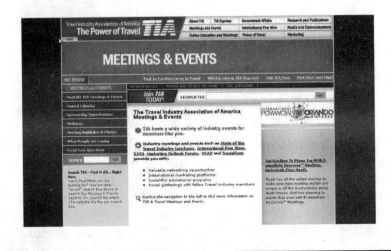

Figure 3.3.   The Travel Industry Association of America provides useful links for travel industry professionals from its site.

window. (It replaces the content of your page with the content of the linked page.) The second and preferred method is to have the link open a new browser window. (Your page stays where it is and the content from the linked page opens up in the new browser window.) This is preferred because once visitors are finished with the new page, they can close the new browser window and your page is still there in the "old" browser window. Try exchanging links with others so you receive a link from their site to your site. As long as the links are of value to your visitors, people will come back to use your resource.

You might consider asking visitors if they are interested in being notified when you update your list of links or just make updates to your site in general. By offering this, if they choose to do so, you have the opportunity to send people an e-mail message and remind them about your site while presenting them with new information about what might be going on with your site.

Providing a Featured Product or Tip of the Day/Week to Encourage Repeat Visits

Have a section that offers cool tips that relate to your business, your products or services, or your target market, as in Figure 3.4. These tips can be from one sentence to one paragraph long. In the example shown in Figure 3.4, WCI

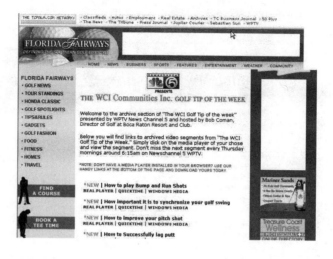

Figure 3.4. WCI's Golf Tip of the Week. Tips of the day or tips of the week can encourage repeat visitors.

provides a golf tip of the week. This golf tip is provided as a video clip. You can be guaranteed that golfers will return to this site on a regular basis to view the video golf tip.

If visitors find your advice helpful, they will return repeatedly to see what interesting piece of information you have displayed that day. Ask your visitors if they would be interested in receiving the tip via e-mail or if they would like to be notified when the tip has been updated so they can then visit your Web site. Encourage people to send the tip to a friend. You can also encourage others to use your tip on their Web site as long as they provide a link back to your site as the source. You can go a step further and syndicate your content, putting it up on appropriate sites to be accessed and available by anyone looking for content for their newsletter, e-zines, or Web sites. You can also make it available to other sites by way of an RSS feed (see Chapter 25 on RSS feeds).

All of these techniques work equally well for a featured section on your site. What is featured will be different for different Web sites.

This technique has been used very effectively by a number of businesses—golf tip of the week by golf courses, featured product of the week by many retailers, featured destination of the week by travel agencies or destination marketing organizations, fitness training tip of the week by fitness clubs, fishing tip of the week for fishing camps. There are as many options for tips and featured sections as there are businesses.

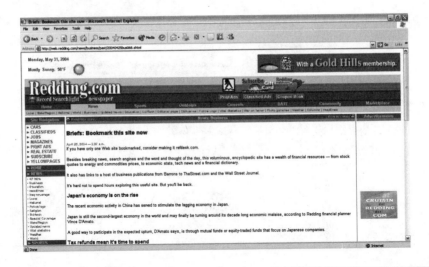

Figure 3.5. When you see a "Bookmark this site now!" or "Bookmark us!" call to action, nine times out of ten you will at least consider it.

Ensuring Your Site Gets Bookmarked

Encourage visitors to add you to their bookmark list. At appropriate parts of your site, display the call to action "Bookmark me now!" (see Figure 3.5). A call to action is often effective—it's amazing how often people do what they are told to do! Make sure the title of the page that has the "Bookmark me now!" clearly identifies your site and its contents in an enticing way, because the title is what appears in the bookmark file as a description. Whenever I see "Bookmark this site now!" I always consider it. Sometimes I do and sometimes I don't, but I always consider it. Often, when the call to action is not presented, I don't think about it and don't bookmark it. Then, days later when I want to go back there, I wish I had remembered to bookmark it.

World Interaction with Bulletin Boards, Forums, Discussion Groups

It can be very satisfying to see people join in from all over the world just to interact with each other on a topic that relates to your Web site. Beware, however, that you will have to keep an eye on the messages and may even have to play referee occasionally.

Inviting Visitors to Contribute with Surveys

Performing surveys is a way to increase the traffic to your site. For people to want to fill out the survey and see the results, the survey topic must be interesting. To encourage input, consider having the survey results available to participants only. Your survey could be on a topic concerning current events or something pertaining to your industry. The more controversial or debatable the topic of the survey, the more people will visit to contribute or see the results. If you want to draw a very targeted audience, pick a topic that is of interest to that market alone.

In performing these surveys, you are building repeat traffic and you are gathering valuable information on your market. If you hold an interesting survey every week or every month, then you will retain a loyal audience of repeat visitors. If your surveys are newsworthy, then you can send out press releases to publicize the results and gain publicity for your site.

Your surveys should be short and to the point. Let people know why you are asking them to do the survey and the submission deadline. Make your questions clear and concise. The responses should be Yes/No or multiple choice. When reporting the results, don't just put them on your Web page; post the results to newsgroups and mailing lists that would be interested. Don't forget to add your signature file. If you are holding weekly or monthly surveys, let people know via your signature file what the next survey topic will be and that there is more information on your Web site.

Again, ask people if they'd like to be notified of survey results, either by e-mail or by prior notification as to when the results will be posted on the site. You might also ask if they'd like to be notified when you are conducting a new survey.

There are many Web-based software tools available at a very reasonable price online.

Encourage Repeat Visits with Your Site of the Day

Having your own Site of the Day or Site of the Week listing means a great deal of work, searching the Internet for a cool site to add or looking through all the submissions. However, if your picks are interesting to your audience, you might find that avid Internet users come back every day to see what great new site is listed. Remember that this must be updated on schedule; displaying a week-old Site of the Day reflects poorly on your site and your company. For more information, see Chapter 19 about hosting your own award site.

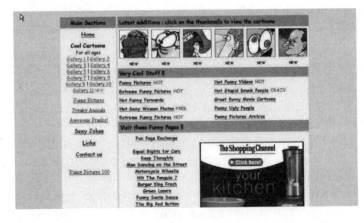

Figure 3.6. The Cartoons4fun site offers amusing cartoons to its viewers and has an e-mail list that informs its visitors when a new cartoon is posted on the site.

Keep Them Happy with Cartoons

Displaying relevant cartoons keeps your site dynamic and fun. You do not necessarily have to create all of the content and features yourself. If you update this weekly, ask if visitors would like to be notified via e-mail when you update your Web site. A good example of a site that uses cartoons is the Myke Ashley-Cooper Cartoons4Fun site (*http://www.cartoons4fun.com/c4f.shtml*), which continuously provides humor to its viewers (see Figure 3.6). Cartoons provide a great viral marketing opportunity.

As with all elements on your site, before you decide to include this type of element, make sure it is appropriate content to help you achieve your objectives with your target market.

Benefiting from Humor with Jokes and Trivia

"Laughter is the best medicine" and could prove to be a popular feature of your Web site. People enjoy trivia, or a Thought of the Day, and there are many sources available. Be sure to update regularly. Again, this gives you the opportunity to ask if your visitors would like to be notified when you update this section of your Web site and offers a viral marketing opportunity as well. Always make sure that whatever you include as content on your Web site is appropriate given your objectives and target market.

Figure 3.7. Station.com has many games for its users to enjoy.

Who Doesn't Love Games?

More and more sites are featuring fun activities and games. Again, your content must be appropriate given your objectives and target markets. (A sample game site is shown in Figure 3.7.) Just about anything goes here. You can host anything from a Star Wars trivia contest to having guests play an interactive game with other visitors. Allow visitors an easy way to "Tell a friend" about your game.

Keep Customers in Touch with Update Reminders

Ask visitors to your site if they would like to be notified when there are updates or content changes to your pages. This is similar to a mailing list except that you write to the "list" only when changes have been made. This is effective when you have a newsletter or a frequently visited calendar of events on your site.

Special Events Reminder Services/Gift Registry

People can sign up to be reminded of something via e-mail on specified dates (see Figure 3.8). This feature was originally thought of by a florist to remind

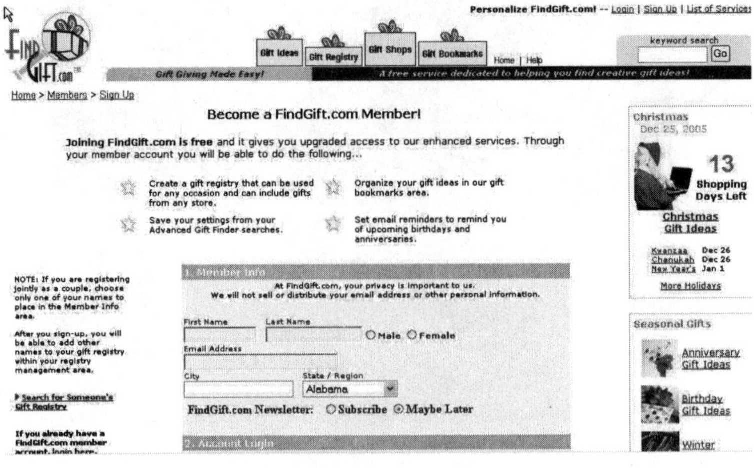

Figure 3.8.   FindGift.com has a reminder service where you can register to receive e-mail reminders for special dates.

people about important dates. You can remind people about any number of things relating to your business. If you own a site that sells fishing and hunting gear, you could get visitors to sign up to be reminded when certain fishing or hunting seasons start. You should try to develop a reminder service that relates to something that you sell from your site. In your reminder you can include suggestions about what fishing fly works best at this time of the year.

Reminder services are becoming very popular with retail sites. Their services are very much appreciated by busy people who are not good with remembering dates. This has saved me on more than one occasion and made it very easy to purchase from the site that provided the reminder. I have five nieces and nephews across the country. I have registered their birthdays with a site that also asked for some details about the reminder—things like what the date is, the relationship that I have with the person, their ages, things they enjoy, and how far ahead of time I want to be notified. Like clockwork, ten days prior to Ryan's birthday, I got this e-mail: "Susan, your nephew Ryan's birthday is in 10 days. He will be 13 years old. Ryan likes PlayStation video games. We happen to have several that might be appropriate as a gift for Ryan. Click here for more details."

I am then able to choose the gift that I want to purchase, the paper I want it wrapped with, and the text that I want on the card that will be attached to the gift. Then I simply provide the address I want it sent to and give them my credit card number, and they send it off. Everyone is happy—especially me.

You might consider adding a gift registry to your site if it is appropriate given your products or services and given your target markets. I have seen a number of interesting registry elements lately incorporated into sites. It is very appropriate for gift sites, toy stores, and many retailers. I have recently seen a Honeymoon Registry on several travel agency sites.

Establish Yourself as an Expert with Advice Columns

Some Web sites are incorporating advice columns. People will return again and again to read the e-mails asking for advice and to see the responses that are given. This also helps perpetuate an image of your company as an expert in your given field.

MP3s/Podcasts

Many information entrepreneurs and other sites are incorporating downloadable audio content and adding new content on a regular basis to encourage repeat visitors. This is appropriate for any sites that have a newsletter that provides educational content. My site would be very appropriate. I have an Internet marketing newsletter that regularly provides Internet marketing tips, tools, techniques, and resources on all kinds of different topics. I could choose to record these tips and make them available as a downloadable MP3 for those interested in listening to the content rather than reading it. Check out my site (*http:// www.susansweeney.com*) to see if I've done it and let me know of any topics you'd like to see covered this way.

This is very appropriate for all kinds of sites. Think about your products or services and your target market to come up with ideas for content that would be appropriately delivered in this format.

This is becoming very popular because people like to download and listen to this type of content at their own convenience; they can do an hour of Internet marketing training while working out, or sitting on the beach, or riding the subway, or traveling by air.

If you plan to do this on a regular basis, you will want to let people know on your Web site that you have new downloads available every week, every two weeks, or every month depending on how often you are prepared to develop these. Leverage it with permission marketing by asking them if they'd like to receive an e-mail when you have new downloads available.

Once you have developed audio downloads, you might want to make them available and downloadable through a number of the online podcast directories like Podcast.net (*http://www.podcast.net*). See chapter 27 for more details on Podcasting.

Distribution through RSS Feeds and Autoresponders

Many of the repeat traffic generators we have discussed in this chapter can be provided to others for their information by way of autoresponders (see Chapter 11 on Autoresponders) or to be used as content on their Web sites by way of an RSS feed (see Chapter 25 on RSS feeds for more details).

Internet Resources for Chapter 3

I have developed a great library of online resources for you to check out regarding repeat-traffic generators in the Resources section of my Web site at *http://www.susansweeney.com/resources.html*. There you can find additional tips, tools, techniques, and resources.

I have also developed a seminar on this topic which can be taken at any time over the Internet, can be taken live over the Internet at a scheduled time, or can be purchased as a seminar on CD. See *http://www.susansweeney.com/store.html*.

4

Spreading the Word with Viral Marketing

Have you ever visited a Web site and found an article, a coupon, a special, or something else that impressed you so much that you immediately sent an e-mail to your friends about it? If you have, you've already been bitten by the viral marketing bug! Viral marketing, which is often referred to as "word-of-mouse" marketing, is a low-cost, highly effective way to market your product or service using the Internet. Just like a flu virus in humans, viral marketing replicates and propagates itself online. Viral marketing enables you to capitalize on referrals from an unbiased third party—the consumer! The power that peers and reference groups have over the purchasing decision is phenomenal. Similar to how a positive testimonial from a reliable source can add credibility to a product or service, the opinions of friends, business associates, and family can also help influence a consumer's purchasing decision. By implementing various viral marketing techniques on your Web site, you are provided with a dynamite opportunity to leverage the opinions of the consumers' reference groups. In this chapter, we will cover:

- How you can use viral marketing to increase traffic

- Word-of-mouth viral marketing

    - Pass-it-on viral marketing

- Tell-a-friend scripts

• Various ways to leverage your viral marketing campaigns

• Incentives to encourage viral marketing.

Capitalizing on Viral Marketing Opportunities

Viral marketing can be one of your most powerful online marketing techniques, using the power of associations to spread the word. Viral marketing is still evolving, but today we see three common forms being used:

1. Word of mouth—such as "Tell a friend," "Send this coupon to a friend," or "Recommend this to a friend"

2. Pass it on—when we receive an e-book, cool tool, or funny or branded video and then forward it to friends

3. Product or service based—when a free tool is used online and that tool includes an embedded marketing message, such as Hotmail.

Word of Mouth

You can use viral marketing techniques in a number of different ways throughout your Web site. By placing a "Tell a friend about this product" or "Share this information with a friend" button on your site, you enable users to quickly and easily spread the word about your site and your products. Visitors can click on the button, provide appropriate information in the "To" and "From" fields (including name and e-mail address of both the recipient and the sender), and a brief message. Although the message is personalized, your business can include additional information about the product, including features, benefits, the price, and a link directly to the page where the recipient can purchase the item. Because the message is personalized from a friend, the recipient is more apt to open the e-mail and visit the site to find out more about the product than he or she would be if the e-mail came from a traditional corporate e-mail campaign.

Amazon.com (see Figure 4.1) is a prime example of a company that has implemented viral marketing features throughout its site. When visitors browse

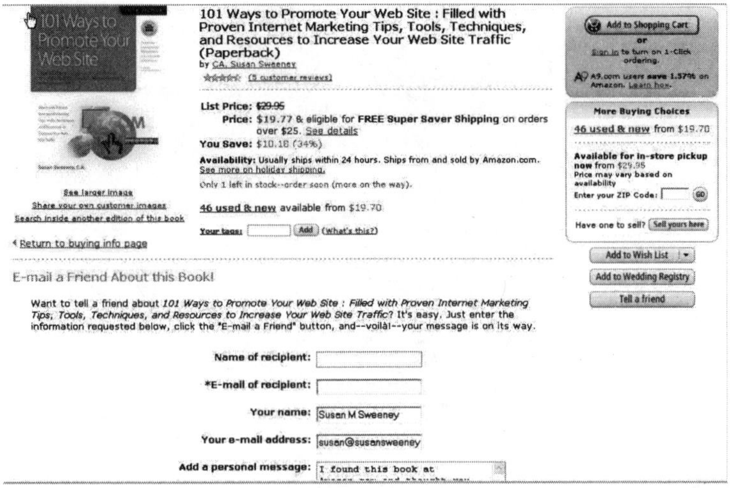

Figure 4.1. Amazon.com leverages the opinions of its customers by incorporating a "Tell a friend about this product" option for all of the products on the Web site.

through Amazon.com's three million plus product listings, they are always presented with the opportunity to "Tell a friend about this product." Providing this feature leverages the effectiveness of the Amazon.com Web site and ultimately results in increased sales for the company.

In addition to the aforementioned techniques, there are many different ways that you can implement viral marketing techniques on your Web site. If you have a newsletter on your site, you can add a "Tell a friend about this newsletter" button on the site. You can also incorporate a message in the body of your e-mail newsletter encouraging readers to forward a copy to friends they think would benefit from the information included in the newsletter. You should also include information in the message on how to subscribe to the newsletter for those recipients who receive the newsletter from a friend. The recipients will then be able to send a copy of the newsletter to their friends, who will in turn be presented with the opportunity to subscribe and regularly receive the newsletter (see Figure 4.2). The opportunities for viral marketing are endless.

A good word-of-mouth viral marketing strategy enables a visitor to your site or a recipient of your e-mail to share your site or e-mail content with others with just one click of a button or link. The design and placement of that link or button is critical to the success of the campaign.

Figure 4.2.   Including a "Send to a friend" button on your newsletter can encourage readers to forward a copy to their friends.

First of all, you should look to every repeat-traffic generator you have on your site for viral marketing opportunities. Repeat-traffic generators like coupons, newsletters, e-specials, and contests all provide ideal opportunities for "Tell a friend" or "Send a copy to a friend" links and buttons. Once you have determined the viral marketing techniques you are going to use, you want to make it easy for the site visitor or e-mail recipient to spread the word.

To be effective, you have to make it obvious what you want your visitors to do. Use a call to action to get them to do it. A button with "Send this coupon to a friend" or "Tell a friend about this e-special" works well. Don't assume that people will take the time to open their e-mail program and send an e-mail to a friend about your e-special or coupon or include the URL to the page on your Web site just because you have a great offer—it doesn't happen! You have to make it easy.

Here are some tips to make your word-of-mouth campaign effective:

- Have a fantastic button or graphic that grabs their attention.

- Provide a call to action telling the visitors what you want them to do.

- Place the button in the appropriate place away from clutter.

- Have the button link to an easy-to-use "Tell a friend" script. The "Tell a friend" script accepts the name and e-mail address(es) of the friend(s) and the name and e-mail address of your site visitor who is sending the message to a friend. You need to provide a section for a message. You might provide clickable options for this, such as "Thought this might be of interest" or "Knew you'd be interested in this."

- Give clear instructions on how to participate; make it simple, intuitive, and easy.

- Offer an incentive to encourage them to do what you want them to do: "Tell a friend and be included in a drawing for [something of interest to the target market]."

- Leverage, leverage, leverage: "Tell five friends and be included in a drawing for [something of interest to the target market]."

- Avoid using attachments in the message you want spread. This will avoid any potential technical problems with the attachments being opened as well as allaying any fears related to viruses.

- Have your privacy policy posted. If the user is going to pass along a friend's e-mail address, he or she wants to be assured that you will not abuse the contact information.

Viral marketing will only be successful if the content is good enough or valuable enough to be passed along.

Pass-It-On Viral Marketing

When we find a great resource, a funny video, or a cool game, we usually forward it to our colleagues or friends who we know will be interested in it. This old "they tell two friends and they in turn tell two friends" formula works very effectively online to enable you (with the right content) to reach a tremendous amount of your target market.

For this type of viral marketing to be successful, you have to start with great content that recipients will want to share with others. It can take many forms:

- E-books

- Small utility programs

- Fun videos

- Digital games

- Checklists

- A sound bite or **audiozine**

- Articles.

Audiozine
A magazine in
audio format.

The pass-it-on viral marketing methodology works best using small files that can easily be spread around.

E-Books

E-books are very big these days. If you have great content that clearly shows your depth of knowledge on a particular topic, an e-book can do wonders to create great exposure for you, your site, and your products and services. Ensure that you have clear references to you and links to your Web site that provide a reason for people to click through. You might provide additional resources on your site or encourage people to visit for copies of other e-books you have developed. Then market, market, market that e-book. Encourage e-zine and newsletter providers to send a copy to their subscribers, and promote it through your sig file, in newsgroups, and in publicly accessible mail lists.

You can provide a shareware or freeware program that might be of interest to your target market. Of course, you want to ensure that you reference your site throughout the program and give them a reason to visit.

Small Utility Programs

You can offer small utility programs for your target market which include your logo. For example, if you own a speakers' bureau, you can offer a small program that helps speakers organize their speaking engagement dates. If you are a car dealer, you can offer a small program that reminds car owners of safety inspections, license renewals, and scheduled tune-ups. If you are a real estate agent, you can offer a program that allows the user to calculate mortgage payments. Think of your target market and what might be handy and helpful for them.

Fun Videos

Nothing seems to spread faster on the Web than funny video clips. We've all seen the enraged employee attacking his computer and the bear taking salmon from the fisherman. Sometimes these video clips are cartoons, seen one slide at a time with embedded audio, and other times they seem to be full-scale productions. Savvy marketers are developing very innovative videos that incorporate their brand or their products with the objective of having a winner that will be passed on many times.

Digital Games

If your organization can develop a digital game or you have access to the rights to use a game, incorporate your logo and link back to your Web site within the game. A good game spreads very quickly.

Checklists

If you have a checklist that others might find useful, why not include links to your site in it and then provide it to your target market for use? For example, you might have a great checklist for making your site search engine friendly, or if you are a travel agent you might provide a handy checklist for travel planning. Think about your target market and what they might find useful. Always remember to encourage them to pass it on through viral marketing.

Podcasts, MP3 or Audiozine

Today's technology enables you to very quickly and easily forward podcasts, sound bytes, MP3s, or audiozines. As long as the content is relevant, pertinent, and of value to your target market or people in the industry you serve, people will pass it on. See Chapter 27 for more on podcasts.

Articles

Writing articles that can be distributed as content for newsletters or e-zines is another form of viral marketing. These articles can be distributed to be used as Web site content as well. Just make sure that you have clearly stated that others are free to use your article as long as they include it in its entirety verbatim and include the Source box. The article should contain links to your site. The Source box should include information on you, your company, and your Web site.

You should track your viral marketing rate of infection. You want to know what is working and how fast it is working. You can always include a graphic in the article or e-book or digital game that is accessed from your site. Then you can use your Web traffic analysis to find information on the effectiveness of your pass-it-on viral marketing campaigns.

Product- or Service-Based Viral Marketing

Two of the most prominent service-based viral marketing campaigns are Hotmail and Blue Mountain.

The Hotmail Example

MSN has capitalized on viral marketing to the fullest extent with its Hotmail service (*http://www.hotmail.com*). Hotmail is a free e-mail service that is provided by MSN.com and is used by millions of people around the world. Why is a free e-mail account a viral marketing technique? Because whenever a message is sent from a Hotmail account, a tag line is automatically inserted into the body of the e-mail message that tells the user about Hotmail's e-mail service. The message reads as follows:

> *Join the world's largest e-mail service with MSN Hotmail http:// www.hotmail.com.*

This small message results in hundreds of new e-mail accounts being opened daily on the Hotmail Web site. Although Hotmail doesn't provide any commercial services (i.e., they don't sell anything), this viral marketing technique creates mass exposure for the Hotmail.com Web site.

Blue Mountain—Taking Viral Marketing to the Next Level

Blue Mountain (see Figure 4.3) is a site that is synonymous with electronic greeting cards, or e-cards. Initially Blue Mountain received thousands of visitors daily who all sent free electronic greeting cards to friends all over the world. Today Blue Mountain still offers this service to the public, although a nominal annual fee is now charged if you want to be a member. With some of their cards you can add your own audio or type in the message you want to send and choose the accent you want it delivered in—male voice, female voice, Valley girl, or English male. Cool or what!

Figure 4.3. Blue Mountain has one of the largest collections of electronic greeting cards on the Internet.

Initially when you visit the Blue Mountain Web site, you are presented with an array of different options such as e-cards, gifts, paper greeting cards, and downloadable screensavers. When you decide to send a friend an electronic greeting card and finally select a greeting card from the thousands of cards available on the site, you are asked to fill out the contact information for the individual who will be receiving the card.

Blue Mountain encourages the recipient to visit the Blue Mountain Web site to reply to the sender with another electronic greeting card. This again provides Blue Mountain with the opportunity to sell a membership. Through viral marketing, Blue Mountain is able to spread the word about its business quickly and in a cost-effective manner.

Virtual Postcards

Today a large number of businesses, especially those that are tourism-oriented, are increasing traffic to their sites by offering virtual postcards on their Web site, which enables them to capitalize on viral marketing opportunities. Visitors can send virtual postcards to their family and friends. The postcard should not actually be sent as an attachment, but rather, an e-mail notice is sent saying that a postcard is waiting for the recipient at a particular Web address. By clicking

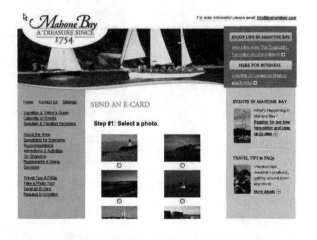

Figure 4.4.   The town of Mahone Bay offers free virtual postcards to generate exposure for its destination and its Web site.

on the Web address, the recipient is sent to the Web site to view the personalized postcard.

An example of this is the very scenic seaport town of Mahone Bay *(http:// www.mahonebay.com)*, a site that gives visitors the opportunity to send their friends colorful postcards depicting scenes of Mahone Bay via e-mail (see Figure 4.4). When you send a postcard to your friend, he or she receives an e-mail containing a link to the page where the postcard can be viewed. When your friend clicks through to view the postcard, there are links to other sections of the Web site. Offering electronic postcards is a great way to generate repeat visitors to your site and to spread the word about your site through the use of viral marketing.

Internet Resources for Chapter 4

I have developed a great library of online resources for you to check out regarding viral marketing in the Resources section of my Web site at *http:// www.susansweeney.com/resources.html*. There you can find additional tips, tools, techniques, and resources.

I have also developed a seminar on this topic which can be taken at any time over the Internet, can be taken live over the Internet at a scheduled time, or can be purchased as a seminar on CD. See *http://www.susansweeney.com/store.html*.

5

Permission Marketing

Permission marketing is an extremely important aspect of Internet marketing. Legislation imposes restrictions on what you can and cannot send via e-mail. When you play your cards right, permission marketing can be a valuable asset to any marketing campaign. In this chapter we discuss permission marketing and its uses to provide you with a greater understanding of this topic. This chapter provides the details on what permission marketing is and how it can be incorporated into your site. Chapter 14 on Private Mail List Marketing provides all the details on how it is sent, how to grow your database, and how to make sure your permission-based e-mail is not treated as spam.

Permission Marketing Explained

Permission boils down to asking your target market and Web site visitors for the authority to perform a specific action—for their permission to do, or send them, something. Many businesses and advertisers compete for the attention of their target market on a daily basis, but it is very difficult to break through all of the advertising clutter. The key to permission marketing is to get your target market to willingly volunteer to participate in the process. In order to do this, whatever it is you are proposing must be of value to your target market—you have to make it clear to the user by answering the question "What's in it for me?" If your target market sees no benefit in participating, then they will not participate—it's that simple.

Chapter 3 discusses many ways to encourage repeat visits to your Web site. Almost every repeat-traffic generator provides an opportunity for permission marketing. Examples include:

- "We change our coupons every week! Click here to join our mail list to be notified as soon as we update."

- "Click here to join our mail list and receive our biweekly Internet marketing tips, tools, techniques, and resources newsletter."

- "We have new specials on a regular basis. Click here to be notified by e-mail when we post our new specials."

- "We have a new contest every three weeks. Keep checking back or click here if you'd like to be notified by e-mail every time we begin a new contest."

- "We constantly update our Calendar of Events. Keep checking back or click here if you'd like to be notified by e-mail every time we update."

You might consider integrating your permission marketing requests with an e-club. I expect that the next round of legislation will allow you to send only those things that people have specifically requested. If someone has given you permission to send them your e-specials, you don't have their permission to send your newsletter or your new contest information. If you have an e-club and encourage people to "Join our e-club to receive our e-specials; new contest information and other great promotions available only to e-club members," you are essentially getting umbrella permission to send all types of marketing information.

What makes permission marketing so effective? Permission marketing is not intrusive. Your target market volunteered to receive the information you're sending because it is of interest to them, and as a result they expect to receive it. This significantly increases the likelihood of your target market viewing the material sent to them and their being receptive to it. When implemented correctly, permission marketing can be a valuable asset in acquiring new customers and maintaining relationships with existing ones. We discuss some of the ways in which you can use permission marketing to increase your online marketing success in the next section.

Uses of Permission Marketing

Permission marketing techniques can be integrated with many Internet marketing tools, including newsletters, surveys, contests, and so on. Chapter 3 covers many repeat-traffic and customer-loyalty-building tools that you can use on your Web site. Permission marketing is an excellent way to enhance and leverage the use of those tools—a few of which are covered in depth in this chapter.

Newsletters are one of the most popular resources for permission marketing. You can ask visitors if they would like to receive notification of new products, updates to your site, relevant tips, advice, industry news, and so on—whatever might be of interest to your target market. People who sign up to receive your newsletter do so because they have a clear interest in what it is you have to say. In your newsletter you can integrate strategic promotional opportunities to encourage users to come back to your site or to take some other course of action. If your newsletter is about recent happenings in your business or new product updates, encourage users to "follow this link" to see the updates or additional details and then, when they do, transport them to your Web site. A newsletter keeps you in front of your target market and constantly reminds them of your presence. Permission marketing opens the door for communication with your target market; this is an important step in building a long-lasting and profitable relationship with them.

Warranty registrations offer you an opportunity to capitalize on permission marketing. On the warranty registration card or online registration form for your product, you can include a section encouraging the consumer to sign up to receive additional information on your products and services. Many software vendors integrate the warranty or user registration process into their software and allow the user to submit it via the Internet once it's completed. On the registration form, the software vendor usually asks consumers if they would like to be notified of upgrades to their product or if they would like to receive additional information on new products being released. The consumer can then click "Yes" to receive additional information or "No" to not receive any additional information. Users usually click "Yes" because they want to be notified when updates become available. Along with the information they requested, you can include relevant promotional opportunities. The simple act of posing the question increases your chances of capturing your consumers because you have put the idea into their heads—something that might not even have crossed their mind.

Contests and sweepstakes represent another ideal opportunity to put permission marketing to work. In this case, the contest is the primary motivator to encourage people to sign up. The e-mail notification sent out to notify each contestant of the winner can also include promotional material and can encourage people to visit your Web site. In order for people to sign up for your contest, it must be of significant interest to them.

Say, for instance, that you are an online electronics retailer. When consumers visit your site, they could immediately be presented with the opportunity to enter a daily contest to win electronic-related merchandise such as the latest and greatest MP3 player. There is a direct correlation with the prize being given, the target market, and the purpose of the site, and as a result of the strategic fit, you would likely receive many entrants into the contests.

Once users enter the contest, they should be sent an e-mail confirmation stating that the entry was received. Also include in the e-mail a viral marketing call to action to tell others about the contest as well as a call to action for the user to visit the site and shop around. Referring back to the contest window, directly under the e-mail address entry field should be the option for the visitor to sign up to receive details on the latest hot deals at your site. This is an excellent example of how to combine contests, newsletters, and permission marketing and maximize the opportunity. Not only is the target market encouraged to enter the contest, but they are also encouraged to sign up for the hot deals newsletter while their interest is piqued.

Legislation Regarding Permission-Based Marketing

Recently, there have been major changes in the privacy and anti-spam legislation in Canada and the United States. This legislation affects every business that does outbound e-mail marketing. Everyone has to be in compliance with the new privacy and anti-spam legislation. If you do not know what the terms of the legislation are, then you might unknowingly be breaking the law and be subject to penalty.

The current Canadian legislation revolves around privacy and rights of an individual to the protection of their private information. Canada's legislation, Privacy Law—Personal Information Protection and Electronics Document Act (PIPEDA for short), came into effect January 1, 2004, for commercial businesses. The latest information on this legislation can be found at the Web site of the Office of the Privacy Commissioner of Canada (*http://www.privcom.gc.ca/legislation/02_06_01_01_e.asp*).

The current U.S. legislation revolves around spam and pornography. The U.S. legislation, Controlling the Assault of Non-Solicited Pornography and Marketing Act (CAN-SPAM for short) came into effect January 1, 2004, for commercial e-mail. The latest information on this legislation can be found at *http://www.spamlaws.com/federal*.

Privacy Concerns

When used correctly, permission marketing can be a very rewarding and cost-effective means of promotion; however, if you make ill use of this technique, you can do more harm than good. In order to avoid this pitfall, remember that you should never send your target market anything that they did not ask to receive, and you should never use their personal information for anything other than what they were told they were signing up for.

If you send your target market information they did not ask for, they will consider it spam. If you use their personal information for anything other than what your visitors expect, you could find yourself in bad public light as well as in significant legal trouble. Misuse of permission marketing also damages your relationship with your target market because you have violated their trust. This can also lead to bad publicity as the target market is very likely to turn around and tell many of their friends and associates about their bad experience with your company, ultimately resulting in lost business for you.

Companies that are successful in their permission marketing endeavors tend to leverage their campaign by prominently displaying their privacy and security policies. People like to know how their personal information is handled and are very reluctant to hand over their details to a company or organization that does not explain how their information is used. Privacy and security policies help build trust and confidence with your target market. These days, people are inundated with junk e-mail and are reluctant at the best of times to provide their e-mail address. You miss out on a lot of permission marketing opportunities if you don't prominently display and clearly state your privacy policy.

Again, make sure you stay current with privacy and anti-spam legislation. Always provide the opportunity for any e-mail recipient to opt out of future mailings.

Personalization

When asking permission to communicate with your target market, you want to make it easy. Don't have visitors complete a long form on which they have to provide all kinds of information. At this point, less is better. Have a simple form on which they provide their e-mail address and their first name. You want the first name so that you can personalize your communication. Most mail list software programs these days allow you to easily personalize the text in the body of the message you are sending and also the text in the subject line. You want to use a software program that manages all the permissions—the unsubscribes as well as the subscribes. See Chapter 14 on private mail list marketing for details.

Sell the Benefits

When you are asking permission to communicate with someone on an ongoing basis, you need to sell the benefits. People are inundated with junk e-mail and need to be "sold" on why they should subscribe to or join your communication list. "Join our weekly newsletter" just doesn't cut it. "Join our weekly newsletter to receive our Internet-only specials, coupons, and tips from our pro" will get you more subscribers. You have to know your target market well and know what is enticing enough to get their permission (see Figure 5.1).

Figure 5.1. MyLeisureTravel.com provides a list of reasons to join its getaway club.

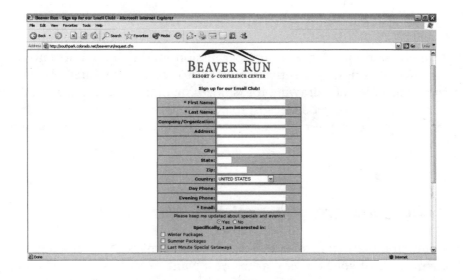

Figure 5.2. Beaver Run asks subscribers questions so it can tailor its future communications.

Data Mining

Data mining is sorting through data to identify patterns and establish relationships. Over time, you might want to ask a question or two in an appropriate manner to learn more about your subscribers so that you can target your communication with them a little better (see Figure 5.2).

Cooperative Permission Marketing

Cooperative marketing is starting to take hold on the Internet. Look for opportunities to form an alliance with other sites that are trying to reach the same target market you are, and then see how you can do some win-win marketing. For example, if you have a monthly newsletter, you can allow subscribers to sign up to receive alliance partners' newsletters at the same time they sign up to receive yours. In return, your alliance partners do the same. The same can be done for many repeat-traffic generators like coupons, e-specials, e-zines, etc. Get innovative!

Incentive-Based Permission Marketing

To increase the response to any permission marketing opportunity, you might consider offering an incentive: "Sign up to receive our Internet-only e-specials and be included in a drawing for (something of interest to your target market)."

You can also offer a free gift to new e-members or subscribers. It could be a sample of one of your products or an e-book on a topic of interest to your target market.

A Closing Comment on Permission Marketing

Permission marketing adds leverage to online marketing campaigns. Once you are in front of your target market, you want to take every opportunity to stay there and continue to communicate with them time and time again. Permission marketing helps you achieve this, but it is a game of give and take. You give them a reason to give you permission to send them e-mail—they provide you with the permission and their personal information; you provide them with valuable content. There is a trade-off and the cycle continues. Over time, you will gain more knowledge about your target market, which will empower you to provide them with a better overall experience in dealing with your company through better targeted promotions and better fulfillment of customer needs.

Why should you use permission marketing? To summarize, permission marketing can return a much higher response rate over intrusive advertising; it can increase sales, build your brand, and help develop relationships with your target market; and it is cost effective.

Visit Chapter 14 for more tips, tools, techniques, and resources related to permission marketing.

Internet Resources for Chapter 5

I have developed a great library of online resources for you to check out regarding permission marketing in the Resources section of my Web site at *http://www.susansweeney.com/resources.html*. There you can find additional tips, tools, techniques, and resources.

I have also developed a seminar on this topic which can be taken at any time over the Internet, can be taken live over the Internet at a scheduled time, or can be purchased as a seminar on CD. See *http://www.susansweeney.com/store.html*.

6

Designing Your Site to Be Search Engine Friendly

When Internet users are looking for a particular product, service, subject, or information pertaining to an area of interest to them, how do they do it? The most common research tool used is the search engine—85 percent of people doing research online use the search engines to find what they are looking for. Because search engines can bring significant volumes of traffic to your site, you must understand how the major search engines work and how the design of your site can influence the indexing of your site by the search engines. You must also know about the elements that are included in the search engines' algorithms or formulas that are outside your Web site and what you can do to ensure that you earn maximum points for those things you can influence.

When people conduct Internet searches, they rarely go beyond the first couple pages of results. If you want to be noticed, you need to appear in the top 10 or 20 search results. But before you submit to the search engines, you have to be sure your site has been designed to be search engine friendly. In this chapter, we cover:

- The methodology to make your site search engine friendly

- The key elements of Web site design to accommodate search engines

- How to use your competition and industry leaders as guidance

- The all-important content

- The importance of keywords in all aspects of your Web site

- The elements that are in the search engine algorithms or formulas that are outside your Web site

- The importance of link popularity and link relevancy to your search engine placement.

Methodology to Make Your Site Search Engine Friendly

To make your site search engine friendly you have to:

- Decide which search engines are critical for your success.

- Learn as much as you can about their ranking criteria and the weighting given to each criteria in their algorithm. It is also important to know which databases they are using.

Then you must:

- Determine the keywords that your target market is using in the search engines to find what you have to offer.

- Assign those keywords to specific pages throughout your site, and then

- Populate the pages with the assigned keywords in the appropriate places given the ranking criteria for your targeted search engines.

The remainder of this chapter walks you step-by-step through this process.

BOTS
Programs used by search engines to search the Internet for pages to index.

Understanding Search Engines

Search engines use programs or intelligent agents, called **bots**, to actually search the Internet for pages, which they index using specific parameters as they read the content. The agent reads the information on every page of your site and then follows the links. For example, Google's spider continually crawls the Web looking for sites to index and, of course, indexes sites upon their submission. Google is obviously very important in the search engine community, so be sure your site is easily accessible to its spider. A detailed discussion on submissions to search engines and directories can be found in Chapter 7.

Registering with search engines is fairly simple. In most cases, you simply have to submit your URL or Internet address on their submission form. Even if your URL is not registered with search engines, a number of the major search engines will eventually find you as their bots are continually roaming the Internet looking for new sites to index. Your odds of being indexed increase significantly if you have a well-developed links strategy. There are millions of sites out there, so I suggest that you be proactive and register your site to ensure a speedier listing. Once you are registered, some of the bots will periodically visit your site looking for changes and updates.

A common problem faced by Internet marketers is how to influence search engines to index their site appropriately and how to ensure that their site appears when people use relevant search criteria. Many of the interesting and creative sites on the Internet are impossible to find because they are not indexed with the major search engines. The majority (85 percent) of Internet users employ search engines or directories to find what they are looking for on the Web. They do this by typing in a keyword or phrase that represents what they are looking for. The following sections explore how to make your Web site more search engine friendly.

Many search engines and directories either partner with or license the use of another search engine's or directory's search technology. If you submit your site to a search engine that uses Google's index, then the design of your site influences how you're indexed in all search engines that rely on Google for their search results. For example, Google's results can be found on AOL, Netscape, and even sites like CNN. Google's paid advertising results appear on many other sites as well.

In a similar fashion, you often find other search engine and directory data intermixed or included in some form with another search engine's or directory's data. For example, with Ask Jeeves its primary search results come from Teoma, while its paid listings originate from Google. To take this example further, some search engines are built on the premise of pooling the search results of many search providers and presenting the results to the end user—they do not maintain their own index, but rather manipulate the results of many other search engines in hopes of providing a better search experience. This type of search tool is called a meta-search engine. Dogpile is an example of a meta-search engine.

When designing your site, you must always keep the search engines in mind. Something as simple as a DHTML drop-down menu on your site or a Flash intro can cause problems with the search engines and the indexing of your site if implemented incorrectly. You want to do everything you can to ensure that your site is designed to meet the needs of your target audience while remaining completely search engine friendly. Search engines can produce a significant amount of traffic to your site if you can manage to be placed in the top search results.

Decide Which Search Engines Are Important

To start this process, you want to decide which search engines you are going to be concerned about when taking steps necessary to rank high in their search results. For this section we are talking about **organic listings** rather than pay-per-click or sponsored listings. Ranking high in the pay-to-play search engines is discussed in Chapter 8. You want to select a number of the most popular search engines for your concentration. You also want to be indexed in topic-specific search engines for your industry.

Organic Listing

A free listing of a site in the search results ranked by the search engine's ranking formula or algorithm.

You can find the most popular search engines by doing your research online through sites such as Search Engine Watch (*http://www.searchenginewatch.com*). You can keep up with what's happening in the search engines by joining one of the many discussion lists on the topic.

There has been much consolidation in the search engine industry lately. Yahoo! now owns Inktomi, AlltheWeb, and AltaVista. AlltheWeb and AltaVista now return results from Yahoo!'s "tweaked" Inktomi engine. As it stands at the time of this writing, the remaining major players in the search engine industry are:

- Google (*http://www.google.com*)

- Yahoo! (*http://www.search.yahoo.com*)

- MSN Search (*http://search.msn.com*)

- AOL (*http://www.aol.com*).

Learn the Search Engine Ranking Criteria

Each search engine has its own unique ranking criteria and its own unique algorithm or formula giving different weighting to each criteria in its formula. For the search engines that you have decided to focus on, you have to learn as much as you can about their ranking criteria and relative weighting.

The search engines are all fighting for market share. The more market share a search engine has, the more valuable the company is. To gain market share a search engine has to provide better results than its competition. It is for this reason that the search engines are changing and improving their formulas on an ongoing basis. You have to keep up with changes in these formulas, tweak your site accordingly, and resubmit when necessary.

The search engines use different databases for their search results. They have different algorithms or formulas for their ranking. They have different weighting for the various elements within their formula. They change their formulas over time and they change their ranking over time. Sound complicated?

Things have changed quite a bit from the early days. Elements that used to have significant weighting may now have very little weight. You have to remember that it is the highest total score you are looking for so, even if an element has reduced weighting, if the element has any points at all you want to incorporate the element to maximize your total score. Sometimes the top sites are within a small number of points of each other.

It is not as daunting as it might sound because the major search engines tend to look at similar information, but weight the relevancy for particular items differently in their algorithms. That having been said, here are the most important areas on a Web page that you must address when performing organic search engine optimization:

- Title tags (page titles)

- Keyword meta-tags

- Description meta-tags

- Alt tags

- Hypertext links (e.g., anchor text)

- Domain names and file names

- Body text (beginning, middle, and end of page copy)

- Headers

- Between the "NOFRAMES" tag of framed Web sites.

Page titles and text-based page content are the most important of the noted placement areas. Keyword meta-tags are not as critical as they once were, but are still applicable for some engines. Remember—it is the absolute highest score you are looking for—if there are any points available you want to design your site to take advantage of them.

Because Google is the favorite search engine for the time being, let's take a closer look at how it ranks pages. Google uses the Open Directory database for its directory listings and its internal index for its primary search listings. Google has many other features as well, some of which include:

- An images search

- Usenet news data database

- A news search feature

- Froogle (a shopping search tool)

- A local search

- A blog search

- A news search

- A catalog search

- Advertising services through the Google AdWords programs.

The ranking formula for Google's main search function looks for the keywords in the visible body text, headers tags, title tags, hypertext links, Alt tags, and gives a very heavy weighting to the link popularity with extra points for quality of links and relevancy of text around the links.

More and more of the search engines are giving heavy weighting to link popularity—that is, the number of links to your site from other sites on the Internet. The search engines are getting very sophisticated in the weighting of link popularity, with the search engines giving extra points for link relevancy—that is, how high the site with the link to your site would rank for the same keyword. Other points are awarded based on the keywords in the text around the link pointing to your Web site. For strategies on generating significant links to your site, see Chapter 16.

Keywords Are Critical

Keywords are the terms and phrases that your target market uses when searching for the products and services you sell in the major search engines and directories. Your keywords are used in everything you do and are the key determining factor in how you rank in the search results among many of the major search engines.

A critical step in natural search engine optimization is to select the right keywords for your business, products or services (including descriptive words), and your target market. Understand whom you are targeting and build your search engine optimization efforts around your audience.

You need to choose keyword phrases that are going to bring sustainable targeted traffic consisting of potential customers—not just anything and everything. What you may think is the perfect keyword phrase may not be used at all by your target market in their search queries, which is why it is so critical to research and validate your keywords.

Ideally, each page of your Web site is going to focus on a different set of keywords that are specific to the content at hand. If you were to focus on the same set of keywords on every page, then you would hit only one small portion of your market potential because you are only going to hit those same keywords over and over again—it is self-defeating. As a general rule, you want to target somewhere between two and five keyword phrases per page.

First, you want to gather a master list of all possible keyword phrases. To make the data easier to manage, you can create different keyword list profiles that represent individual topics as opposed to trying to cover all topics in a giant master list. For example, if you have two product lines, you can create a keyword list for each. Naturally, some keywords are shared across the lists, but it is important to understand that the people looking for one topic (e.g., "jobs") are not necessarily the same people looking for another topic (e.g., "autos"), and as such they are going to use different keyword combinations in their searches.

How do you create your master keyword list? Here are four solid techniques for generating a list of potential keyword phrases:

1. Brainstorm, survey, and review promotional material.

2. Review competing and industry-leading Web sites.

3. Assess your Web site traffic logs.

4. Use keyword suggestion and evaluation tools.

Be sure to record the keywords you gather in a text document in your word-processing program or in a spreadsheet. Including them in a spreadsheet or database makes them much easier to sort when it comes time to prioritize the keywords and weed out the junk.

As you work your way through the list of techniques, you want to cycle back to some of the techniques because you will come across search terms that can expand the scope of your original efforts and open the door to new, more targeted phrases that you might have missed the first time around.

Brainstorming, Surveying, and Reviewing Promotional Material

At this stage, the idea is to gather all the keyword phrases you can, within reason. Sit down with a pen and paper and jot down all keywords that come to mind. Bring other members of your team in on this process to fuel ideas. There is nothing scientific or technical to be concerned with here—the sky's the limit, but try to put yourself in your customers' shoes.

Try to think as your target market would if they were to do a search for information on a topic contained within your site. Do not just think about what people would do to find your site, but what they would do if they didn't know your company existed and were looking for the types of products and services you sell.

Here are several questions to help you with your brainstorming process:

1. What industry are you in (e.g., travel)?

2. What is the focus of your Web site (e.g., a resource, a guide, a store)? What would people search for if they were looking for a Web site like yours?

3. If your customer were to take a guess at your Web address, what would it be? Remember, they do not know who you are, but they know what kind of products or services they are looking for.

4. What products and services do you sell? What are some of the descriptive words or benefits of your products and services that might be familiar to your target market? For example, if your site offers information on resort spas, then one descriptive keyword you might choose could be *massage*. Also, include words that describe the benefits of these services or the service in more detail, such as *massage therapy* and *full-body massage*.

5. Are there any regional or geographic implications to consider? For example, there could be spelling differences to account for. In the United States, the target market might look for *color laser printer,* and in Canada the target market might look for *colour laser printer.* Depending on the audience you are trying to communicate with, you need to tailor keyword phrases accordingly. Also, people typically blend a destination or major landmark with their keyword search. If you are going to Dallas, you are going to look for Dallas hotels, not just hotels.

Your current corporate materials, brochures, and other marketing collateral can be a valuable source of keyword phrases. Begin by indiscriminately highlighting any words that people might search for if they are looking for products or services your company has to offer.

To assist you in developing your keyword list, consider asking your customers for their input. Ask what keywords they might use to find a site like yours. You can always turn to a thesaurus for additional ideas if you get stumped.

Review Competing and Industry-Leading Web Sites

Check out your online competition. The term *competition* is referenced quite loosely in that industry leaders with whom you may not directly compete are also included here. Look at the sites for which you have a record and look for sites in the major search engines using some of the keyword phrases you have gathered so far.

You want to see what sites are in the top 20 positions and understand them. By reviewing top-ranking Web sites, you can look for themes and patterns in the sites that give you a good indication of what they are going after and how they are doing it. You can then turn around and apply this newfound knowledge to your own Web site.

When reviewing competing Web sites, you should look at the same general areas you would optimize on your own Web site. As mentioned before, the most critical keyword placement areas include:

- Title tags (page titles)

- Keyword meta-tags

- Description meta-tags

- Alt tags

- Hypertext links (e.g., anchor text)

- Domain names and file names

- Body text (beginning, middle, and end of page copy; headers)

- Between the "NOFRAMES" tag of framed Web sites.

By searching for your most important keywords and observing what the top-ranking sites are using with respect to their page content, title tags, description meta-tags, keyword meta-tags, and so on, you can formulate a good plan of attack. Remember that if you don't appear in the first two or three pages of search results, it is unlikely that prospective visitors will access your site through the search engine.

Check to see what meta-tags your competitors have. Not only can you learn from the sites that catch your eye, you can also learn from your competitors' mistakes. After you have done a thorough job of this market research, you are in a good position to develop a description that is catchy and adequately describes your site.

To check your competition's meta-tags in Microsoft Internet Explorer, you simply go to their site, then click "View" on your menu bar and select "Source" from the drop-down menu. This brings up the source code for that respective page in whatever your default text browser is.

Pay special attention to the title tag of the top-ranked Web sites. To get a little more specific, you can narrow your search to keywords in a title tag. The reason for doing this is that optimizing a title tag is a given when it comes to search engine optimization, so it only makes sense to look at who else is doing it as well. On Google you can enter "allintitle: keyword phrase," without the quotes, to search for all pages with the noted keywords in their title tag. This approach is a little more focused than simply looking for all pages with a certain set of keywords because the keywords might just be there in passing, as a part of an article, and not something the site is intentionally trying to target. If the keywords are found in the title tag, there is a better chance their reason for being there is intentional.

As noted earlier, you can not only learn from the sites that catch your eye, you can also learn from your competitors' mistakes.

Assess Your Web Site Traffic Logs

Your Web site traffic logs can be a source of pertinent keyword information. You can view your traffic logs to see what search terms and search engines people are using to locate your Web site and to help you fine-tune future search engine optimization efforts.

If you are not sure whether you have access to a Web site traffic analysis program, check with your current Web site host to see if they provide one to you. If not, there are plenty of tools available to you. See Chapter 32, "Web Traffic Analysis," for helpful information.

Understand that the search terms displayed may not be the most relevant; they just happen to be the search terms people are executing to find your site during the selected time frame. Applying new search engine optimization techniques with relevant keywords changes how people find your Web site. The Web site traffic analysis package you use gives you the power to measure the impact of your optimization efforts.

Your traffic logs can be a source of inspiration for generating your master keyword list. Note the search terms people are currently using and add them to your list. For a more complete look at the search phrases reported on your Web site, expand the date range to cover a larger spread—say, over the period of a year.

When your site is optimized, your Web traffic analysis tool will become your best friend in monitoring your success.

Keyword Suggestion and Evaluation Tools

There are a number of services available that can help you with selecting the most appropriate keywords for your site. These services base their suggestions on results from actual search queries. Wordtracker is an example of such a service.

Keyword research tools can help meet your current needs, whether you're looking for a place to start, are plum out of ideas, or simply feel like you're missing something. Here are the most common tools my team uses on a daily basis:

WordTracker (*http://www.wordtracker.com*)—WordTracker is the most popular keyword research tool and is an absolute must for doing your research. WordTracker does have a fee associated with it. You can expect to pay approximately US$250 per year or $8 for a day.

WordTracker maintains a database of over 350 million keywords gathered from several meta-search engines. The tool is easy to use and provides a valuable source of information. When you run a search for a term, it shows you related keywords, including misspellings, the plural and singular versions of the word or phrase, and references from its thesaurus if desired.

WordTracker allows you to build your list of keyword phrases through a process similar to adding items to a shopping cart. The tool enables you to drill down a bit further by selecting keyword phrases of particular interest that are related to the specific phrase with which you are concerned. Figure 6.1 shows WordTracker's interface.

A nice feature of this tool is that it provides you with an indication of the popularity for your keywords as well as the predicted volume of competition for said keywords. This is a handy feature when trying to determine which keywords are worth going after and which are a waste of time.

Overture's Search Term Suggestion Tool (*http://inventory.overture.com/d/searchinventory/suggestion*)—Overture's Search Term Suggestion Tool is free. The tool enables you to enter keyword phrases and search for related keywords based on the previous

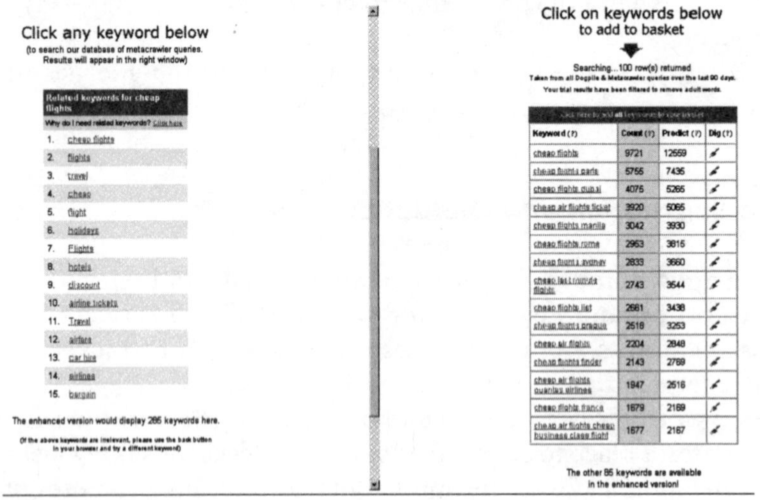

Figure 6.1.   WordTracker in action.

Keyword Selector Tool

Not sure what search terms to bid on?
Enter a term related to your site and we will
show you:

• Related searches that include your term

• How many times that term was searched
  on last month

Get suggestions for: (may take up to 30
seconds)

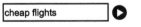

Note: All suggested search terms are subject
to our standard editorial review process.

*No suggestions for **cheap flights**.*

Figure 6.2. Overture's Search Term Suggestion tool.

month's search data. Up to 100 results per query are displayed. The results are displayed in order of popularity and only search terms with a minimum of 25 queries during the previous month are displayed. An example of the tool in action can be seen in Figure 6.2.

The Overture tool does have some notable ways of doing things that you need to keep in mind. For one, it always converts the word you are questioning from the plural to the singular, so it is not possible to tell whether someone is searching for the plural or the singular version of a word (e.g., stores versus store). Second, the Overture tool always displays the correct spelling of a word, but in some cases you may want to know what a common misspelling is along with how often it is searched for (e.g., accommodation versus accomodation). A final note is that the tool just shows results that include the exact phrase you searched for. If you search for the keyword *cheap flights,* as is done in Figure 6.2, all of the results will include only *cheap flights;* it does not suggest *discount flights, discount airlines, cheap airfare,* and so on, as alternatives. You have to enter more specific phrases to drill down.

Google AdWords: Keyword Suggestions (*https://adwords.google.com/select/main?cmd=KeywordSandbox*)—Another useful free tool. You can use the Google AdWords: Keyword Suggestions tool to generate new keyword ideas and compare the results from the other tools. The Google tool also makes suggestions on related terms you should consider. An example can be seen in Figure 6.3.

WordTracker and Overture are essential keyword suggestion tools; however, the Google tool can offer some support and it can help gener-

More Specific Keywords	**More Specific Keywords**
These are popular queries that include your keyword. If you're showing your ads on broad-matched keywords, these queries may trigger your ads. To increase your click-through rate, you should consider replacing your general keywords with any relevant, more specific suggestions you see here. You should also identify any irrelevant terms and add them as negative matches otherwise your ads will show for terms that don't pertain to your busines).	**Expanded Broad Matches** Your ads may automatically show for these related queries. To stop your keywords from being expanded, add the unwanted keywords as negative matches, or change your keyword matching option from broad matching to phrase or exact matching.
• cheap flights • cheap international flights • cheap air flights • flights cheap • cheap flights to europe • cheap flights uk • cheap flights london • cheap flights to hawaii • cheap flights europe • cheap flights to paris	• cheap airfares • cheap flight • lowest airfares • cheapest airfares • cheapest flight • airfare discount • discounted airfare • discounted airfares • bargain airfare • airfares cheap **Here are additional keywords to consider:**

Figure 6.3.   Google AdWords: Keyword Suggestions tool.

ate new ideas. The Google tool's primary purpose is for researching keywords for its AdWords program.

Related searches on search engines and directories—A lesser known technique is to run a query on a search engine and watch for the related search options it suggests. Some search engines such as Teoma and Lycos make suggestions on related keyword phrases that you can use to refine your search. You can use these suggestions as a means of generating additional keywords or opening a new theme of search phrases you hadn't previously considered. Figure 6.4 shows an example of search suggestions made by Teoma for a query on cheap flights.

Fine-Tuning Your Keyword Phrases

Now that you have your master keyword list, probably with a few hundred keyword phrases, you have to drill down and figure out which keywords you are going to target for each page of your Web site that you want to optimize. Realistically, you can emphasize two to five keyword phrases on a single page, and maybe a few others as spillover. Keep in mind that each page you optimize should lean toward a different set of keywords. Why? What good is buying 100 lottery tickets for the next drawing if they all have the same number? It is the same idea here.

Refine
Suggestions to narrow your search

Cheap Flight To Malaga

Cheap Flight To Tenerife

Cheap Cyprus Flights

Cheap Flight To Turkey

Cheap Flights In UK

Cheap Flight Florida

[Show All Refinements]

Figure 6.4. Teoma search suggestions.

Your efforts should focus around those keyword phrases that bring in a fair volume of traffic and that are highly targeted. The return on investment for such keywords will be much higher. When reviewing your keyword list, you need to consider:

- Which keywords are vital to your objectives

- Which keywords are popular enough to generate reasonable, sustainable traffic

- Which keywords do not have so much competition that it would be counterproductive considering the time and effort necessary to target them.

For a hotel to have the keyword *travel* stand alone on the hotel's Web site would prove a waste of effort. *Travel* is a vastly popular keyword, which is good, but it is too generic and too competitive to be worthwhile. You have to make judgment calls from time to time. In some cases a word is relevant and popular, but also competitive to the point of being intimidating. If this word is essential to your business, however, then go for it.

Organize your keywords according to their level of importance. When completed, you will have a refined master keyword list that you can refer to when optimizing your Web site. Also, different directories allow different numbers of keywords to be submitted. Because you have organized the list with the most important words first, you can simply include as many of your keywords as the directory allows.

You can begin editing the list by deleting words that either are too generic (for example, *business*) or are not appropriate for keyword purposes. Review each word and ask yourself, "Would people search using this word if they were looking for the products and services available through my Web site?"

For each page that you are optimizing, take a copy of the comprehensive master list and delete words that are not appropriate for that particular page. Reprioritize the remaining keywords based on the content of the page you are indexing. Now take the keyword phrase you have assigned to this page and put it at the top of the list. This is the keyword list for that particular page. Repeat this procedure for every page you are optimizing. This is also a great procedure when you are developing the keyword meta-tag for each page of your site.

What I covered above is a very basic approach to organizing keywords. If you are up to the challenge, you can take it further by adding weights and multipliers to your keyword list to further refine it. Review some of the resource Web sites provided at the end of this chapter to learn advanced techniques.

You can choose to keep it basic while you are learning the ropes, but as you become more familiar you might want to be more critical in selecting your keywords to boost your performance in the search engines. The more knowledge with which you are armed, the better prepared you are to optimize your Web site. Here are some additional tips to keep in mind when refining your keywords master list:

- **Plural and singular keywords**—There is some debate about whether it is better to use only the plural version of a keyword or whether it is best to use both the plural and singular forms of the keyword. Is your target market looking for both? As an example, some people might search for *game,* and others might search for *games.* Google matches exactly what the user searches for, so it is important to use both where possible.

- **Using the names of your competitors**—There is often the question as to whether to include your competitor's name in your keywords. The idea here is that if someone looks for your competitor, they are going to find you as well. Never include a competitor's name in your keywords. Because several search engines read only a small amount of content for keywords, you lose valuable page real estate to irrelevant keywords when you use your competitor's name. In addition, there have been recent legal battles regarding the use of competitors' names within one's keywords.

- **Common misspellings of words**—There are many words that people misspell on a frequent basis. The question here is, do you include those misspelled keywords in your site or not? My stance is "No." Although people use them in their searches, it hurts your credibility in that you come off as a company incapable of spelling its own products and services. There are exceptions to every rule. Canadian sites often have U.S. customers as their target market and U.S. sites often have Canadian customers as their target markets. There are a number of words that are spelled differently by these countries—*theatre* in Canada is *theater* in the United States, *centre* in Canada is *center* in the United States, *colour* in Canada is *color* in the United States are just a few examples. If you are caught with one of your important keywords spelled differently by your target market, you might want to optimize a page of your site to accommodate this. Perhaps you might offer a page that is designed for Our Canadian Friends or for Our American Friends.

- **Case sensitivity**—Some search engines are not case-sensitive and others are. Regardless, most people search in lowercase, and to keep the process simple, for now you should record your original keyword master list using lowercase. Once you begin finalizing your keyword list, you might notice that people are actually searching for the proper spelling of a word, in which case you would reflect the changes in your keyword list.

- **Stop and filter words**—Filter words are words that search engines simply ignore during searches. Stop words are extremely common words that search engines use as triggers to stop grabbing content on a given page, such as "and," "a," and "the." Some search engines view stop words and filter words as the same thing, but you need to remember only one thing: search engines bypass these words to save time as these words are not considered to add any value to the search. It is best to try to avoid using stop words where possible in your keyword phrases. Following is a sample list of some of the more common stop words on record from a list compiled by Search Engine World (*http://www.searchengineworld.com/spy/stopwords.htm*):

a	ii	about	above	according
across	39	actually	ad	adj
ae	af	after	afterwards	ag
again	against	ai	al	all
almost	alone	along	already	also
although	always	am	among	amongst
an	and	another	any	anyhow
anyone	anything	anywhere	ao	aq
ar	are	aren	aren't	around
arpa	as	at	au	aw
az	b	ba	bb	bd

be	became	because	become	becomes
becoming	been	before	beforehand	begin
beginning	behind	being	below	beside
besides	between	beyond	bf	bg
bh	bi	billion	bj	bm
bn	bo	both	br	bs
bt	but	buy	bv	bw
by	bz	c	ca	can
can't	cannot	caption	cc	cd
cf	cg	ch	ci	ck
cl	click	cm	cn	co
co.	com	copy	could	couldn
couldn't	cr	cs	cu	cv
cx	cy	cz	d	de
did	didn	didn't	dj	dk
dm	do	does	doesn	doesn't
don	don't	down	during	dz
e	each	ec	edu	ee
eg	eh	eight	eighty	either
else	elsewhere	end	ending	enough
er	es	et	etc	even
ever	every	everyone	everything	everywhere
except	f	few	fi	fifty
find	first	five	fj	fk
fm	fo	for	former	formerly
forty	found	four	fr	free
from	further	fx	g	ga
gb	gd	ge	get	gf
gg	gh	gi	gl	gm
gmt	gn	go	gov	gp
gq	gr	gs	gt	gu
gw	gy	h	had	has
hasn	hasn't	have	haven	haven't
he	he'd	he'll	he's	help
hence	her	here	here's	hereafter
hereby	herein	hereupon	hers	herself
him	himself	his	hk	hm
hn	home	homepage	how	however
hr	ht	htm	html	http
hu	hundred	i	i'd	i'll
i'm	i've	i.e.	id	ie

if	il	im	in	inc
inc.	indeed	information	instead	int
into	io	iq	ir	is
isn	isn't	it	it's	its
itself	j	je	jm	jo
join	jp	k	ke	kg
kh	ki	km	kn	kp
kr	kw	ky	kz	l
la	last	later	latter	lb
lc	least	less	let	let's
li	like	likely	lk	ll
lr	ls	lt	ltd	lu
lv	ly	m	ma	made
make	makes	many	maybe	mc
md	me	meantime	meanwhile	mg
mh	microsoft	might	mil	million
miss	mk	ml	mm	mn
mo	more	moreover	most	mostly
mp	mq	mr	mrs	ms
msie	mt	mu	much	must
mv	mw	mx	my	myself
mz	n	na	namely	nc
ne	neither	net	netscape	never
nevertheless	new	next	nf	ng
ni	nine	ninety	nl	no
nobody	none	nonetheless	noone	nor
not	nothing	now	nowhere	np
nr	nu	nz	o	of
off	often	om	on	once
one	one's	only	onto	or
org	other	others	otherwise	our
ours	ourselves	out	over	overall
own	p	pa	page	pe
per	perhaps	pf	pg	ph
pk	pl	pm	pn	pr
pt	pw	py	q	qa
r	rather	re	recent	recently
reserved	ring	ro	ru	rw
s	sa	same	sb	sc
sd	se	seem	seemed	seeming
seems	seven	seventy	several	sg

sh	she	she'd	she'll	she's
should	shouldn	shouldn't	si	since
site	six	sixty	sj	sk
sl	sm	sn	so	some
somehow	someone	something	sometime	sometimes
somewhere	sr	st	still	stop
su	such	sv	sy	sz
t	taking	tc	td	ten
text	tf	tg	test	th
than	that	that'll	that's	the
their	them	themselves	then	thence
there	there'll	there's	thereafter	thereby
therefore	therein	thereupon	these	they
they'd	they'll	they're	they've	thirty
this	those	though	thousand	three
through	throughout	thru	thus	tj
tk	tm	tn	to	together
too	toward	towards	tp	tr
trillion	tt	tv	tw	twenty
two	tz	u	ua	ug
uk	um	under	unless	unlike
unlikely	until	up	upon	us
use	used	using	uy	uz
v	va	vc	ve	very
vg	vi	via	vn	vu
w	was	wasn	wasn't	we
we'd	we'll	we're	we've	web
webpage	website	welcome	well	were
weren	weren't	wf	what	what'll
what's	whatever	when	whence	whenever
where	whereafter	whereas	whereby	wherein
whereupon	wherever	whether	which	while
whither	who	who'd	who'll	who's
whoever	NULL	whole	whom	whomever
whose	why	will	with	within
without	won	won't	would	wouldn
wouldn't	ws	ww	wx	y
ye	yes	yet	you	you'd
you'll	you're	you've	your	yours
yourself	yourselves	yt	yu	z
za	zm	zr		

- **Modifiers**—A modifier is a keyword you add to your primary keyword phrase to give it a boost. Who simply searches for a hotel at random? It doesn't make sense. You look for a hotel in combination with a destination. In this case, the destination is the modifier. As a side note, local search is becoming increasingly popular, so if the local market plays a significant role in the success of your business, be sure to use geographic modifiers accordingly.

- **Multiple-word keyword phrases**—Two- or three-keyword phrases perform better than single keywords. According to OneStat.com (*http://www.onestat.com*), people tend to use two- and three-word phrases when performing a search online. Here is a list of the most popular number of words used in a search phrase:

  - two words—32.58%

  - three words—25.61%

  - one word—19.02%

  - four words—12.83%

  - five words—5.64%

  - six words—2.32%

  - seven words—0.98%.

Not only are multiple keyword phrases used more often by searchers, but it also enables you to be more descriptive in the modifiers to your keyword phrases.

Assign Specific Keywords to Specific Pages

The next step is to allocate specific keywords to specific pages of your site for search engine optimization. You then populate each page in the appropriate places with the assigned keyword. You do this because you want to ensure that no matter which keyword or keyword phrase your target market decides to search on, one of the pages on your site is likely to rank in the first couple of pages of search results.

Many sites populate all their pages with the same keywords in the hopes that one of their pages will rank high in the search results. They use the same meta-tags for every page on their site. Again, this is the same as buying 100 tickets on the lottery but selecting the same numbers for every single ticket.

Some search engines rank sites by how early the keyword appears on the site. The earlier a keyword is mentioned on your site, the more points earned and the higher your site may be positioned in search results. And remember what was stressed earlier: though you don't want to repeat a keyword hundreds of times (some search engines are on to this), you do want to repeat the keywords assigned to that particular page a number of times on that page of your site.

When you have allocated your keywords to the various pages on your site, you will populate or include the keyword phrases assigned in the appropriate places for that particular page: Let's take a closer look at all those appropriate places.

Title Tags—Use Descriptive Page Titles

It is extremely important that all Web pages have titles. Title tags are viewed as one of the most important elements of search engine optimization when it comes to keyword placement. Each of the pages on your Web site should be given a title.

The title is inserted between the title tags in the header of an HTML document. <HEAD> indicates the beginning of the header, and the ending of the header is marked by </HEAD>. A simplified version might look like:

- <HTML>

- <HEAD>

- <TITLE>Document Title Here</TITLE>

- <META-NAME="keywords" CONTENT="keyword1, keyword2, keyword3">

- <META-NAME="description" CONTENT="200-character site description goes here">

- <META-NAME="robots" CONTENT="index, follow">

- <!—Comments tag, repeat description here>

- </HEAD>

Title tag information identifies and describes your pages. Titles tell readers where the information contained on a page originated. Most Web browsers display a document's title in the top line of the screen. When users print a page from your Web site, the title usually appears at the top of the page at the left. When someone bookmarks your site or adds it to their "Favorites," the title appears as the description in his or her bookmark file. These are all reasons that it is important that a page's title reflects an accurate description of the page. More importantly, the title tag is typically what the target market sees in search results in some of the major search engines. In Figure 6.5 you can see that a typical search result consists of the title tag as the link to the Web site, a brief description of the Web site, and the URL.

Every page of your Web site should have a unique title tag and each title tag should accurately describe the page content. Your target market should be able to read the title tag and understand what the page they are about to view contains.

Keep your title tags brief—in the realm of five to ten words. The longer your title tag is, the more diluted your keywords become and the more likely your title tag is to be truncated by a search engine. Google displays a maximum of 66 characters. Yahoo!Search, on the other hand, permits up to 120 characters for a title tag. Presently Google and Yahoo!Search are the two most important search engines; use their requirements as an approximation when designing your title tag.

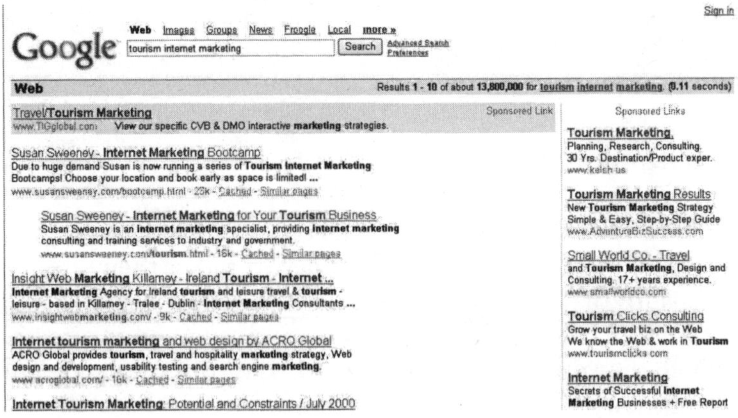

Figure 6.5. The title tag of a Web site appears as the first line of information about a Web site.

My advice is to include your most important keyword phrases first, within Google's 66-character range. Overspill, or less important keywords, can run into the excess space Yahoo!Search allows. By including your most important keywords first, you secure their position for use by the search engines and for browser bookmarks.

The shorter and more accurate the title tag is, the higher the keyword density and relevancy for that title tag. Try to keep your use of a keyword phrase to a single instance if possible, unless the title tag truly warrants duplication. In the case of a hotel, the word *hotel* might appear twice in a title—once for the hotel's proper company name and once in a descriptive term such as a targeted geographic area.

Match the keywords you use in your meta-tags with the words you use in your page titles. Search engines check page titles, meta-tags, and page content for keywords. For certain keywords, your pages will be more relevant and, therefore, will place higher in the search engines if these keywords appear in each of these three sections. Position your keywords near the beginning of your page titles to increase your keyword relevancy.

Some of the search engines retrieve your page, look at your title, and then look at the rest of your page for keywords that match those found in the title. Many search engines use title tags as one of the elements in their algorithm to determine search engine ranking. Pages that have keywords in the title are seen as more relevant than similar pages on the same subject that don't, and may thus be ranked in a higher position by the search engines. However, don't make your title a string of keywords such as *cuisine, French cuisine, imported food,* because this is often considered spam by the search engines and you end up worse off in the rankings or removed altogether. Also keep in mind that people will see that title in the search results, and they're more likely to click on a site that has a title that flows and is descriptive—not a list.

Keywords Meta-Tag

As we noted earlier in this chapter, a common problem faced by Internet marketers is how to influence search engines to index their site appropriately and how to ensure that their site appears when people use relevant search criteria. The majority of Internet users employ search engines or directories to find Web sites, which they do by typing in a keyword or phrase that represents what they are looking for.

Retaining a certain measure of control over how search engines deal with your Web site is a major concern. Often Web sites do not take advantage of the techniques available to them to influence search engine listings. Most search engines evaluate the HTML meta-tags in conjunction with other variables to decide where to index Web pages based on particular keyword queries.

Although in recent years fewer points have been allocated to content in the keywords meta-tags, it is important to keep your eyes on the total score—if there are any points at all allocated to this element, you want them all. The site with the highest total score appears at the top of the search results, so you are going after every point you can get.

The Web Developer's Virtual Library defines an HTML meta-tag as follows:

> *The META element is used within the HEAD element to embed document meta-information not defined by other HTML elements. The META element can be used to identify properties of a document (e.g., author, expiration date, a list of keywords, etc.) and assign values to those properties.*

> *An HTML tag is used in the HEAD area of a document to specify further information about the document, either for the local server or for a remote browser. The meta-element is used within the HEAD element to embed document meta-information not defined by other HTML elements. Such information can be extracted by servers/clients for use in identifying, indexing, and cataloging specialized document meta-information. In addition, HTTP servers can read the contents of the document HEAD to generate response headers corresponding to any elements defining a value for the attribute HTTP-EQUIV. This provides document authors with a mechanism for identifying information that should be included in the response headers of an HTTP request.*

To summarize this lengthy definition, meta-information can be used in identifying, indexing, and cataloging. This means you can use these tags to guide the search engines in displaying your site as the result of a query. There are many meta-tags, including:

- Abstract

- Author

- Copyright

- Description

- Expires

- Keywords

- Language

- Refresh

- Revisit

- Robots.

Most of the above meta-tags are not useful for optimization purposes. The most recognized meta-tag is the keywords meta-tag.

<META-NAME="keywords" CONTENT="..."> tells search engines under which keywords to index your site. When a user types one of the words you listed here, your site should be displayed as a result. A space or comma can be used to separate the words. Do not frequently repeat the keyword; rather, repeat the keyword about five times in different phrases. You do have the option of using more than 1,000 characters in your keywords meta-tag, but be wary of keyword dilution. You should create a unique keywords tag for each page of your site that lists the appropriate keywords for that particular page.

Description Meta-Tag

<META-NAME="description" CONTENT="..."> should be included on every page of your Web site. The description meta-tag is used to supply an accurate overview of the page to which it is attached. The description meta-tags can influence the description in the search engines that support them.

It is best to keep the description meta-tag to somewhere in the realm of 200 to 250 characters in total. Be sure to use the same keywords applied elsewhere on the page being optimized in the description meta-tag for consistency and relevancy; however, do not duplicate your title tag in your description meta-tag or you may run the risk of being accused of keyword stacking. Also, it helps to include a call to action encouraging the target market to visit your Web site or some other action.

Alt Tags

Some search engines use the information within Alt tags when forming a description and determining the ranking for your site. Alt tags are used to display a description of the graphic they are associated with if the graphic cannot be displayed, such as in text-only browsers. Alt tags appear after an image tag and contain a phrase that is associated with the image.

Ensure that your Alt tags contain the keywords assigned to the particular page wherever you can. This gives your page a better chance of being ranked higher in the search engines. For example:

<image src="images/logo.gif" height="50" width ="50"
alt="Games Nation – Computer Games Logo">

You do not want your Alt tags to look something like "Game Nation" or "Company Logo" because this does not include any keywords. Be sure you apply proper Alt tags to all images on your site to achieve best results. Keep in mind that users who browse with graphics disabled must be able to navigate your site, and proper use of Alt tags assists them in doing so.

Hypertext Links

A hypertext link consists of the description of a link placed in between anchor tags. Here is an example of an absolute link, where the link includes the total path to where the document can be found:

<a href="http://www.susansweeney.com/speakingkit.html">.
This is the anchor text for the sample link</A>

The text inside a hyperlink, or anchor text, is increasingly important for search engine optimization. The major search engines have points available for including the keyword phrase being searched on in the text around the link pointing to your Web site. There is a strong relevancy pattern.

Good places to use links include the primary and sub-navigation aspects of a Web site, as well as links to external resources from within the page copy. Likewise, if links on other Web sites pointing to your Web site include the same string of keywords, your site's relevancy gets a boost. When you encourage other Web sites to link to yours, be sure to provide them with the link text they should use and make sure you get the keyword phrase you have assigned to that particular page in the text around the link. Similarly, when you submit your Web site to directories and other link sources, provide the comparable link or title text.

Domain Name and File names

Use of keywords within your domain name and file names can help with search engine positioning. Some professionals argue that including dashes to separate keywords makes it easier for search engines to distinguish keywords, which can help boost your rankings. Personal experience leads me to believe that if it actually does make a difference, the difference is so small that you are better off spending your time optimizing your Web site in areas that really count. This also applies to file names.

Examples of domain names are:

1. www.thisisadomainname.com

2. www.this-is-also-a-domain-name.com.

Examples of file names are:

1. www.thisisadomainname.com/samplepage.html

2. www.thisisadomainname.com/samples-page.html.

It does not take much effort to give your images and file names meaningful names—names that include the keyword phrase you have assigned to that page—so take the time to do it. For example, instead of using *http://www.susansweeney.com/bcs.html* for a page that is focusing on my Internet Marketing Bootcamp, it would be much better to use *http://www.susansweeney.com/bootcamp.html.*

Body Text—Header Tags and Page Copy

The body text of a Web page consists of all the visible text between the <body> and </body> tag, such as headings and the page copy encased in paragraphs. Along with page titles, body text is the next important area on which to focus your search engine optimization efforts. Body text is where you want to spend the bulk of your time.

Headings—<H1>Header Tags</H1>

Use your HTML <H1> header tags effectively to indicate the subject and content of a particular page. Most people use them only as a method of creating large fonts. Some search engines, including Google, use the content included within the header text in their relevancy scoring. The H1 tag is the most important, followed by H2. Include your most important keywords in your header tags. If you can, work a couple of H2 tags into your page to sort content and improve the relevancy of your page.

Page Copy

You want to ensure that the keyword you have assigned to a specific page appears in the first 200 characters on that page as close to the beginning as possible. The higher up on a page, the greater the keyword prominence. Search engines tend to lend more weight to page content above the fold. The fold is where your browser window ends and where vertical scrolling begins, if necessary.

The assigned keyword should appear at the beginning of the text on the page, in the middle, and again at the end. You want to build a theme on your page, and to do so you have to spread your keywords throughout the page, not just focus on the first paragraph.

Always have a descriptive paragraph at the top of your Web page that describes what can be found on the page for your target market and for the major search engines. Search engines use this as their source for a site description and keywords on your site. In addition, search engines use the content found within the opening paragraph in influencing the ranking of your site among search results. Again, be sure to use the most important keywords first, preferably within the first two or three sentences. This is enormously important. Make sure that the keywords you use flow naturally within the content of the opening paragraph and relate to the content and purpose of your site. You don't want the search engines to think you're trying to cram in words where they don't fit.

As you can tell, textual HTML content is extremely important to the search engines, which brings me to my next point. Never create a page that is excessive in graphical content. For example, don't display information that should be displayed in text as a graphic file. I've seen this done numerous times. A site may have the best opening statement in the world, but the search engines can't use it because the information is presented in the form of a graphic. No matter how great it looks, the search engines can't read text embedded in your graphics for content. Very often I see a site that has the company name used every time in a graphic logo. If someone were to do a search on the company name, they may not earn enough points to score on the first page of results.

Do not make your home page excessively lengthy. The longer your page is, the less relevant the information on the page becomes to the search engines. I recommend that you keep your home page short and to the point. A page consisting of between 250 and 800 words provides the major search engines with the information they need.

Little things such as how often you update your site can have an effect on how well your site places in search engine results. Spiders can determine how often a page is updated and will revisit your site accordingly. This may lead to higher rankings in some of the major search engines. Fresh content is good for your target market and for search engine rankings. After all, who wants to view stale content?

As a final note, before you submit your site, be sure the content on the page you are submitting is complete. Some of the major search engines will ignore your submission if you have an "under construction" or similar sign on your page.

Do not get too muddled down in the science of search engine optimization. No two search engines' formulas or algorithms are identical, so if you spend all of your time tailoring your site for just one engine, you may have many missed opportunities on your hands. You generally will do just fine if your application of relevant keywords is related to your page at hand, tied together with the different optimization elements that make-up a Web page, and are used consistently and creatively enough to build a theme. A tool such as Web Position (*http://www.webposition.com*) can assist you in analyzing your pages for keyword density and relevancy.

Spamming

Search engines want to provide the most accurate and complete search results they can to their target market. After all, this is what drives all aspects of their business model. If people have no faith in a search engine, the traffic dries up and the sponsored listing fees as well as other advertising fees cease to exist.

In the olden days, Internet marketers used various techniques to trick the search engines into positioning their sites higher in search results. These tricks do not work with the search engines today, and if it is discovered that you are trying to dupe the search engines, some may not list you at all. Search engines are programmed to detect some of these techniques, and you will be penalized in some way if you are discovered. A few of the search engine tricks that used to work—BUT DO NOT WORK TODAY; DON'T USE THEM—pertaining to Web site design are included below. I include them so you can go back to look at your site to see if they have been used on your site, and if they are, this is probably the reason you are having difficulty with search engine placement.

- **Repeating keywords**—Some Web sites repeat the same keywords over and over again, by hiding them in the visible HTML, in invisible layers such as the <NOFRAMES> tag, and in meta-tags. Repeating keywords over and over again by displaying them at the bottom of your document after a number of line breaks counts as well! For example:

  – . . . games, games, games, games, video games, games, games, board games, online games, games, games, games, games . . .

- **Keyword stacking**—It is quite obvious when a site is using this ill-fated technique. Its not so obvious cousin is called keyword stuffing, which is when you exercise the same stacking techniques to aspects of the Web site that should not be optimized, such as spacer images. A spacer image is used by Web developers for just that—properly spacing items on a page. It is not good practice to include descriptive text in an Alt tag for a spacer image.

- **Jamming keywords**—If you are displaying keywords on your Web pages using a very small font, then you are jamming keywords. Why would you even do this unless you were specifically trying to manipulate search results? Don't do it. This spam technique is called "tiny text."

- **Hidden text and links**—Avoid inserting hidden text and links in your Web site for the purpose of getting in more keywords. For example, you can hide keywords in your HTML document by making the text color the same as the background color. Another example is inserting keywords in areas not visible to the end user, such as the hidden layers in style sheets.

- **Misleading title changes**—Making frequent and regular title changes so that the bots think your site is a new site and list you again and again is misleading. In the case of directories, you could change the name of your site just by adding a space, an exclamation mark (!), or "A" as the first character so that you come up first in alphabetical lists.

- **Page swapping**—This practice involves showing one page to a search engine, but a different one to the end user. Quite often you find people hijack content from a top-ranking site, insert it on their page to achieve a top ranking, then replace that page with a completely different page when a desired ranking is achieved.

- **Content duplication**—Say you have one Web page and it is ranking pretty well. You decide it would be nice to improve your ranking, but hey, it would be good to keep your current position too. You decide to duplicate your page, fine-tune a few things, and call it something different. You then submit that page to the search engine. Your ranking improved and now you have two listings. Not bad! Why not do it again? And so on and so forth. If you are caught duplicating Web pages, you will be penalized. Search engines want to provide unique content, not the same page over and over again.

- **Domain spam (mirrored sites)**—Closely related to content duplication, this is when an entire Web site is replicated (or slightly modified) and placed at a different URL. This is usually done to dominate search positions and to boost link popularity, but in the end all it does it hurt you when you get caught. You will get banned for practicing this technique.

- **Refresh meta-tag**—Have you ever visited a site and then been automatically transported to another page within the site? This is the result of a refresh meta-tag. This tag is an HTML document that is designed to automatically replace itself with another HTML document after a certain specified period of time, as defined by the document author—it's like automatic page swapping. Do not abuse this tag. Additionally, don't use a redirect unless it is absolutely necessary. A permanent redirect (HTTP 301) can be used to tell the search engines that the page they are looking for has a new home; this tells them to go there to index it.

Refresh Meta-tag
A tag used to automatically reload or load a new page.

If you do use a refresh meta-tag to redirect users, then it is suggested that you set a delay of at least 15 seconds and provide a link on the new page back to the page they were taken from. Some businesses use refresh meta-tags to redirect users from a page that is obsolete or is no longer there. Refresh meta-tags also may be used to give an automated slideshow or force a sequence of events as part of a design element.

- **Cloaking**—This technique is similar to page swapping and using the refresh meta-tag in that the intent is to serve search engines one page while the end user is served another. Don't do it.

- **Doorway pages**—Also known as gateway pages and bridge pages, doorway pages are pages that lead to your site but are not considered part of your site. Doorway pages lead to your Web site but are tuned to the specific requirements of the search engines. By having different doorway pages with different names (e.g., indexa.html for AltaVista or indexg.html for Google) for each search engine, you can optimize pages for individual engines.

  Unfortunately, because of the need to be ranked high in search engine results and the enormous competition among sites that are trying to get such high listings, doorway pages have increasingly become more popular. Each search engine is different and has different elements in its ranking criteria. You can see the appeal of doorway pages because this allows you to tailor a page specifically for each search engine and thus achieve optimal results.

  Search engines frown upon the use of doorway pages because the intent is obvious—to manipulate rankings in one site's favor with no regard for quality content. Do not use them.

- **Cyber-squatting**—This term refers to stealing traffic from legitimate Web sites. If someone were to operate a Web site called "Gooogle.com" with the extra "o" or "Yahhoo" with an extra "h," that would be considered cyber-squatting. Domain squatting is when a company acquires the familiar domain of another company, either because the domain expired or the original company no longer exists. The new company then uses the familiar domain to promote completely unrelated content. Google, in particular, frowns on cyber-squatting.

- **Links farms**—These are irrelevant linking schemes to boost rankings based on achieving better link popularity. Having thousands of irrelevant links pointing to your Web site does more damage than good. The search engines are on to this technique and they don't like sites that try to manipulate placement. For best results, only pursue links that relate to your Web site and are of interest to your target market.

How do you know if you are spamming a search engine? If the technique you are employing on your Web site does not offer value to your end user and is done solely for the intention of boosting your search engine rankings, then you are probably guilty of spam.

Search engines post guidelines for what they consider acceptable practices. It is advised that you read each search engine's policy to ensure that you conform to their guidelines. Following is Google's policy (*http://www.google.com/ webmasters/guidelines.html*) on quality:

Quality Guidelines—Basic Principles

- Make pages for users, not for search engines. Don't deceive your users, or present different content to search engines than you display to users.

- Avoid tricks intended to improve search engine rankings. A good rule of thumb is whether you'd feel comfortable explaining what you've done to a Web site that competes with you. Another useful test is to ask, "Does this help my users? Would I do this if search engines didn't exist?"

- Don't participate in link schemes designed to increase your site's ranking or PageRank. In particular, avoid links to Web spammers or "bad neighborhoods" on the Web as your own ranking may be affected adversely by those links.

- Don't use unauthorized computer programs to submit pages, check rankings, etc. Such programs consume computing resources and violate our terms of service. Google does not recommend the use of products such as WebPosition Gold that send automatic or programmatic queries to Google.

Quality Guidelines—Specific Recommendations

- Avoid hidden text or hidden links.

- Don't employ cloaking or sneaky redirects.

- Don't send automated queries to Google.

- Don't load pages with irrelevant words.

- Don't create multiple pages, subdomains, or domains with substantially duplicate content.

- Avoid "doorway" pages created just for search engines, or other "cookie cutter" approaches such as affiliate programs with little or no original content.

These quality guidelines cover the most common forms of deceptive or manipulative behavior, but Google may respond negatively to other misleading practices not listed here (e.g., tricking users by registering misspellings of well-known Web sites). It's not safe to assume that just because a specific deceptive technique isn't included on this page, Google approves of it. Webmasters who spend their energies upholding the spirit of the basic principles listed above will provide a much better user experience and subsequently enjoy better ranking than those who spend their time looking for loopholes they can exploit.

If your Web site is mistakenly penalized for spam, your best course of action is to contact the search engine and discuss remedies. If you are applying a technique that is considered spam, get rid of it. Know what is considered search engine spam and avoid it before it ever becomes a problem for you.

Other Important Design Factors

It is not always possible to have a Web site that meets all requirements of a search engine and your target market. Perhaps you are coming in on the tail end of a Web development project or simply want to make your Web site as search engine friendly as possible, without having to do a significant redesign. Here are some common issues and how you deal with them to improve the search engine friendliness of your Web site, whether you are building a new site or are improving your current one:

- Frames

- Robots.txt, meta-robots tag

- Clean code is king

- Navigation techniques

- Revisit Meta-tag

- Cascading style sheets

- Dynamic pages and special characters

- Splash pages and the use of rich media

- Use of tables

- Custom error pages

- Image maps

- Optimization for search localization.

Frames

From a marketing perspective, you should avoid building a Web site entirely based on **frames** when you develop your Web site. This is probably the most recognized hurdle when it comes to search engine optimization.

Frames
The division of a browser's display area into two or more independent areas.

Frames may result in some search engines' being unable to index pages within your site, or they can result in improper pages being indexed. Also, many people simply prefer sites that do not use frames. Frames also cause problems when someone wants to bookmark or add to their favorites a particular page within a framed site. Usually only the home page address is shown.

What I mean by "improper pages being indexed" is that content pages will be indexed, and when the search engines direct users to these content pages, they will likely not be able to navigate your site because the navigation frame probably will not be visible. To prevent this one technique, you can use a robots meta-tag in the header section of your HTML that does not allow bots to proceed beyond your home page. As a result, you can really submit only your home page, which means you have less of a chance of receiving the high rankings you need on the major search engines. Alternatively, you should include textual links to all major sections within your site to accommodate those users who enter your site on a page other than a home page, and to assist the search engines with indexing your site.

Some search engines can read only information between the <NOFRAMES> tags within your master frame. The master frame identifies the other frames. All too often the individuals who apply frames ignore the <NOFRAMES> tags, which is a big no-no. If you do not have any text between the <NOFRAMES> tags, then the search engines that reference your site for information have nothing to look at. This results in your site being listed with little or no information in the indexes, or you are listed so far down in the rankings that no one will ever find you anyway. To remedy this situation, insert textual information containing your most important descriptive keywords between the <NOFRAMES> tags. This gives the search engines something they can see, and it also helps those users who are browsing with browsers that are not frame-compatible.

Now that the search engines have found you, you still have a problem. They can't go anywhere. Create a link within your <NOFRAMES> tags to allow search engines and users with browsers that aren't frame-compatible to get into your site. Frames are a headache when designing your site to be search engine friendly. To make your life easier and from a marketing perspective, it's better to avoid them altogether.

Robots.txt, Meta-Robots Tag

<META-NAME="robots" CONTENT=" "> tells certain bots to follow or not follow hypertext links. The W3 Consortium white paper on spidering (spiders are defined below) offers the following definition and discussion:

- <META-NAME="ROBOTS" CONTENT="ALL | NONE | NOINDEX | NOFOLLOW">

- default = empty = "ALL" "NONE" = "NOINDEX, NOFOLLOW"

- The filler is a comma-separated list of terms:

- ALL, NONE, INDEX, NOINDEX, FOLLOW, NOFOLLOW.

Note: This tag is for users who cannot control the robots.txt file at their sites. It provides a last chance to keep their content out of search services. It was decided not to add syntax to allow robot-specific permissions within the meta-tag. INDEX means that robots are welcome to include this page in search services.

FOLLOW means that robots are welcome to follow links from this page to find other pages. A value of NOFOLLOW allows the page to be indexed, but no links from the page are explored. (This may be useful if the page is a free entry point into pay-per-view content, for example. A value of NONE tells the robot to ignore the page.)

The values of INDEX and FOLLOW should be added to every page unless there is a specific reason that you do not want your page to be indexed. This may be the case if the page is only temporary.

Clean Code Is King

Clean code is essential to search engine success. You want to ensure that you do not have stray tags, HTML errors, or bloated code. Problematic code is bad for the user experience and bad for search engine placement.

Navigation Techniques

JavaScript embedded in anchor tags, drop-down menus, and pull-down menus can cause many headaches for a Web site looking to be indexed by the major search engines. The rollover effect on navigation links is quite common and can add visual appeal to a Web site. A problem arises when JavaScript is encased within the anchor tag, which can cause problems for the search engines.

The rollovers look good, so odds are that if your site is using them you are not going to want to get rid of them. A quick and simple solution to ensure that your site is indexed is to include text-based navigation along the bottom of your Web page as supportive navigation. This approach also gives you the opportunity to get in your keywords twice—once in the Alt tag for your main navigation and the second time around the anchor tag for the supportive text links. In addition, it is to your benefit to include all your JavaScript material in external files to keep the Web site code as clean as possible.

Drop-down menus (e.g., DHTML) and pull-down menus pose similar concerns because of the coding script necessary for them to execute. If you choose to use them, be sure to have an alternative means of navigation available.

Revisit Meta-Tag

You cannot tell a search engine when to visit your Web site, though the theory behind the Revisit Meta-tag is that you can define how often you want a search engine to come back to your Web site. Use the Revisit Meta-tag if you like, but it is not needed.

Cascading Style Sheets (CSS)

CSS is common practice in the Web development world. It gives developers more control over how they want their Web page to be laid out, plus it requires less coding. Less coding means less room for error and better site performance. Like JavaScript, CCS benefits from being stored in external files as opposed to being embedded in each page's individual source code.

Dynamic Pages and Special Characters

Dynamic content has historically caused many problems for search engines because they do not like to be fed duplicate content and the query strings can cause spiders confusion. Times are getting better, but these elements can still cause some difficulties.

Dynamically driven content typically has a query string in the URL such as question marks (?), an ampersand (&), or the percent sign (%). The lengthy URL contains a number of calls to database information and to a template to put together the Web page you see in your browsers. Search engines struggle to figure out what exactly they are supposed to index because they have difficulty understanding what information is actually meaningful and how to present it.

There is no question that dynamically driven sites are common. Your challenge is to work around the needs of the search engines and include pure HTML-based information pages that the search engines can index as a standard part of your Web site . Likewise, there are methods of reducing the complexity of URLs into a form the search engines can process—Amazon.com has been very successful at this. Amazon.com has eliminated all stop symbols from its page URLs. Depending on the technology used to create your Web site (e.g. ASP, CFP, PHP), tools exist to help you rewrite your URLs at the server level to make them more friendly for search engine indexing. This is the same logic applied behind services such as *http://www.tinyurl.com.*

Splash Pages and the Use of Rich Media

A splash page is basically an opening page that leads into a site. Often splash pages consist of a Java or a Macromedia Flash intro that can be slow to load for some users and contain little meaningful content for search engines.

Some Web sites use splash screens that consist of an eye-pleasing image and an invitation to enter the site. Many splash pages implement techniques that automatically send you to the home page once you've seen the splash page, and others invite you to "Click here to enter" in some form or another. Why do people use splash pages on their sites? For one, they usually look nice. Another reason is to provide the user with something to look at while images or content for the home page loads in the background. Individuals also use splash pages as a means of advertising. Splash pages are usually very attractive in appearance, but they often lack content relevant to search engines.

If you do use a splash page on your site, be sure you include the proper meta-tags within your HTML header. This is necessary for search engines that use meta-tags to access this information. This ultimately affects your ranking and how your site is displayed to users in the search results.

Include a paragraph or statement on your splash page that pertains to your site's content. This can help boost your rankings on some of the major search engines that both do and do not use meta-tags. Some search engines will review your opening paragraph and use this information when developing a description for your site that is presented in their search results.

Lastly, include a link into your Web site for the target market and the search engines. Many splash pages exercise the Refresh meta-tag, and this should be avoided.

Use of Tables

Tables can pose indexing problems with some of the search engines. Tables are a common feature found on many Web sites to display information and position content, but if implemented incorrectly, they can cause the search engines some confusion. Also, by using tables close to the top of a page, you are potentially forcing the content you want search engines to see farther down on your page. Because some search engines look only so far, you might be hurting your chances of receiving a high ranking. If you are using tables, place any important information pertaining to the page content above the table, if possible, to help prevent any potential problems.

Tables
Information arranged in columns and rows.

Here's an interesting problem with some search engines. Assume you have a Web site; the main color of the background is white, and you have a table on the page with a dark background. If you were to use white text in the table, some of the major search engines would pick this up as using text that is the same color as the background and ignore your site's submission because it is considered spam to search engines. Using tables is okay; many people do it—just be careful with your choice of colors.

Custom Error Pages

A custom 404 error (page not found) page should be created for your Web site. This page is displayed when a user attempts to access a page that does not exist. The custom error page should contain your company's branding and contain links to all major pages of your Web site, similar to the site map.

If you redesign or rework your Web site, then odds are pages are going to get moved or no longer exist. It is possible that people have pages of the old

Web site bookmarked and those pages may no longer be a part of the new Web site. Also, search engines index select pages of the current Web site, and those pages may also no longer exist under the new design. The custom error page allows people and search engines to easily make updates to their references.

Image Maps

Image maps are single graphics that are split into "hot spots" or sensitive areas that when clicked lead you to different pages or resources within the Web site. The problem with image maps is they basically lock search engines out and prevent them from indexing your Web site properly.

If you do decide to implement image maps, always include text hyperlinks so that the search engines trying to give you a more accurate index can use them. Another option is to include a site map, which is basically the entire layout of your Web site in the form of hypertext links. Submitting your site map to the search engines is also a good idea as it can assist the search engine in making sure it indexes all the pages within your Web site.

Optimization for Search Localization

A recent study by comScore Networks (*http://www.comscore.com*) discovered that 60 percent of consumers search for local content. Much of the local searches surround such topics as restaurants, travel, hotels, and car rentals. With the introduction of Google Local, optimizing your site for local searches has become important.

Search localization is simply when searchers put in their keyword phrase and hit the Local tab while searching on Google or when they simply add a geographic modifier to their query in any search engine in order to get more accurate results from a search engine. If you want to go out to dinner, then odds are you're going to want to go to some place in your area. Common modifiers include:

- ZIP or postal code

- Street

- City or town, along with descriptive words such as "Northern," "Central," "East," "West," and "Southern"

- State or Province, entirely spelled out as well as the abbreviation

- Country, entirely spelled out as well as the abbreviation

- Area code and phone number

- Recognizable landmarks and destinations (e.g., right next door to . . .).

Search localization presents a good opportunity for companies optimizing their Web site. Naturally, any company looking to speak to a local market should be considering search localization when optimizing its Web site. You may not care where the book you ordered comes from, but when you are looking for a house you want a real estate agent in the local area with knowledge of the area.

Optimizing your Web site to speak to the local market is no different from regular search optimization; it just requires a bit of creativity. The same optimization areas, such as page titles, page copy, and meta-tags, are relevant to search localization. Here are some examples to get you started:

- Include geographic keywords in page headers and footers. For example, you can insert a copyright notice at the bottom of each page of your Web site that includes your location: "© 2004, Prince George Hotel, a Centennial Hotels Property. 1725 Market Street in downtown Halifax, Nova Scotia B3J 3R9. Hotel Reservations 1-800-565-1567 • tel 902-425-1986 • fax 902-429-6048."

- Include geographic-related keywords in your page titles. Instead of Fine Italian Dining—il Mercato Restaurant, you could have Fine Italian Dining in Downtown Halifax—il Mercato Restaurant.

- Include geographic-related keywords in your page copy. For example, a paragraph can include a statement such as "Come visit us on the Halifax waterfront, right next door to Historic Properties" to capture high-profile local destinations. You could also have "Just south of Halifax in Peggy's Cove" or "Ten minutes from Halifax." In this case you are adding a modifier to include a nearby city to capitalize on a market that might not think to look for your exact location.

- Include comprehensive geographic-related information throughout your Web site, on your contact page, a maps and directions page, and in your Frequently Asked Questions (FAQs).

- Pay-to-play or PPC is covered in another chapter, but you can use the same geographic modifiers in your paid search placement campaigns to zero in on local markets and increase your return on investment. Yahoo!, Google, SuperPages.com, Findwhat.com, AskJeeves, and Overture are all examples of search providers that offer some means of search localization.

- Add your GPS coordinates to your site as well. With more and more mobile devices equipped with GPS as well as the likelihood that the search engines will include this information in their search query, this will become standard practice. I know that we at Verb Interactive are incorporating this information in most of our client sites these days.

Monitoring Results

As with any business endeavor, you want to know how successful you are. There are a number of ways to measure your search engine placement success.

Web site traffic analysis—You can check the effectiveness of your keyword placement and utilization by using Web traffic analysis reports. This is discussed fully in Chapter 32. You can use Web traffic analysis reports to determine what sites are referring people to you and how often the search engine spiders are visiting your Web site looking for new content. You can strip down this information further to view only search engine referrals. By looking at this information, you can also see exactly what keywords people are using to find you and you can alter the keywords used based on this information. Refining your keywords is one of the key elements to success—you're letting the search engines tell you what you're doing right and what you could be doing better.

Early in the chapter we looked at how Web traffic analysis can contribute to your master keyword list. Figure 6.6 illustrates how WebTrends package (*http://www.webtrends.com*) can show you the keyword phrases the target market is using to locate a Web site.

The amount of targeted traffic and the return on investment (ROI) achieved through your optimization efforts are the true measure of success. How much business you generate online ultimately depends on how well constructed your Web site is. Just because you perform well in the search rankings does not mean the target market automatically does business with you. Once the target market reaches your Web site, it is up to your Web site to sell your business. As with

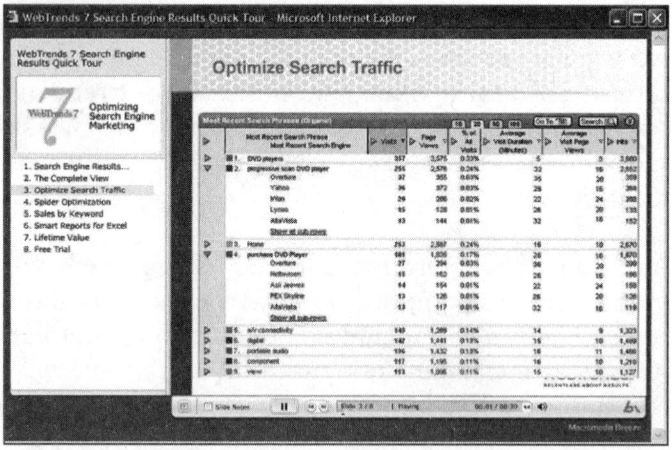

Figure 6.6.   WebTrends reports the keywords used to locate a site.

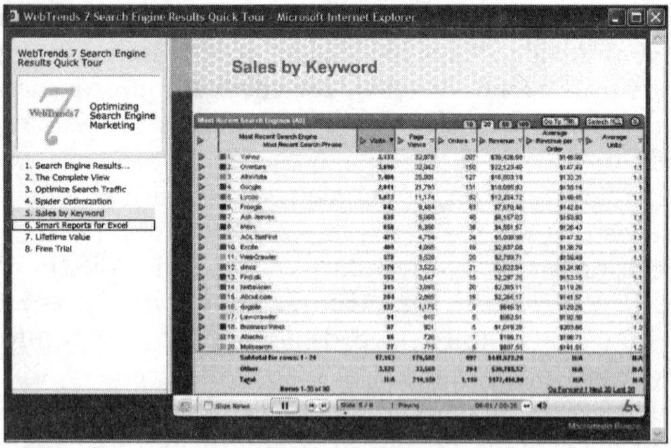

Figure 6.7.   WebTrends tracks sales from their point of origin.

many popular Web traffic analysis and metrics packages, WebTrends can show you sales data as it relates to particular search engines and keywords, which can then be used to calculate your ROI. Figure 6.7 again uses WebTrends to show the number and value of sales that resulted in a referral from a search engine.

Also look at entry pages and paths through your Web site. Because you optimized specific pages for specific keywords, people should be entering your Web site on those pages. If the page is designed to the needs of your target market, it should push them deeper into the Web site or to a point where a transaction takes place, which you can monitor by looking at paths through your Web site and entry pages. For example, say you created a Web page to address a particular special at a hotel with a goal of having the target market fill out a reservation request form. If the specials page is performing well in the engines, but people are staying on the page only a few seconds and are then leaving the Web site, you know it is the page itself that is not performing. Odds are the copy and images do not have the right appeal to the target market, so you can tweak it. The page may not require a complete redesign—it could be that the call to action to fill out the reservation form is not obvious, so make minor changes and monitor performance.

Search engine rankings—You can check the performance of your Web site for a particular keyword phrase by hand or through the use of an application such as WebPosition (*http://www. webposition.com*). If you are checking your results by hand, then you simply need to go to the search engine in which you're interested, enter your keyword phrases, and observe where your Web site ranks. You can hire someone to do this for you as well. Using an application to check your rankings allows you to check more rankings, faster, by automating the process. Search engines tend to frown on this because of the added stress it puts on their system when you have many people using these automated packages to run many searches. Figure 6.8 shows a sample report from the WebPosition software that summarizes search rankings for a series of keywords.

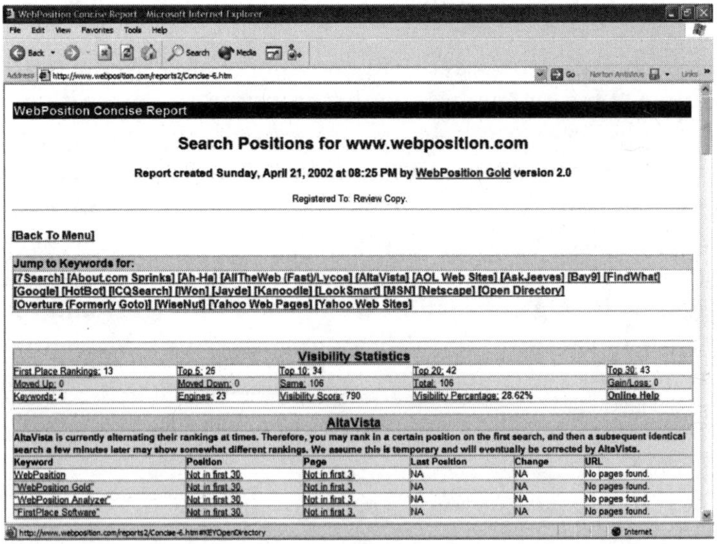

Figure 6.8. WebPosition concise report sample.

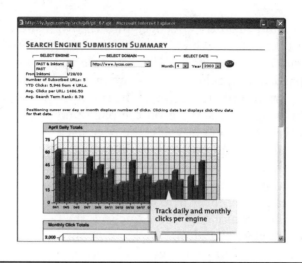

Figure 6.9.   The Lycos InSite program offers basic tracking information.

Checking your search rankings tells you how well your Web site is ranking for particular keyword phrases. You can use this information to keep your rankings current and target your optimization efforts toward gaining increased ratings on any particular engines you wish.

Paid inclusion accounts—The search engines that have paid inclusion features usually give the customer the means to track some search information. This includes basic information such as the keywords searched for and the number of referrals the search engine sent through to the destination Web site. See Figure 6.9 for an example report from the Lycos InSite program.

Pay-to-play accounts—At the heart of all pay-to-play campaigns (PPC) is the tracking functionality. You are paying for each and every click, so it is important to know which search terms are working and which are not. One of the most well known pay-to-play providers is Yahoo! Search Marketing. When you sign up with Yahoo! Search Marketing, you can track all aspects of your campaign, including conversion rates, click-throughs, and revenue generated. Figure 6.10 illustrates Yahoo! Search Marketing's Marketing Console where you can monitor and adjust your marketing campaigns.

Internet Resources for Chapter 6

I have developed a great library of online resources for you to check out regarding designing your site to be search engine friendly in the Resources section of

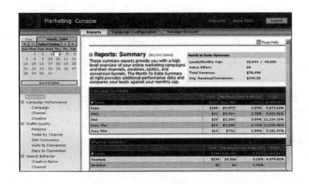

Figure 6.10. Yahoo! Search Marketing's Marketing Console helps you monitor your success.

my Web site at *http://www.susansweeney.com/resources.html*. There you can find additional tips, tools, techniques, and resources.

I have also developed a seminar on this topic which can be taken at any time over the Internet, can be taken live over the Internet at a scheduled time, or can be purchased as a seminar on CD. See *http://www.susansweeney.com/store.html*.

7

Search Engine and Directory Submissions

There are billions of Web pages on the World Wide Web, so how can you increase your chances of being found? One method is to submit your Web site to the many search engines and directories. Once you've optimized your Web site to be search engine friendly, you are ready to face the challenge of submitting it to the most important search engines. By "search engines," I'm referring to the combination of search engines, directories, spiders, and crawlers. You need to be within the first two pages of search results to ensure your best possible success online. This is no easy feat, but this chapter will provide you with the knowledge necessary to get on the road to success. This chapter covers:

- Search engines, directories, and their ranking criteria

- Search engine and directory submission pointers.

Submission Process

Although people often use the term *search engine* interchangeably for search engines and directories/portals, there is a major difference when it comes to submission protocols. The search engines (Google, Yahoo! Search, Teoma, and soon the new MSN/Microsoft Search Engine) allow you to simply "Add your URL." Your URL is your uniform resource locator—also known as your Web address, your www.yourcompanyname.com. When you add your URL, it is put in a queue and when it is your turn, the search engine's spider or crawler visits your site and includes it in its database.

On the other hand, to submit to directories such as the Yahoo! Directory, Open Directory, and Business.com, you have to go to the directory site, select a category, and find the link to its submission form. For the directories, you generally have to complete a detailed form filling in all the blanks of required information.

Paid advertising placements and pay-per-click campaigns are covered in Chapter 8.

A Closer Look at Search Engines and Directories

Search engines and directories share a common goal in providing the searcher with relevant, meaningful results; however, there are many differences in their functionality. In general, search engines have a much larger index than directories and utilize spiders to add sites to their index. In contrast, directories typically have a smaller index and often are maintained by humans. When you're submitting to a site, you can usually tell the difference between a directory and a search engine by the information they request. A search engine typically asks only for the URL you wish to submit and sometimes your e-mail address. A directory usually asks for much more information, including your URL, the category you wish to be added to, the title of your site, a description, and your contact information.

When you do a search on the Internet, in seconds the search engine has digested what you are looking for, searches the millions of pages it knows about, and responds to your request with appropriate sites ranked in order of importance. Amazing! How do they do it?

Search engines use spiders to index your site. Some search engines are free, while others require you to pay for inclusion. Usually, a search engine's spider will include the pages on your site in its database once you have submitted the request to be added, but sometimes they can't for a number of reasons. They might have problems with frames or image maps on a Web site, they might simply miss a page, and so on. Even though a number of spiders constantly crawl the Web looking for sites, I suggest you take a proactive approach and submit all appropriate pages on your site to the search engines to guarantee that all your important pages are properly listed. But before you submit, check the search engine's submission document to be sure submitting more than one page is permitted, because you don't want your site to be rejected. A search engine might also have restrictions on the number of pages you can submit in a single day—perhaps only five or ten pages are allowed to be submitted.

As covered in the previous chapter, some of the search providers share technology. Many search engines and directories either partner with or license the use of another search engine's or directory's search technology. Being indexed by these engines means your Web site is likely to be found in other major search services. For example, Google's results can be found on AOL and Netscape. Google's paid advertising results appear on many other sites as well. Bruce Clay has a fantastic site that shows the relationship among the various search engines. See Figure 7.1 for the chart, which Bruce keeps updated on his site (*http://www.bruceclay.com*).

The ranking criteria can differ to determine who gets top placement, so even though two search engines might use the same database, they can provide different search results. For example, some search engines determine how often a keyword appears on the Web page. It is assumed that if a keyword is used more frequently on a page, then that page is more relevant than other pages

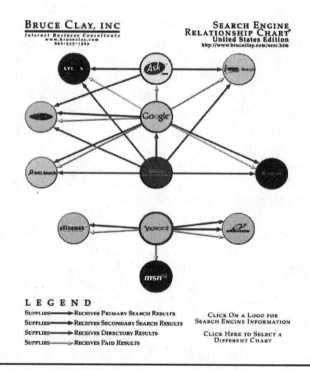

Figure 7.1. Bruce Clay's search engine relationship chart.

with a lower usage of that keyword. Some search engines look for the keyword in the title of the Web page and assume that if the keyword is in the title, then that page must be more relevant than those that don't have the keyword in their title. Some search engines determine where keywords are used and assume that pages with keywords in the headings and in the first couple of paragraphs are more relevant. Some search engines use the number of links pointing to a particular page as part of their ranking criteria. Some search engines use information contained in meta-tags; others don't look at the meta-tags at all.

To summarize, search engines all have different ranking criteria, and this is why you receive different results when you search on the same keyword with different engines. You should learn as much as you can about each of the major search engines' ranking systems and make sure your site is optimized for the search engines before you submit. One particularly useful site with this information is *http://searchenginewatch.com*.

As covered in Chapter 6, the remaining major players in the search engine industry are:

- Google (*http://www.google.com*)

- Yahoo! Search (*http://www.yahoo.com*)

- MSN Search (*http://search.msn.com*).

Let's turn our attention to directories now. Directories are maintained by human administrators. Some directories permit free submissions, while others require you to pay—just like the search engines. Popular directories include:

- Yahoo! (*http://www.yahoo.com*)

- LookSmart (*http://www.looksmart.com*)

- Open Directory (*http://www.dmoz.org*)

- About.com (*http://www.about.com*)

- Business.com (*http://www.business.com*).

When submitting your Web site to a directory, you can expect to wait a longer period of time before seeing your page appear in its index. In general, you can expect to wait from two to eight weeks unless you pay a fee for an expedited review.

For example, the directory aspect of Yahoo! charges US$299 for an expedited review. When you pay the fee, Yahoo! will review your site for inclusion within seven business days. There is no guarantee they will include you; just a guarantee they will review your site and consider including you.

In contrast to a search engine, your site's position in directories depends much less on its design and much more on the initial submission process itself. For this reason, you will be asked for much more information when you submit to a directory.

Directories catalog a smaller number of pages than search engines. Search engines are known for their enormous databases of indexed Web sites. Google currently claims that it has the largest index, with an excess of 8 billion indexed pages! Open Directory, Yahoo!, and LookSmart are popular directories, and each has a few million indexed Web pages.

Submitting to the Search Engines

Registering with search engines is fairly simple. In most cases, you simply have to submit your URL or Internet address on their submission form. Figure 7.2 shows Google's search submission page.

Even if your URL is not registered with search engines, a number of the major search engines may eventually find you, since their bots are continually roaming the Internet looking for new sites to index. There are millions of sites and billions of pages out there, so I suggest that you register your site to ensure

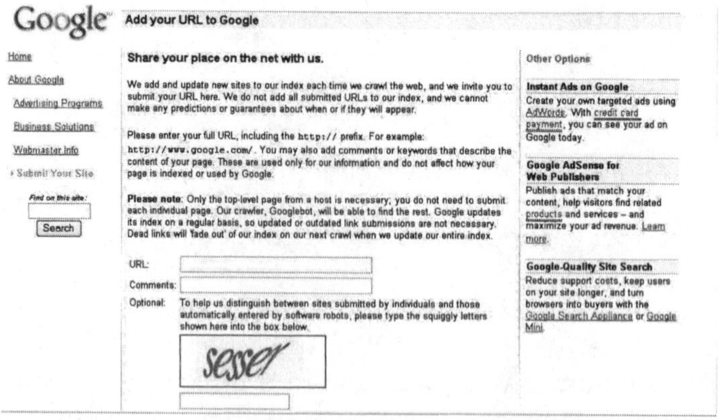

Figure 7.2.   Google's Web page submission form.

a speedier listing. Once you are registered, some of the bots will periodically revisit your site looking for changes and updates. How high you rank depends largely on how well your Web site is optimized, along with other proactive marketing activities such as links strategy development.

Outside of pay-to-play advertising options covered in Chapter 8, you will basically encounter two search submission options:

1. Free submission

2. Paid inclusion.

Free Submissions

Submitting your Web site is free, but no promises are made. Your site might or might not be indexed, and indexing it might take a couple of days or even a few months. There are no guarantees with free submissions.

For free submissions, the search engines have guidelines that indicate how many pages and how often you can submit from a single site. It might be one page in total, one page per day, five pages at a time, or even 50 pages at once. Take the time to read their guidelines to improve your chances of being indexed. Your home page is the most important page on your Web site to be indexed, so if you can submit only one page, be sure that is the one.

Paid Inclusion

With paid inclusion you have more control over your destiny, but it comes at a price, which implies the need to create a search submission budget based on your available resources and the submission fees requested by the search engines.

With paid inclusion you are guaranteed to be indexed by the search engine, up to the number of pages you have paid for, within a short, defined period. Paid inclusion options tend to offer other perks as well, such as guaranteed revisits to update your listings (e.g., every 24 hours), guaranteed inclusion on any partners' Web sites, reporting to track your performance, and in some cases a review of your Web site to ensure its relevance. Just because you paid to have your site indexed does not mean it will rank well. How well your Web site performs depends on how well it is optimized for a particular search engine.

Search engine submissions need to be handled manually rather than by an automated application. Google requires you to type in your Web address as well as a code that is embedded in a graphic on the submission form page. The text that is embedded on that page is different for each visitor. Submission software would be unable to read the text embedded in the graphic and, therefore, would be unable to input the required code into the submission form.

All of the submission suggestions assume you are interested in being indexed by the major U.S.-based search engines. If you plan to submit your Web site to international search engines or international editions of the major search engines, then you need to take into consideration search engine optimization for specific languages and cultures.

Is Your Page Already Indexed?

Before you submit or resubmit to a search engine, check to see if your page is already indexed. Perform a search using the most important keywords you think people will use to find your page. Also, perform a search using your company name.

With many of the search engines, you can narrow the search to your specific domain. Check out the help files for each search engine for more information on how to verify that your URL is included in their index. To check for your Web site in Google, all you have to do is enter the following information into the search field, where "yourwebsite" is replaced by the name of your real Web site:

site:yourwebsite.com

If your page is found and you're happy with the results, you need not submit or resubmit.

Submitting to the Directories

When you submit to a directory, you have to take the time to find the best category for your site. Submitting your site to the wrong category could mean a minimal increase in traffic if no one thinks to look for you in the category you submitted to. Also, your site might not be added if you select an inappropriate category.

When choosing categories you want to pick one (or two if the directory permits you to do so) that consistently gets listed near the top of results for popular searches and that accurately represents your Web site. Use the keyword phrases you have gathered to help you identify good categories. If local traffic is important to your business, you should look at submitting to the regional categories found on most directories. You can also look at where your competitors are listed in the directory for an indication of where you should be focusing your efforts.

LookSmart's Travel category contains subcategories including Activities, Destinations, Lodging, Transportation, and so on. These categories are then often broken down further into other categories within the subcategories. The deeper you go, the more specific the category becomes.

Your site's ranking in a directory depends on the information you provide the directory on the submission form. As such, it is critical that you review each directory's submission procedure and tips. Compared to a search engine, you will be asked for much more information when you submit to a directory. The title, description, and any other information you give them during submission are what is used to rank your site. Figure 7.3 illustrates Open Directory's submission form.

The keyword research you performed for optimizing your Web site is every bit as important when it comes to directories. You must use your important keyword phrases when filling out the directory submission forms. Again, for best results be sure to review each directory's submission guidelines.

Preparing your Directory Submission

Before submitting to the directories, you should go to each one you are interested in submitting to and print the input form. Then develop a Word file with

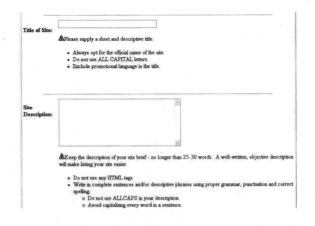

Figure 7.3. Open Directory's submission form.

all the required fields for all the submission forms you will be completing. Take the time up front to develop the submission material carefully. Organize the information in a logical order in a text file. Then, when you go to submit, you can copy and paste the content to the appropriate fields on each of the submission forms.

This approach gives you a starting point and will save you time when submitting your Web site. You may need to adjust your information for each directory submission, though, because they all have unique submission requirements. You need to be careful to follow them to the letter to reduce the risk that a directory editor might change your submission entry. You want your listing to appear in your words, with no editing.

Be sure to spell-check, check, and recheck everything before you start. Spell-checkers won't pick up misspelled "works" if that word is also in the dictionary.

After you print the submission forms, you'll find that there are many common elements requested by the different directories. The information prepared for each page on the site to be indexed should include:

- URL

- Page title

- Ten-word, 25-word, 50-word, and 100-word descriptions for the page (different engines allow different lengths of description)

- List of keywords for each page (based on the master keyword list you generated in the previous chapter)

- Description of the ideal audience for the site

- Categories and subcategories you should be listed under for the different directories you plan to submit to

- Contact information:

  - Company name

  - Contact name

  - E-mail address

– Company address

– Telephone and fax numbers.

Pay Careful Attention to Titles and Descriptions

Pay careful attention to your titles and descriptions. When it comes to supplying a page title, a directory typically wants you to restrict it to your company name. In some cases, they will provide you with additional direction on supplying a descriptive tag line; however, your company name will be required to accurately represent your company or organization. Proper punctuation and capitalization are a must.

It is a good idea to create a number of different descriptions of varying lengths because the different directories allow different description sizes. Start off by creating descriptions consisting of 10, 25, 50, and 100 words. Make sure that you use the right length for each directory, because you won't want it to be altered when it is displayed in search results. Editors are notorious for editing descriptions if your submission does not meet the directory's guidelines, or even a particular editor's style. When submitting to a specific directory, it does not hurt to read the other entries in your category to look for a common theme in the descriptions and then modify yours to follow suit.

Your description should be compelling. When you get your site to appear in the first page or two results of a search, the description is what differentiates your site from the rest. It is the description that entices a prospective visitor to click and visit—or pass by and go to a more exciting site.

Always use your important keywords or keyword phrases in your description. Apply the most important keywords first because keywords used further along in the description are generally given less weight by the major search engines. If possible, use keywords in combination with other keywords, but make sure your description flows naturally. Round off your description with a call to action. It is amazing how many people do what they are told.

Pay Careful Attention to All Fields on the Submission Form

When submitting forms to directories, be careful to fill in every field on the form. Some of the directories reject your registration automatically if you have not filled in all the blanks. When you have to choose categories, select them carefully. It would be a shame to have a great product, great price, and a great site, but be listed in a place where your potential customer would never think about looking for you. I cannot emphasize this enough: read the FAQs or instructions first to ensure that you understand exactly what information is being requested.

Proofread your submission at least twice before you hit the Submit button. It isn't quick or easy to change listings if you make a mistake. Your listing might be wrong for quite a while before it gets corrected. To change a listing you typically have to either contact a category editor directly or fill out a change request form.

More Directory Submission Tips

It generally takes longer to be indexed in a directory because, often, you have human administrators who review every page submitted before adding it to the database. Make sure your page contains quality content, is easy to use, is visually appealing, is free of errors, and is free of performance issues such as a poor load time. It is the administrators who decide if your page is worthwhile before they include it. Pages that do not meet the requirements of the administrator will not be added to the directory—whether or not you abide by best practices in Web site development can make or break you when it comes to getting listed in directories.

Consider Yahoo!'s directory. Yahoo! won't add you if you have Under Construction signs on your site. Yahoo! likes sites that are complete; contain good, pertinent information; are aesthetically pleasing; and are easy to use. Before you submit, be sure to check if you're already in their directory. You may not want or need to submit your site if you're already where you want to be. If you are in their directory but want to change the information displayed, then you can fill out a form located at *http://add.yahoo.com/fast/change* that is specifically used for changing information already listed in the directory.

The following are some other tips to remember when submitting your site to Yahoo!:

- Remember, your submission counts for almost everything here, so do it right. Yahoo! is a directory, not a search engine. Yahoo! Search is the search engine. Designing your site to be search engine friendly means very little here.

- Make sure that what you submit is actually what your site is about. Yahoo!'s administrators will review your site, and if they feel the description you provided does not match your site, you will not be added to their directory.

- Keep your description to 150 characters or less, and use descriptive keywords that fit naturally within the description. Yahoo! reserves the right to modify your description if they see fit. You're the only one who knows what information is important to include in your description, so you probably do not want Yahoo!'s administrators to modify your description because you might lose an important part of your description, resulting in less traffic. Keep in mind that Yahoo! does not like submissions that sound like an advertisement—they like concise, pertinent information.

- Submit a short, relevant title, not something such as "The Best Gardening Site on the Web." Be sure to use descriptive keyword phrases in your title as well. That way, when searches are performed, your page title will be referenced.

- When you submit your site, develop your page title and descriptions to use keywords in combination with others, as this can also give you a boost. Check out your competitors to see who's on the top and what they're doing right.

- If you're looking for local traffic, then submitting to a regional category might be a good approach for you.

- Don't fill out the submission form using ALL CAPITALS—they hate that. Use proper grammar and spelling. Before you submit, be sure to check and recheck your submission.

- If your domain name contains keywords, you can benefit here. Keywords can help your page stand out when a user performs a search on a keyword that is in your domain name.

- Don't forget to fill out Yahoo!'s submission form exactly as requested! Read the help documentation and FAQs, beginning with "How to Suggest Your Site," which can be found at *http://docs.yahoo.com/info/ suggest*.

Keep a Record of your Submissions

Keep a record of the directories and search engines to which you have submitted. The information recorded should include the following:

1. Date of the submission

2. URL of the page submitted

3. Name of the search engine or directory

4. Description used

5. Keywords used

6. Password used

7. Notes section for any other relevant information, such as the contact person for the search engine or directory

8. Date listed.

This list can come in handy when checking the status of your submissions or if you encounter any problems in the future where you need to contact the search provider or resubmit.

Effective Use of Submission Tools and Services

There are many search engine submission services available on the Net that will submit your site to varying numbers of indexes, directories, and search engines. They will register your URL, description, and keywords. Use these services only after you have manually submitted to the most important search engines and directories. Check them to see how comprehensive they are before using these services. Here are a couple of sites for you to look at:

Web Position
http://www.webposition.com
Search engine submission and evaluation software that tells you where your site is positioned in search results of the most popular search engines and directories. Builds traffic by tracking your search engine positions and helping you to improve your rankings.

Position Pro
http://www.positionpro.com
Position Pro is a powerful combination of tools providing you with the ability to analyze your entire Web site like a search engine would. Offers search engine submission services.

SubmitPlus
http://www.submitplus.com
Successfully promoting Web sites around the world since June 23, 1998. Its programs and promotion packages were developed with the input of major search engines to assure precise and search engine friendly results.

Although these services save a great deal of time, it is essential that you be registered accurately in search engines and directories. For the best results, register individually in those search engines you have decided to focus on before you resort to multiple-submission sites. There aren't that many search engines or directories that have long submission forms, so submit manually to ensure the best results. If you have taken the time to do the work described earlier, submit to the major engines yourself. This way you can take full advantage of the legwork you have done targeting the differences between the engines.

To summarize, each search engine is different. Know the unique qualities of each before you submit.

Complete Your Site before You Submit

Before you submit to any of the search engines and directories, take the time to complete your site. Many of the major search engines and directories are not fond of receiving submissions from people who have pages that are not yet complete or that are full of sloppy code. You do not want to spend your time submitting your page only to find out it has not been added because it is still under construction.

Be sure to validate your HTML before submitting. You want your site to be free of errors to ensure your success with submissions. A few of the tools you can use to validate your HTML are:

W3C HTML Validation Service
http://validator.w3.org

NetMechanic
http://www.netmechanic.com/toolbox/html-code.htm

Search Engine World
http://searchengineworld.com/validator

WDG HTML Validator
http://www.htmlhelp.com/tools/validator

Get Multiple Listings

One way to have your site listed many times is to submit many times. Because each page on your site is a potential entry point for search engines and each page has a unique URL, you can submit each URL (each page) in the various search engines, directories, and so on. Each page of your site should be indexed to improve your chances of having your site listed in the top ten search engine results. And because every page on your site is different, each page should have a different title, a different description, and different keywords all tied in to the keyword phrase you have assigned to that page. That way, you increase your chances of being found by people searching for different criteria and keywords.

It is important to abide by netiquette. In some search sites, the previously discussed practice of submitting multiple times is acceptable and might even be encouraged. In others it is considered abuse and is discouraged. Check each search engine's rules, and use your judgment on this one.

Some Final Pointers

Here are some important final pointers you should keep in mind. Always read the submission guidelines before submitting. Search engines and directories often provide a number of valuable tips that can help you to achieve better rankings.

Periodically review your rankings in the major search engines and directories. To make this manageable, I suggest you make a list of the search engines and directories to which you have submitted. Divide your list into four groups. Every week check your ranking with each of the search engines and directories in one group. If you have dropped in the ranking or don't appear in the first couple of pages of search results, then you want to resubmit to that particular search engine or directory. The next week, check your ranking with the next group. By doing so you can set a regular schedule for yourself, keep organized, and determine which search engines and directories you need to resubmit to. Sometimes your site may be removed from an index because the search engine has flushed its directory, or maybe it is just one of those things no one can explain—either way, you will be on top of things. If you make any significant changes to your site, you also might want to resubmit. You want to be sure that your listing reflects your fresh content.

Internet Resources for Chapter 7

I have developed a great library of online resources for you to check out regarding search engine and directory submission in the Resources section of my Web site at *http://www.susansweeney.com/resources.html*. There you can find additional tips, tools, techniques, and resources.

I have also developed a seminar on this topic which can be taken at any time over the Internet, can be taken live over the Internet at a scheduled time, or can be purchased as a seminar on CD. See *http://www.susansweeney.com/store.html*.

8

Developing Your Pay-to-Play Strategy

It used to be that you could simply optimize your Web site using traditional organic search engine optimization techniques, as described in Chapter 6, which would enable you to place high in the major search engines and create a great deal of exposure for your product or service offerings. This can still be accomplished; however, with thousands of people competing for the top positions on a given search results page, it is becoming an increasingly more challenging task. This is why many businesses are leaning toward **PPC** online advertising models to generate targeted exposure for their sites, and in turn their products and services. So what options are available to enable businesses to create targeted exposure for their Web sites, and how can businesses with minimal advertising budgets utilize these advertising models to increase their visibility online? In this chapter, we cover:

PPC
PPC, or pay per click, refers to the advertising model in which advertisers pay for click-throughs to their Web site. Ads or sponsored listings are served based on keywords or themes.

- Maximizing exposure through the Google, Yahoo! Search, and MSN advertising networks

- Expanding your reach with contextual advertising

- Geo-targeting ads to better communicate with your target market

- Dayparting, and how you can capitalize on increased traffic levels during specific time periods

- Developing effective landing pages for your ads.

Generating Targeted Traffic Using PPC Advertising

At the end of the day, the success of your search engine positioning strategy boils down to one thing—results! Over the last several years, many search engines have adopted various PPC advertising models that enable advertisers to pay for exposure on their search results pages, based on targeted keyword sponsorship. Businesses can bid on specific keywords or phrases to have their search engine listings appear only when a searcher conducts a particular query using their engine. If the searcher clicks on a particular listing, the business pays the amount they bid for the click, but they receive a targeted lead delivered to their site for the fee.

The key is that the lead is "targeted." Using traditional organic search engine optimization techniques can cause your site to appear at the top of search results, generating targeted traffic to your Web site, but even the leading search engines often return results that are not exactly what the searcher desires. What if your Web site always appeared when a searcher conducted a query using a targeted keyword relating to the product or service being promoted on your site? What if you could ensure that everyone interested in your products or services had the opportunity to click on your search engine listing to learn more about what you have to offer?

These are the true benefits of developing your PPC or pay-to-play online promotional strategy. By participating in PPC, you generate targeted traffic to your site and you increase brand awareness for your organization, which ultimately results in increased sales for your organization. Over the years some programs have proven successful while others have failed, but at the end of the day, a handful of PPC programs have proven to be extremely successful. These programs include:

- Google AdWords (*http://adwords.google.com*)

- Yahoo! Search Marketing (*http://searchmarketing.yahoo.com*)

- MSN adCenter (*http://advertising.msn.com/msnadcenter*).

All of the major PPC programs have in-depth tutorials, case studies, white papers, and tools to help you learn more about their programs and make them easy for you to use. Things are changing rapidly in this area, as the competition for your advertising dollar is fierce. Changes to these programs, whether we're talking about program updates, program features, new pricing, new tools, new offerings, or program enhancements, are being made on a regular basis.

In this chapter I'll provide an overview of Google AdWords and the Yahoo! Search Marketing programs. Other programs you will want to check out include MSN's adCenter and Kanoodle. The information included in this chapter is current as of the date of publication. For the absolute latest information on these programs, I strongly suggest you visit the advertising sections of all of the major search engine Web sites.

Exploring Google AdWords

Google AdWords has quickly become one of the premier online advertising vehicles for businesses for several reasons. First and foremost, why wouldn't you want to place targeted ads on the Internet's top search engine to generate exposure for your products and services? In addition, by sponsoring keywords and phrases on a cost-per-click basis on such a prominent Web portal, you are guaranteed one thing—targeted exposure.

Some PPC programs provide businesses with the opportunity to outbid each other for top placement of their ads. This means that businesses with large advertising budgets can dominate the top placements using these particular programs, which is not exactly fair to those businesses that cannot afford a high CPC.

CPC

CPC or cost per click refers to the price paid by the advertiser each time a visitor clicks on the advertiser's ad or sponsored listing.

Google AdWords helps to create a level playing field for all advertisers, meaning that even small businesses with a minimal budget can compete with large enterprises for premium listings. Businesses can set their CPC for particular keywords well above their competitors', but this doesn't mean that their ads will appear above the competitions'. AdWords ranks each ad based on a combination of the ad's CPC and the ad's click-through rate. What this means is that if a business with a high CPC creates an irrelevant ad that does not generate any clicks, that ad slowly moves to the bottom of the listing of ads that appears on Google's search results page and is ultimately removed. This enables businesses with a lower CPC, but more relevant ads, to position higher—at no extra cost!

How AdWords Works

Setting up an AdWords account can be accomplished in 15 to 20 minutes by following a few simple steps. When preparing to launch a campaign with AdWords, you first determine where you would like your ads to appear on Google's network of Web sites, and which languages you plan to target with your ads. You can choose to communicate your ads to the masses, or you can opt to geographically target your ads to specific locations—even locations within a specific distance from your business's physical location. Now that's targeted advertising!

You then need to design an Ad Group for your campaign. An Ad Group is a collection of one or more ads that you wish to display on Google's network of sites. Each ad consists of a headline and description that, if designed correctly, relates specifically to the keywords that are associated with the overall Ad Group. Once each ad in a given Ad Group is designed, you select targeted keywords that you wish to be associated with the Ad Group.

Why does an Ad Group contain one or more ads? The AdWords program is designed to work effectively for advertisers, weeding out ads that are not generating targeted traffic for them. To illustrate, assume that a given Ad Group consists of five different ads relating to a specific topic, each with a unique headline and description. When an advertiser launches a campaign, AdWords randomly displays each ad in the Ad Group to the advertiser's target market. Eventually, certain ads in the Ad Group perform better than others, generating more click-throughs. When this happens, AdWords then displays only ads within the Ad Group that are generating results for the client, and slowly removes the others from the rotation. This helps to maximize the effectiveness of the overall ad campaign.

When launching an ad campaign, you are given the opportunity to set a budget for your campaign. You can set a maximum CPC for each Ad Group along with a maximum daily budget for your campaigns. By default, AdWords provides advertisers with a recommended maximum CPC for optimal results with their campaign. The maximum CPC can range anywhere from US$0.01 to US$50.

If you are unsure of what your maximum CPC should be, AdWords provides an excellent traffic-estimation tool that can help you estimate daily traffic for selected keywords and phrases. The traffic-estimation tool helps you fine-tune what your maximum CPC should be based on your overall online advertising budget and campaign objectives. By manipulating the maximum CPC, you are able to determine what your daily expenditures would be based on traffic patterns associated with the keywords that you have selected, along with where your ads will be positioned during the campaign.

Figure 8.1. Google AdWords' strategic advertising network.

Where Do Your Ads Appear?

When you implement a campaign on the AdWords network, your ads appear in more places than just within Google's search results. Through building relationships with some of today's top industry-specific Web sites and search portals, Google expands the reach of your ads to the masses. Popular Web sites such as the New York Times, AOL, Ask Jeeves, and Netscape all display AdWords' advertisements when a Web surfer conducts a search using those sites' search tools. Figure 8.1 shows some of AdWords' more prominent advertising partners.

Extending Your Reach with Yahoo! Search Marketing

Yahoo! Search Marketing, another prominent leader in PPC advertising, boasts that it reaches over 90 percent of the Internet population through its network of advertising affiliates. As a subsidiary of Yahoo! Inc., Yahoo! Search Marketing displays its pay-for-performance sponsored search results on prominent Web sites such as Yahoo!, MSN, CNN, and AltaVista.

Ads that appear on Yahoo! Search Marketing's search results page appear in the form of a sponsored listing. Yahoo! Search Marketing's Sponsored Listings are provided to searchers as the first three search results for any given search. This increases the likelihood that a searcher will click on a listing as it

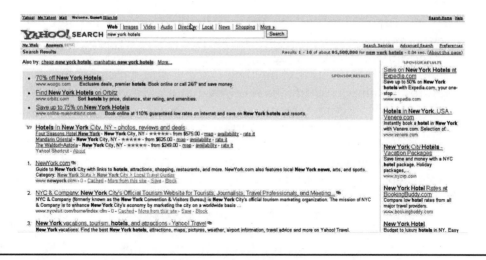

Figure 8.2.   Yahoo! Search Marketing sponsored listing results appear at the top of the results page for the keywords where they were one of the top bidders.

appears as a standard search result to an Internet user. To view an example of a Sponsored Listing, refer to Figure 8.2.

Unlike with programs such as Google AdWords, placement of ads on Yahoo! Search Marketing's network is heavily dependent on the advertiser's online advertising budget. Advertisers with large budgets quite often become "squatters" by bidding into the top three positions for a given keyword or phrase. Yahoo! Search Marketing does not regulate the ads that are displayed based on performance like AdWords does. As long as an advertiser continues to outbid the competition for top placement, it can remain on the top of all listings. Although this seems unfair, it is important to remember that maintaining top placement for prominent keywords often comes at a high price, which is an easy way to blow through an advertising budget in a hurry.

How Yahoo! Search Marketing Works

Launching a campaign using the Yahoo! Search Marketing advertising network is similar in some ways to setting up an AdWords account; however, there are distinct differences between the two. On Yahoo! Search Marketing, there are no Ad Groups with multiple ads that are randomly presented to searchers. Instead, individual ads are developed and associated with each keyword or phrase that is being promoted on the site. Although a single ad can be associated with more than one keyword or phrase, Yahoo! Search Marketing's advertising network does not possess the logic to display one particular ad over another.

The Support Center is the headquarters for all information related to your Yahoo! Search Marketing campaign. Once you become an advertiser, you can log into the Support Center, where you can manage every aspect of your Yahoo! Search Marketing campaign, including payment methods, keyword sponsorships, advertising options, and reporting. You can easily create and launch new ads directly within this section of the site.

To create an ad listing using Yahoo! Search Marketing, you follow a few simple steps. The process begins by researching the different keywords and phrases that you wish to sponsor. You can conduct a query within the Support Center to identify keywords that are being utilized by those who conduct searches on the Yahoo! Search Marketing network. Included within the results, you are presented with the current top bid price, the number of searches conducted within the previous month using the keyword or phrase, and the estimated number of clicks that an ad should receive based on historical statistics. Yahoo! Search Marketing's keyword suggestion tool is a great way for you to identify targeted keywords relating to products and services similar to yours that are being utilized by your target market.

Once you have selected the keywords or phrases that you wish to sponsor, you are prompted to create either a unique headline and description for your advertisement or a common ad listing that will be shared with each keyword selected. Similar to AdWords, to be effective the headline and description should relate specifically to the keyword being sponsored. This will increase the likelihood that a searcher will click on the ad.

As you build your ad campaign, all keywords that are being sponsored are listed within the Support Center, which provides you with a dashboard to view the performance of each ad listing. Within this dashboard you can view the top five bids for each keyword being sponsored and can manage your current CPC with a few clicks. The minimum CPC per keyword using Yahoo! Search Marketing is US$0.10 per click. The user-friendly interface of the Support Center makes it very easy for you to manage your campaigns. The snapshot view of campaign activity makes it very easy for you to identify ad listings that are performing well or are not performing at all, allowing you to take action to improve the performance of the listing.

Where Do Your Ads Appear?

Similar to AdWords, Yahoo! Search Marketing's vast network of affiliated Web sites ensures that you receive maximum exposure for your online marketing efforts. The network of Yahoo! Search Marketing affiliates that are responsible for promoting Yahoo! Search Marketings Premium Listings (ranks 1–3), and Classic Results (ranks 4 and below) includes many prominent search engines and directories, prominent content sites, ISPs, and even the default search results in the world's most prominent Internet browser—Microsoft Internet Explorer. The network sites change from time to time. At the time of this book's publication, the following is a brief listing of current Web sites that display Yahoo! Search Marketing's PPC listings in their search results:

- AltaVista (*www.altavista.com*)

- Excite (*www.excite.com*)

- MSN (*www.msn.com*)

- Sympatico.ca (*www.sympatico.ca*)

- Yahoo! (*www.yahoo.com*)

- Juno (*www.juno.com*)

- Netzero (*www.netzero.com*)

- Metacrawler (*www.metacrawler.com*)

- AlltheWeb (*www.alltheweb.com*)

- CNN (*www.cnn.com*)

- ESPN (*www.espn.com*).

Maximize Exposure with Contextual Advertising

Imagine that a consumer is currently in the market for a home theatre system and is viewing a recognized electronics Web site to learn more about the latest innovations in home theatre technology. If you were a salesperson in a traditional brick-and-mortar store and a consumer wandered into your department, you would approach the consumer as he or she was already semi-engaged in the sale, just trying to figure out what to buy. In a similar way, the latest advancement in contextual advertising enables you to reach those same consumers, but in the online marketplace.

To further illustrate the example, assume that you are that same consumer on the electronics Web site and you are viewing a page of content that strictly provides information on plasma televisions. Accompanying the content on this page is a listing of ads for online retailers who are promoting plasma televisions online. Because the ads relate directly to your area of interest, you click on a link, are directed to a Web site, and ultimately place an inquiry with the online retailer about its product.

Similar to how a Web surfer searches for information using a major search engine and is presented with PPC ads, contextual ads enable advertisers to promote their ad listings on content sites that relate to specific information (e.g., electronics). Contextual advertising provides advertisers with yet another opportunity to target specific customer segments with targeted advertisements. Both AdWords and Yahoo! Search Marketing currently offer advertisers the ability to take advantage of contextual advertising opportunities by promoting their ad listings on related content sites within their respective advertising networks.

Geo-Targeting Your Campaigns

Implementing a PPC strategy enables you to advertise to a mass audience, or to target Internet users in a specific geographic location. As explained earlier in this chapter, AdWords provides you with the opportunity to target customers not only on a state or provincial level, but also on a local level, by displaying advertisements only to potential customers conducting searches in your business's local area.

With AdWords alone, you can choose to target over 250 different countries in up to 14 different languages. You can also choose to advertise within over 200 different regions throughout the United States. Geo-targeting provides you with an increased level of control over where your ads are displayed and how they figure into your advertising budget. By targeting only those locations where you wish your ads to appear, you can maximize your online advertising dollars whether you are working with a small or a large budget.

Dayparting

When you are analyzing your Web traffic logs, you will most likely notice that your traffic levels spike on a particular day of the week or during a specific time period throughout the day. When monitoring the performance of your PPC strategy, you can also note when searchers are more apt to click on one of your ads to visit your site and learn more about what you have to offer. If you notice a significant increase in your click-through rates at a specific time, you can capitalize on this increased visibility.

Adjusting your PPC advertising strategy to capitalize on traffic during a particular point of the day is what is referred to as "dayparting." Reports reveal that when you capture your target market when they are more apt to visit your Web site (e.g., during a particular time of the day, or on a particular day of the week), they will be more apt to click on your ad and ultimately convert to a customer. This strategy requires in-depth analysis of conversion rates, click-through rates, and general traffic levels. The basic premise behind dayparting is that advertisers increase their CPC during the time of the day when searchers will be most apt to view information on their products and services. By increasing your CPC during this timeframe, you maximize the exposure for your products or services—provided that you are presenting the searcher with optimized ads.

Maximizing Your Exposure

Developing ads for your PPC strategy is not just a matter of throwing together a headline and description in the hopes that a customer will click on one of your ads. Well, it could be, but this strategy will not result in your meeting your campaign objectives of click-throughs and conversions. Your ads should be designed to entice the searcher, but be wary that if you create ads that are too inviting, you can rack up your click-through rate quickly without converting any customers at all. The bottom line is that you do not want to entice uninterested searchers to your Web site, as you would be wasting your online advertising budget.

To avoid this issue, make sure that your ads relate specifically to the keywords they are associated with and make sure your message is clear. When a true potential customer views one of your ads, you want that person to say, "Wow, that's exactly what I am looking for." This ensures that your click-throughs are more targeted.

In addition to developing targeted ads for your campaigns, you also want to be sure that when searchers click on your ad, the page they are directed to provides them with information about what you are promoting. Too often, businesses simply point click-throughs to their Web site's homepage, which requires the potential customer to navigate further through the Web site to find more information about the company and its product or service offerings. This often results in wasted clicks and fewer conversions.

Instead, try pointing Web surfers to landing pages that are tailored to specific advertisements. You have to remember that people are not going to buy simply by clicking on your ads—they want information. That's why you would never simply point a new customer to your online order form. However, if you develop a landing page that communicates the features and benefits of the promotion and provides the visitor with a clear "Order Now" call to action, you can increase the likelihood that the visitor will convert to a buyer.

When developing landing pages for your PPC strategy, you should design various pages and test their effectiveness. The key thing to remember is that if someone is searching for "New York Hotels," you do not want your landing page to say something unrelated, but rather to include a call to action that says "Click here for New York hotels." You want to make sure that you provide the viewer with the information that she or he is looking for. In addition, make sure that you do not overwhelm the visitor with navigation options that would distract the visitor from understanding the message you are trying to communicate. Clear communication of your value proposition is the key.

Maximizing Your Budget

One of the biggest mistakes that organizations make is assuming that they have to bid into the number one position to make their PPC strategy work. Being number one is associated with being the best; thus it is very easy to let your ego get in the way of your marketing objectives. Bidding into the top positions for more competitive keywords generates optimal exposure, but it also blows through your budget more quickly than if your ads were appearing in the lower ranks. Constantly bidding into top positions can result in having to start and stop your campaigns if the budget is not available to constantly maintain them.

To maximize the effectiveness of your budget, try bidding into the lower ranks to minimize your average CPC. This helps you to stay under your daily budget and lets you implement longer campaigns with your advertising dollars. Also, bidding on the most competitive keywords is not always the best strategy. Use the tools that are available with your PPC program to identify keywords that are proven to be effective but are not being capitalized on by your competitors. Advertisers typically focus their efforts on the keywords that are most utilized by their target market and avoid keywords that are less popular.

To illustrate, assume that using the Yahoo! Search Marketing PPC program, the most popular keyword related to New York hotel accommodations is the phrase *New York Hotels*. This is the most popular keyword phrase used by your target market, but its CPC is US$5.55. However, after conducting additional research, you discover that the keyword phrase *New York Accommodations* is used slightly less by your target market, but only has an average CPC of US$0.30. This is a much more attractive keyword to sponsor as it still generates targeted exposure for your site, but at only a fraction of the cost. Identifying popular keywords that are cost-effective is an excellent way to stretch your advertising budget—it just requires a little more upfront work to conduct the appropriate keyword research.

Internet Resources for Chapter 8

I have developed a great library of online resources for you to check out regarding search engine pay-to-play strategies in the Resources section of my Web site at *http://www.susansweeney.com/resources.html*. There you can find additional tips, tools, techniques, and resources.

I have also developed a seminar on this topic which can be taken at any time over the Internet, can be taken live over the Internet at a scheduled time, or can be purchased as a seminar on CD. See *http://www.susansweeney.com/store.html*.

9

Utilizing Signature Files to Increase Web Site Traffic

A signature file, or sig file as it is commonly referred to, is your electronic business card. It takes the form of a short memo and is attached at the end of your e-mail messages. You can use your signature file in a number of clever ways, from just giving out phone numbers and addresses, to offering more substantial information. Sig files can be used to let people know about a special event or to inform people about an award or honor your company has received. In this chapter, we cover:

- The appropriate size of sig files

- The content and design of sig files

- Creating sig files to add statements to your messages

- The benefits of sig files.

Presenting Your e-Business Card

A signature file is your e-business card. It should be attached at the end of all your e-mails—those that are sent to individuals and especially those that are sent to forums, discussion groups, newsgroups, and mail lists. Most, if not all, e-mail programs allow for the use of a signature file. If yours doesn't, you should consider switching e-mail programs because sig files can be effective in drawing traffic to your Web site when used appropriately.

Your sig file should always include all basic contact information: name, organization, snail mail address, phone, fax, e-mail, and URL. You should provide every way possible for recipients to reach you; do not provide only the way in which you would like to be contacted. The customer is king and it is the recipients' choice if they would rather call than e-mail you.

Some businesses also have a "Click here" on their sig file, which takes you directly to their Web site. This is a nice idea, but you must also remember to include your URL so that the recipients have it. Sometimes people just print their e-mail to take home that night, and they can't get to your Web site by trying to click on a piece of paper.

You should also include a tag line offering information about your company, its products and services, a current sales promotion, where you will be located at a trade show, a special event you are hosting, an award your company has received, or other marketing-focused information. Sig files are readily accepted online and, when designed properly, comply with netiquette.

Always remember to place *http://* before Web site URLs and *mailto:* before e-mail addresses to make them hypertext links. This allows readers to click on the links to take them directly to a Web site or to e-mail you without having to copy and paste the address in their browser or e-mail program. Without the *http://* before the *www*, some older e-mail programs don't recognize it as a link, meaning that, to get to your site, the recipient has to copy the address, open their browser, and paste the address in the address field to get to the page you are recommending.

How to Develop Your Signature File

In preparation for designing and developing your sig file, you should decide what information you want to include and what you want your e-business card to look like. Depending on the e-mail program you use, you can create your sig file using Windows Notepad, Microsoft Word, or any other word processor and save it as a text file (with a .txt extension), or you can create your sig file within your e-mail program.

All e-mail programs have instructions on setting up your signature files in their "help" text. If you are using Microsoft Outlook, take the following steps to develop your sig file:

Microsoft Outlook

1. On the menu bar, click "Tools."

2. In the drop-down menu, click "Options."

3. Click the "Mail Format" tab.

4. Click the "Signatures" button.

5. Then click the "New" button to add your new signature.

6. Enter a name for your signature, and select the "Next" radio button and click "Next."

7. Enter your signature and click "Finish."

8. If you have more than one signature, pick one that will be used as a default.

9. Click "Ok," then "Ok" again.

The Do's and Dont's of Signature Files

It is a good idea to develop several signature files to use with different groups of recipients. You can use an appropriate sig file for each different group you are targeting. You should update your sig file often to reflect current marketing-related information.

Some e-mail programs allow a maximum of 80 characters per line for sig files. You should design your sig file to fit well within the limits of all programs. Use no more than 65 characters per line to be assured that your sig file will be viewed as you have designed it, no matter what reader is being used. As a matter of fact, the fewer characters the better to ensure that what you have on one line appears on one line (and not two) in your viewers' browsers. Sometimes people open and view their e-mail in a small window and not the full screen.

Some people get really innovative in the design of their sig files. They often include sketches, designs, or logos developed by combining keyboard numbers and punctuation. Including graphics in your sig file is not a good idea. This might look quite nice on your screen, but when you send it to other people who have a different e-mail program or are using different screen resolutions, it could look quite different on their monitors. You should also stay away from using icons or sketches in your signature files. Check out sig files attached to messages you receive or those posted to newsgroups to see what you like, what you don't like, and what suits you best. You can always build it, test it on your colleagues, and then decide whether you should use it or not.

The use of sig files offers a number of benefits to your company. If you use sig files appropriately, you promote your company and your online presence in the following ways:

- The use of sig files increases your company's online exposure. By merely placing a sig file at the end of a posting to a newsgroup, you ensure that your company name will be seen by thousands of people. A great **tag line** with a call to action can encourage people to visit your site.

> **Tag line**
> Advertising message, usually included in your signature file, attached to an e-mail.

- As with any advertisement, the design and content of your sig file can be used to position your business and create or complement a corporate image.

- Using your sig file can enhance the reputation of your company based upon the e-mail that it is attached to. If your postings to newsgroups and mailing lists are helpful and continually appreciated, this will become associated with your company name.

- Using appropriate sig files signals to the online community that you are a member who respects proper netiquette.

Sig File Do's	Sig File Don'ts
Do list all appropriate contact information.	Don't list prices of any kind.
Keep it short, say four to eight lines.	Don't use a sales pitch.
Keep it simple.	Don't use too many symbols.
Provide an appropriate and professional tag line.	Don't list the company's products or services.

Sig Files to Bring Traffic to Your Web Site

The major benefit of sig files is that they can attract visitors to your Web site. Use your signature file as a mini-advertisement for your company and its products and services (called sigvertising). With sigvertising you can go beyond offering the basic contact information. Use your sig file as a tool to bring traffic to your Web site. Instead of simply listing your company's phone number and URL, give the reader some insight into your company and a reason to visit your site.

One of the most important elements of your signature file from a marketing perspective is the tag line. Your signature file should always include a one-line tag line or catch phrase. A tag line is a small sentence that is used in branding and is often recognizable without even the mention of the company or product name. Does your tag line give the reader a real and compelling desire to visit your Web site?

Do you recognize any of these tag lines?

- "We try harder."

- "It's the real thing."

- "Like a rock."

- "Just do it."

- "Kills bugs dead."

A catch phrase might be something that catches the reader's attention and intrigues him or her to find out more. You should include a call to action in the catch phrase wherever possible to have your reader take action. I often include the catch phrase "Check out our Internet Marketing Bootcamp" in my signature file with a hypertext link to my Web site, with positive results. The recipients often do check out our Internet Marketing Bootcamp, ask for additional information on the Bootcamp, and often attend. It works!

Consider some of the following tag line or catch phrase possibilities to increase the traffic to your Web site:

- Announce a sale or special offer. Briefly mention that your company will be having a sale, or inform people that there is a special offer available on your Web site.

- Offer something for free. Inform readers of free information or samples that they can access if they visit your site.

- Announce an event. If your company is organizing or sponsoring a special event, inform people through your sig file, and invite them to your site for more information.

- Announce a contest. If your site is holding a contest, tell readers that they can enter by visiting your site.

- Announce an award or honor. If your company or your Web site has received special recognition, tell people about it through your sig file.

Sig files are accepted online in e-mail, newsgroups, mail lists, and discussion groups. However, be cautious when developing your sig files to ensure that they will be well received. Sig files that are billboards, or sig files that are longer than most of your text messages, are to be avoided. Sig files that are blatant advertisements definitely are not appreciated. The online community reacts unfavorably to hard-sell advertising unless it is done in the proper forum. Here is an example of a sig file that might offend Internet users:

xxxxxxxxxxxxxxxxxxxxxxxxxxxxxxxxxxxxxxxxxxxxxxxxxxxxxxxxxxxxxxxxxxxxxx
Are you in need of a reliable vehicle?
If you are, come on down to Sunnyvale Volkswagen!
We have the best deals in town and will beat any of our competitors' prices
on new and used cars!
Money-back guarantee!
Great deal on a 2006 Diesel Jetta . . . $16,995.
Talk to Jane Doe about our new lease incentives!
101 Main Street, Woodstock, New York 10010
Tel: (800) 555-0000
Cell: (800) 555-1010
Fax: (800) 555-1020
www.bug.com
xxxxxxxxxxxxxxxxxxxxxxxxxxxxxxxxxxxxxxxxxxxxxxxxxxxxxxxxxxxxxxxxxxxxxx

Another mistake that people make is that they try to make their sig files too flashy or eye-catching. Using a lot of large symbols might catch people's eyes, but the impression it leaves will not be memorable. Here is an example of what not to do:

```
??      :):):)?:):):):)?:):):):)?:):):):)?:):):):)?:):):):)?:):):):)?:):):):)    ??
??      !Sunnyvale Volkswagen !                                                  ??
??      !Jane Doe, Marketing Assistant !                                         ??
??      ! jdoe@bug.com !                                                         ??
??      232 Main Street ?      ?800) 555-0000                                    ??
??      Woodstock, New York ?      ? (800) 555-0002                              ??
??      30210                                                                    ??
??                  "Test drives @ www.bug.com"                                  ??
??      :):):)?:):):):)?:):):):)?:):):):)?:):):):)?:):):):)?:):):):)?:):):):)    ??
```

Here are some examples of what sig files should look like:

```
=========================================================
Sunnyvale Volkswagen
Jane Doe, Marketing Assistant
mailto:jdoe@bug.com
101 Main Street, Woodstock, New York, 10010
Tel: (800) 555-0000  Fax:(800) 555-0002
```
"Our once-a-year sales event is on now @ http://www.bug.com"
```
=========================================================
```

Jane Doe, Marketing Assistant
Sunnyvale Volkswagen
jdoe@bug.com

101 Main Street	Tel: (800) 555-0000
Woodstock, New York, 10010	Fax: (800) 555-0001

Check out our online contest **http://www.bug.com** today and WIN!

```
>>>>>>>>>>>>>>>>>>>>>>>>>>>>>>>>>>>>>>>>>>>>>>>>>>>>>>>>
```
Jane Doe, Marketing Assistant
Sunnyvale Volkswagen

101 Main Street	jdoe@bug.com
P.O. Box 101	Tel: (800) 555-0000
Woodstock, New York 10010	URL: www.bug.com

"2006 Winner of the Best Dealership Award"
```
>>>>>>>>>>>>>>>>>>>>>>>>>>>>>>>>>>>>>>>>>>>>>>>>>>>>>>>>
```

Internet Resources for Chapter 9

I have developed a great library of online resources for you to check out regarding signature files in the Resources section of my Web site at *http://www.susansweeney.com/resources.html*. There you can find additional tips, tools, techniques, and resources.

I have also developed a seminar on this topic which can be taken at any time over the Internet, can be taken live over the Internet at a scheduled time, or can be purchased as a seminar on CD. See *http://www.susansweeney.com/store.html*.

10

The E-mail Advantage

E-mail is one of the most crucial forms of communication you have with your clients, potential customers, suppliers, and colleagues. E-mail is a widely accessible and generally accepted form of business communication. We are seeing a huge increase in commercial e-mail volume. The reason for this significant increase is understandable given that e-mail is a very cost-effective, time-efficient tool that has a high response rate. E-mail is used to build your community online, sell products and provide customer service, reinforce brand awareness, and encourage customer loyalty.

In the online community, e-mail is an extremely efficient way to build and maintain relationships. As a marketing tool, e-mail is one of the most cost-effective ways to maintain an ongoing dialogue with your audience.

However, with the overabundance of spam, spam-detection software, filtering of e-mail, and the new anti-spam legislation, things are changing rapidly in the e-mail world. It is becoming a challenge to make sure that your e-mail is received, opened, and responded to.

This chapter focuses on individual e-mails that you send. Mass-marketing e-mails sent to your target market is more fully discussed in Chapter 14 on private mail list marketing.

In this chapter, we cover:

- Strategies for creating effective e-mail messages

- E-mail netiquette

- E-mail marketing tips

- Sending HTML versus ASCII (text-based) e-mail messages.

Making the Connection

E-mail is a communication medium, and, as with all forms of communication, you do not get a second chance to leave a first impression. E-mail must be used appropriately. People receive large amounts of e-mail each day, and the tips in this chapter will help to ensure that your e-mail is taken seriously.

One of the greatest benefits of e-mail is the speed with which you can communicate. E-mail takes seconds rather than weeks to send a message around the world. The cost of this form of communication is negligible, compared to making a long-distance phone call or sending a fax. The economies of scale are significant. One e-mail message can be sent to millions of people across the globe simultaneously. This type of mass mailing is done at a fraction of the cost and a fraction of the time (and internal resources) it would take with **snail mail**.

> **Snail mail**
> Slang term for the regular postal service.

All kinds of files can be sent via e-mail, including sound, video, data, graphics, and text. With an autoresponder, information can immediately be sent automatically to customers and potential customers 24 hours a day, 7 days a week, 365 days a year in response to their online requests. We discuss autoresponders in Chapter 11.

E-mail is interactive. Your current and potential customers can immediately respond to you and carry on an ongoing dialogue with you. E-mail is seen much more like a conversation than a text document. It is perceived as being more personal than snail mail and can go quite a long way in building relationships.

E-mail Program versus Mail List Software

The time has come where mail list software is essential for sending mass, permission-based, marketing e-mail. In this chapter we'll talk about regular, day-to-day e-mail. See Chapter 14 for the discussion on marketing e-mail sent to a group or private mail list marketing.

Effective E-mail Messages

Most people who use this medium get tons of e-mail, including their share of junk e-mail. Many use organization tools, filters, and blockers to screen incoming e-mails. The following tips will increase the effectiveness of your e-mail communication to ensure that you have the best opportunity for your e-mail to be opened, read, and responded to.

The Importance of Your E-mail Subject Line

The first thing most people do when they open their e-mail program is start hitting the delete key. They have an abundance of mail in their inbox and they want to get rid of the clutter, so they delete anything that looks like spam or an ad. How do they determine what is junk? The subject line is usually the deciding factor. It is essential that your e-mail subject line not look like ad copy.

Never send an e-mail message without a subject line. Subject lines should be brief, with the keywords appearing first. The longer the subject line is, the more likely it will not be viewed in its entirety because different people set the viewable subject line space at various widths.

The subject line is equivalent to a headline in a newspaper in terms of attracting reader attention. When you read a newspaper, you don't really read it; generally you skim the headlines and read the articles whose headlines grabbed your attention. The same is true with e-mail. Many recipients, especially those who receive a significant number of e-mails daily, skim the subject lines and read only the articles whose subject line grabs their attention. The subject line is the most important part of your e-mail message because this phrase alone determines whether or not the reader will decide to open your e-mail or delete it.

Effective subject lines:

- Are brief, yet capture the reader's interest

- Don't look like ad copy

- Build business credibility

- Attract attention with action words

- Highlight the most important benefits

- Are always positive

- Put the most important words first.

Effective subject lines should grab the reader's attention, isolate and qualify your best prospects, and draw your reader into the subheads and the text itself. Avoid SHOUTING! Using CAPITALS in your subject line is the same as SHOUTING AT THE READER! DON'T DO IT!! Stay away from ad copy in your subject lines—it is the kiss of death for an e-mail. When most people open their e-mail, they delete all the ads as the first step.

E-mail "To" and "From" Headings Allow You to Personalize

Use personal names in the "To" and "From" headings whenever possible, to create a more personal feeling. People open e-mail from people they know and trust. If your message is coming from 257046@aol.com rather than Jane Doe, will your friends know it is coming from you? Most e-mail programs allow you to attach your own name to your e-mail address.

If you are using Microsoft Outlook, the following are the steps to set up your name in the "From" heading:

1. On the menu bar, click "Tools."

2. On the drop-down menu, click "E-mail Accounts."

3. In the E-mail Section make sure that "View or change existing email accounts" is checked. Then click Next.

4. Highlight the e-mail account you want to edit and click Change.

5. In the User Information section, put your name as you want it to appear in your recipient's From field in the Your Name area. Then click Next.

6. Click Finish and you're done.

For all other e-mail programs, consult the Help file included in the program.

Blind Carbon Copy (BCC)

Have you ever received an e-mail message in which the first screen or first several screens were a string of other people's e-mail addresses to which the message had been sent? Didn't you feel special? Didn't you feel the message was meant just for you? This sort of bulk mailing is very impersonal, and often recipients will delete the message without looking at it.

A few years ago I would have suggested using the BCC feature when sending bulk or group e-mails. Today, a number of Internet service providers look for multiple addresses in the BCC area to determine if an incoming message is spam. If your message is deemed to be spam, it will probably not go through to your intended recipient. This is one of the reasons I recommend moving to private mail list software for marketing messages that are going out to a group. See Chapter 14 on private mail list marketing.

BCC

When blind carbon copy is used in an e-mail message, all recipients' names are hidden so that no one sees who else has received the e-mail.

Effective E-mail Message Formatting

The content of the message should be focused on one topic. If you need to change the subject in the middle of a message, it is better to send a separate e-mail. Alternatively, if you wish to discuss more than one topic, make sure you begin your message with "I have three questions" or "There are four issues I would like to discuss." People are busy; they read their e-mail quickly and they assume you will cover your main points within the first few sentences of your message.

E-mail is similar to writing a business letter in that the spelling and grammar should be correct. This includes the proper use of upper- and lowercase lettering, which many people seem to ignore when sending e-mail. However, e-mail is unlike a business letter in that the tone is completely different. E-mail correspondence is not as formal as business writing. The tone of e-mail is more similar to a polite conversation than a formal letter, which makes it conducive to relationship building.

In general, you should:

- Keep your paragraphs relatively short—no more than seven lines.

- Make your point in the first paragraph.

- Be clear and concise.

- Use *http://* at the beginning of any Web address to ensure that you make it "live." When you provide the URL starting with the *www*, the reader sometimes has to copy and paste the Web address into the address field in the browser if he or she wants to visit your site. When you place *http://* before the *www,* the link is always "live" and the reader just has to click on the address to be taken directly to your site. Make it as easy as possible for your reader to visit your Web site.

- Give your reader a call to action.

- Avoid using fancy formatting such as stationery, graphics, different fonts, italics, and bold, because many e-mail programs cannot display those features. Your message that reads: "I *loved* the flowers. **Love ya**" could be viewed as "I <I>loved<I> the flowers. <B>Love ya<B>" if the recipient's e-mail software can't handle formatting. That kind of loses the impact!

- If your e-mail software doesn't have a spell-check feature, you might want to consider composing your message first in your word-processing program. Spell-check it there, then cut and paste it into your e-mail package. If your e-mail software does have the spell check option, turn it on!

- Choose your words carefully. E-mail is a permanent record of your thoughts, and it can easily be forwarded to others. Whenever you have the urge to send a nasty response, give yourself an hour or two (maybe even 24) to reconsider. Those words can come back to haunt you—and they usually do.

A Call to Action

When you give your readers a call to action, it's amazing how often people will do as they're told. I'll give you an example of something we did at Verb Interactive. We ran a series of ten Internet marketing workshops for a large organization. Their staff and selected clients were invited to participate in any, some, or all of the workshops. Their clients could include up to three employees. Because the workshops extended beyond noon, lunch was provided.

Because we were responsible for organizing and managing the project, we needed to know the approximate number of people who would be attending each of the workshops to organize the luncheons. When we contacted each company's representatives by e-mail looking for participation RSVPs, we conducted an experiment. We sent half the representatives one version of the message and the other half a slightly different version. The only difference between the two messages was that in one, we included a call to action. In that message we asked: "RSVP before Wednesday at noon indicating if you will be attending as we must make arrangements for lunch," and in the other, this same line read: "Please let us know if you are planning to attend as we must make arrangements for lunch."

There was a 95 percent response rate from the group who received the first message. This is because we gave people a call to action and a deadline, and they felt obligated to respond more promptly. Meanwhile, fewer than 50 percent of the people in the second group responded to our message. What does this tell us? To improve your response rate, give your readers a call to action when you send them e-mail. People respond when told to do something; they act with more urgency when there is a deadline.

Appropriate E-mail Reply Tips

Do not include the entire original message in your replies. This is unnecessary and is aggravating to the original sender of the message. However, use enough of the original message to refresh the recipient's memory. Remember to check the "To" and "CC" before you reply. You would not want an entire mail list to receive your response intended only for the sender. The same applies for selecting "Reply to All" instead of "Reply."

HTML or Text?

Should you send e-mail messages as text or as HTML? HTML messages allow you to send what looks like a Web page with graphics and nice formatting via e-mail. These HTML messages are far prettier and eye-catching than text, and studies have shown that HTML messages deliver significantly higher click-through rates.

Today, the rule of thumb is that you send text e-mail for your routine, individual communication and you use HTML for mass, permission-based marketing communication like your newsletter or e-specials. You send your routine e-mail with your e-mail program and you send your HTML marketing e-mail with your private mail list software. See Chapter 14 on private mail list marketing.

Always Use Your Signature Files

As discussed previously, signature files are a great marketing tool. Always attach your signature file to your online communication. See Chapter 9 for information on signature files. Remember to be sure that the signature files are right for the intended audience.

Discerning Use of Attachments

If you are sending a fairly large amount of data, you might want to send it as an attached file to your e-mail message. However, only include an e-mail attachment if you have the recipient's permission to send an attached file. You would never consider going to someone's home, letting yourself in, finding your way into their living room, and then leaving your brochure on the coffee table. However, people do the online equivalent of this when they send an unsolicited attachment. The attachment is sent across the Internet to the recipient's computer and is downloaded and stored on the computer's hard drive. This is considered quite rude and, in most cases, unwanted.

Also, unless the recipient of your e-mail is aware of the file size and is expecting it, don't send an attachment that is larger than 50K. Although your Internet connection might be a cable modem or a T1 line, and a 3 MB file is sent in seconds, the person who is receiving your message and attachment might be using a 14.4 Kbps modem and a slow machine. If you send a 3 MB file, it might take the person with the 14.4 Kbps modem two hours to download the file. Needless to say, he or she won't be too pleased.

Another factor to consider when sending an unsolicited attachment is that the attachment you are sending might be incompatible with the operating system or the software on the recipient's system. You might be using a different platform (Mac/PC) or different operating system, and the recipient might not be able to open and read your file. Even PC to PC or Mac to Mac, the recipient might not be able to open and view the attachment if that particular program is not installed on his or her machine. Someone using a 1994 version of Corel WordPerfect might not be able to read a Microsoft Word 2003 document sent as an attachment. Thus, you have wasted your time sending the file and the recipient's time downloading the file.

Finally, it is a well-known fact that e-mail attachments can act as carriers for computer **viruses.** Many people will not open anything with an attachment, even if it is from someone they know, unless they have specifically requested a file. You might unknowingly send someone an attachment with a virus, and even if the file you send is virus-free, you could still take the blame if recipients find a virus on their system, just because you sent them an attachment. Basically, avoid sending e-mail attach-

Viruses
Programs that contaminate a user's hard drive, often with unwanted results.

ments of any type unless you have the recipient's permission. Be mindful of the size of the file you intend to send, compatibility with other platforms, and computer viruses. One alternative to sending a large attachment is to post the file on a Web server, and in your e-mail message direct users to a URL from which they can download the file.

Expressing Yourself with Emoticons and Shorthand

In verbal communication, you provide details on your mood, meaning, and intention through voice inflections, tone, and volume. You also give clues about your meaning and intention through facial expression and body language. E-mail does not allow for the same expression of feeling. The closest thing we have to this online is the use of emoticons.

> **Emoticons**
> Symbols made from punctuation marks and letters that look like facial expressions.

Emoticon is a combination of "emotion" and "icon." Emoticons are combinations of keyboard characters that give the appearance of a stick figure's emotions. They have to be viewed sideways and are meant to be smiling, frowning, laughing, and so on. Emoticons let you communicate your meaning and intentions to your reader. For example, if your boss gives you an assignment via e-mail and your response is, "Thanks a lot for unloading your dirty work on me," your boss might become upset at your obvious defiance. But if you replied with this: "Thanks a million for unloading your dirty work on me :-)," your boss would understand that you were jokingly accepting the assignment.

Emoticons enable you to add a little personality and life to your text messages. However, their use is not universal and generally should not be used in business correspondence. Some of the more commonly used emoticons include:

:-)	Smiling
:-@	Screaming
:-0 or :-o	Wow!
:-p	Tongue wagging
;-)	Wink
(-:	I'm left-handed
:-V	Shout
:-&	Tongue-tied
:-r	Tongue hanging out
;-(or ;-<	Crying

:-#	My lips are sealed!
:-*	Oops!
:-S	I'm totally confused.
8-0	No way!
:-	Skeptical
:-<	Sad or frown
~~:-(	I just got flamed!
%-0	Bug-eyed
:\	Befuddled
:-D	Laughing, big smile
}:->	Devilish, devious

E-mail shorthand is used in newsgroups and other e-mail to represent commonly used phrases. Some common abbreviations are:

- BTW   By the way

- IMHO   In my humble opinion

- IMO   In my opinion

- IOW   In other words

- JFYI   Just for your information

- NBD   No big deal

- NOYB   None of your business

- TIA   Thanks in advance

- PMFJI   Pardon me for jumping in

- OIC   Oh, I see . . .

- OTL   Out to lunch

- OTOH   On the other hand

- LOL   Laughing out loud

- LMHO   Laughing my head off

- ROFL   Rolling on the floor laughing

- BFN   Bye for now

- CYA   See ya!

- FWIW   For what it's worth

- IAE   In any event

- BBL   Be back later

- BRB   Be right back

- RS   Real soon

- WYSIWYG   What you see is what you get

- <g>   Adding a grin

Because e-mail shorthand is most commonly used in newsgroups and chat rooms, you will be most successful when using these acronyms with others who are familiar with them.

E-mail Marketing Tips

Be prepared. You will receive a number of e-mails requesting information on your company, your products, your locations, and so on, from people who have seen your e-mail address on letterhead, ads, business cards, and sig files. Don't wait for the first inquiry before you begin to develop your company materials. Here are some tips. Following them will make you more prepared to respond.

Include a Brochure and Personal Note

Have an electronic brochure or corporate information available that you can easily access and send via e-mail. Try to send a personal note in your e-mail along with any material requested.

Gather a Library of Responses

Different people will ask a number of the same questions, and over time you should develop a library of responses to these frequently asked questions. When responding to an e-mail, ask yourself if you are likely to get the question again. If your answer is "yes," then consider developing a document in your word processor called "Frequently Asked Questions," or "FAQs." In the future, when you get a question that you have answered before, simply cut and paste your response from your FAQs file into your e-mail message. Always make sure to appropriately edit and personalize your responses.

Following Formalities with E-mail Netiquette

When writing e-mails, remember these points:

- Be courteous. Remember your pleases and thank-yous.

- Reply promptly—within 24 hours.

- Be brief.

- Use upper- and lowercase characters appropriately. ALL CAPITALS indicates SHOUTING!

- Use emoticons only where appropriate—that is, if the person you are sending the e-mail to is a personal friend or colleague.

- Check your grammar and spelling.

- Use attachments sparingly.

- Do not send unsolicited bulk e-mail.

Reply Promptly

People expect an answer the same day or the next day at the latest. E-mail communication is like voice mail. If you do not respond within 24 hours, you send a very clear message to your clients, potential clients, and colleagues: "Your communication is not important to me." Respond within 24 hours, even if the message is only, "Sorry, I can't get to this immediately. I'll try to have a reply for you by the end of the week." This might be a response you will want to save in a readily available file, from which you can copy and paste into an e-mail message. A prompt reply, even if it says you can't respond immediately, is better than a delayed full response. The people writing you for information will appreciate the fact that you felt their message was important enough to respond to immediately.

Internet Resources for Chapter 10

I have developed a great library of online resources for you to check out regarding e-mail in the Resources section of my Web site at *http://www.susansweeney.com/resources.html*. There you can find additional tips, tools, techniques, and resources.

I have also developed a seminar on this topic which can be taken at any time over the Internet, can be taken live over the Internet at a scheduled time, or can be purchased as a seminar on CD. See *http://www.susansweeney.com/store.html*.

11

Autoresponders

Autoresponders act much like fax-on-demand systems. With fax-on-demand systems, you call from your fax machine, dial the specified code, and get back the requested document on your fax machine. The **autoresponder** works much the same way—you send an e-mail to an autoresponder e-mail address and you get back the requested information via e-mail. In this chapter, you will learn:

> **Autoresponder**
> A computer program that automatically returns a prewritten message to anyone who submits e-mail to a particular Internet address.

- What autoresponders are

- Why you should use autoresponders

- What types of information to send via autoresponders

- Autoresponder features

- Tips on successful marketing through autoresponders.

What Are Autoresponders?

An autoresponder is a program located on a mail server that is set up to automatically send a preprogrammed reply to an e-mail address that sends mail to it. The reply can be a single message or a series of preprogrammed messages. They are known by many names, such as infobots, responders, mailbots, autobots, automailers, or e-mail-on-demand.

Why Use Autoresponders?

One of the major benefits of using an autoresponder is the immediate response—24 hours a day, 7 days a week, 365 days a year—providing immediate gratification for the recipient.

Autoresponders are a real time saver, eliminating the need for manual responses for many mundane and routine requests. They also enable you to track responses to various offers to assist you in your ongoing marketing efforts.

One big advantage with today's autoresponders is the ability to schedule multiple messages at predetermined intervals. The first response can go immediately, with a second message timed to go two days after the first, a third message to go five days after the second, and so on. Market research shows that a prospect needs to be exposed to your message multiple times to become a motivated buyer.

Today's autoresponders are getting even more sophisticated in terms of mail list administration. These programs gather the e-mail addresses of people requesting information, and store them in a database. The program adds new names to the database and eliminates e-mail addresses that no longer work. Today's autoresponder programs also provide reports about site visitors requesting information. This technology is very cost-effective when compared to manual responses by a human, not to mention the associated telephone and fax costs.

Personalization is a standard feature of today's autoresponder programs. Autoresponders are used to send all kinds of information:

- Price lists

- Welcome letters

- Thank you letters

- Out-of-office advice

- Order confirmations

- Sales letters

- Catalogs

- News releases

- Brochures

- Job lists

- Spec sheets

- Assembly instructions.

You can provide a copy of your newsletter so people can read a copy before subscribing, or anything else in which your target market might be interested.

Why use an autoresponder when you could just provide the information on your Web site? There are many reasons. With the autoresponder you have the interested party's name and e-mail address; you don't get that from a visitor to your site. The autoresponder also provides you with the opportunity to send multiple messages to your potential customer.

Types of Autoresponders

There are three different types of autoresponders:

- Free

- Web host

- Other autoresponder providers.

There are many free or minimal-fee autoresponders available that come with an ad on your responder page. Some Web hosting companies provide autoresponders in their Web hosting packages. Some storefront providers are including autoresponders in their product offerings. There also are many autoresponder service providers that offer packages for a fee if you don't want to have ads placed on your responder page.

The important thing is to get the autoresponder that has the features you are looking for.

Autoresponder Features

When you are looking for an autoresponder, you want to make sure it has all the features to enable you to make the most of this marketing activity. Today's autoresponders keep getting better—new features are being added all the time. Some of the things you want to look for are discussed below.

Personalization

Today's autoresponders capture the requester's name as well as e-mail address, allowing personalized responses.

Multiple Responses

Studies have shown that a potential customer has to be exposed to your message multiple times before he or she is ready to buy. Many autoresponders allow multiple messages on a scheduled time line.

Size of Message

Some autoresponders have a limit on the size of the message that can be sent. Ensure that your autoresponder can handle any message you would want to send to prospective customers.

Tracking

You must have access to tracking reports that provide you with information to enable you to track the results of your marketing efforts. You need to be able to determine what is working and what is not.

HTML Messaging

Choose an autoresponder that can handle HTML and plain text e-mails. Studies have shown that HTML marketing e-mails get a higher click-through rate. Autoresponders are constantly being enhanced. Stay current.

Successful Marketing through Autoresponders

The technology itself is only one piece of this marketing technique. The content of the messages sent out by the autoresponder is the determining factor in converting recipients of your message to customers. The following tips will help you produce effective messages:

- Personalize. Personalize your messages using the recipient's name throughout the message and in the subject line.

- Tone. Selling is all about relationships. Give your messages a tone that builds relationships.

- Focus on the reader's needs, and how your product or service provides the solution. Focus on the benefits.

- Subject line. Have a catchy subject line, but don't use ad copy. Ad copy in a subject line is a sure way to get your message deleted before it is read.

- Include a call to action. It is amazing how often people do what they are told to do.

- Use correct spelling, upper- and lowercase letters, grammar, and punctuation. This correspondence is business correspondence and is a reflection of everything related to how you do business.

- Get to the point quickly. Online readers have little patience with verbose messages.

- Write for scannability. Have a maximum of six or seven lines per paragraph.

Internet Resources for Chapter 11

I have developed a great library of online resources for you to check out regarding autoresponders in the Resources section of my Web site at *http://www.susansweeney.com/resources.html*. There you can find additional tips, tools, techniques, and resources.

I have also developed a seminar on this topic which can be taken at any time over the Internet, can be taken live over the Internet at a scheduled time, or can be purchased as a seminar on CD. See *http://www.susansweeney.com/ store.html.*

12

Effective Promotional Use of Newsgroups

People participate in newsgroups by "posting" or e-mailing comments, questions, or answers to other participants' questions, thus taking part in a conversation or thread. Using proper netiquette is important. To do this, read the FAQ files and rules, "lurk" first, and stay on topic. In this chapter, we cover:

- The benefits of using newsgroups in your marketing plan

- Newsgroup netiquette

- Reading the FAQ files, abiding by the rules, and lurking

- How to advertise if advertising is not allowed

- Developing your Usenet marketing strategy

- Identifying your target newsgroups

- Participating in this online community

- Responding correctly to messages

- Cross-posting and spamming

- Using signature files.

Newsgroups—What Are They?

Every day, people from all over the globe enter a virtual community with others who are interested in the same topic. These people are brought together by their common interest in the topic of discussion. While they are in this virtual community, only that specific topic is discussed. There are many communities discussing different topics. You can visit and participate in as many of them as you wish. These virtual communities are called **newsgroups.**

Newsgroup
A discussion group on the Internet that focuses on a specific subject.

Newsgroups are hierarchical and are arranged by subject. Each newsgroup is dedicated to a discussion of a particular topic, such as antique cars, home schooling, travel, artificial intelligence, or the latest hot band.

Visitors to these virtual communities can "post" messages. These messages might be questions or comments or may be responses to other participants. Everyone who visits the newsgroup has the opportunity to view these "postings." Often, many visitors participate in these discussions, and every side of the issue is presented.

There are three types of newsgroup visitors:

- People asking questions or wanting advice

- People providing answers or advice

- People who read the discussion without taking part.

The Changing Face of Newsgroups

Back in the early days, Usenet newsgroups started out as places where academics conducted discussions on research. They quickly expanded to include newsgroups on every topic imaginable, with participants having wonderful conversations relevant to the topic. Usenet newsgroups had to be accessed using your newsgroup reader. Today newsgroups can be accessed through the Web.

Then commercialization saturated the Web, and today there are many newsgroups overrun with advertisements with very little topical discussion taking place. However, there are still many newsgroups that have vibrant discussions with loyal participants that provide a great opportunity for communicating with your target market.

Every visitor to a newsgroup made an effort to get there. He or she chose the specific newsgroup for a reason, usually an interest in the topic being discussed. If your business's products or services are related to that topic, you have found a group of your target market (they have prequalified themselves) in one place interested in discussing what you have to offer.

The Benefits of Newsgroups

There are many ways online marketers can benefit from participating in newsgroups:

- Reaching prospective customers. You can immediately reach thousands of your targeted potential customers with a single message.

- Communicating with existing customers. You can provide your loyal customers with valuable information.

- Market research. You can use newsgroups to find out the latest trends, customer needs, what people are looking for, and what they are talking about. These newsgroups can be beehives of information where you can check out your competition and gather invaluable data on your market.

- Reputation building. By answering people's questions and helping to solve their problems, you build your reputation as an expert in the field.

- Increased traffic. You can direct people to your commercial Web site if you do it in an informative way.

Thousands of Newsgroup Categories

Newsgroups are organized into different types of discussions or categories. Each of the major categories has lots of individual newsgroups in which you can participate. Major newsgroup categories include:

- alt—Discussions on alternative topics.

- biz—Discussions on business topics. You might find groups that allow advertising here.

- comp—Discussions on computer hardware- and software-related topics.

- humanities—Discussions on fine arts, literature, and philosophy topics.

- misc—Discussions of miscellaneous topics that don't have their own categories such as employment, health, and other issues.

- news—Discussions on Usenet news and administration.

- rec—Discussions on recreation topics such as games, hobbies, and sports.

- sci—Discussions on science.

- soc—Discussions on social issues.

- talk—Making conversation.

Each of the major categories has a number of subgroups, and each of the subgroups has a number of sub-subgroups. For example, under the rec major group you can find a subgroup rec.sports. Here the discussion revolves around all kinds of sports. Under the subgroup rec.sports you can find sub-subgroups and sub-sub-subgroups—for example:

- rec.sports

- rec.sports.hockey

- rec.sports.hockey.NHL

- rec.sports.hockey.NHL.BostonBruins.

As you can see, the longer the name, the narrower is the discussion that is taking place.

Target Appropriate Newsgroups

With the large number of Usenet newsgroups that currently exist and additional groups being introduced every day, it is a formidable task to identify appropriate newsgroups for your company's Internet marketing activities. First, you need to determine which newsgroups your prospective customers frequent.

Look for a close fit between a newsgroup and the product or service you are offering. For example, if your company sells software that aids genealogical work, then one fruitful newsgroup for your business might be soc.genealogy.methods. Try finding newsgroups that your target market would enjoy reading, or ask your clients or customers which newsgroups they participate in or find interesting.

There are many ways to find appropriate Usenet newsgroup listings. You can do a search using the newsgroup functions of the two leading browsers, Netscape Navigator and Microsoft Internet Explorer, and most newsreader programs have a search capability.

Search the newsgroups for keywords that relate to your target market, your product, or your service to identify possible newsgroups for your marketing effort. A good place to start is Google Groups (*http://groups.google.com*), or you can go to *http://www.google.com* and select "Groups" from the four tabs (Web, Images, Groups, or Directories). Here you can conduct a keyword search of the Usenet newsgroups by typing your keywords into the search box and clicking "Google Search." The search results are displayed in chronological order, with the results at the top being the most recently used. You should choose keywords right for your target customer or client. These methods can identify a fairly large list of potential newsgroups to be considered for your marketing activities.

If your company specializes in providing exotic vacations to Mexico, search for keywords like *Mexico, vacation, travel, tropical, resorts, beaches,* and so on, to find potential newsgroups for your marketing effort. A benefit of the Google site is that you can post to the newsgroups directly from the site. You don't have to go through alternative software to do so.

Read the FAQ Files and Abide by the Rules

Read the FAQ files, **charter,** and rules about posting and advertising for each of your target newsgroups. It is very important that you abide by all the rules. If the FAQ files do not mention

Charter
Established rules and guidelines.

the group's stance on commercial advertising and announcements, then go back to Google Groups. Conduct a search based on the group's name and charter. This tells you where the newsgroup stands on commercial activity.

Lurking for Potential Customers

Once you have narrowed your potential newsgroup list, visit each one to determine whether its participants are, in fact, potential customers. Spend time **lurking.** Monitor the types of messages being posted. Is there likely to be an opportunity for you to contribute? Are the participants your target market? Research the newsgroup to ascertain if it might appeal to your customers. The name of the newsgroup might not reveal what the newsgroup is about, so take your time and make sure.

Lurking
Browsing without posting.

Tips on Posting Messages

After you have become familiar with the rules of your selected newsgroup, have spent some time lurking, and have decided that the newsgroup is one where your target market is participating, you can begin to post messages. Remember to abide by the rules! If the rules do not allow advertising, then do not blatantly post an ad. To take full advantage of the newsgroup, you have to gain the trust of its members. With one wrong message, you could outrage all of the potential customers who participate in the newsgroup.

It is a good idea to run a test before you post a message to a newsgroup. Doing a test shows you how the posting works and prevents you from making a mistake when it comes to the real thing.

Becoming a respected member in a newsgroup is a way to promote yourself as well as your company. Provide valuable responses—the readers can tell when you are making a valuable contribution and when you are just advertising. In time you might forget that you began reading the newsgroup to promote your business. You will find yourself reading newsgroups in order to participate in stimulating discussions. You will be discussing anything and everything about the newsgroup subject. Only mention your Web site when you find an opportunity to bring your business knowledge into the conversation.

Newsgroups exist for specific purposes. They can be designed for discussions, news announcements, postings related to particular topics, and even buying and selling goods. They might have hundreds of messages sorted and available for access at any moment. Newsgroup participants will decide whether to open or pass up your posted message based on the words in the subject area. Make your subject short and catchy so that your message will be read. Try to put the most important words of the subject first. This is a critical part in posting a message to a newsgroup. Some people adjust the screen to see only the first few words in the subject area. When deciding on the text for the subject area, think about what keywords someone would use to search for information on the content of your message. The worst thing that you can do is post a message to a newsgroup with no subject at all. This will definitely receive no attention and is a waste of your time.

Start your message with a short description of how it relates to the group's main topic. People are looking for answers to specific questions, so it is rude to jump into the conversation with a topic that doesn't match the one in the subject line. You should attempt to get your message across right away. You should get to the point of your message in the first sentence. By doing so, you catch the readers' attention and ensure that they read the entire message.

Message length should be short—no longer than 24 lines. Short paragraphs of six or seven lines work well. Write for scannability.

When responding to a message in a newsgroup, you have the option of privately responding to the individual who posted the message or of responding through the newsgroup. Determine which is better under the given circumstances. If your message is of value to the entire group or promotes your company's capabilities, then post the response to the newsgroup for all to see. If you think that your company has a solution for the individual and would like to provide details to the "target customer," but feel that it would not benefit the other members of the group, then deliver a private response. Often you do both because once the answer to a question has been received, the original poster might not visit the newsgroup for awhile and you want to make sure he or she has the benefit of your posting. Whichever approach you take, make sure that you respond as quickly as possible so that the first message is still fresh in the mind of the recipient.

Tips to Ensure That Your Messages Are Well Received

Here are some basic rules to help you post well-received messages.

Keep to the Newsgroup Topic

Make sure you always stay on the newsgroup's topic of discussion. People participate in specific newsgroups because of that subject and don't appreciate off-topic postings.

Stay on the Thread

When responding to a message, use the Reply option. When you reply without changing the subject line, your message will appear immediately below the message you are responding to in the newsgroup. This is referred to as "staying on thread" and makes it easy for others to follow the discussion.

Make a Contribution

Informed, quality responses to people's questions give you credibility with the group and reflect well upon you and your company. If you post positive and useful information, visitors will return to the newsgroups and look for your posts.

Don't Post Commercials or Advertisements

Advertising is not welcome in most newsgroups, and many charters specifically forbid the posting of ads. Read the FAQ files before posting a message. If the newsgroup does not allow commercial messages or ads, don't post them.

You Don't Have to Have the Last Word

Don't post gratuitous responses in newsgroups. Never post a message with just a "Thanks" or "I like it" if you have nothing else to contribute. If you feel such a response is warranted or would like to discuss the issue privately, send a private e-mail to the person to convey your appreciation or opinion.

Newsgroup Advertising Hints

Newsgroups have been developed for different audiences and different topics. Some newsgroups are dedicated to posting advertisements. If advertising is appropriate for your company, the following newsgroup types might be included in your Internet marketing strategy. Most of the newsgroups that allow advertising are readily identifiable. The newsgroup name itself might include one of the following:

- biz

- classified

- for sale

- marketplace.

Again, read the FAQ files and lurk to determine if the newsgroup is appropriate for your target market before you post. Use a short, catchy subject line with keywords at the beginning—the subject will determine whether your message warrants a read or a pass. Avoid ALL CAPITALS. This is equivalent to shouting on the Internet. Stay away from !!!!, ****, @@@@, and other such symbols.

When you have found a newsgroup whose participants include your target market but the newsgroup does not allow advertising, don't despair. When responding to queries or providing information that is of genuine interest to the newsgroup, you have the opportunity to attach your sig file. A sig file can be as effective as an ad if it is designed properly. Your message should offer valuable information pertinent to the discussion. (A thinly veiled excuse to get your sig file posted will not be appreciated.) If your information is relevant and of value to the participants of the newsgroup, the fact that the tag line in your sig file is an advertisement will not matter—in fact, it could add credibility to the information you have provided and enhance your company's reputation. See Chapter 9 for discussion on signature files.

Cross-Posting and Spamming

Cross-posting is posting identical messages to a number of relevant newsgroups. Doing this is considered to be inappropriate because of the number of common users in associated newsgroups. Spamming is posting identical or nearly identical messages to irrelevant newsgroups without care or regard for the posting guidelines, the newsgroup topic, or the interests of the group. Cross-posting and spamming annoy the readers of the newsgroup. Doing these things reflects badly on you and your company and prevents you from achieving your online marketing objectives.

Earning Respect with Newsgroup Netiquette

Following are ten rules for netiquette. Incorporating them in your newsgroup posting will gain you respect by the other participants.

1. Don't use CAPITALS. They are akin to shouting on the Internet.

2. Don't post ads where they are not welcome.

3. Do provide valuable, on-topic information for the newsgroup.

4. Don't be rude or sarcastic.

5. Don't include the entire message you are replying to in your response. Only quote relevant sections of the original message.

6. Do a thorough review of your message before you post. Check your spelling and grammar. Check your subject line; it should be short and catchy with the keywords first.

7. Do provide an appropriate sig file.

8. Don't post messages that are too lengthy. Online communication tends to be one screen or less.

9. Don't spam or cross-post.

10. Don't post replies that contribute nothing to the discussion (e.g., "I agree" or "Thanks").

Internet Resources for Chapter 12

I have developed a great library of online resources for you to check out regarding newsgroup marketing in the Resources section of my Web site at *http://www.susansweeney.com/resources.html*. There you can find additional tips, tools, techniques, and resources.

I have also developed a seminar on this topic which can be taken at any time over the Internet, can be taken live over the Internet at a scheduled time, or can be purchased as a seminar on CD. See *http://www.susansweeney.com/store.html*.

13

Effective Promotion Through Publicly Accessible Mailing Lists

Internet mailing lists are quick and easy ways to distribute information to a large number of people. There are thousands of publicly available online lists. You can also create your own Internet mailing lists to keep your clients and prospects informed of company events, product announcements, and press releases. In this chapter, we cover:

- How to identify useful publicly accessible mailing lists (discussion lists)

- Subscribing to the mailing list

- Writing messages that will be read

- Mailing list netiquette

- Creating your own mailing list.

Connecting with Your Target Audience

Discussion mailing lists are publicly accessible and are focused on a particular subject. Participating in a discussion list relevant to your line of business can help you attract new customers. Discussion lists are organized hierarchically by subject in a way similar to Usenet newsgroups. Likewise, the membership of each discussion mailing list varies. People subscribe to particular lists to participate in that list and to receive all of the postings that are sent to the group, generally because they have an interest in the topic. When you post a message to a mailing list, the message is sent out by e-mail to everyone who has subscribed to the list.

Discussion mailing lists offer an efficient way to distribute information to masses of people interested in a particular topic. The difference between discussion mailing lists and newsgroups is that while anyone on the Internet can visit newsgroups at any time and anonymously read any articles of interest, a discussion list delivers all messages posted directly to the subscribers' e-mail. Only discussion list subscribers can receive these messages. To subscribe to a discussion list, you have to send a subscription message to the list administrator and request permission to join the mailing list.

Types of Publicly Accessible Mailing Lists

Publicly accessible mailing lists can be one of several types, each with varying degrees of control. Following is a discussion of the two major types of lists.

Moderated Discussion Lists

This type of list is maintained by a "gatekeeper" who filters out unwanted or inappropriate messages. If you try to post an advertisement where it is not permitted, your message will never make it out to the list of subscribers. Similarly, flames (i.e., publicly chastising another list member) are screened out. The gatekeeper also keeps the topic of discussion on track.

Unmoderated Discussion Lists

An unmoderated list is operated without any centralized control or censorship. Many publicly accessible lists are of this type. All messages are automatically forwarded to subscribers. Unmoderated lists tend to have more blatant advertisements and flame wars because there is no gatekeeper to guide the discussion. It is then the responsibility of the list members to police their own actions. If the list participants aren't rigidly abiding by the rules and reprimanding others who stray, the list could end up being a landfill for spammers. When this happens, many members simply leave the list.

Targeting Appropriate Discussion Mailing Lists

There are four types of mailing lists:

- Publicly accessible mail lists

- Direct mail lists

- Private mail lists

- Bulk mail lists.

There are thousands of publicly accessible lists on-line and a number of sites that provide lists of these mailing lists. Two of the most popular and comprehensive are:

- Topica at *http://lists.topica.com* (Figure 13.1)

- Tile.net at *http://tile.net/lists.*

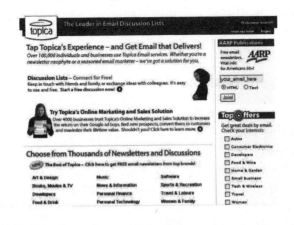

Figure 13.1. Topica provides access to thousands of mailing lists and discussion groups.

There are also companies on-line that specialize in providing targeted lists for a fee, much like purchasing a direct-mail list in the offline world. One company that provides this type of list is Post Master Direct Response at www.postmasterdirect.com. This company rents e-mail lists of people who have requested information on a particular topic. These direct-mail lists are discussed fully in Chapter 15.

Another option is to develop your own private mailing list. This concept is discussed in Chapter 14.

Still another option is to purchase bulk e-mail lists—not. We've all received e-mails that say, "Reach 5 million with our mailing list available for $29.95."

SPAM
Sending the same message to a large group of people who didn't ask for it, or Sending People Annoying Mail.

After all, one of the major benefits of the Internet is reaching large numbers of people quickly—right? Wrong! Do not use these! This is an unacceptable practice because it involves **spam.** Bulk e-mail lists are generally sold without the permission of the addressees, much like junk mailing lists. The recipients did not ask to be put on a mailing list and often do not appreciate being sent unsolicited e-mail. Another drawback is that usually these lists are not targeted. By using bulk e-mail lists, you run the risk of not reaching any of your target market. You also risk annoying those addressees who under other circumstances might have been interested in what you were trying to sell.

The best approach is to choose a list whose subscribers fit your target market as closely as possible. For example, if you are selling geographic information systems to municipalities, a shotgun approach is a waste of both your time and your resources. By using bulk e-mail, you raise the ire of thousands of recipients, destroy your corporate image, and potentially damage your professional credibility. In this case, a targeted list, even though much smaller, would get a much higher-quality response rate. Less is sometimes better.

Finding the Right Mailing List

Whether you join a publicly accessible discussion mailing list or choose to purchase an opt-in e-mail list from one of the many online sources, you want to find a list whose members are your target market. You need to do your homework here, because there are thousands of lists to choose from.

There are various meta-indexes of publicly accessible mailing lists where you can search by title or by subject. Some of these sites provide detailed information on the lists, such as their content and the commands used to subscribe. We have provided information on a number of these in the Internet Resources section at the end of this chapter.

Once you have identified mail lists that have your target market as members, subscribe to those lists. To confirm that the list is right for your marketing purposes, lurk a while to monitor the discussion taking place. Then you can begin participating in the list by providing valuable content. If advertising is not allowed, abide by the rules. However, signature files are generally allowed, and you can always have that one-line tag line or mini-ad to advertise where advertising isn't allowed.

Subscribing to Your Target Mailing Lists

Topica (*http://lists.topica.com*) and tile.net/lists (*http://tile.net/lists*) are great resources that provide a huge roster of accessible mailing lists plus specific instructions for joining those that interest you. After you subscribe, you generally receive an e-mail response with the rules, FAQs, and instructions on how to use the list.

For the most part, the rules for posting to newsgroups apply to mailing lists as well. Read the rules carefully and abide by them. A lurking period should be considered before you post a message. This helps you observe what types of messages are posted and the commonly accepted practices for that particular group.

List Digests

When subscribing to a mail list, quite often you are given the option to subscribe or to subscribe to the digest. When you subscribe, you receive each message as it is posted. When you subscribe to the digest, the messages are accumulated and sent in one e-mail, usually overnight. The compilation of many individual messages is sent to each subscriber as one bulk message. Many digests contain a table of contents. The good thing about a digest is that you do not receive so many separate e-mail messages and your mailbox doesn't become clogged.

Composing Effective Messages

As discussed in the previous chapter, your e-mails must be carefully prepared before you post to a mailing list. Remember to make your subject line relevant, keep your messages short and to the point, and always include your sig file. If you are unsure whether your posting is right for the group, you can send a test message to the moderator asking for advice.

Unlike newsgroups, the members of mailing lists receive all the messages directly into their mailbox every day. Some people prefer to receive the postings in digest form; that is, all the messages for that day are compiled into one e-mail sent to the recipient at the end of the day. At the beginning of the e-mail, the digest provides a listing of all the messages with the "From" and "Subject" identified, followed by the complete messages. Just as individuals who visit a newsgroup don't read all the messages, subscribers to publicly accessible discussion lists do not read every posting. They decide which messages to review based on the subject line. Thus, the content of the "Subject" field is extremely important.

Never repeat the same or similar messages to a mailing list, as you might do in a newsgroup. Once members of a mailing list have seen your posted message, they don't appreciate seeing it again, whereas a newsgroup has different readers all the time and similar postings are acceptable if they are timely. The following tips on mailing list postings should assist you in becoming a respected member of their online community:

- Make sure that your messages are on the subject. List subscribers don't want to receive announcements unrelated to their topic.

- You should be a regular contributor to your list before making any commercial announcement. If your mailing list does not allow advertising (most do not), use your sig file. Sig files are generally accepted. Be sure to make effective use of your tag line to get your mini-ad into discussion mailing lists where blatant advertising is not permitted.

- Track and record your responses when you use a new mailing list. You should have a call to action in your posting, encouraging the readers to visit a specific page on your site or to send e-mail to an address designated solely for this purpose. Only by tracking responses can you know with any certainty which mailing lists are successful and which are not. It's amazing how well calls to action work. For some reason, people tend to do what they're told.

- Set reasonable and achievable goals. As a benchmark, in most e-mail marketing campaigns, a one to three percent response rate is considered a good response. However, if your mailing list is well targeted and you are offering something of interest or value to a particular group, your response rates should be significantly higher.

Building Your Own Private Mailing Lists

You might want to build your own private mailing list. Generating your own lists is often beneficial because of their many marketing uses. They can be used to maintain dialogue with existing customers regarding updates, support, specials, and so on. They can also be used to communicate with current and prospective customers through distribution of corporate newsletters, price lists, new catalogs, product updates, new product announcements, and upcoming events. A full discussion of private mail lists is provided in Chapter 14.

Starting Your Own Publicly Accessible Mailing List

You can create your own publicly accessible Internet mailing list. This is something you should carefully consider before you make your final decision. It takes lots of time and effort to do this right, so be sure you're ready and that it would bring sufficient return on your investment. First you must give it a name that reflects the desired discussion and is enticing for your target market. You must draft an FAQ file or charter containing information on what the list is all about. You must develop guidelines for participation.

You should create a Web page for your list to provide information about the list as well as its charter and guidelines. You should provide an opportunity to subscribe from the Web site as well. This adds credibility to your mailing list.

Once the list is up and running, advertise it so that people actually subscribe. You can promote your list by participating in newsgroups that relate to your mail list topic. Remember not to post blatant ads where advertising is not allowed. Contribute to the newsgroup with your postings and use a tag line in your signature file to promote your mail list. You can also trade e-mail sponsorships with other mailing lists for promotion purposes.

There are a number of places to announce your list. Get your mail list linked from the many lists of lists on the Internet. We provide some of these in the Internet Resources section at the end of this chapter. Make your list worth reading by ensuring that you and others have valuable information on the topic to share. You should make sure to include an opportunity for your subscribers to spread the word or to recommend your mail list to others. You can do this in your mail list messages and also through the companion Web page. In the newsletter or announcement mail lists where messages go only one way, it is easy to encourage your subscribers to send a copy to a friend who they think might be interested. If you encourage viral marketing in this way, you want to make sure you have included the how-to-subscribe information in the messages as well. When encouraging viral marketing through the companion Web page, make sure you include a call to action. It's amazing how well this works!

Internet Resources for Chapter 13

I have developed a great library of online resources for you to check out regarding publicly accessible mail lists in the Resources section of my Web site at *http://www.susansweeney.com/resources.html*. There you can find additional tips, tools, techniques, and resources.

I have also developed a seminar on this topic which can be taken at any time over the Internet, can be taken live over the Internet at a scheduled time, or can be purchased as a seminar on CD. See *http://www.susansweeney.com/store.html*.

14

Establishing Your Private Mailing List

Private mailing lists enable you to create one-way communication to your target market and are a tremendous vehicle for building relationships and a sense of community. Generating your own mailing lists is highly recommended because a targeted opt-in list has many marketing uses. The list can be used to maintain dialogue with customers and potential customers regarding updates, support, specials, and so on. It can also be used to distribute corporate newsletters, price lists, new catalogues, product updates, new product announcements, and upcoming events. In this chapter, we cover:

- Why have your own mailing list?

- The issue of privacy

- Managing your mail list

- Building your mail list

- Promoting your mail list

- Tips to stay under the spam radars

- Recent legislation.

Why Have Your Own Mailing List?

There are numerous reasons to own and use your own mail list. They include some of the same reasons that make it imperative to join someone else's list. Running a private mailing list can be beneficial in many ways, including:

- Permission-based marketing

- Establishing yourself or your business as an expert in your field

- Networking

- Conserving contacts

- Building repeat traffic to your Web site (as discussed in Chapter 3)

- Branding

- Promotion of your business's products and services

- Potential source of revenue.

Permission-Based Marketing

Permission and privacy are critical to the success of any e-mail marketing campaign. Although unsolicited direct "snail mail" might be generally accepted or at least tolerated by many consumers, the rules are completely different on-line. Unsolicited e-mail (known as spam) runs the risk of damaging your company's reputation, not to mention the very real possibilities of flames, public blacklisting, hack attacks, or having your Internet services revoked. For serious spammers, recent legislation adds heavy fines and the possibility of prison. Online consumers are quick to let you know when you have crossed the line, and unsolicited e-mail definitely crosses the line. Because of this, online marketers are using many techniques to get their customers, potential customers, and Web site visitors to give them "permission" to send e-mail on a regular basis.

Permission marketing is really a win-win situation. Recipients receive information that they asked to receive, and the marketer is communicating with an audience that has expressed interest in what is being marketed. Online marketers claim that permission e-mail marketing is one of the best ways to improve customer retention and boost sales. Permission e-mail marketing generally yields response rates ten times that of banner advertising.

So how do you get this coveted permission? Generally you have to provide something of value and of interest to your target market. There are many opportunities on your Web site to ask for permission. The more repeat-traffic generators on your site, the more opportunities you can provide for visitors to give you the permission. (See Chapter 3 for repeat-traffic generators.) You should leverage repeat-traffic generators with permission marketing that "sells the sizzle" and accelerate responses with a call to action. On my Web site I have a call to action that says "Sign Up Now" for Susan's biweekly newsletter filled with tips, tools, techniques and resources to assist you in achieving your Internet marketing goals. Here are some typical examples:

- "We change our coupons every week! Click here to join our mail list to be notified as soon as we update."

- "Click here to join our mail list and receive our biweekly Internet marketing tips, tools, techniques, and resources newsletter."

- "We have new specials on a regular basis. Click here to be notified by e-mail when we post our new specials."

- "We have a new contest every three weeks. Keep checking back or click here if you'd like to be notified by e-mail every time we begin a new contest."

- "We constantly update our calendar of events. Keep checking back or click here if you'd like to be notified by e-mail every time we update."

- "Join our e-club to receive our e-specials, coupons, our great newsletter, and other great offers available only to our e-club members!"

You get the picture. Almost every page on your Web site provides an opportunity for you to offer permission marketing. Of course, when site visitors click, they are taken to a screen where they add themselves to your mail list. Your mail list program should keep track of the element the visitor gave you permission to send. Your mail list should be integrated with the Web site so when someone gives you permission, his or her name is automatically added to your database.

Permission marketing enjoys its success because it is personal, relevant, and anticipated. Your messages should be personalized, enhancing the one-to-one relationship marketing element.

Privacy is a very big issue when a Web site visitor is deciding whether to give you an e-mail address or not. It is very important to assure your visitors that you will not pass on their e-mail address to others or use it for anything but the purpose intended. Your privacy policy should clearly be evident on your Web site on every page that asks for permission. The privacy policy can read like a legal document or be short and to the point.

Benefits of Private Mail Lists

- *Establish Yourself as an Expert.* By operating your own private industry-specific mailing list and offering your advice to members of your list, you can establish yourself as an expert in your field. As a result, you can quickly earn the respect and admiration of your peers and develop new business contacts and clients.

- *Networking.* Having your own private list permits you to network closely with others in your industry and with current and potential clients. Very often, new business relationships and opportunities develop when people with similar interests are brought together. Use your mailing list to create these sorts of relationships. It could be that you find new business partners, establish new clients, or start another business venture.

- *Conserving Contacts.* You develop many great contacts every day in business. Often businesses develop a relationship with a client firm, complete a project with it, and then lose contact as time goes on. Starting your own private mailing list enables you to stay in constant contact with these individuals. This helps you to maintain these relationships in the long term, and ultimately results in more business and a stronger reputation for your business.

- *Branding.* Once you develop your own private mailing lists and generate a loyal list of subscribers, people relate the value of your list to your company's products or services. Mailing lists are an effective way to brand your business's products and services online. If you send messages to your subscribers on a regular basis, they will be exposed again and again to your corporate ID and products and services.

- *Promotion of Your Business's Products and Service.* It is important to remember that people are subscribing to your mail list to receive valuable information that helps them in some way. If your mail list messages consist solely of blatant advertising, the retention rate of your subscribers will drop dramatically. However, to take advantage of your mailing list's potential as a branding tool, you should always include a call to action that encourages a subscriber to click through to your Web site and learn more about your products and services. This is a great way to generate exposure for your products and services.

- *Potential Source of Revenue.* Once your list becomes established and has many subscribers, you might be able to sell advertising to people interested in marketing to your list members. Needless to say, a mailing list becomes an excellent revenue source as its credibility and membership numbers expand. In the end, the time and effort you exert nurturing your list to prominence can pay for itself and more. If you are already a member of a publicly accessible mailing list, take note of the number of advertisements that appear in each posting you receive from the list. Administer your own private mailing list and earn advertising revenue for yourself. However, be ever mindful of the number and type of ads you have in your mail list. The ads should not detract from your message or your credibility.

The Issue of Privacy

Privacy is a growing concern among many online users. You can boost your mailing list's sign-up rate by guaranteeing that subscribers' e-mail addresses are kept confidential and are not sold to or shared with anyone else. If you cannot assure them that your company will use their e-mail address solely for your correspondence with them, they will not feel comfortable giving their e-mail address to you. Provide people with your privacy policy statement. Make them feel comfortable about divulging their e-mail address to your business. To do this, you should have your privacy policy everywhere you ask permission or, alternatively, place a link to your business's privacy policy in a prominent location on your Web site, especially on your mail list sign-up page.

You should never add someone's name to your mailing list without his or her permission. People really resent receiving unsolicited mail, even if you give them the option to unsubscribe.

Where We Need To Be

There are only two ways to do more business on-line:

- Have more people receive your offer.

- Improve your conversion rate of Web site visitors to Web site customers.

There are only a few ways to have more people get your offer:

- Increase the number of visitors to your Web site.

- Increase the number of people whom you reach with your online marketing in newsgroups, public mail lists, affiliate marketing, or any of the 101 ways in this book.

- Increase the number of people in your mail list who have given you permission to send them e-mail on an ongoing basis.

Ideally, where we'd like to be in terms of mail list marketing is:

- Have the right mail list technology.

- Grow your mail list through permission-based marketing as big as you can as fast as you can.

- Provide consistently valuable content to your list on an ongoing basis.

- Learn as much as you can about everyone on your list, building a profile on each person, so that you can send more targeted communication.

The Right Mail List Technology

There are several ways that you can manage your mail list:

- Use your e-mail program (not recommended).

- Use mail list software.

- Outsource your mail list management.

Using Your E-mail Program

Although managing your mail list through your e-mail program might look like a great option in that it doesn't cost you anything and is run from your desktop, giving you ultimate control, there are limitations. Your e-mail program doesn't easily afford you the opportunity to segment your mail list—those who asked to receive your newsletter versus those who asked to receive notification when you update your What's New section, for example. Your e-mail program doesn't generally provide the technology to quickly and easily personalize your communication—that is, insert the recipient's first name in designated areas within the e-mail. E-mail programs do not provide much in the way of tracking information, either. It would be nice to be able to track such things as how many people opened your e-mail, how many sent a copy to a friend, how many clicked through and visited your Web site. The tracking technology is generally available only through mail list software or from the third party that manages your mail list marketing if you choose to outsource this activity.

Another drawback is the administrative headache of manually managing all the "Subscribes," "Unsubscribes," and "Changes of E-mail Address," particularly when you have multiple sign-up opportunities on your Web site—for example, someone wants to unsubscribe from your e-specials but still wants to receive your newsletter and coupons. The time really has come when you need to invest in mail list software or outsource if you want to take this element of online marketing seriously.

Using Mail List Software

There are numerous mail list management software programs available to help you organize your list distribution (See the Internet Resoureces at *http:// www.susansweeney.com/resources* for links to mail list software programs). This software enables you to easily add or remove subscribers. Mail list management software enables you to draft and send properly formatted messages directly from within the software. Mail list software generally allows you to personalize your e-mails quickly and easily. Most of these programs can be integrated with your Web site so that people can add themselves to your list right from the site. You can also use this software to set up notification mechanisms to reply to subscribers confirming that they have been added to the list. This makes running your mail list less time-consuming, as the software does most of the work for you.

Using your own mail list software requires an initial investment to purchase the program or an ongoing cost if you use an Application Service Provider (ASP)—a company that develops the mail list software and provides it to you as a monthly or annual service rather than as a product. The major advantage to this model is that as new bells and whistles are introduced, they are immediately available to all users of the software.

The cost to purchase software can range from an entry-level program at $99 to a robust, full-featured program at $2,500. The ASP model could cost you from $30 a month to several thousand if you use an application that charges you per e-mail sent and you have a very large database.

Some of these programs run from your desktop; others have to be run from your server or through your Internet service provider. Many of the ASP model programs are run from the ASP's server. Most of these programs are sophisticated enough to allow you to segment the e-mail addresses in your database so you know who has asked to receive what from your Web site.

Most of these programs today have the personalization capability to allow you to insert a recipient's first name throughout the correspondence and in the subject line of the message as well. For this to work, you have to capture the first names for each e-mail address in your database. Keep this in mind when asking people if they'd like to give you permission to send them e-mail for whatever reason—in addition to their e-mail address, have a mandatory field for their first name.

More and more of these programs are incorporating tracking features to let you know what's working and what's not. From an administrative perspective, many of these programs do a great job of adding new "Subscribes," deleting "Unsubscribes," and managing undeliverable addresses. This feature alone is worth its weight in gold.

Features to look for in mail list software include:

- Personalization capability—You want to be able to personalize each e-mail by inserting the recipient's first name in the subject line, in the salutation, and throughout the body of your message.

- HTML capability—You want to be able to send HTML e-mail (e-mail that looks like a Web page rather than text), which gets much higher readership than text e-mail.

- Message editor—You want to be able to bring up a past e-mail, edit it, and re-send it to a group.

- Previews—You want to be able to preview your message before you send it to make sure the formatting is correct, the personalization is working, and the message looks great before you send it.

- Spam checker—The spam checker is a valuable tool to ensure that your message has the best chance of being received and not being rejected as spam. You want to be able to run your message through the spam checker to see how you score before you send any message. Today, if you score 5.0 or higher in the spam checker, you will want to edit your message to reduce your score before you send.

- Multi-threaded sending—This feature is important for large lists. It divides a list and sends multiple messages at one time through different streams.

- Filtering—This feature allows you to send specific messages to parts of your list. You could send a message only to those individuals in a specific state by filtering on the name of the state. You could send a message only to those interested in golf if you have that information in a field in your database.

- Scheduling—This allows you to prearrange to send your e-mail at a specific future time and date. Great if you want to set up all of your "Tips of the Week" in advance or if you are going to be traveling when you want your newsletter to be sent out.

- Autoresponders—Some mail list software applications have autoresponders built in. See Chapter 11 for details on their uses.

- Web site integration—You want your mail list software to work with your Web site so when someone subscribes from your site, his or her contact information is automatically included in your mail list software. If someone wants to unsubscribe or change contact information, this can be taken care of through your site or through the e-mails you have sent. This really cuts down on the administration you have to deal with.

- Reporting and tracking—Some mail list software provides reports on messages sent (audience selected, date sent, clicks, total sent, number of bounces), subscriber activity (subscribes, unsubscribes, e-mails opened), link tracking, and bounce activity (number of undeliverables, hard bounces, soft bounces).

Outsourcing Your Mail List

A third option is to outsource your mail list management to a third party. There are companies that specialize in this service with great depth of experience. One such company that we have had the pleasure to work with is Inbox360.com (*http://www.inbox360.com*).

When you outsource this activity, of course you have a monthly service fee. The software is run from the outsource company's server or its ISP's server.

Virtually all of the mail list service providers have the latest software, allowing you to personalize your messages, segment your lists, and get great tracking reports. Generally, administrative issues like adding the "Subscribes," deleting "Unsubscribes," and managing the undeliverables are handled by software used by the outsource company.

On the down side, you might lose some control—over content, over your customer, and over timing of your message release. It is imperative to have a clearly laid-out contract with the outsource company, addressing:

- Ownership of e-mail addresses

- Use of e-mail addresses

- Timing of correspondence

- Final approval of content

- Responsibility and timelines for replies to subscribers.

It is important that you retain ownership of all e-mail addresses and that the contract clearly states that all subscribers' names and e-mail addresses are the property of your company. Also include in the contract that you are provided the current list in digital format every month. This way, if you decide to change service providers, your list goes with you. It takes a lot of effort to build your list, and it is a very valuable asset. Make sure you protect it.

Make sure that your contract clearly states that your e-mail addresses are not to be used by anyone else or provided to anyone else for any purpose whatsoever. People on your list have given you their e-mail addresses in confidence.

They trust that you will not abuse the relationship. Make sure it is in your power to live up to that expectation.

Make sure that you have final control over the timing of your communications. It is important that your messages be delivered when you want them delivered. Timing is everything. We discuss timing later in this chapter.

Make sure that your contract has a clause that permits you to approve the final content going out to your list. You want to see and approve everything. You want to make sure the formatting is the way you want it; you want to be sure the personalization is working as it should; and you want to make sure there is no problem with graphics or word wrap.

You want to have a clear understanding with the outsource company regarding replies from messages going out to your list. Often the "From" field, although it looks like it is coming from you, is actually an address that resides with the outsource company. Discuss and agree on what happens when a recipient replies to your communication. Where does it go? When does it go? To receive a batch of replies three weeks after your communication went out is not acceptable.

There are certain benefits to outsourcing this activity to a third party that specializes in mail list marketing. This is their core responsibility. Often the outsource company has been involved in many campaigns—gaining expertise in what works and what doesn't. Often they can help you tweak your content or format to help achieve your objectives. Also, outsourcing this activity to a competent third party frees up your time and allows you to focus on other priorities.

Building Your Database or Mail List

Once you are committed to private mail list marketing, you want to focus on building your database of e-mail addresses. The more people you can reach in your target market with your message, the better.

There are many ways to grow your list:

- Depending on where your database resides and current legislation, you may be able to import from your existing database. You probably already have a customer or prospective customer list that you can import into your mail list. You may be able to send a one-time message asking them if they'd like to be on your list or join your e-club. Tell them what they'll be receiving and how often, and stress the benefits. Provide them with a link to the sign-up page on your Web site. You need to be careful here with current legislation and where your database members are located (particularly if they reside in Canada).

- Use permission marketing techniques to ask if site visitors would like to be included in your list to receive your newsletter, your e-specials, your coupons, or anything else you want to use to entice them to join your list. See Chapter 5 for more information on permission marketing.

- Collect names and e-mail addresses at your point of contact—registration desk at a hotel, checkout counter in a retail environment, member renewal or registration forms for membership associations or organizations. Ask permission to add them to your e-club—remember to "sell the sizzle."

- Have employee contests and reward the employee who collects the most sign-ups for your e-club.

- Have posters in your bricks-and-mortar location promoting your e-club and letting people know how to join. Think about providing an incentive: Join our e-club and get a 10 percent off coupon for your next purchase or a free gift.

- Promote your e-club in all your direct-mail pieces and ads.

- Use direct e-mail rental lists to ask for sign-ups.

- Use brokers to run campaigns on complementary sites to get targeted sign-ups.

- Promote your e-club in your signature file.

- Encourage viral marketing via existing list members: "Send a copy to a friend" works for a number of repeat-traffic generators such as coupons, newsletters, e-specials, contest information, special offers, and promotions. Make sure that every viral marketing communication includes sign-up information so recipients can add their names and e-mail addresses to your list as well: "If you've received a copy of this newsletter . . . or coupon . . . or e-special from a friend and would like to be included on our list to receive your own in the future, click here." The link should take them to a sign-up page on your Web site or open a new message in their e-mail program with "Subscribe" in the subject line and details of what exactly they would like to subscribe to in the body of the e-mail message.

- If you use tele-sales, add an element that promotes your mail list and asks if the person would like to join.

Promoting Your Private Mail List

Promote your private mail list wherever you can reach your target market: on your site, online through various online marketing techniques, and offline. You will:

- Encourage your Web site visitors to join your list by making sure you have "Join our mail list—click here" calls to action throughout your site. You might enhance this with an incentive "Join our mail list to receive our biweekly tips, tools, and techniques and to be included in our drawing for a Palm Pilot—Click here."

- Include a viral marketing element as previously described to encourage your subscribers to recommend your mail list to others.

- Invite your friends, colleagues, current clients, and potential clients to join your list.

- Remember to mention your mailing list in your e-mail signature file. This is an easy way to promote the list.

- If you are looking for a large distribution list, you might even register your mailing list with Topica (*http://www.lists.topica.com*) or other public mail lists (see Chapter 13 on Public Mail Lists).

Your Communication with Your Mail List

To be successful with private mail list marketing, you have to have a great targeted list and you have to know how to communicate effectively with your subscribers. How often should they receive your messages? When do you start to become an irritant? What time and day are your recipients going to be most receptive? How should your communication be formatted? Should it be text or

HTML? These all are important questions to be answered if you want to improve the response.

How often should you communicate? It depends on what you're sending and what they asked to receive. Newsletters should generally be sent out every couple of weeks or once a month. Special promotions, coupons, and e-specials generally will be sent out weekly or bi-weekly at a consistent time. What's-new updates would generally be sent monthly unless you've got something "hot." Tips of the day should be sent . . . daily. Tips of the week should be sent . . . weekly.

When should your communication be delivered? There have been many studies on this topic, and consensus has it:

- Never send your message late in the day or first thing in the morning. If you do, your e-mail is included in that large group that is in the recipient's in-box first thing in the morning. You know what happens to all that e-mail because you do it yourself—the first thing you do is see how much you can delete—starting with anything that looks remotely like an ad or promotion.

- Not after 2 p.m. on Friday or at all in the afternoon on Friday in the summer months. Being buried in that huge pile awaiting a recipient on Monday morning is the kiss of death for your e-mail.

- Lunch hour is best for business-to-business messages. Generally, people clean out their e-mail first thing in the morning and again before they go to lunch. After their lunch break they are a little more relaxed and the first thing they do is check their e-mail. This is the best chance for your e-mail to get noticed.

When it comes to the formatting of your correspondence, if you communicate in a newsletter, coupons, e-specials, or this type of marketing content, an HTML message has a better chance of grabbing the viewer's attention. If your message is meant to look like a personal one-on-one message, then text-based is better. Your communications should be personalized using the recipient's first name appropriately throughout the correspondence and in the subject field.

Your content should always be valuable, fresh, relevant, and succinct. One bad message could result in many "Unsubscribes."

Each paragraph should be written so it can be easily scanned, containing no more than six or seven lines. Include calls to action. Always encourage viral marketing—"Send a copy to a friend"—and provide instructions for the friend to subscribe to be included on your list.

Use a personal name in the "From" field. You want to build a relationship! Take time with your subject field:

- Avoid ad copy.

- Avoid gimmicky slogans.

- Build business credibility.

- Use action words.

- Be positive.

- Personalize.

Stay under the Spam Radar

These days anywhere between 5 and 20 percent of legitimate, permission-based e-mail is filtered out by the spam detectors and never reaches the intended recipients. Always run your marketing messages through a spam checker before sending out. The spam checkers will give you a spam rating score and tell you how you received that score. Today, if your score is 5.0 or higher it will be deemed to be spam by most of the spam filters. If your message scores too high, you should edit your message to eliminate or change the items that gave you the score. Then you should run your new message through the spam checker to make sure you have an acceptable score before sending your message out.

Many ASP mail list software programs have an integrated spam checker. If yours does not, there are a number of free spam checkers online and others that charge a fee.

Some of the e-mail elements that add points to your spam rating include:

- Using software and listservers that are commonly used by spammers. The header identifies the software that you are using.

- Spam words in the subject line. Things such as:

  - FREE in CAPS

  - GUARANTEED

- – Subject talks about saving

- – Starts with Hello

- – $

- Hyperlinks—Using links without the http:// prefix or using IP numbers instead of domain names.

- Color discrimination:

  - – Color tags not formatted correctly

  - – Using colors not in the 217 Web-safe colors

  - – Hidden letters (same color as background)

- Background other than white

- HTML issues:

  - – HTML message with more than 50 percent HTML tags

  - – JavaScript within the message

  - – HTML forms within your e-mail

  - – HTML comments that obfuscate text

- Using excess capital letters

- Using large fonts and characters. Fonts larger than +2 or 3 can cause you to have points added to your score. Use H1, H2, H3 instead.

- Using spam words or phrases in the body of your message adds points to your score. There are way too many of these to list. Your spam checker lets you know what words are adding points. The following are the type of words and phrases that they are looking for:

  - – Great offer

- Risk free

- You have been selected

- Guarantee

- Call now

- Amazing

- Act now

- Millions

- Order now

- Carefully word your Unsubscribe. Claims that a recipient can be removed, claims that you listen to removal lists, and list removal information all add points to your score. Use text like "Use this link to unsubscribe."

- If your communication is a newsletter, say so. The spam rating also allows points to be deducted from your score for certain elements. When the subject contains a newsletter header, or contains a newsletter frequency, month name or date, you might be spared some unwanted points.

- Use a signature file. This is another element that can cause points to be deducted from your score. Spammers never include their signature file.

- Don't mention spam compliance—only spammers do this.

- Keep your message size over 20k. Spammers' messages are very small in file size because they often send millions in a mailing.

- Always make sure you update your list and do your housekeeping regularly. Remove any addresses that have bounced back to you as undeliverable if your software doesn't automatically do this for you. Remove any "spam flag" addresses in your database—those that begin with spam@, abuse@, postmaster@, or nospam@.

- Set up test accounts for yourself at the popular e-mail hosts to ensure that your mail is getting through. Set up test accounts at MSN, Hotmail, Yahoo, AOL, and some of the popular ISPs.

- Always monitor the Blacklists to make sure you are not included.

Recent Legislation

It is essential to make sure you are in compliance with legislation regarding anti-spam (in the U.S.), privacy (in Canada), and other rules and regulations related to commercial e-mail throughout the world.

The U.S. legislation, which took effect January 1, 2004, is called the Controlling the Assault of Non-Solicited Pornography and Marketing Act (CAN-SPAM). This legislation provides regulations for commercial e-mail. The full details can be found at *http://www.privcom.gc.ca/legislation/index_e.asp*.

The main rules for CAN-SPAM include:

- You must provide accurate header information. The sender has to identify himself/herself/itself accurately.

- You must provide an accurate Subject line for commercial e-mails.

- You must provide a functioning return e-mail address that is clearly and conspicuously displayed and permits a recipient to decline future commercial e-mails (opt-out) from that sender.

- Commercial e-mail must include the (snail mail) postal address of the sender.

- Commercial e-mail must include clear and concise identification that the content of the e-mail is an advertisement or solicitation.

- If a person opts out of your mailings you must remove that individual from your database within 10 days and you are not allowed to transfer, sell, or give that individual's contact information to anyone else after they have asked to be removed.

The Canadian legislation is the Personal Information Protection and Electronic Documents Act, commonly referred to as PIPEDA. The Canadian legislation establishes rules to govern the collection, use, and disclosure of personal information. It recognizes the "right of privacy" of individuals with respect to their personal information. Full details on the Canadian legislation can be found at *http://www.privcom.gc.ca/legislation/index_e.asp*.

The main rules for PIPEDA include:

- Accountability—An organization is responsible for personal information under its control and shall designate an individual or individuals who are accountable for the organization's compliance with the following principles.

- Identifying purposes—The purposes for which personal information is collected shall be identified by the organization at or before the time the information is collected.

- Consent—The knowledge and consent of the individual are required for the collection, use, or disclosure of personal information, except where inappropriate.

- Limiting collection—The collection of personal information shall be limited to that which is necessary for the purposes identified by the organization. Information shall be collected by fair and lawful means.

- Limiting use, disclosure, and retention—Personal information shall not be used or disclosed for purposes other than those for which it was collected, except with the consent of the individual or as required by law. Personal information shall be retained only as long as necessary for the fulfillment of those purposes.

- Accuracy—Personal information shall be as accurate, complete, and up-to-date as is necessary for the purpose for which it is used.

- Safeguards—Personal information shall be protected by security safeguards appropriate to the sensitivity of the information.

- Openness—An organization shall make readily available to individuals specific information about its policies and practices relating to the management of personal information.

- Individual access—Upon request, an individual shall be informed of the existence, use, and disclosure of his or her personal information, and shall be given access to that information. An individual shall be able to challenge the accuracy and completeness of the information and have it amended as appropriate.

- Challenging compliance—An individual shall be able to address a challenge concerning compliance with the above principles to the designated individual or individuals accountable for the organization's compliance.

Measure, Measure, Measure

You want to improve your effectiveness as you learn from experience. This can happen only if you keep track of past performance. You want to track such things as delivery rate, how many undeliverables, how many unsubscribes, click-through rates, gross response, and net response. You want to compare response rates within different timings, different types of creativity, different formats, different segments of your list, and different target markets. Once you analyze what is working and what is not, you'll be in a better position to improve your conversion ratios.

Where to Go from Here

In this chapter, we discussed reasons you might want to have your own mailing list, how you can set up your list, and other issues you might face once your list goes live. Private mailing lists are prime marketing vehicles if you manage them correctly and actively promote them. You can reach out to your target market with a mailing list. This technique of permission, or opt-in, e-mail marketing is the key to your success. If you have something to offer to people in your industry and it is feasible for you to establish and administer a mailing list, give the idea strong consideration.

Internet Resources for Chapter 14

I have developed a great library of online resources for you to check out regarding private mail list marketing in the Resources section of my Web site at *http://*

www.susansweeney.com/resources.html. There you can find additional tips, tools, techniques, and resources.

I have also developed a seminar on this topic which can be taken at any time over the Internet, can be taken live over the Internet at a scheduled time, or can be purchased as a seminar on CD. See *http://www.susansweeney.com/store.html.*

15

Effective Promotion Through Direct Mail Lists

For years, marketers have been renting mail lists from reputable companies for direct-marketing purposes. These companies take their customers' marketing materials and manage the process of printing labels, affixing the labels, postage, and sending the materials out. The same type of service is available online—only the marketing message is sent via e-mail rather than snail mail. In this chapter, we cover:

- How direct mail list companies work

- How to select a company to work with

- How you work with a direct mail list company

- Costs related to direct mail list marketing

- Tips on how to make the most of your direct mail list marketing.

How Direct Mail List Companies Work

Online direct mail list companies work on the same premise as offline direct mail list companies. They provide a service to organizations that want to directly market to a particular demographic or geographic segment of the population. To do this effectively, they develop large databases of individuals who fit specific criteria.

How they generate these databases is what differentiates the good from the bad. The not-so-reputable companies and the bulk mail list companies tend to "grab" e-mail addresses from newsgroups, public mail lists, and a number of other places on the Internet, using programs built just for that purpose. Reputable companies, on the other hand, have a number of strategic ways to build their lists of people interested in receiving information on specific topics. They partner with sites that have significant targeted traffic to offer relevant and interesting information to each site's visitors. They offer the site visitors the opportunity to "opt in" to receive updates or information on the specified topic.

To opt in, there has to be an offer for information on the topic and the visitor has to ask to be put on the list, provide his or her e-mail address, and often also provide his or her first name. The list company wants the first name so that future correspondence can be personalized.

Some of the more reputable companies require a "double opt-in" to increase the value of their list and to ensure the validity of the names on their list. With a double opt-in, the site visitor asks to be put on the list to receive updates or information on a particular topic. When the mail list company receives this request, it follows up with an e-mail notifying the individual that the request has been received and asking for confirmation of the request by a reply to the e-mail.

These direct mail list companies organize their databases by area of interest. They continually improve their lists by doing a little data mining with their correspondence to the people on their lists. Sometimes they use tracking techniques to hone in on specific areas of interest, sometimes they ask a question or two to access more demographic or psychographic information about the individuals on the list, and sometimes they send a detailed survey-type questionnaire asking for feedback so they can better tailor the information being sent to the individual.

How to Select a Direct Mail Company

There are a number of factors to consider when selecting a direct mail list company to work with. First and foremost, the company must be reputable.

The company should have a topic list that meshes with your target market. If you sell tropical fish, the company should have a category that fits. Not all direct mail list companies focus on the same categories. Some concentrate on business topics, others on individual leisure topics, still others on technology topics, and some focus on a combination.

When you have narrowed down the reputable companies with topic lists that relate to your product or service, look at costs, tracking, policies on content, and opt-in policies. You want to work with a company that personalizes its correspondence to the individuals on the list. You also want to be able to encourage recipients to visit your Web site, so you don't want to have any restrictions on hypertext links. Some direct mail list companies provide tracking statistics for their customers. It is useful to know how many people read the message, and how many people merely "clicked through" to your Web site rather than taking the action you wanted them to.

How to Work with a Direct Mail List Company

Once you have selected the direct mail list company or companies you want to work with, you should:

- Fine-tune the specific list to receive your message.

- Provide the message content to the direct mail list company.

- Approve the sample message.

Then, the mail list company will:

- Compile the specific list.

- Develop or format the message you provided.

- Send you a sample for final approval.

- Merge the list with your message so that each person on the list receives a personalized message.

- Send out the message to the list.

- Track specific actions taken by recipients once they have received the message.

You work with the direct mail list company employees to have them develop the specific list that meets your objectives and fits your budget. These companies usually can segment their lists to come up with just the right grouping to meet your needs and budget. For example, you might want your message to go out to people interested in white-water rafting. If the direct mail list company's list for outdoor adventure enthusiasts is segmented, the white-water rafting segment can be pulled out. If that list provides more names than your budget can afford, the list might be able to be segmented further to include only white-water rafting enthusiasts in specific states.

Costs Related to Direct Mail List Marketing

The costs for direct mail list marketing are always on a per-name basis. Often there is a sliding scale based on volume. The costs per name generally include all the services you need from the direct mail list company, including segmenting and rental of the list, merge and personalization, and delivery of the message. Different companies charge different amounts per name.

Postmaster Direct (*http://www.postmasterdirect.com*) is one of the oldest and most reputable direct mail list companies around (see Figure 15.1). It has more than 400 topic lists, with more than 30 million e-mail addresses. It has the largest database of business-to-business double-opt-in e-mail addresses. One hundred percent of the names on its list are opt-in. It partners with high-traffic

Figure 15.1. Postmaster Direct is one of the oldest and most reputable direct mail list companies around.

reputable sites to generate its lists—the cost per name on sites like About.com, Internet.com, and CNET. Postmaster Direct ranges from 10 cents to 35 cents, including rental, merge, and delivery. A minimum order is 5,000 names.

There are a number of direct mail list companies to consider. I have provided a link to many of them from the free Internet Resources section of my Web site (*http://www.susansweeney.com/resources.html*). Although the pricing information and numbers of topic lists or categories were correct at the time of printing this book, check the direct mail list company sites for updates before making any decisions.

Make the Most of Your Direct Mail List Marketing

Direct mail list marketing is a great way to reach a significant number of your target market with your message in a short period of time. Ideally, you would like to have each of these names on your private mail list. If you're smart about the content of the message you have the direct mail list company send out, you can go a long way toward converting the direct mail list recipients to your private mail list subscribers.

In your direct mail list message, you want to give recipients a compelling reason to visit your Web site. The URL or specific page reached by the hypertext link in your direct mail message should provide them with not only the content they are expecting, but also a compelling reason to join your private mail list and an opportunity to easily sign up.

To ensure that your message is opened and read, put in the time and effort to have a dynamite subject line. Often the subject line determines whether the message is read or is one of the many that are deleted unopened. Consider personalizing the subject line with the recipient's name. And make sure the subject line copy does not read like an ad. Ads and junk mail are the first to be deleted.

Write your message so it can be easily scanned. That's how busy people read their e-mail—they scan it. Grab the reader's attention in the first sentence. If you don't, he or she won't read any further.

Of course, be sure you have used the proper upper- and lowercase, correct grammar, and correct spelling. You yourself know how many business e-mails you get that don't take this seriously. Your e-mail is a reflection of the attention to detail you give everything in your business.

Make sure you access and analyze any tracking information available from the direct mail list company. Notice what copy works best. Notice what subject lines give a better response rate. Notice the different responses from different direct mail list companies.

Internet Resources for Chapter 15

I have developed a great library of online resources for you to check out regarding direct mail list marketing in the Resources section of my Web site at *http:// www.susansweeney.com/resources.html*. There you can find additional tips, tools, techniques, and resources.

I have also developed a seminar on this topic which can be taken at any time over the Internet, can be taken live over the Internet at a scheduled time, or can be purchased as a seminar on CD. See *http://www.susansweeney.com/ store.html*.

16

Developing a Dynamite Link Strategy

The more strategically chosen **links** you have to your site, the better. Increase your traffic and improve your search engine ranking by orchestrating links from related Web pages. In this chapter, we cover:

Links
Selectable connections from one word, picture or information object to another.

- Developing a link strategy

- How to arrange links

- Getting noticed—providing an icon and tag line hypertext for links to your site

- Link positioning

- Tools to check your competitors' links

- Using links to enhance your image

- Web rings and meta-indexes

- Getting links to your site

- Reciprocal link pages

- Associate programs

- How links can enhance your search engine placements.

Links Have an Impact

Developing your link strategy is one of the most crucial elements of Internet marketing. It is a time-consuming task, but it is time well spent. Links are important for several reasons.

1. Strategically placed, they can be a real traffic builder.

2. A number of the frequently used search engines use link popularity and link relevancy as part of their ranking criteria. The more links to your site, the more popular it is, so the number of links you have to your site can significantly impact your placement with those search engines.

3. The more links you have to your site, the more opportunities search engine spiders have to find you.

Links Have Staying Power

When you post a message to a newsgroup where you promote your Web site through your brilliant contributions and your signature file, you receive increased traffic while the message is current and is being read by participants in the newsgroup. As time passes, your message appears farther and farther down the list until it disappears, and then your traffic level returns to normal. The same goes for a promotional effort in a mail list. You can expect increased traffic for a short while after your mail list posting, but as soon as everyone has read your posting and visited your site, traffic levels return to normal.

This is not the same for links. Traffic from links does not go away as easily as other forms of Internet marketing. Links generally stay active for a long time. When a link to your site is placed on another Web site, you hope people see it and are enticed to click through to visit your site. As long as the site that hosts your link has new traffic, you continue to receive traffic through it. The beauty of links is that in three months, that link will still be there and people will still be clicking through!

Links are very important because if you have links placed on a high-traffic Web site, they can turn into traffic builders for your own site. They also are important because they can have a major impact on your ranking in search engines, because some of the busiest ones use link popularity in their ranking criteria. Some of these search engines include:

- Google (*www.google.com*)

- Yahoo! Search (*www.search.yahoo.com*)

- AltaVista (*www.altavista.com*)

- HotBot (*www.hotbot.com*)

- MSN (*www.msn.com*)

- Inktomi (*www.inktomi.com*).

Once your link strategy is implemented and you begin to see an increase in the number of sites linking to your Web site, you will see your ranking in the previously mentioned search engines improve. For more information on search engines and their ranking criteria, see Chapters 6 and 7.

A Quick Talk about Outbound Links

The more links to your site, the better chance that someone will be enticed to visit. However, a quid quo pro usually applies, and this means providing reciprocal links, giving people the opportunity to leave your site with the click of a button. To minimize this "flight effect," make sure you place outbound links two or three layers down in your site. Never place outbound links on your home page. You want your visitors to come into your site and see and do everything you want them to before they have the opportunity to go elsewhere.

There are two ways you can provide outbound links. The first is by providing a hypertext link, which transports the visitor from your site to someone else's with a single click. The second and preferred method is to have each outbound link open a new browser window when clicked. This way your visitors get to see the referred Web site, but when they are finished and close that

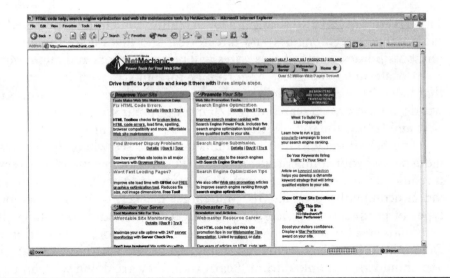

Figure 16.1. The NetMechanic site provides many valuable tools. Its HTML Toolbox can be used to find out if you have dead links on your site or if you have any HTML errors that need correcting.

window, the original browser window with your Web site is still active. The browser window with your site should still be visible on the task bar during their visit to the referred site.

Regularly test all of the links from your site to ensure that they are "live" and are going to the intended locations. Dead links reflect poorly on your site even if they are out of your control. There are tools available online to help you determine whether you have dead links. These tools include NetMechanic at *http://www.netmechanic.com* (see Figure 16.1) and Dr. Watson at *http://watson.addy.com*. Each of these tools is discussed in more depth in the Internet Resources section of my Web site, referenced at the end of this chapter.

Strategies for Finding Appropriate Link Sites

Ideally, you should be linked from every high-traffic site that is of interest to your target market. Develop a strategy to find all of these sites and arrange links.

Start with the popular search engines. Most people use search engines and directories to find subjects of interest on the Internet. Most of the people searching never go beyond the first 10 to 20 results that the search engine returns.

Thus, these top 10 to 20 sites get a lot of traffic. Search relevant keywords in all the popular search engines and directories, and investigate these top sites for link possibilities. Some of these sites will be competitors and might not want to reciprocate links. The best opportunity for links is with noncompeting sites that have the same target market. I suggest you take your most important keywords, do a keyword search in the 20 most popular search engines and directories, and review the top 30 sites in each for potential link sites.

Another strategy to find useful link sites is to see where the leaders in your industry and your competitors are linked. I use the term *competitors* very loosely. It would include your direct competitors, your industry leaders, companies selling noncompeting products to your target market, companies selling similar types of products or services to your target market, and companies that compete with you for search engine ranking. See what your competition is doing. Determine where they are linked from, and decide whether these are sites that you should also be linked from. Learn what they are doing well, and also learn from their mistakes. You should be linked everywhere your competition is appropriately linked, and then some.

Explore These URLs

There are many tools on the Internet to help you identify a Web site's links. These tools can be used to see which sites are linking to your Web site. But they can also be used to see what sites are linking to your competition. This is a great way to research where your site could be linked from but isn't—yet! Let me walk you through a step-by-step process to increase the number of links to your Web site.

When determining which sites you should be linked from, you first have to develop a lengthy list of competitors. A competitor can be any business or site that offers the same products or services as you do or anyone targeting the same demographic group. Because the Internet creates a level playing field for all businesses, you are competing against large and small companies from around the globe. Someone using a search engine to find information on services that your company can provide might see results from companies from all across the world in the top ten results.

Once you have developed your extensive list of competitors and have gathered their URLs, you must then find out what sites they are linked from. Tools have been developed to assist you in finding who is linking to your site. In most cases you enter your URL, and then these tools provide a list of sites linking to it. However, by entering the URL for a competitor's site you can just as easily determine which sites are linking to your competition and industry leaders.

The more organized you are for this exercise, the better. I suggest that you:

1. Gather an extensive list of competitors and their URLs.

2. Choose the tool(s) from the next section that you are going to use for this exercise.

3. Enter the first competitor URL to find the sites linking to it.

4. Copy and paste the results into a Word, Notepad, or other file that you can access later.

5. Enter the next competitor URL to find the sites linking to it.

6. Copy and paste the results into the same Word, Notepad, or other file, adding to your list of potential link sites.

7. Repeat steps 5 and 6 until you have found all the sites linking to your competition. When this is done, you have your potential link sites list.

8. Now develop a link request (see below for details) and keep it open on your desktop so that you can copy and paste it into an e-mail when you find a site you'd like to have a link from.

9. Next, visit every one of the potential link sites to determine whether the site is appropriate for you to be linked from. If so, send your link request. If the site is not appropriate for whatever reason, delete it from your list. Also delete duplicates. When you get to the bottom of your list, it has changed from a potential links list to a request links list.

10. Follow through and follow up. Follow through and provide an appropriate link to those who agree to a reciprocal link. Follow up to make sure that they provide the link to your site as promised, that the link works, and that it is pointing to the correct page on your site.

11. Submit the Internet address of the page that has provided the link to the popular search engines so that they know it's there. This will help boost your link popularity scores.

Tools to Identify Your Competitors' Links

The following tools can be used to obtain a list of locations on the Internet that are linked to your competitors' Web sites:

AltaVista
http://www.altavista.com
To find out where your competitors are linked using AltaVista, simply enter the competitor's URL in the search area like this: *link: yourcompetitorsdomain.com*. This returns all pages in AltaVista with a link to your competitor's Web site.

Excite and Other Search Engines
Just enter your competitors' URLs and see what comes up. (Be sure to include *http://*.) If anything, the search query will include all indexed Web sites that contain the URL searched.

Google
http://www.google.com
Enter your competitor's URL in the search box like this: *link: yourcompetitorsURL.com*. The results will contain all Web sites linking to your competitor's Web site.

HotBot
http://www.hotbot.com
Enter your competitor's URL in the search box and change the default from "all the words" to "links to this URL." When you type in the URL, remember to include *http://*. The results will contain all Web sites linking to your competitor's Web site.

Link Popularity
http://www.linkpopularity.com
Simply type in your competitor's URL and it will give you a list of all the sites linking to that particular site (see Figure 16.2).

Link Popularity Check
http://www.linkpopularitycheck.com
Use this tool to compare your Web site to up to three other competitors' sites using their link popularity check. In addition to a comparison graph of the number of links each site has, it also gives details on where those links are coming from.

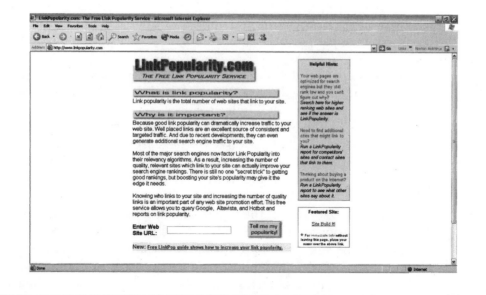

Figure 16.2. LinkPopularity.com offers a free link popularity check service.

Other Potential Link Strategies

Another strategy for finding potential link sites is to visit the many different search engines and do a search on keywords you feel people would search on if they were looking for your site. The top results get a lot of visits from your target market, so they are always good potential link sites.

The following is a step-by-step strategy to get linked from these sites.

1. Make a list of your most important keywords for your Web site using your master keyword list and meta-tags (see Chapter 6).

2. Develop a list of the top ten search engines (check SearchEngineWatch.com).

3. Go to each of the ten search engines and input your most important keyword as identified in step 1.

4. Copy and paste the top 30 results into a Word, Notepad, or other file that you can access later.

5. Enter the next keyword and copy and paste the results into the same Word, Notepad, or other file, adding to your list of potential link sites.

6. Repeat step 5 until you have used all the keywords in your list. When this is done, you will have 300 potential sites for each keyword. You now have your potential link sites list.

7. Now develop a link request (see the next section for details) and keep it open on your desktop so that you can copy and paste it into an e-mail when you find a site you'd like to have a link from.

8. Next, visit every one of the potential link sites to determine whether the site is appropriate for you to be linked from. If so, send your link request. If the site is not appropriate for whatever reason, delete it from your list. Also delete duplicates. When you get to the bottom of your list, it has changed from a potential links list to a request links list.

9. Follow through and follow up. Follow through and provide an appropriate link to those who agree to a reciprocal link. Follow up to make sure that they provide the link to your site as promised, that the link works, and that it is pointing to the correct page on your site.

10. Submit the Internet address of the page that has provided the link to the popular search engines so that they know it's there. This will help boost your link popularity scores.

Winning Approval for Potential Links

Now that you have a list of Web sites you would like to be linked from, the next step is to determine from whom to request the link. Usually this can be found on the site. Titles such as Webmaster@ or any variation on that theme are usually a safe bet. If the site does not have an obvious contact, try feedback@. You can either send the request there or ask for the e-mail address of the right person.

If you cannot find an e-mail address on a Web site, you can visit a domain registration service such as Network Solutions (*www.networksolutions.com*) to find out contact information for that domain name. Click on the "WHOIS Lookup" link and submit the URL to do a search. The results will include the contacts, both technical and administrative, for that Web site. The technical contact most likely is the person you are looking for, because that is who most likely looks after the Web site. The administrative contact is usually responsible for the renewal of the domain name, and the billing contact is usually the bill payer for the domain name.

Generally, a short note with the appropriate information in the subject line is most suitable. Your note should be courteous, briefly describe your site's content, and provide the rationale for why you think reciprocating links would result in a win-win situation. It doesn't hurt to compliment some aspect of the site that you think is particularly engaging.

It is a good idea to develop a generic "link request" letter that you can have on hand when you are surfing. You should always keep this letter open on your desktop when surfing the Internet so that you can easily copy and paste the letter into an e-mail.

Here is an example of a link request e-mail:

> *Dear Web Site Owner,*
>
> *I have just finished viewing your site and found it quite enjoyable. I found the content to be very valuable, particularly [customize here]. My site visitors would appreciate your content as I think we appeal to the same demographic group. My site, http://ww.mysitename.com, focuses on [my site content] and would likely be of value to your visitors. I'd like to suggest we trade links.*
>
> *Sincerely,*
>
> *John*

A typical response might say that they would appreciate the link to their site and offer to provide a reciprocal link. To facilitate this, you should either have the HTML for the link ready to send or have it available on your site, or both. Make sure you have your most important keyword in the text around the link to your site to ensure that you score as high as possible in the link relevancy category.

Make sure to follow through and follow up. If you said that you would provide a reciprocal link, do so within 24 hours. Follow up to make sure that your site has been linked from theirs, the link works properly, and it is linked to the right page on your site.

Then remember to send a thank you. Because they are doing you a favor by adding your site to their Web page, you should strive to develop a good relationship with them. This way they might be more generous with the link they give you. They might place it higher on the page, or even offer you the opportunity of having a small graphic link on their page, which would be dynamite for increasing traffic to your site. These graphic links are explained in more detail later in the chapter.

Another way to get links is to ask for them on your site. In a prominent location on your site, place a link that says something like, "Would you like to provide a link to this site? Click here." Link this message to a separate page that holds several options for links. You can provide viewers with several different sizes of banner ads they could place on their Web site. You can also provide them with a thumbnail icon, the HTML, and your tag line, which they could simply copy and paste into the HTML code on their Web site. Again, remember to select appropriate keywords to include in the text around the link to increase your link relevancy score with the popular search engines.

Quite often, if you offer viewers these opportunities for links, you have a better chance of receiving these enhanced link features. If you make it easier for them to add the link, they will be more willing to provide it. Figure 16.3 shows an example of a site that provides the relevant coding and images for people who want to provide a link.

Figure 16.3. By providing the HTML text and icons on your site, you can make it very easy for visitors to add your link to their site.

You might want to offer an incentive to people who provide you with a link. It could be something that can be downloaded or a free sample of your product in exchange for a link. This provides you with another opportunity to market your site because you are giving something away for free, and thus you can be listed on the many Internet sites that identify sites for freebies. Another useful tactic is to include viewers who provide a link to your site in a drawing for a prize.

You might run a contest such as "Provide a link to us and win," where you include all those sites linking to you in a drawing once a week or once a month, depending on the size of the prize.

Meta-indexes and **Web rings** are other sources for links. For a complete discussion of meta-indexes and Web rings, see Chapters 18 and 23, respectively.

Web rings
Interlinked Web sites.

You might need to prompt sites to provide promised links. If you have made an arrangement for a link and find that the link is not there, it is appropriate to send an e-mail reminder. When sending the follow-up e-mail, include your icon, HTML, URL, and any other helpful information.

Making Your Link the Place to Click

There are links and then there are links. Usually links are your company name hyperlinked to your home page, and your company's site link is listed with a number of other companies' links. Sometimes, if you are lucky, there is a brief description attached to the link.

You should take a proactive approach with linking arrangements. Explore every opportunity to have your link placed prominently and, if possible, to have it differentiated from the other links on the page. Figure 16.4 demonstrates how having an image associated with your link can make your link stand out among all of the other links.

Once you have an agreement with a site willing to provide a link, you should ask if you could send them an **icon** and the HTML for the link. The icon (GIF or JPG format) should be visually pleasing and representative of your company. Within the HTML, include a tag line or call to action that entices people to click on the link. With the icon or logo, the tag line, and your company's name, your link will stand out. Again, remember to include appropriate keywords to add to your link relevancy score to improve your search engine ranking.

Icon
An image that represents an application, a capability, or some other concept

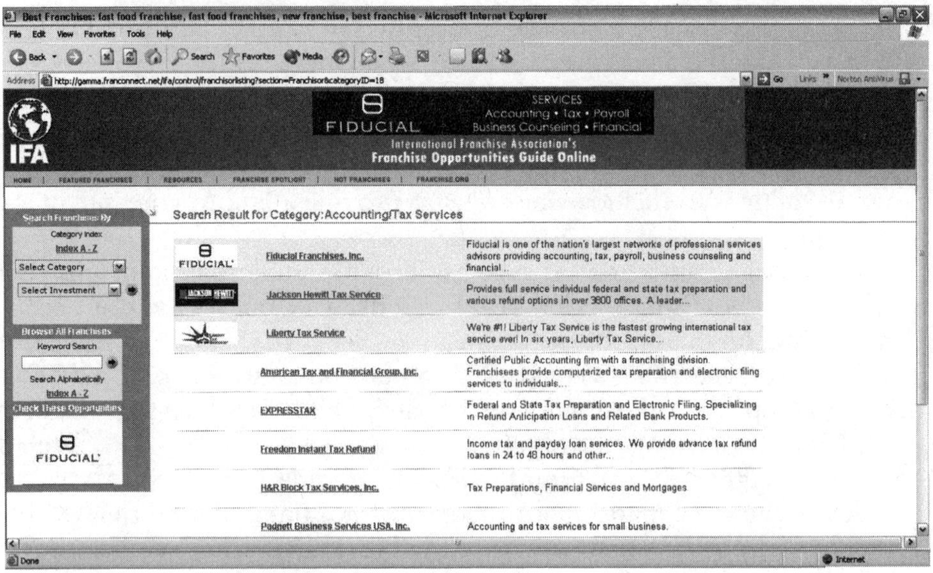

Figure 16.4. By adding a small graphic to your link, you can definitely make your link stand out from the others.

If another Web site is generous enough to provide a link to your site, your image should be only a thumbnail, for you don't want to take up too much space. This image could be your corporate logo or a graphic from a current promotion for one of your products or services. By having this image and tag line strategically placed on a Web site, the chances that a viewer will click through to visit your Web site are much higher. Here is an example of what it should look like:

<IMG SRC="images/nameofgraphicfile"><A HREF="http:// www.yourdomainname.com"> Catchy tag line here.</a>

To Add or Not to Add with Free-for-All Links

There are thousands of free-for-all links sites on the Net. These sites allow you to add your URL to a long list of links, but they provide little traffic and the search engines don't like sites that try to manipulate the search placement. I'd suggest you stay away from these types of link sites.

Add Value with Affiliate Programs

Another way of benefiting from links to your Web site is by developing an affiliate program. Affiliate programs (also called reseller or partnership or associate programs) are revenue-sharing arrangements set up by companies selling products and services. When another site agrees to participate in your affiliate program, it is rewarded for sending customers to your business. These customers are sent to your site through links on your associates' or affiliates' Web sites. By developing and offering this type of program, you generate increased business and increased links to your site and increased link popularity for search engines. Affiliate programs are explained in more depth in Chapter 17.

Maintaining a Marketing Log

Record all new links to your site in your Internet marketing log. It is important to maintain this log and review it regularly. You must periodically check to make certain that links to your site are operational and are going to the appropriate location. Along with the URL where your site is linked from, you should also keep track of all contact information gathered when communicating with the Webmaster.

A Word of Caution with Link Trading

You must be aware when trading links that all links are not created equal.

- If you provide a prominent link to another site, make sure you receive a link of equal or greater prominence.

- Be aware, when trading your links with sites that receive substantially less traffic than you do, that you will probably have more people "link out" than "link in" from this trade. Consider trading a banner ad and a link from their site for a link from your site, thus making it more of an equal trade. If their site has more traffic than yours, don't mention it unless they do.

- Never put your outbound links directly on your home page. Have your outbound links located several levels down so that visitors to your site will likely have visited all the pages you want them to visit before they link out.

- When incorporating outbound links, make sure that when the link is clicked, the Web page is opened in a new browser window so that the visitor can easily return to your Web page.

- Sometimes when people update their site, they change the Internet address or delete a page altogether. If you have placed a link on your page to that page, and one of your viewers tries to link out to that page and receives an HTTP 404 error, this reflects badly on your site. You should frequently check your Web site for dead links.

- When you change content on a page within your site, don't create totally new pages; just update the content on your current pages and keep the same file names. There might be links to your pages and if you delete them, anyone trying to click on a link to your site from another site will get an HTTP 404 error. This results in a dead link on the referring page as well as in any search engine listings you might have.

Internet Resources for Chapter 16

I have developed a great library of online resources for you to check out regarding link strategies in the Resources section of my Web site at *http://www.susansweeney.com/resources.html*. There you can find additional tips, tools, techniques, and resources.

I have also developed a seminar on this topic which can be taken at any time over the Internet, can be taken live over the Internet at a scheduled time, or can be purchased as a seminar on CD. See *http://www.susansweeney.com/store.html*.

17

Affiliate Programs

It is a well-known fact that referral business is the easiest and most efficient business to generate. When doing business on-line, affiliate programs enable you to capitalize on this concept. The concept of setting up a referral business model was first started in 1996 when Amazon.com started paying other Web site owners for referring customers to their Web site. This referral business model caught on, and now many sites are incorporating this model into their everyday business activities. The idea and the corresponding software technology have come a long way since 1996. The software available today makes the process so simple that anyone with basic Web skills can set up an affiliate program.

There are many different affiliate programs available on the Internet. These programs vary in terms of reliability, quality, and the amount of commissions offered. E-tailers use these programs to develop repeat business and increase sales. A side benefit to having an affiliate program is that every affiliate provides a link to your site, which in turn improves link popularity, which in turn improves your ranking in a number of the popular search engines. On the downside, developing and implementing the affiliate program takes time and effort, and you must be competitive with other affiliate programs to encourage participation. In this chapter, you will learn:

- How to distinguish among the different types of affiliate programs

- How to pick the appropriate affiliate program for your Web site

- Tips to succeed with affiliate programs

- The benefits of affiliate programs

- How to start your own affiliate programs

- Important features for affiliate-tracking software

- Affiliate program resources.

Affiliate Programs: Increase Traffic to Your Web Site

To understand the opportunities available, you must first understand the different types of affiliate programs. They all pay for referral business, but in different ways. Before you decide to implement an affiliate program, you must first look at your objectives, your products and services, and your target market, and then decide whether an affiliate program is appropriate for your site. If so, choose the type of program that works for you.

Commission-Based Affiliate Programs

The most common type of affiliate program is commission based. This type offers the referring Web site a percentage of sales income resulting from its referrals. Commissions typically range from 1 to 15 percent. Some programs offer a two-tier commission structure, and some offer an increased commission for higher-traffic sites. In a two-tier commission program, an affiliate is paid a commission on each sale (or lead or click-through) it refers plus a commission on each sale referred by any affiliate it tells about your program. Some examples of commission-based affiliate programs include:

- Amazon.com (*http://www.amazon.com*)

- WebPositionGold (*www.webposition.com*—see Figure 17.1).

Flat-Fee Referral Programs

Flat-fee referral programs pay the owner of a Web site a fixed amount for every new visitor who links from the referring site to the host site and takes certain

Figure 17.1.   WebPosition has a very popular affiliate program.

Figure 17.2.   e-Bay.com has a very well developed affiliate program.

predefined actions. The required action often is making a purchase on the host site. Some flat-fee programs do not require a purchase; the predetermined actions might be joining its e-club, signing up to receive its e-specials or newsletter, downloading a free demo, ordering a catalogue, requesting a quote, or taking another action desired by the host site. A good example of this is eBay (http://www.ebay.com), which offers affiliates compensation when visitors to their Web site click through and bid on an item (see Figure 17.2).

Click-Through Programs

A click-through program is one in which affiliates receive a fee for every unique visitor who clicks through on the referring link on the affiliate's Web site or from a link the affiliate has included in a signature file, e-zine article, advertising, or elsewhere. There are many click-through programs on the Internet. For example, Google AdSense (*http://www.google.com*) has a click-through program that eliminates the problems of finding individual advertisers and allows you to place banner advertisements on your Web site. Whenever a visitor links out from your site through one of these banner ads, you receive a flat fee.

Selecting an Affiliate Program That Is Right for You

The first step in deciding whether to start an affiliate program is to ask whether this fits in with your Web site objectives. Click-through programs can serve to increase traffic to your Web site as long as your banner ad, signature file, e-zine article, or whatever method is used to refer is designed with your target market in mind and that element is placed on sites that are of interest to your target market. Commission-based and flat-fee affiliate programs can further encourage the referred visitors to do what you want them to do when they get to your site. The referring site knows that it receives a commission only when a certain action has been taken by the visitor, whether that action be a purchase, a quote request, or something else. The referring site has a vested interest in having the referred visitor take the desired action and is in a position to suggest or recommend that the visitor take that action.

How to Succeed with Your Affiliate Site

You may have an affiliate program, but are you really doing all you can to exploit it? Times have changed. In the olden days the strategy was to get as many affiliates as possible, and there was little interaction between the owner of the affiliate program and the affiliates. Today the focus is on getting great affiliates who are going to perform and giving them the tools to do the job. Often the owner of the affiliate program will conduct weekly online affiliate meetings to provide affiliates with new materials on a regular basis.

There are several things you could do to be successful with an affiliate program. You should go out of your way to help make the links stand out on your affiliates' sites. Provide different-sized icons that grab visitors' attention and are designed with the target market in mind. Also prepare the proper HTML coding and a tag line linking to your Web site incorporating your important keywords for the search engines, and you help your affiliates get the attention of their visitors as well as helping yourself in terms of search engine ranking. You can also inspect your affiliates' Web sites regularly to determine whether there is anything you can do to help them add value to the links on their pages. You could offer them advice about where they should locate your links if they are in an obscure place on their Web site. Remember, though, that you don't run their Web sites, so be diplomatic.

Other affiliate program operators offer more advanced tools to their affiliates. For example, a program operator might offer affiliates a generic e-mail newsletter, which the affiliate could easily download, personalize, and send out to its mailing list. This generic newsletter is written in an enticing manner and encourages the affiliate's mail list subscribers to visit the affiliate Web site and click on the affiliate program link.

Some affiliate program operators provide a weekly e-mail to their affiliates with new material, icons, articles, banners, etc., as well as recommended actions to be taken by the affiliates for the coming week.

The key point is that you should take advantage of as many opportunities as possible to leverage the power of your affiliate program. Through providing your affiliates with these value-added services, you not only strengthen the power of your affiliate program, but you also show your affiliates your commitment to seeing that they are successful with your program.

You should also make sure that you, the affiliate administrator, do your best to be prompt with reporting and referral payments. People will not want to participate in your program if you are late with payments or don't provide them with detailed reports of their referrals from the previous reporting period. By sticking to the program schedule and doing the best you can for your affiliates, you not only keep your affiliates happy, you also advance the interests of your affiliate program.

Benefits of Creating an Affiliate Program

There are many benefits to having an affiliate program. With an affiliate program you could generate a significant increase in traffic to your own Web site.

When your affiliates place links on their Web sites linking to your site, you will increase your link popularity and, if you're strategic about the keywords that you include in the text around the link to your site, you will increase your link relevancy score as well.

The affiliate links can generate a significant amount of traffic to your site and also help to increase your search engine rankings. Some of the major search engines use link popularity in their ranking criteria. Once you have successfully launched your affiliate program and have developed a wide sales force on the Internet, you might be surprised by the amount of new traffic coming to your Web site.

Your greatest advantage is the opportunity to expand your sales force to thousands of people. If you run a good affiliate program, your sales force could consist of people all over the world, thus expanding your target market into different cultures that your personal sales force otherwise might not have been able to penetrate.

Another benefit of launching an affiliate program on your Web site is that you increase the brand awareness for your business. For example, how many times have you seen an Amazon.com logo on a personal or commercial Web site? Many hundreds of thousands have subscribed to Amazon.com's affiliate program, making it one of the largest programs on the Internet. All of Amazon.com's affiliates place banner ads, buttons, text links, and other promotional tools on their Web site and in their outbound marketing in an effort to encourage their visitors to click through to the Amazon.com Web site and make a purchase. Even though not everybody clicks through to the Amazon.com site, their Web site visitors are still exposed to the Amazon.com brand, thus increasing the brand exposure for Amazon.com's products and services. This could ultimately result in those visitors' going directly to the Amazon.com Web site in the future to make a purchase, thus bypassing the affiliate's Web site and the need to pay that affiliate a referral for their business.

Purchasing Affiliate Software

There are several options when it comes to purchasing Affiliate software:

- You can use an Application Service Provider, or ASP. An ASP is a third-party entity that manages and distributes software-based services and solutions to customers usually over the Internet.

- You can purchase software.

- You can build your own.

- You can use a storefront software solution that includes an Affiliate module.

Depending on what features you would like to provide to your affiliates, the cost of tracking software ranges from $300 to $15,000. Sometimes this software is provided as part of your shopping cart service.

There are many varieties of affiliate software. Some programs are quite unsophisticated and offer few features, and others offer all the bells and whistles. There are some features that you should watch for when purchasing your software. They can help you to run a smooth affiliate program and can save you a lot of time. Here are some of the more important features available:

- Automated Signup. You should always look for this feature because you want to make it as easy as possible for your affiliates to sign up for your program. It should not take them days to officially sign up; they should be able to do so automatically. You want them to get started as quickly as possible, so as soon as they sign up, they should automatically be sent all information that you feel is necessary for them to quickly incorporate your program on their Web site.

- Automated Tracking System. This is one of the most important features that you must look for. You want to make sure that your software is capable of tracking all sales made so that you can reward your affiliates with the appropriate commission. You don't want to have to calculate which Web sites the sales came from at the end of the month. You want to be able to let the software do all of the tracking for you, and at the end of the reporting period provide you with a report outlining payment due to your affiliates.

- Automatic Contact Systems. You should be able to contact all of your affiliates whenever you find it necessary. Some software allows you to send messages to all of your affiliates at the click of a button. It compiles their e-mail addresses in a database.

- Real-Time Statistics. Real-time statistics allow your affiliates to view their current sales statistics. This lets them know how many people clicked through from their site and how many of those people actually purchased something. This is a very good feature because it is important to keep your affiliates informed about their current sales status in your program.

- Variable-Payment Option. Another important feature that you should look for is the variable-payment option. Some forms of affiliate software let you work with only so many variables, meaning the fixed fee, percentage, or flat rate per click-through that you multiply by the referrals from your affiliates' sites. Some software is designed for only certain types of programs. You might purchase software designed to calculate payments for a click-through program. If you wanted to have a commission-based program that pays a percentage of sales resulting from each click-through, this software would not be good for you. It would not be able to comprehend and manipulate data to calculate the payments, for it is incapable of using the percentage-of-sales variable. Check this out before you purchase any software.

- Automatic Check Payment. Once your affiliate program is up and running, and you have developed an extensive list of affiliates, it can become a hassle to write checks at the end of each payment period. Some software comes equipped with an automatic check payment option that allows your computer to print the checks. This can make your affiliate program run more smoothly and can save you time.

- Automatic Reporting-Period Statistic Distribution. Some of the more advanced affiliate-tracking software automatically e-mails each of your affiliates at the end of the reporting period. This tells your affiliates how much success they are having with your program and allows them to adjust their marketing strategy to help them succeed with your program.

Internet Resources for Chapter 17

I have developed a great library of online resources for you to check out regarding affiliate marketing in the Resources section of my Web site at *http://www.susansweeney.com/resources.html*. There you can find additional tips, tools, techniques, and resources.

I have also developed a seminar on this topic which can be taken at any time over the Internet, can be taken live over the Internet at a scheduled time, or can be purchased as a seminar on CD. See *http://www.susansweeney.com/store.html*.

18

Maximizing Promotion with Meta-Indexes

Meta-indexes are designed to be useful resources for people who have a specific interest in a particular topic. Meta-indexes are a large and valuable resource for reaching your target audience and should be utilized to their full potential. In this chapter, we cover:

- What meta-indexes are

- Why meta-indexes are useful

- How to make the links to your site stand out

- Creating your own meta-index.

What Are Meta-Indexes?

Meta-indexes are lists of Internet resources pertaining to a specific subject category and are intended as a resource for people who have a specific interest in that topic. These lists, such as the one for Internet shopping sites shown in Figure 18.1, consist of a collection of URLs of related Internet resources that

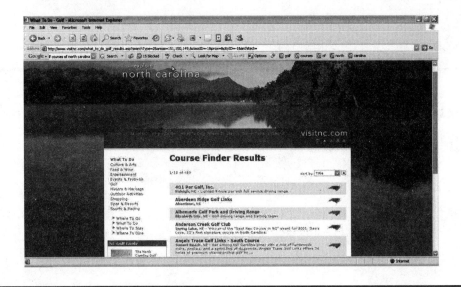

Figure 18.1. VisitNC.com provides a meta-index with links to Web sites of golf courses in North Carolina.

are arranged on a Web page by their titles. The owners or creators of meta-indexes put a lot of effort into compiling these lists and are eager to find new sites to add to them. It used to be that the owners of these sites would list your site for free because they desired to have the most meta of the meta-indexes—they strived to have the largest of the large indexes, and more sites mean a larger index. Today, many of these meta-indexes are commercial and charge a fee for the link to your site.

Some of these meta-indexes have a "Submit" or "Add Your Site" area; for others, you have to develop an inclusion request e-mail and send it to the owner of the site. In your inclusion request e-mail, let the owner know that you visited the site and feel that your site would be appropriate to be included. Give the reasons you think your site is appropriate and request the link. You should provide the HTML for the link as well. Review the techniques discussed in Chapter 16 to have your link stand out with a graphical icon, hypertext link, and tag line as well as including targeted keywords to enhance your link relevancy scores for enhanced search engine placement.

Meta-indexes are directed at a specific topic, such as "Connecticut Country Inns" or "Antique Car Sites." Meta-indexes provide easy access to a number of sites on a specific topic, and they are a great way to draw targeted, interested people to your Web site. In addition, some users might rely on meta-indexes as their only search effort. They might not use a search engine to perform a query on Mexican resorts, for example, if they know a certain meta-index contains 200 sites on Mexican resorts. Where search engine results might show books on Mexican resorts, personal Web pages relating to family vacations at Mexican resorts, etc., experienced Web users know that meta-indexes provide links to the actual Web sites of Mexican resorts. Meta-indexes can increase your chances of being found by people who are interested in what you have to offer.

You might want to consider placing a banner ad on one or more of the meta-indexes you find, given that the target audience you want to reach will be the people using these indexes. Choose carefully, though; you don't want to buy a banner ad on a meta-index that is not up to par and doesn't provide the traffic you are looking for. Take your time and investigate the meta-index before advertising on it. Does it appeal to the eye? Is it of good quality? Are there many dead links? Is it updated frequently? Does it have sufficient traffic?

Meta-indexes can be an effective way to increase traffic to your Web site. Word spreads quickly about the best meta-indexes because they are a great resource. Your target market will tell two friends and they will tell two friends, thus increasing traffic. In addition, more people may add links to your meta-index, and the more links you have to your Web site, the more traffic your site gets.

How to Find Appropriate Meta-Indexes

Now that you know what a meta-index is, how do you find one? You might be browsing on the Web and happen to come across one. A better way to find meta-indexes is through the search engines and directories on the Web.

You need to know how your particular search engine of choice works. Most search engines have advanced search capabilities, so be sure to explore them. When you're looking for meta-indexes, we recommend that you create a more focused search by adding an extra word such as *directory, list, index, table, resource, reference,* or *guide.* By adding one of these words in conjunction with another word—for example, *travel*—you're increasing your chances of finding appropriate meta-indexes. Performing a search on travel alone will return far less-targeted results. Looking for a travel directory alone might not work for you.

Why not? A search for a travel directory on the search engines often means looking for all sites that contain the word *travel* and all sites that contain *directory.* You should refine your searches to achieve more accurate results. Some general techniques that use the words *travel* and *directory* as examples you can apply in your search for meta-indexes are:

- Entering *travel directory* generally means: Look for all sites containing the word *travel* or *directory,* but try to gather those sites with *travel* and *directory* together.

- Entering *"travel directory"* (with quotation marks) often means: Look for all sites containing the words *travel* and *directory* next to each other.

- Entering *+travel directory* generally means: Find all sites with the word *travel* and preferably the word *directory* as well.

- Entering *+travel+directory* generally means: Find all sites with both words.

Search engines look for information in different ways and allow different techniques to be applied in order to narrow or broaden the search criteria. This information can be obtained by looking at the respective search engines' Help page (Figure 18.2).

Many search engines and directories offer an Advanced Search or Search Options page that lets you perform more detailed searches without using the parameters outlined above. Yahoo! (Figure 18.3) and Google (Figure 18.4) are two such sites.

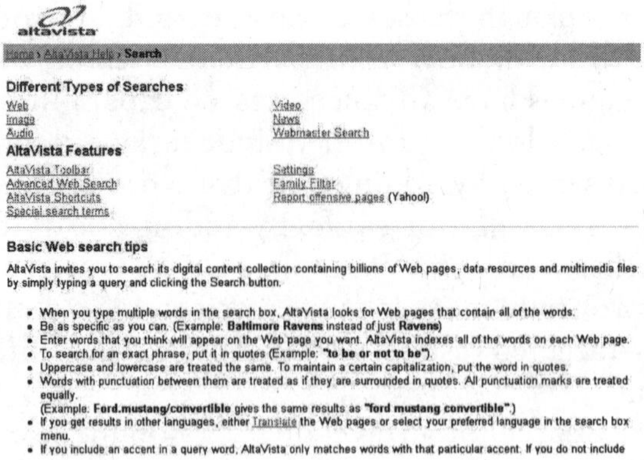

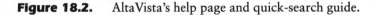

Figure 18.2. AltaVista's help page and quick-search guide.

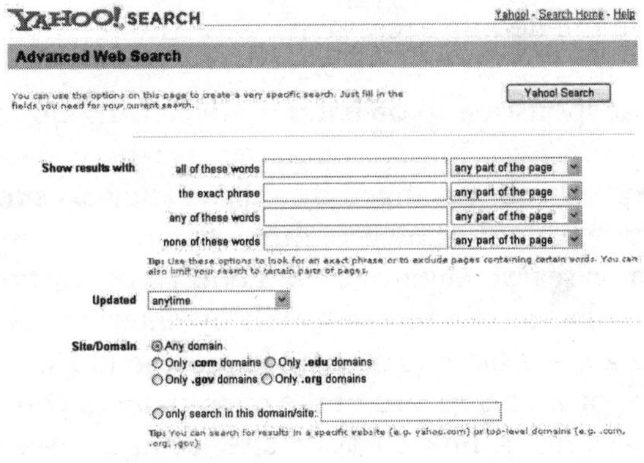

Figure 18.3. Yahoo!'s advanced search.

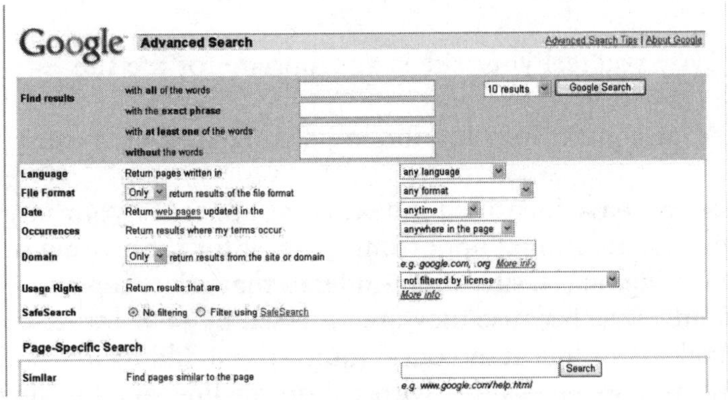

Figure 18.4. Google's search options.

Enlisting Meta-Indexes for Optimal Exposure

To ensure that you are taking full advantage of meta-indexes:

- Search for appropriate meta-indexes.

- Request a link.

- Provide the details necessary.

- Look at sponsorship or banner advertising opportunities.

Meta-indexes can be arranged by subject (such as sites that provide information on book publishing) or by geography (tourist sites in Alaska). As mentioned before, the major search engines are a good place to start. For example, to find tourist sites in Alaska, conduct a search by entering +*Alaska+tourist+directory*. Once you find a good list and start to check the links, you will likely find other lists. Bookmark or keep a record of the meta-indexes you like for future reference.

When requesting a link to your site, send an e-mail with "Site addition request" in the subject area of your message. Include the following in the body of the message:

- URL

- Description of your site

- Why you feel your site is appropriate for the site

- Your contact information in your signature file (see Chapter 9).

Once you have identified indexes that appeal to your target market, determine whether additional opportunities exist for sponsoring or purchasing banner advertising on the site. Meta-indexes that relate to your market are a great place to advertise because they are accessed by your target customers.

To make your link stand out, inquire about adding a prominent link or icon to the meta-index page along with a short tag line, in addition to your company name. If you provide the GIF and the HTML, the meta-index owner might be happy to include it.

Keep in mind that the compilers of the free meta-indexes are motivated by noncommercial reasons and are under no obligation to add your site to their list or process your request quickly. However, more and more meta-index sites have a commercial focus.

A listing on a meta-index might be free, but there could be a fee charged for placing a hypertext link within the listing. However, there also are meta-indexes that charge a fee for the listing. If you are considering paying a fee to be included in a meta-index, consider the volume of traffic the meta-index receives, whether the traffic is targeted, and the cost involved in relation to the return on investment. It might be wise to contact those already listed in the meta-index to see if the listing has been a good investment for them.

Internet Resources for Chapter 18

I have developed a great library of online resources for you to check out regarding meta-index marketing in the Resources section of my Web site at *http://www.susansweeney.com/resources.html*. There you can find additional tips, tools, techniques, and resources.

19

Winning Awards, Cool Sites, and More

There are literally hundreds of Cool Sites, Sites of the Day, Hot Sites, and Pick-of-the-Week Sites. Some of these sites require you to submit; others are selected based on such things as:

- Awesome graphics

- Dynamite content that is useful and interesting

- Uniqueness

- Fun features.

If you are selected for one of these sites, it can mean a huge increase in the number of visitors to your site. You must be prepared for the increased traffic flow as well as the increased demand for online offerings. In this chapter, we cover:

- Where to submit your site for award consideration

- How to win Site of the Day—tips, tools, and techniques

- Getting listed in What's New

- Posting your awards on your site

- Hosting your own Site of the Day.

It's an Honor Just to Be Nominated

There are sites that find and evaluate other sites on the Internet and recognize those that are outstanding by giving them an award. The award sites are generally quite discriminating in terms of selecting which sites are the recipients of their award. They have established criteria defining what they consider "hot" or "cool" and base their award selection on those criteria. Figure 19.1 shows a variety of awards.

What's New Web sites are designed to inform Internet users of new sites and updates to existing sites, and are often selective in which new sites they promote. The owner of each site also selectively chooses awards for Site of the Day, Week, Month, and Year. As mentioned earlier, some of these sites require you to submit an announcement or site description, and the awards are granted based on criteria such as graphics, dynamic content, uniqueness, and the "fun" quality of your site. Other sites grant their awards based solely on the personal likes and dislikes of the owner of the site and do not adhere to any criteria at all.

Some awards are taken just as seriously as the Academy Awards. The Webby Awards have a very comprehensive nomination procedure. Information regarding the Webby is available on their Web site at *http://www.webbyawards.com.*

Figure 19.1. A collage of some of the more popular award sites.

When you win an award, you post it on your site for all to see. The award icon is usually a link back to the site that bestowed the honor on you.

Choosing Your Awards and Submitting to Win

There are different levels of prestige associated with the award sites. Some are an honor to receive. Some are highly competitive because of the number of submissions they receive.

Some awards are easier to receive than others, such as those from commercial sites that give out awards in an attempt to increase the traffic to their own site. Traffic increases because the award is a graphic link displayed on the winner's site that visitors can follow back to the award giver's site. Other Webmasters give out awards to anybody and everybody who makes a submission. The award is granted with the sole purpose of building traffic.

The bottom line is that awards are valuable assets. The average Web user cannot tell which awards are the prestigious ones and which are given to anyone who submits. So, submit for any awards that you choose to, as long as your site is ready.

Where you place these awards is important. If you win many awards, consider developing an Awards page to house them with a link from your navigation bar.

Something to consider before you submit for an award is whether the huge amount of new traffic would benefit your site. If you sell T-shirts emblazoned with WWW cartoons, then any traffic is good traffic, and awards could benefit your site. On the other hand, if you are a marine biologist specializing in red tides in the Arctic, then the traffic that Site of the Day would bring might be more of a hindrance than a help in marketing your services. Always determine if the marketing tools and techniques will increase visitors from your target market before deciding to include them in your online marketing strategy.

Getting mentioned on one of the popular Cool Sites lists is probably the single biggest way to draw a tremendous amount of traffic to your site. However, that traffic is like a flash flood—fast and furious. Be careful what you wish

FTP (File Transfer Protocol)

The simplest way to transfer files between computers on the Internet.

for—you just might get it! Be prepared! Have a plan that you can implement on a moment's notice. If you offer something free from your site, be sure that you can access a huge volume of whatever it is and that you have a plan to distribute quickly. If you offer a free download from your site, plan to have a number of alternative FTP sites available to your visitors. If you have a call-in offer, make sure you have a telephone response system in place and staff to handle the huge volume of calls you might get. You need a plan to handle a huge volume of e-mails as well.

Once you have decided that the type of traffic that comes along with winning awards fits with your marketing strategy, make sure your site has the makings of a winner and then submit to as many award sites as you can.

- First, make a list of the URLs of the award sites you are interested in.

- Understand the submission form and guidelines. Review a number of forms to determine the information commonly requested.

- To save time, develop a document with the answers to the various questions from which you can copy and paste into the different submission forms.

- Submission forms capture the following types of information:

  - URL

  - Title of your site

  - Contact person (name, e-mail, phone, address)

  - Owner of the site.

- Submission guidelines tell you what types of sites can be submitted. (Some awards do not accept personal pages; others do not include commercial sites.) The submission guidelines also tell you what meets the definition of "cool" or "new" and what doesn't.

- Some award sites require that you display their award icon on your site. Posting an award on your site can provide a number of positive results—including enhanced credibility.

What's Hot and What's Not in the Name of Cool

Most of the award sites provide their selection criteria. Some base their selection on valuable content; others look for innovative and unique capabilities. Sites vary on what they consider "hot" or "cool," but they are fairly consistent on what doesn't make the grade, as summarized next.

What's Hot	What's Not
Awesome graphics, animation, audio, video	Single-page sites
Great, original content	Single-product promotion
Broad appeal	Offensive language or graphics
Fun features	Lengthy download time

Posting Your Awards on Your Site

If you have managed to collect a few awards for your Web site, you want to display them. After all, any award is a good award, and the site that granted you one expects you to display it in return for the recognition. Posting the awards on your home page might not be the best idea, though. For one thing, the additional graphics that will have to be downloaded will slow the load time for your home page. Second, by posting the awards on your home page, you are placing links leading out of your site on the first page. Thus, you are giving people the opportunity to leave your site before they have even had a chance to explore it. Where should you post your well-deserved awards, then? Simply create an awards section on your Web site. Here, you can list all of your awards without adversely affecting the load time of your home page or losing traffic.

Becoming the Host of Your Own Awards Gala

You can also create your own awards program to draw traffic to your site; however, this requires a considerable amount of work to maintain. The benefits of having your own awards program include having links back to your site from the awards placed on winners' sites, which is important for search engine placement because of link popularity. Because you control the text around the link back to your site, make sure you include your most important keywords to enhance your link relevancy score to further improve your search engine ranking. There are also great opportunities for permission ("Click here to be notified via e-mail when we have a new award winner") and viral marketing ("Tell a friend about this award—click here"). In addition, having your own awards program provides you with "bragging rights" and the opportunity for press releases to announce your awards, which gain exposure for your Web site and increase traffic. You need to work at it daily or weekly, so you must be committed to it. Be sure there is a benefit from a marketing perspective before you design and develop your own awards program. You must also be prepared to conduct your own searches to find sites worthy of your award if the quality of sites being submitted to you is not up to your standard.

There are a number of steps involved in getting your awards program up and running:

- Develop the criteria to use in your site selection.

- Develop several Web pages related to the award (information on selection criteria, submission forms, today's or this week's award winner, past award recipients page, etc.) in order to promote the award. (Be sure that you stipulate whether you are looking for submissions from commercial sites or personal pages and what criteria will be used in judging submissions.)

- Develop your award icon. Have this icon link back to your site. The award distinguishes the winner; thus, the link might be displayed prominently on its site. This is a great traffic builder.

- Finally, announce the award and market, market, market.

Internet Resources for Chapter 19

I have developed a great library of online resources for you to check out regarding awards in the Resources section of my Web site at *http://www.susansweeney.com/ resources.html*. There you can find additional tips, tools, techniques, and resources.

20

Productive Online Advertising

The world of banner advertising is changing rapidly. In the early days when banner advertising was in vogue, visitors were clicking through, good banner space was hard to find, and prices were rising. Then we saw the big decline. Click-through rates were poor and, as a result, advertisers were looking at alternative online advertising mediums. We saw banner advertising prices decline significantly. Quality space was not difficult to obtain and banner advertising was being used primarily to meet branding objectives. Over the last few years we have seen more and more pay-per-click targeted advertising opportunities, and this type of advertising is now on the rise. I have chosen to discuss the two types separately. I deal with pay-per-click or pay-to-play search engine advertising in Chapter 8 and deal with traditional banner advertising in this chapter.

Despite all the doom and gloom and bad press, traditional banner ads can still be an effective advertising medium if the banner ad is properly developed and is placed on a well-chosen site. We are starting to see a shift toward ads using rich media. Advertising on-line provides visibility—just as offline advertising does. You must develop a banner advertising strategy that works with your product, your marketing objectives, and your budget.

In this chapter, we cover:

- Your online advertising strategy

- Advertising opportunities on the Web

- Banner ad design and impact on click-throughs

- Banner ad sizes and locations

- Placing classifieds

- Tips to creating dynamite banner ads that work

- The cost of advertising online

- Measuring ad effectiveness

- Banner ad exchange networks

- Using an online advertising agency

- Sources of Internet advertising information.

Expanding Your Exposure through Internet Advertising

Today, Internet advertising is being recognized in the advertising budgets of businesses around the globe. Banner ads are a way to create awareness of your Web site and increase the traffic to it. Banners are placed on the sites that your target market is likely to frequent, thus encouraging this market to click-through and visit you.

The Internet offers many different advertising spaces. Banner ads can be placed on search engines, content sites, advertising sites, portals, and online magazines. The choice of where your ad is displayed is based on the objectives you wish to achieve with your online advertising strategy.

There are a number of advantages to online advertising:

- The response from these ads can easily be measured within one day through Web traffic analysis.

- The amount of information that can be delivered, if your Web site is visited, far surpasses that of a traditional advertising campaign.

- The cost of developing and running an online advertising campaign is much less than using traditional media.

Let's compare online advertising to traditional advertising. In traditional offline advertising, you generally work with a public relations (PR) firm or advertising company to come up with your marketing concept. As clients, businesses review and approve (usually after several attempts) the concepts before they are ever released to the public. The PR or advertising firms are responsible for developing TV, radio, and print ads for the businesses. They come up with the media-buy strategy after reviewing appropriate publications, editorial calendars, pricing, and the discounts that they receive for multiple placements. The ads are then gradually released over the period of the campaign and finally are viewed by the public. At the end of the campaign, the PR or advertising company evaluates the success of the marketing campaign. This is very easy if the objective of the campaign is to achieve X number of sales, but it is much more difficult if the goal of your campaign is to generate brand awareness.

Today, online banner ads are developed in much less time and are placed on Web sites quickly. Web traffic analysis software can tell you the next day if the banner ad is working or not by tracking the number of visitors who clicked through and visited your site through the ad. This provides you with the opportunity to change the site on which you are advertising or to change the banner ad to see if it attracts a greater audience.

Nielsen Net Ratings (*http://www.nielsen-netratings.com*—Figure 20.1) offers great up-to-date resources to find out who is doing the most online advertising. You can check this resource to find the top ten banners displayed on the Internet each week and the top ten advertisers on-line.

Figure 20.1.   Nielsen/Net Ratings provides you with continuously updated statistics on who is doing the most advertising on the Internet. The site also provides you with interesting information and popular banner ads.

Maximize Advertising with Your Objectives in Mind

When developing your advertising strategy, start with the objectives of your advertising campaign. The most common objectives for an online advertising campaign include:

- Building brand awareness

- Increasing Web site traffic

- Generating leads and sales.

You have a number of choices to make, such as what type of advertising to use and where to advertise. These decisions should be based on your objectives. If your objective is to increase overall brand recognition, a nicely designed banner ad on several of the high-traffic search engines would be effective. If you would like to develop leads and find new clients, then a more targeted approach should be taken, such as placing a banner ad on a high-traffic Web site that is frequented by your target market.

When deciding how to proceed with your advertising strategy, consider how many people you want to reach. Do you want a high-quality response from a small number of much targeted people, or do you want to reach a mass audience of grand proportions?

Think about the people you are targeting. If you sell dentistry supplies to dental practices, then you want to target dentists and hygienists. It would not make much sense to put an ad on CNN when you could advertise on a site about new medical discoveries in dentistry.

Always keep your budget in mind when you are devising your online advertising strategy. If you have a reasonable budget, you will work with several online advertising agencies. If your budget is small or nonexistent, there are many ways to stretch your advertising dollar. If you have the time, you can find promising sites to trade banners.

Online Advertising Terminology

Banner Ads

Banner ads are small advertisements that are placed on a Web site. Companies usually develop their banner ads, find sites for placement, and then either purchase or trade banner space.

Click-Throughs

When a viewer clicks on a banner ad with the mouse and goes to the site advertised, it is called a "click-through." Sometimes banner advertising prices are determined by the number of click-throughs. You don't pay every time your ad is displayed. You pay only for those that actually click on your ad and are delivered to the appropriate page on your Web site.

Hits

Hits to a site are the number of times that another computer has accessed that site (or a file on a site). This does not mean that if a page on your site has 1,000 hits, 1,000 people have visited it. If your home page has a number of graphic files on it, this number could be misleading. A hit is counted when the home page main file is accessed, but a hit is also counted for every other file that loads along with the home page. Each one of your pages will have a number of files on it—you have a file for each graphic, a file for each banner you display, often a different file for each navigation button on the page, etc. So if a person visits 10 pages on a site and each page has 15 files included on it, then at least 150 hits would be generated.

Impressions or Page Views

When a banner ad is viewed, it is called an impression. Banner advertising prices are often calculated by impressions. If a person visits a page where your ad is displayed six times, this generates six impressions.

CPM

Cost per thousand, or CPM, is a standard advertising term. CPM is often used to calculate the cost of banner advertising if a site sells advertising based on impressions. If the CPM of banner advertising on the site was US$40 (that is $40 per thousand impressions) and the number of impressions the ad had was 2,000, then the advertiser would have to pay US$80 for displaying the ad.

Keywords

You can purchase keyword advertising on search engine (see Chapter 8) sites that have sophisticated advertising programs, or sites whose advertising real estate is maintained by online advertising agencies that have sophisticated advertising programs. Your ad appears when someone does a search on the keyword that you purchased. This is good for zooming in on your target market.

Geo-targeting

Purchasing geographically targeted banner advertising is one of the latest trends in Internet marketing. This is done by purchasing banner advertising for a range of IP addresses. Every device that connects to the Internet has its own unique IP address. These are assigned centrally by a designated authority for each country. We are now seeing search engines sell advertising by IP addresses to help businesses pinpoint their target geographic group. For example, John Doe is building a new home in Utah and is searching for a company selling lumber in his area. Dooley Building Supplies, a lumber company in Utah, happens to be marketing over the Internet, and as part of Dooley's advertising campaign they have purchased ads by keyword and by IP address. Simply stated, they have said that they want their ad to appear only when the keyword *lumber* is searched on by individuals whose IP address is within a certain range (the range being those existing in Utah). When John Doe does his search on the word *lumber,* the Dooley Building Supplies ad is displayed at the top of the page holding the search results. Someone in Michigan searching for lumber would see a different ad.

Jump on the Banner Wagon

Banner advertising is the most common and most recognized form of online advertising. Banner ads are available in various sizes. (See Figure 20.2 for some of the more popular banner ad sizes.)

Banners usually have an enticing message or call to action that coaxes the viewer to click on it. "What is on the other side?" you ask. The advertiser's Web site, of course. Banner ads can also be static, just displaying the advertiser's logo and slogan, or can be animated with graphics and movement.

If you use an advertising or PR company to develop your offline ads, quite often they provide you with a library of banner ads that you can use for your online advertising campaign. If you choose not to use an advertising or PR company, you can outsource the creation of a banner ad to another company or create your own.

The banner ad should be designed to have a direct impact on the number of click-throughs it achieves. There are a number of resources on-line to assist you in developing dynamic banner ads. Animation Online at *http://*

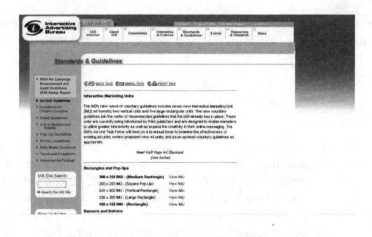

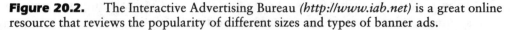

Figure 20.2.   The Interactive Advertising Bureau *(http://www.iab.net)* is a great online resource that reviews the popularity of different sizes and types of banner ads.

www.animationonline.com allows you to create banners on-line at no charge. The Media Builder at *http://www.mediabuilder.com* allows you to develop animated banner ads directly from its site. Other resources to assist you in designing and building banner ads are identified in the Internet Resources section of my Web site, referenced at the end of this chapter.

As noted previously, there are a wide variety of banner ad sizes available. You should consult with the owners of the Web sites on which you want to advertise before creating your banner ad or having one created professionally for you.

The objective of your banner ad is to have someone click on it. Do not try to include all of your information in your ad. A banner that is too small and cluttered is difficult to read and is not visually appealing. Many banners simply include a logo and a tag line enticing the user to click on it. Free offers or contest giveaways are also quite effective for click-throughs because they tend to appeal to the user's curiosity.

Exploring Your Banner Ad Options

Static banners are what the name suggests. They remain static on the same Web page until they are removed. Your banner ad will be visible on that particular page until your reader moves to another page.

Figure 20.3a   This is the first stage in an animated banner ad. It catches visitors' attention and makes them think the banner is doing a search on popular keywords related to skiing.

Figure 20.3b   This is the second stage in the animated banner ad. It acts as though the banner is continuing the search.

Figure 20.3c   This is the final stage in the animated banner ad series. It looks as though the search was completed. Now they have the viewer's complete attention.

Animated banners are banners that move on a Web site. Animated banners are usually in **GIF** format and contain a group of images in one file that are presented in a specific order (see Figures 20.3a through 20.3c). When using animated banner ads, you can choose to loop the file so that the banner continues to move between the images in the files or you have the option to make it stop after a complete cycle.

GIf
Graphics Interchange
Format.

Rotating banners are banner ads that rotate among different Web pages on the same site. Some rotating banners rotate every 15 or 30 seconds, so a visitor might see several ads while remaining on the page. Other rotating banner ads rotate every time there is a new visitor to the page. Rotating banners are commonly used in high-traffic Web sites.

Scrolling banners are similar to modern billboards. Here the visitor sees a number of billboard ads, scrolled to show a different advertisement every 10 to 30 seconds.

Banner Ad Tips

Follow these tips to ensure that your banner ad achieves your marketing objectives:

- Make sure that your banner ad is quick to load. If the Web page loads in its entirety before the banner, then the viewer might click away before ever seeing it. Ideally, you should have a very fast banner ad on a relatively slow-loading site. This way your viewers have nothing to do but read your banner ad while they are waiting for the site to load. You should always try to keep your banner ad size under 5K.

- To see how big files are when using any version of Internet Explorer, you can follow these steps:

  - Right-click on the banner ad.

  - Select Properties.

  - In the Properties window you will see a Size line which will tell you the banner size.

- Keep it simple! If your banner contains too much text or animation, or too many colors and fonts, viewers experience information overload and will not be encouraged to read or click on your banner.

- Make sure your banner ad is easily viewed. Many banners on the Internet are nicely designed but difficult to read. Use an easy-to-read font with the right size. Be careful in your choice of color.

- Always use Alt tags for those visitors who surf the Internet with their graphics turned off or cannot see your banner ad for whatever reason.

- Make sure your banner ad links to the optimum page on your site. It is not uncommon to click on an interesting banner only to find an error message waiting for you. This is annoying to Internet users and counterproductive for your marketing effort. Check your banner ads on a regular basis to verify that the link remains active and is pointing to the right page on your Web site.

- If you are using animated banner ads, limit your ads to two to four frames.

- You should always include a call to action such as "Click here." It is amazing how many people do what they are told. However, you still have to make your ad interesting and one that grabs their attention. Don't simply say "Click here"—give your audience a compelling reason to do so.

- Test your banner ads with the different browsers, the different versions of these browsers, and at different screen resolutions to make sure that they look the way you want them to.

- If you know absolutely nothing about advertising and graphic design, do not try to create a banner on your own. Go to a professional. If you do design your own banner, get a second opinion and maybe a third.

- Have your link send your target customer to an appropriate landing page rather than your home page. (See Chapter 24 for tips on landing pages.)

Interesting Banner Ads

The following are more technologically advanced forms of banner advertising. They are interesting to viewers because they have attributes that are unique or unusual in some way. These attributes might be more apt to grab viewers' attention and entice them to click on the banner ad.

- Expanding Banner Ads. An expanding banner ad (see Figures 20.4a and 20.4b) is one that looks like a normal banner ad but expands when you click on it, keeping you on the same site rather than transporting you to another site on the Internet. Usually these say "Click to Expand," and the viewer then can learn more about what the banner is promoting. Some of the more advanced expanding banner ads have e-commerce capabilities, which allow you to actually order products from the banner without ever going to the Web site.

- Animated Banner Ads. Animated banner ads contain a group of images in one file that rotate in a specific order. These banner ads are more likely to receive a higher click-through than a normal banner ad because moving images increase chances of the viewers' reading the banner. These banners also allow you to deliver more information than in a normal banner ad because you can show different files, which contain

Figure 20.4a   This expanding advertisement displays the ad and then prompts the viewer to expand the banner ad.

Figure 20.4b   When the banner expands, it explains more about the product while remaining on the site that hosts the banner ad.

different data. Limit your banner ads to two to four frames to keep your load time fast and to make sure your viewers read your information before they continue to surf the Internet.

- Drop-Down Menu Banner Ads Containing Embedded HTML. Lately we are seeing an increase in banner ads containing embedded HTML (see Figures 20.5 and 20.6). This allows viewers to select from a drop-down menu which site they want to visit. These banners are great because instead of making viewers click through and then navigate through your site, as with a conventional banner, these direct your viewers to the page of interest on your site. This type of banner ad also is great for co-op advertising programs. Several companies selling noncompeting products or services to the same target market can use this type of banner advertising to get more exposure for their dollar.

- Interstitial Ads. These are advertisements that appear in a separate browser window while your visitors wait for a Web page to load. Interstitial ads are more likely to contain large graphics, streaming presentations, and

Figure 20.5. Trip.com advertises using banners with embedded HTML which allows the viewer to choose from different sites in the drop-down menu.

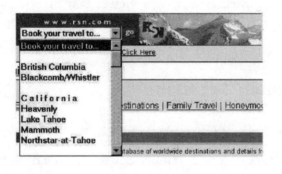

Figure 20.6. Another embedded HTML banner allowing different selections for the viewer to choose from.

more applets than a conventional banner ad. However, some users have complained that interstitial ads slow access to destination pages.

- Java, Flash, and Shockwave Ads. These banner ads allow you to use rich media in your advertisements. By using these technologies, you can incorporate animation and sound into your banner advertisement. Although Java banners are more technologically advanced and offer more features, they also take longer to download and risk not being viewed. Flash was designed to generate faster-loading Web sites, online animation, and advertising. If you want to incorporate rich media into your banners, you may want to go with Flash or Shockwave because you want your visitors to see your banner ads as quickly as possible.

- Floating Ads and DHTML. These ads appear when you first view a Web page, and they appear to "fly" or "float" over the page for anywhere from five to 30 seconds. They tend to obscure your view of the page, and they often disable mouse input until the ad is finished loading so that you must watch it before being able to access the page content. They have a high click-through rate and are great for branding, although their intrusiveness has been questioned.

- Unicast Ads. A Unicast ad is basically like a television commercial that runs in a pop-up window. It has animation and sound and can last from 10 to 30 seconds. Although they are like television commercials, they go a step further in that a viewer can then click on the ad to obtain further information. They have a higher-than-average click-through rate.

Location, Location, Location

As with all types of advertising, the location of the ad is extremely important. There are any number of targeted sites where you can place your banner ads. Always make sure that your banner advertising location is consistent with your objectives.

Search Engines

Advertising with search engines is covered in Chapter 8.

Content Sites

If your objectives include bringing interested people from your target market to your site, then advertising on strategically chosen content sites would be extremely effective. These are sites that concentrate on a specific topic. The CPM of advertising on content sites ranges drastically depending on the traffic volume they see and the focus of their visitors.

Banner Ad Price Factors

The price of banner ad space varies from site to site. Banner ads often are sold based on the number of impressions or number of click-throughs. As stated earlier, an impression is an ad view, and click-throughs are the actual clicking on the banner ad and being sent to the advertiser's Web site. The price per impression should be less than the price per click-through.

When site owners charge per impression, there is usually a guarantee that your ad will be seen by a certain number of people. The burden is on the seller to generate traffic to its site. When the charges are per click-through, the responsibility is on you, the advertiser, to design an ad that encourages visitors to click on it. Sites that charge per impression are more common than those that charge per click-through.

There are obvious advantages to the advertiser when paying per click-through. The advertiser doesn't have to pay a cent for the 10,000 people who saw the banner but did not pursue the link. Sites that do not have a large volume of traffic often charge a flat rate for a specified period of time.

Considerations When Purchasing Your Banner Ad

Before you sign on the dotted line to purchase banner advertising, there are a few things you should consider:

- How closely aligned is the target market of the site you want to advertise on to yours?

- How many sites are there like the one you are considering advertising on? Are there other sites you could use to reach the same audience?

- What banner sizes are allowed? Generally, the larger the banner, the more it costs.

- How many ads are on each page? The more ads on a page, the lower the click-through rate for any particular ad on that page. Generally, the more ads on a page, the lower the price per ad.

- Where on the page will your ad appear? Top? Bottom? Side? Above the fold or below?

- What banner rotation system is being used? Is there a comprehensive program that automatically profiles the visitors and provides the best banner? The more targeted the audience, the more expensive the ad; these profiling systems can provide ads to a very targeted audience.

- What are the site's competitors charging?

- Does the site have a sliding-scale ad rate?

Make Sure Visitors Can See Your Banner

A major fact that is often overlooked is that some people still surf the Internet with their graphics turned off. Not a big deal, right? What if you purchased a banner ad and you're paying based on impressions? They are not going to see it, so how could they click through? An easy way to make sure that the viewer still knows that your banner is there is to attach an Alt tag to your banner. An Alt tag is a small piece of HTML code that is added to a Web site. It tells the browser what is supposed to be displayed if the graphic cannot be viewed. It is here that you should develop a clever tag line that still entices the viewer to click through to your Web site. Remember that it is important to include an Alt tag on all of the graphics on your Web site.

Making It Easy with Online Advertising Networks

If your objective is to reach a large number of users through a wide variety of sites, Internet ad networks could be right for you. Ad networks manage the banner advertising real estate on a wide range of different Web sites that people look at every day. If you are going to join an ad network, you are known as an advertiser. You supply your banners to the ad network and determine how you want it to promote you. ValueClick (*http://www.valueclick.com*) is an example of a popular ad network (see Figure 20.7). ValueClick has 17 channels comprising 6,000 properties in its network and is emerging as an ad network leader. It can target a specific industry of your choice or advertise your banner to a mass audience. For a more targeted audience, your CPM would be higher. Even though you have to pay a little more initially, it saves you in the long run.

The benefit of joining an ad network is that the network not only targets your audience, it also provides you with real-time reports that indicate the success of your banner ads. This allows you to evaluate the success of your current banner ad campaign and offers you the chance to change your marketing strategy if you are not happy with your results. Maybe you want to take a different approach, or maybe a different banner design might work better for you. What-

Figure 20.7. ValueClick is a large ad network offering advertisers the opportunity to target their audience using ValueClick's network.

ever it might be, the data that the ad network can provide you with is beneficial to determining the strength of your banner ad campaign.

You can also join an ad network as a publisher. Publishers are the Web sites that banners are placed on. If you have a Web site and would like to make some additional online revenue from your site without the administrative and technical headaches, you can join an ad network, which will place banner ads on your site and pay you for the usage of this space. Very similar to an affiliate program, or banner exchange, by joining an ad network you can dramatically increase your online revenue.

Bartering for Mutual Benefits with Banner Trading

Using this technique requires you to barter with other Web sites to trade banners with their sites. If you are browsing the Internet and find a site that you think appeals to your target market, then ask for a trade. Send the Webmaster an e-mail outlining your proposition. Include the reason you think it would be mutually beneficial, a description of your site, where you would place that site's banner on your site, and where you think your banner might go on its site.

When you make arrangements like this, be sure to monitor the results. If the other site has low traffic, then more visitors could be leaving your site through its banner than are being attracted. Also, check the other site regularly to make sure that your banners are still being displayed for the duration agreed upon.

Tips for Succeeding with Classified Ads

Classified ads are also displayed on various Web sites. Some sites offer to display classified ads for free; others charge a small fee. Here are some tips for creating effective classified ads:

- Headlines. The headline of your ad is very important. The subject line determines how many people read the rest of your ad. Look at the subject lines of other ads and see what attracts your eye.

- Entice. Use your classified ad to get people to request more information, not to make immediate reservations. You can then send them a personalized letter outlining all of the information and make a great pitch to attract an order.

- Be Friendly. Your classified ad shouldn't be formal and businesslike. Make your ad light and friendly.

- Call to Action. Do not only offer information about what you are selling. Call the reader to action—for instance, to order now!

- Do Some Tests. Run a number of different ads and use a different e-mail address for each one. This way you can determine which ad receives the most responses. You can then run the best ad in a number of places to find out which place gets the biggest response.

- Keep a Record. Keep records of your responses so that you know which ads were the most successful.

Form Lasting Advertising with Sponsorships

Sponsorships are another form of advertising that usually involve strong, long-lasting relationships between the sponsors and the owners of the sites. Sponsors might donate money, Web development, Web hosting, Web site mainte-nance, or other products and services to Web site owners in this mutually ben-eficial relationship. By sponsoring Web sites on the Internet, you can achieve great exposure for your site. People appreciate sponsorships and look at banner ads that are from a sponsor. The benefits of sponsorships on the Internet are that you can target a specific audience, you usually get first call on banner ad placement, and you show your target market that you care about their interest. Overall, by sponsoring sites on the Internet, you have the opportunity to get directly in the face of your target market.

There are a number of ways in which you can advertise online through sponsorships. The following is a list of the more common forms of online sponsorship:

- E-Zines and Newsletters. An example of this would be Nike sponsoring a Golf Digest e-zine.

- Content Sites. An example would be DuPont sponsoring a NASCAR racing Web site.

- Online Chat Sessions. An example would be CDNow sponsoring a chat on the Ultimate Band List.

- Events. An example would be a search engine such as AltaVista or Google sponsoring a seminar on search engine strategy.

Commercial Links

Another form of online advertising is commercial links. A number of targeted sites provide lengthy lists of URLs related to a specific topic. See Chapter 18 on meta-indexes. These sites sometimes provide your listing for free but charge a fee to have a hypertext link activated from their site to yours. These are great sites, especially because they are targeted toward your demographic group. An example of this would be Franchise Solutions (*http://www.franchisesolutions.com*). This site (Figure 20.8) has a database of franchise and business opportunities targeted toward entrepreneurs wanting to open their own business. If you are a franchiser and are interested in expanding your business, you would want to have a link on this Web site because your target market visits sites like this.

Figure 20.8. Franchise Solutions allows franchisors to purchase links from its site.

Sponsoring a Mailing List

Another online advertising opportunity is presented by mailing lists. Mailing lists provide a much-targeted advertising vehicle. Mailing list subscribers are all interested in the list topic and are therefore potential clients, if you select the mailing list carefully. The rates for sponsoring lists can be quite low. The cost would be determined on a price-per-reader basis and is usually between one and 10 cents per reader. Subscribe to the lists that appeal to your target market and read the FAQ files to determine whether advertising or sponsorship opportunities exist for each mailing list. If the mailing list allows sponsorship, contact the mailing list administrator to inquire about the cost of sponsoring and, if it is reasonable, check availability and sponsors. All of the members of the mailing list have subscribed and want to be on the list; therefore, they are likely to read your e-mail. This is an excellent opportunity for you to expose your products and services to these potential consumers. A good example of this would be Trip.com's sponsoring a mailing list about vacation destinations around the world. Readers are interested in the topic, so they might be encouraged to click through and book a trip.

Online and Offline Promotion

Your advertising strategy shouldn't be limited to online activities. It is important to integrate your offline advertising strategy with your online advertising strategy. When you run an online campaign, you will want to consider running a consistent campaign offline. For more information on offline promotion, see Chapter 31.

Internet Resources for Chapter 20

I have developed a great library of online resources for you to check out regarding online advertising in the Resources section of my Web site at *http://www.susansweeney.com/resources.html*. There you can find additional tips, tools, techniques, and resources.

I have also developed a seminar on this topic which can be taken at any time over the Internet, can be taken live over the Internet at a scheduled time, or can be purchased as a seminar on CD. See *http://www.susansweeney.com/store.html*.

21

Maximizing Media Relations

Your online media strategy can be extremely effective in building traffic to your site. News release distribution can be done easily. Build the right list of e-mail addresses or make use of one of the online news release distribution services. All reporters and writers have e-mail addresses. Some still don't like to receive e-mailed news releases; others prefer the e-mail versions. When e-mail news releases are sent out, reporters reply by e-mail. They will expect your response within 24 hours. Develop a media kit that you can e-mail out to editors. In this chapter, we cover:

- Developing your online media strategy

- Public relations versus advertising

- Online public relations versus traditional public relations

- Effective news releases

- News release and distribution services online

- How to distribute news releases online

- Providing an area for media on your site

- How to find reporters online

- How reporters want to receive your information

- Encouraging re-publication of your article with a direct link to your site or the article

- Providing press kits online

- Electronic newsletters.

Managing Effective Public Relations

Media relations are very important to your marketing efforts. The best results are achieved when you integrate both online and offline publicity campaigns. News release distribution can be accomplished easily if you have an established list of reporters and editors, or if you make use of a news distribution service.

Maintaining effective public relations delivers a number of benefits to your company. Your company and products gain exposure through news releases, and a positive image for your company is portrayed. Your relationship with current customers is reinforced, and new relationships are formed.

Benefits of Publicity versus Advertising

Media coverage, or publicity, has a major advantage over paid advertisements. Articles written by a reporter carry more weight with the public than ads do because the media and reporters are seen as unbiased third parties. The public gives articles printed in media publications more credibility than they do paid advertisements. Another advantage of distributing news releases is that it is more cost-effective than advertising. You have to pay for advertising space on a Web site or time on the radio, but the costs of writing and distributing news releases are minimal.

One of the disadvantages of news releases compared to advertising is that you don't have control over what is published. If the editor decides to cast your company in a negative light, there is nothing you can do to stop him or her. If the writer of the piece does not like your company, for whatever reason, this might come across in the article. Basically, after your news release is distributed, you have no control over what will be written about your company.

It is important to note that when generating publicity, you might lose control over the timing of your release as well. For example, you might want an article released the day before your big sale, but the editor could relegate it to a date the following week. There is nothing you can do about this. It is not a good idea to rely exclusively on publicity for important or newsworthy events, because if the release is not reviewed or is not considered newsworthy, you might be stuck with no promotion at all.

What Is a News Release?

Before you begin your media campaign, you should know what news releases are and how to write them. News releases are designed to inform reporters of events concerning your company that the public might consider newsworthy. News releases can get your company free public attention. A news release is a standard form of communication with the media. News releases must contain newsworthy information. Companies that continually send worthless information in a blatant attempt to get their name in the press do not establish a good relationship with the media.

Writing a News Release

Journalists are bombarded with volumes of news releases. To improve the chances that your story will interest the journalist enough to publish it, you must make the journalist's job easier by presenting your news release in an appealing format and style. Your news release should be written as if it were prepared by an unbiased third party. The news release should follow a standard format, which is described in the following paragraphs.

Notice of Release

The first thing the reader sees should be . . .

FOR IMMEDIATE RELEASE

. . . unless you have sent the information in advance of the time you would like it published. In that case, state it as follows:

> FOR RELEASE: *Wednesday, April 12, 2006 [using the date you want it released].*

Remember that no matter what date you put here, the publication can release the information before or after that date. If the news is really big, it is unlikely that the publication will hold it until the date you have specified.

Header

The header should be in the upper-left corner. It should contain all of the contact information for one or two key people. These contacts should be able to answer any questions regarding the news release. If reporters cannot get in touch with someone to answer their questions, they might print incorrect information or even drop the article altogether.

Contact:

Susan Sweeney

Verb Interactive

(902) 468-2578

susan@susansweeney.com

http://www.susansweeney.com

Headline

Your headline is critically important. If you get it right, it will attract the attention you are looking for. Your headline should be powerful, summarizing your message and making the reader want to continue reading. Keep the headline short—fewer than ten words.

City and Date

Name the city you are reporting from and the date you wrote the news release.

The Body

Your first sentence within the body of the news release should sum up your headline and immediately inform the reader why this is newsworthy. With the number of news releases reporters receive, if you don't grab their attention immediately they won't read your release. Begin by listing all of the most relevant information first, leaving the supporting information for later in the article.

Ask yourself the five W's (who, what, where, when, and why) and answer them up front. Write the news release just as if you were writing a newspaper article for publication. Include some quotes from key individuals in your company and any other relevant, credible outside sources. If there are any statistics that support your main message, include them as well, providing references.

Your last paragraph should be a short company description.

The Close

If your release is two pages long, center the word *more* at the bottom of the first page. To end your release, center the word *end* at the end of your message. A sample news release is shown in Figure 21.1.

Figure 21.1.   This news release from Destination Hotels & Resorts contains several hypertext links, enabling a journalist to quickly access additional information and perform due diligence.

Advantages of Interactive News Releases

Online news releases take the same standard format as offline news releases, but the online news release can be interactive, with links to a variety of interesting information that supports your message. When your news release is provided by e-mail and you provide a hypertext link in that e-mail, the journalist is just a click away from accessing all the information he or she needs to complete the story. Helpful links to include in your interactive news releases are:

- A link to the e-mail address of the media contact person in your organization so that with the click of the mouse a journalist can ask a question via e-mail.

- A link to the company Web site so that the journalist can quickly and easily access additional information as part of his or her due diligence or can find required information.

- Links to articles that have been written about the company and related issues, both on the corporate Web site and on other sites. Don't provide a link to a magazine site that has written the article; rather, get a copy of the article and place it on your own Web site to ensure a live link.

- Links to graphics and pictures for illustration. If your story relates to a product, have a link to a graphic that can be used.

- Links to key corporate players, their biographies, their photos, and possibly some quotes. Journalists usually include quotes in their stories.

- A link to an FAQ section where you can have frequently asked questions and a few that you wish were frequently asked.

Figure 21.2 is an example of an online news release.

Sending News Releases on Your Own versus Using a Distribution Service

When distributing news releases on your own, you save the money it would cost to have a service do it. You can also be more targeted in your efforts than

Figure 21.2.   This news release from Apple.com contains textual URLs within the release.

a service would be. Some services' lists could be outdated or incomplete. Their lists of reporters and editors might not be comprehensive and might not have been updated. On the other hand, some services could get your news release taken more seriously. A reporter who recognizes the name of the service might be more receptive than if the release were to come from an unknown company. Using a service is bound to save you a lot of time.

If you decide to send your news releases on your own, you have to build a list of journalists. When reading publications, look for the names of reporters and find out their contact information. If you don't know whom to send a news release to at any publication, you can always call and ask for the name of the appropriate editor. Subscribe to a personalized news service to receive articles about your industry. This is a great way to find the names of journalists who might be interested in what you have to say.

There are a number of online resources to assist you in building your news-distribution list, such as the one shown in Figure 21.3. Mediafinder (*http://www.mediafinder.com*) is a Web site that might be useful. It provides access to a database of thousands of media outlets including magazines, journals, newspapers, newsletters, and catalogues. Bacon's (*http://www.bacons.com*) is a public relations resource that has detailed profiles on more than 20,000 media contacts, including their phone numbers, fax numbers, e-mail addresses, and work preferences (Figure 21.4). They also have editorial calendars that tell you who will be writing a scheduled story, what the topic of the story is, and when it will be written.

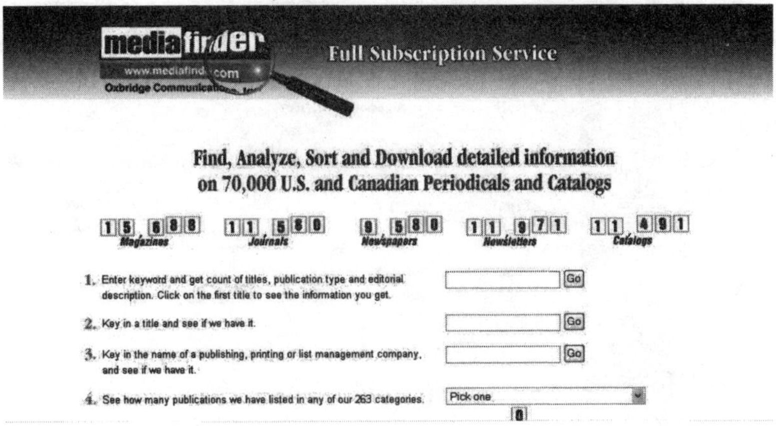

Figure 21.3. Use Mediafinder.com to locate appropriate magazines, journals, newspapers, newsletters and catalogs.

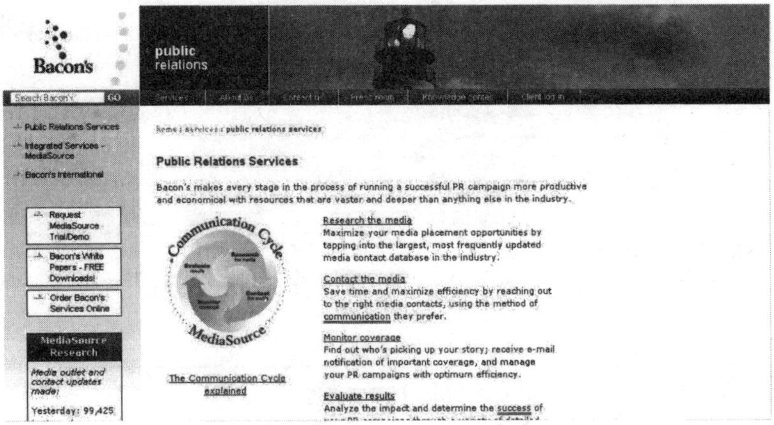

Figure 21.4. Bacon's is a media information company.

There are a number of news release distribution services online (Figures 21.5 and 21.6). Several of them are listed in the Internet Resources section of my Web site, referenced at the end of this chapter.

Figure 21.5. Internet News Bureau is an e-mail news release service company that provides distribution and also the writing of e-mail news releases.

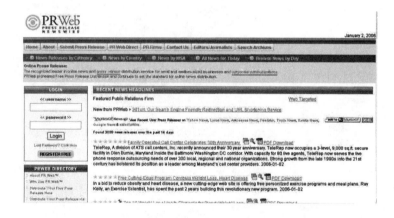

Figure 21.6. You can submit your news release to PRWeb.

Golden Tips for News Release Distribution

When distributing your news releases, don't send them to the news desk unaddressed. Know which editor handles the type of news in your release, and address the news release to that person. Don't send the news release to more than one editor in any organization unless there is more than one angle to the information in the news release. Call ahead, if possible, to discuss and solicit the editor's interest in your news release before sending it. Also, follow up with a phone call a few days later to make sure that it was received and to answer any questions. Be sure to review editorial calendars of publications in your industry to see if there are upcoming articles where your story could make a contribution.

News Release Timing and Deadlines

One of the most important things to remember when sending a news release or advisory is the deadline. Know how far in advance you should send your information for each of the media. Here are some time guidelines for your news release distribution.

Monthly Magazines

For monthly magazines, you should submit your news releases at least two to three months before the issue you want it to appear in. Magazines are planned far in advance, because it often takes a number of weeks to have the magazine printed and in subscribers' mailboxes.

Daily Newspapers

It is a good idea to have your news release arrive on the editor's desk at least several weeks in advance. If it concerns a special holiday, you should send it even earlier.

TV and Radio

When submitting news releases to TV and radio, remember that you might be asked to appear on a show as a guest. Be prepared for this before you submit the release. TV and radio move very quickly; a story that has been given to the news director in the morning might appear on that evening's news.

Formatting Your E-mail News Release

Your news releases can be e-mailed. Some reporters prefer e-mailed releases; others say they prefer mailed or faxed releases. Check the reporter's preference before you send your news release. If you e-mail your news releases, make sure that your e-mails are formatted properly. Refer to Chapter 10 for guidelines on how to create effective e-mail messages.

Keep your e-mailed news releases to one or two pages with short paragraphs. It is best to insert the news release in the e-mail. Do not send your news release as an attachment. You don't know which platform or word-processing program the reporter is using. You might be using the latest Microsoft Word program on a PC, but the reporter could be using an incompatible program on a Mac and will not be able to open the file. There could also be problems downloading, which would prevent your release from being read. The person on the receiving end of your e-mail could be using an old computer with a slow dial-up connection, so what might take you 2 minutes to transfer might take the recipient 20 minutes or two hours to download. In addition, you may be using a PC platform but the reporter may be using a MacOS-based computer. Someone who spends 20 minutes or longer downloading your e-mail only to find that it's useless won't be impressed—great start to getting the journalist to do a positive story on you!

Make sure the subject line of your e-mail is compelling. Journalists can easily delete e-mailed releases unopened, and quite often they do, because journalists receive large volumes of these daily. Make sure your e-mail is clear and concise. Get to the point with the first sentence. If you don't grab the reader's attention at the beginning of the release, the recipient might not keep reading to find out what your news is.

It's important to be able to send news release information in digital format within the body of the email. With a quick copy-and-paste, the journalist would then have the "first draft" of the story. You have made it easy for him or her to then edit the draft and have a story quickly. Everybody loves to save time, and nearly all journalists are under tight deadlines.

What Is Considered Newsworthy

Your news release has to contain newsworthy information for it to be published. One of the main concerns for public relations representatives is figuring out what is considered newsworthy and what isn't. You have to have a catch, and, if possible, it should appeal to some sort of emotion. Here is a list of newsworthy items:

- A merger or partnership between your company and another

- A free service or resource offered by your company to the general public

- A survey or forum that your company is holding to discuss an already hot news topic

- The appearance of a celebrity at a company event or upcoming online promotions

- Your participation in a trade show

- The findings of a report your company has conducted

- A breakthrough in technology resulting in a significant new consumer product

- The development of new strategic alliances or partnerships

- A charitable contribution by your company

- A milestone anniversary that your company is celebrating

- An award presented by your company

- Holiday event tie-ins

- Tips, articles, or advice

- Stories with a human interest element.

What Isn't Considered Newsworthy

Some things that aren't news to the general public might be news to targeted trade magazines and journals. Use your own judgment when trying to determine if your news release is news or just an excuse to get your company's name in print. If your release focuses on any of the following, it is probably not newsworthy enough to publish.

The launch of a new Web site has not been news for a number of years now. Unless the site is based on a breakthrough in Internet technology or serves the public interest in an innovative way, you won't get a mention in the news. Nor is a new feature or change to your Web site newsworthy information. Even if your site has undergone a major overhaul, this is not news to the general public.

Launching a new product is not newsworthy unless the product represents a significant breakthrough in some area. The upgrade of an old product simply won't cut it.

Developing an Online Media Center for Public Relations

If publicity is a significant part of your public relations strategy, you should consider developing an online media center as part of your site (see Figure 21.7). The media center should be easily accessible from your navigation bar. It would include all the components a journalist needs when doing a story on your company. Journalists should be able to find pictures to include in the story and all the information necessary to do their due diligence. They should be able to send a question to the appropriate media contact within the organization with one click. The media center should include:

- A chronology of news releases distributed by the company. Make sure you put the latest news release at the top.

- The company's history and background information

Figure 21.7.   Squaw Valley provides a great media center on its site, complete with a Story Ideas section readily available to the press.

- An electronic brochure

- Links to other articles written about your company. Make sure you have these on your site and not as a link to the magazine site that published the article.

- Links to story ideas for future articles

- Links to pictures of a related product or products that can be used by the journalist. Perhaps have a gallery where journalists can choose the pictures they want to include in their story. The TIFF (Tag Image File Format) is preferred by journalists for crispness and clarity and works best for desktop-publishing applications. The file will have a .tiff or .tif extension. The .tif format is not supported by Web browsers, so you can make it easy for journalists to acquire the photos by placing thumbnails on your Web site and then having an autoresponder send them the specific photos they request in the preferred format. There are also great online media tools available such as CleanPix (*http://www.cleanpix.com*).

- Background information on key company personnel, along with their pictures, bios, and quotes

- A link to your company's media contact and contact information

- FAQs and answers to anticipated questions.

By having a media center on your site, you are sending a clear message to the journalist. You are saying, "You're important to me! I want to provide you with everything you need to quickly and easily complete your story on our company." With the media center you are providing all the information, in a format that journalists can use, to enable them to do the story no matter what time they choose to do it.

You will want to encourage permission marketing by offering visitors the opportunity to be notified to receive your news releases "hot off the press." Place a "Click here to join our media list and to receive notification of our news releases" link on your Web site. In addition, make it easy for visitors to send a copy of your news release to a friend. Sometimes journalists work on stories together, so give the journalist the option to send the news release to a colleague or even to his or her editor through viral marketing.

Internet Resources for Chapter 21

I have developed a great library of online resources for you to check out regarding online media relations in the Resources section of my Web site at *http://www.susansweeney.com/resources.html*. There you can find additional tips, tools, techniques, and resources.

I have also developed a seminar on this topic which can be taken at any time over the Internet, can be taken live over the Internet at a scheduled time, or can be purchased as a seminar on CD. See *http://www.susansweeney.com/store.html*.

22

Increasing Traffic Through Online Publications

More than 60 percent of Internet users frequently read online publications, or **e-zines.** You can identify marketing opportunities by searching for and reading e-zines that are relevant to your business. In this chapter, we cover:

e-zines
Electronic magazines.

- What electronic magazines are

- Finding online sites on which to advertise or arrange links

- How to find appropriate e-zines for marketing purposes

- Submitting articles to e-zines

- Advertising in e-zines

- E-zine resources online.

Appealing to Magazine Subscribers on the Net

Many Web users frequently read e-zines. This is one of the reasons they are among the most popular marketing tools on the Internet. Five years ago there were a few hundred e-zines in publication. Now there are thousands of e-zines dedicated to a wide variety of topics such as travel, business opportunities, food, child care—you name it. For any topic you are interested in, there quite likely are several e-zines dedicated to it.

What Exactly Are E-zines?

E-zines, or electronic magazines, are the online version of magazines. They are content-rich and contain information regarding a certain topic in the form of magazine articles and features. Many e-zines display ads as well. Some e-zines are Web site-based and others are e-mail-based.

Many offline magazines provide a version online as well (Figure 22.1). *Coastal Living, Southern Living, Time, People,* and *Sports Illustrated* are all accessible via the Internet. Some of these provide the full version of their traditional magazine; others are selective about the articles they provide; and still others provide the previous month's edition.

Figure 22.1. *Southern Living* is an example of an offline magazine that has an online version.

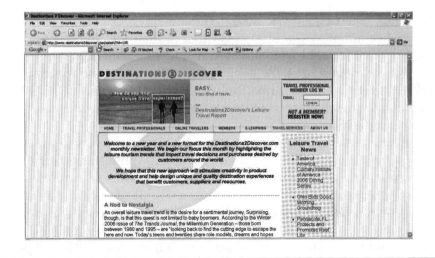

Figure 22.2. Destinations2Discover provides a great e-zine of interest to travelers, travel professionals and destination marketing organizations.

Web-Based E-zines

There are Web-based e-zines that have only an online presence (Figure 22.2). These e-zines are accessed through their Web sites by browsing from page to page. They have the look and feel of a traditional magazine. They include lots of glossy pictures and advertisements. Usually there is no charge to view the Web-based e-zines, but some do charge a subscription fee. These Web-based e-zines tend to be as graphically pleasing as offline magazines.

E-mail E-zines

Although e-mail e-zines can come as text or as HTML, these days we are seeing more and more HTML as they get a much higher readership and most e-mail viewers have no problem displaying HTML e-mails, which look like a Web page. Today we are seeing a blur between newsletters and e-mail e-zines as most newsletters now are sent as HTML and most are content-rich on a specific subject.

E-mail-based e-zines tend to be very content-rich and, as such, tend to be more of a target-marketing mechanism. E-mail e-zines tend to be several screens in length with one main or several short articles and, sometimes, classified advertising. The benchmark is that these e-zines should be able to be read in about five minutes. Circulation is often in the thousands. Most run weekly or biweekly editions. Most e-zines are free to subscribers.

People interested in the subject have taken the time to subscribe and have asked to receive the information directly in their e-mail box. Once you have found an e-zine that caters to your target market, the e-zine could be a valuable marketing vehicle.

Every subscriber to an e-mail-based e-zine has access to the Internet. These people regularly receive and send e-mail and quite likely surf the Net. If you advertise in this type of medium and place your Internet address in the ad, your prospective customer is not more than a couple of clicks away from your site.

People subscribe because they are interested. Even if they don't read it immediately when it is received, they usually read it eventually. Otherwise, they would not have subscribed. Subscribers will see your URL and product advertisements. For this reason, e-mail e-zines are a great marketing tool.

Using E-zines as Marketing Tools

Online publications are superior marketing tools for a number of reasons. They can be used in a number of ways to increase the traffic to your Web site. You can:

- Advertise directly

- Be a sponsor

- Submit articles

- Send press releases

- Start your own.

Finding Appropriate E-zines for Your Marketing Effort

There are many locations online to find lists and links to both Web-based and e-mail e-zines. A number of these resources are listed in the Internet Resources section of my Web site, referenced at the end of this chapter.

You evaluate an e-zine's marketing potential by its audience, reach, and effectiveness. The most important element of choosing an e-zine is to find one that reaches your target market. E-zine ads are effective because there is a high correlation between the target customer and the magazine's subscribers. If you advertise in an e-zine simply because it has the largest subscriber rate, you will probably be disappointed unless your products or services have mass-market appeal.

You should review a number of the e-zine-listing sites, such as the one shown in Figure 22.3. Some of these sites have keyword search capabilities. Others have their e-zines listed by category. Once you have a list of e-zines you feel fit well with your marketing objectives, you should subscribe and begin reviewing these e-zines.

The Multiple Advantages of E-zine Advertising

One of the major advantages of e-zine advertising is the lifespan of your ads. E-zines that are delivered to e-mail addresses are read by the recipient and sometimes saved for future reference. Many e-zines archive their issues with the ads intact. Advertisers have received responses to ads that are several months old!

When you place an ad in an e-zine, you see it in a relatively short period of time, perhaps the next day or the next week depending on how often the e-zine

Figure 22.3. eZINESearch.com provides a searchable directory of e-zines.

is published. Most traditional magazines close out their ad space months before the issue is available on the newsstand.

Your ad in an e-zine is also much more likely to be noticed because there are so few of them. In a traditional magazine every second page is an ad, whereas e-zines have a much greater focus on content and far fewer ads.

When your ad appears in an e-zine, your customer is just a click away because your ad is usually hyperlinked to your Web site. This brings your customer that much closer to being able to purchase your products or services.

Another advantage of e-zine advertising is that e-zines are often shared with friends and associates. Most e-zines use viral marketing effectively, encouraging readers to send a copy to a friend. Your ad might be passed around a number of times after it first enters the mailbox of the subscriber. You are being charged for the ad based on the number of e-mail subscribers. Therefore, the extra viewers of your ad cost you nothing.

One of the most tangible advantages of e-zine advertising is the relatively low cost due, in part, to the low overhead for development, production, and delivery. E-zines need to fill all of their available space. If an e-zine advertising section has empty spaces, the publisher might be willing to negotiate. Some will even barter with you—advertising space at a discounted price in exchange for their e-zine promotion on your Web site.

E-zines provide a very targeted advertising medium. People subscribe to various e-zines because they have a genuine interest in the topics covered. This provides a major advantage over other advertising mediums. E-zine ads have been shown to have very high response rates due to their targeted nature.

Because they are distributed via the Internet, e-zines reach a far wider audience geographically than most traditional magazines. It is not uncommon for an e-zine to have subscribers from all around the world.

There are thousands of e-zines out there related to every topic imaginable. Most e-zines have thousands of subscribers. When you couple the low cost to advertise in these e-zines and the many e-zines that might reach your target market, it is no wonder many companies are allocating more and more of their advertising budgets to online activities.

Guidelines for Your Advertising

Once you have found e-zines that reach your target market, you should consider a number of other factors before you make a final decision on placing your ad.

- Check the ads displayed in the e-zine for repetition. If advertisers have not advertised more than once, then they probably did not see very positive results.

- Respond to some of the ads and ask the advertisers what their experiences were with advertising in that particular e-zine. Be sure to tell them who you are and why you are contacting them. If you are up front, they will probably be receptive to your inquiry.

- Talk to the e-zine publisher and ask questions (e.g., how many subscribers there are). Ask what other advertisers have had to say about their results. Find out what types of ads they accept and if there are any restrictions. Check to see if the publisher has a policy of never running competing ads. Maybe the e-zine has a set of advertising policies that you can receive via e-mail.

- Find out if the publisher provides tracking information and, if so, what specific reports you will have access to.

- Find out if your ad can have a hyperlink to your Web site. If the e-zine allows hyperlinks, make sure you link to an effective page—one that is a continuation of the advertisement or a page that provides details on the item you were advertising. Provide a link to the order form from this page to assist the transaction.

- In some cases e-zines have an editorial calendar available to assist you with the timing of your ad. The editorial calendar will tell you what articles will be included in upcoming issues. If an upcoming issue will have an article relating to your type of product or service, you could choose to advertise in that issue. You might contact the editor regarding a product review or submit an article relevant to the issue topics.

- Make sure that the advertising rates are reasonable based on the number of subscribers, and ask yourself if you can afford it. Find out the "open" rate, or the rate charged for advertising once in the e-zine. Ask what the rate is for multiple placements. If you are not in a position to pay for the advertising now, ask if there are other arrangements that could be made. For example, the publisher might accept a link on your Web site in exchange for the ad.

- Develop your ads with your target customer in mind. They should attract your best prospects. Wherever possible, you should link to your site or provide an e-mail link to the right individual within your organization.

- Develop a mechanism to track advertising responses. You could use different e-mail accounts for different ads to determine which ads are bringing you the responses. You can also use different URLs to point viewers to different pages within your site. If you have a good traffic-analysis package, you can track the increase in visitors as a result of your ad.

- Make sure you are versed in the publication's advertising deadlines and ad format preferences.

Providing Articles and News Releases to E-zines

Besides advertising, a number of other marketing opportunities can be explored with e-zines. Once you have found the e-zines that cater to your target market, these e-zines could be fruitful recipients for your news releases. Refer to Chapter 21 for recommendations on news release development and distribution. The editors might also accept articles of interest to their readers. You might be able to incorporate information on your products and services in an interesting article that would fit the editor's guidelines.

There are many e-zines looking for great content. If you can write articles for them that provide great content for their readers and at the same time provide a little exposure for you, it's a real win-win situation. You'll want to target those e-zines that have the same target market you do and have a broad subscriber base. You'll want to make sure the e-zine includes a resource box at the end of the article crediting you as the author and providing a hyperlink to your Web site or your e-mail address. Having articles published enhances your reputation as an expert, and people like to buy products and services from people who are experts in their field. You might see if you can be a contributing editor or have a regular column or feature in their e-zine.

Besides sending your articles directly to targeted e-zines, you can also submit them to "article banks" online. Article banks are online resource sites for e-zine publishers. E-zine publishers search through these banks for appropriate articles for their e-zine and, if they use one, they include the resource box of the author.

Reasons You Might Start Your Own E-zine

You can start your own e-zine. Today, this is relatively easy. There are lots of resources online regarding e-zine development and administration. Don't make this decision without much thought, though, as you can damage your reputation if you don't deliver consistent, valuable content.

There are a multitude of reasons that you should consider developing and distributing your own e-zine. E-zines can be an extremely effective online marketing tool for the following reasons:

- You become established as an "expert." By providing your readers with valuable articles related to your area of expertise, you become, in their eyes, a valued and trusted expert.

- You establish trust. The first time someone visits your Web site, he or she has no idea who you are, how capable you are, or how professional you are. Sure, visitors get an impression from the look and feel and content of your site, but are they ready to do business with you? By providing them with free, valuable content over a period of time, you earn your visitors' trust, and they are more likely to turn to you when they need the type of product or service you provide.

- You generate significant traffic to your Web site. Your e-zine should always reference and provide a hyperlink to something available from your Web site. Once your visitor links through, there should be elements that encourage him or her to stay awhile and visit a number of pages on your site. The more often people visit your site, the more likely they are to do business with you.

- You build loyalty. Relationship marketing is what it's all about on the Web. You build relationships over time, and your e-zine will help you do just that. Your subscribers receive something free from you every month. Whom are they going to do business with when they have a need for your product or service? People prefer to spend their money with businesses they know and trust.

- You stay current with your customers and potential customers. When you are in front of your subscribers every month, you're not too easy to forget. You can keep them up to date on what's new with your company and your products and services, or what's new in your area of expertise.

- You grow your database. See Chapter 14 for tips on how to build your database.

Developing Your Own E-zine

If you do start your own e-zine, you should spend sufficient time planning and testing before you publish to ensure that you do it right. You don't get a second chance to make a first impression, and you want your readers to subscribe and tell others about the great e-zine they found. You want them to be excited to read your e-zine every time it is delivered to their e-mail box. The following tips will help you in your e-mail–based e-zine planning and preparation:

- Provide great content. This goes without saying. If you have content that people want to read, they will remain subscribers. Don't think that shameless self-promotion is great content; your target audience certainly won't. As a rough guide, make sure your e-zine is 80 percent rich content and no more than 20 percent promotion and ads. Your e-zine should be full of what your target market considers useful information.

- You should keep length a consideration because you want your e-zine to be read and not put aside for later because it is always too long to read quickly. In this case, less is more. Subscribers should be able to read your e-zine in five minutes or less. If you do have a lengthy article, you might give a synopsis in the e-zine with a hyperlink to more detail on your Web site.

- Limit your content to four or five dynamite articles for an e-mail-based e-zine. Provide a brief table of contents at the beginning of the e-zine. Keep the copy short and to the point.

- Keep your line length under 60 characters including spaces to avoid word-wrap issues.

- Encourage your readers to send a copy to others they feel might be interested in your great content. Make sure you provide subscribing instructions as well for those who receive these forwarded copies (Figure 22.4). You should also provide instructions on how to opt out, or unsubscribe.

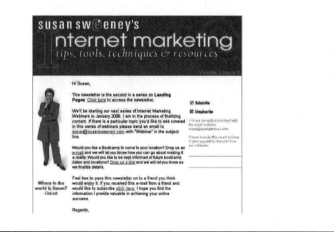

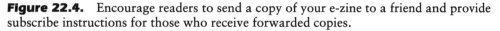

Figure 22.4. Encourage readers to send a copy of your e-zine to a friend and provide subscribe instructions for those who receive forwarded copies.

- Test your e-zine with different e-mail programs to ensure that your e-zine looks the way you designed it no matter which e-mail program your reader uses. Send test copies to friends with different e-mail readers such as Outlook Express, Netscape Mail, Pegasus Mail, and Eudora. See how it looks, make sure that word-wrap is not an issue, and make sure the hyperlinks work.

- Make sure you run your e-zine through a current spam checker to ensure that your e-zine will not be seen as spam by the spam filters.

- Have an unsubscribe button at the bottom of every e-mail enabling anyone in your database to opt out.

- Keep your subscriber addresses private and let subscribers know your privacy policy.

As word about your e-zine spreads, a large community of people who fit your target market will be reading it.

Once you have your own e-zine, you'll have to:

- Promote it to your target market through newsgroups, mail lists, your Web site, and your e-mail signature file. If you do promote your e-zine in newsgroups and mail lists, be sure it is appropriate to advertise your e-zine in a given newsgroup or mail list before you post. You do not want to be accused of spamming. However, promote your e-zine shamelessly on your own site (let people subscribe to the e-zine on your site) and in your signature file.

- Provide an opportunity for subscribers to let others know. In your online e-zine, have a form that allows subscribers to e-mail a copy of the e-zine to their friends and colleagues. Use a call-to-action statement such as "Do you know someone who might be interested in this e-zine? Click here to send them a copy." This is a great way to pick up additional subscribers because some of the nonsubscribers who read your e-zine might then become subscribers if your content is interesting to them.

- Make it easy for people to subscribe to your e-zine. Provide clear subscription instructions in each e-mail version of your e-zine and on the online version. Have a form handy on your site to collect e-mail addresses from people who wish to subscribe. Always ask for the first name so that you can personalize your e-zine.

- Provide an archive of past issues on your Web site so that visitors can sample your wares before subscribing. Make sure you provide an option for visitors to subscribe from that page as well.

- Don't provide your list of subscribers to anyone. This protects your subscribers' privacy and keeps your list spam-free. People will not be happy if they start receiving spam as a result of your e-zine.

Internet Resources for Chapter 22

I have developed a great library of online resources for you to check out regarding e-zine marketing in the Resources section of my Web site at *http://www.susansweeney.com/resources.html*. There you can find additional tips, tools, techniques, and resources.

I have also developed a seminar on this topic which can be taken at any time over the Internet, can be taken live over the Internet at a scheduled time, or can be purchased as a seminar on CD. See *http://www.susansweeney.com/store.html*.

23

Web Rings as a Promotion Tool

Web rings provide a different way to organize sites. They are a free service offered to the Internet community. Web rings arrange sites with similar content by linking them together in a circle, or a ring. Each link in the ring is directed to a CGI script on the Web ring's server that sends the viewer on to the next site in the ring. There are literally thousands of rings with subjects such as communications, games, art, real estate, and so on. If there isn't a ring suitable for your site, you can create your own. The visitors you receive from participating in the Web ring will be potential customers who are responsive to the content of your site and curious about your products or services. In this chapter, we cover:

- What are Web rings and how do they work?

- What promotion possibilities are available with Web rings?

- How do I participate and what will it cost?

- Where will I find Web rings that work for my company?

- What Web ring resources are available on the Net?

An Effective Alternative to Search Engines and Directories

Web rings are a fast-growing service on the Internet, providing one of the easiest ways for visitors to navigate the Internet. In each of its tens of thousands of topic-specific rings, member Web sites have linked their sites together, thus permitting more targeted visitors to reach the joined sites quickly and easily.

People increasingly are becoming dissatisfied with search engines and directories as tools to identify specific topic-related sites. Searches on a specific keyword sometimes yield results that include totally unrelated sites. For instance, if you were planning a vacation to Mexico and you wanted to search for resorts in Mexico, the search engine results would likely include sites only vaguely related to what you were looking for. The results might include book titles at Amazon.com related to Mexican travel, personal pages with other people's experiences traveling in Mexico complete with pictures from their family vacation, travel agencies, and tour company sites. The Web ring provides an alternative to these tools.

Site owners typically trade links with other Web sites to help promote each other's sites. The Web ring was developed to enlarge the scope of link trading. A Web ring joins together many sites with a common topic.

The major Web ring sites are:

- WebRing (*http://dir.webring.com/rw*)

- CrickRock WebRing System (*http://www.crickrock.com*)

- World of Webrings (*http://www.webringworld.org*).

What Are Web Rings?

A Web ring is made up of a number of topic-specific sites that are grouped together. There are country inn Web rings, Star Trek Web rings, prenatal-care Web rings, BMW Web rings, and remote-sensing Web rings in the huge list of Web rings that exists today. All of the Web ring directories have different categories and subcategories. At WebRing the major categories include:

- Business and Finance

- Computers and Internet

- Cultures and Community

- Entertainment and Arts

- Family and Home

- Games

- Government and Politics

- Health and Wellness

- Hobbies and Crafts

- Music

- Recreation and Sports

- Regional

- Religion and Beliefs

- Relationships and Romance

- Schools and Education

- Science.

Each of these major categories has a number of subcategories, and each of the subcategories has a number of individual rings.

Rings can contain any number of sites. There must be at least three before the ring is listed in the directories. Generally, the rings contain between 20 and 200 sites. Some rings are smaller and some are substantially larger, with close to a thousand sites included.

Each ring was started and is maintained by an individual Web site owner. Through navigation links found most often at the bottom of member pages, visitors can travel to all or any of the sites in a ring. They can move through a ring in either direction, going to the next or previous site, or listing the next five sites in the ring. Visitors can also jump to a random site in the ring or survey all the sites that make up the ring.

An extraordinary system, Web rings are entirely open and free of charge to both visitors and members. As more and more people discover Web rings, we will see phenomenal growth in this as a preferred method to surf the net.

How Do Web Rings Work?

To surf a ring, all you have to do is use the links at the bottom of the page in the Web ring block. At the bottom of a Web ring participant's pages, you find the Web ring navigation aid. A common Web ring graphic includes links to the "Next" site in the ring, the "Previous" site in the ring, or a "Random" site in the ring. You also have the option, in many cases, to see a list of the "Next 5" sites in the ring or to view the entire "Index" of the ring's sites. Once you begin surfing a ring, there is no clear beginning or end, just a circle of related material. The Web ring program compensates for sites that are unreachable because they no longer exist or have server problems. You will always be able to navigate the ring.

When using a search engine, you are provided with a list of sites, only some of which are relevant. You visit the sites listed and then, depending on which browser you are using, you may use your "Back" button to return to the Results page to make another selection. With a Web ring this backing out is unnecessary. Once you've finished reviewing a site in the ring, you proceed to the next site that is of interest or simply surf through the connected sites one by one.

How to Participate in Web Rings

The first thing to do is find Web rings that are right for your product or service—those that cater to your target market. You can review the directories at the WebRing site *http://dir.webring.com/rw*, the CrickRock WebRing System at *http://www.crickrock.com*, and also at the World of WebRings site *http://www.webringworld.org*.

Once you have found a promising Web ring, you contact the owner to ask permission to join. The owner reviews your site to determine your "fit" with the theme. Once you are accepted, the owner provides you with the required code and accompanying graphics, which you insert on your page. The ring owner provides all the required material; you slip it into your HTML file, and that's that.

Once the code is on your site, the Web ring monitors the traffic and collects the statistics for your site, as they do for all Web ring sites. This is beneficial to you because you can see how much traffic you are getting through the Web ring.

Any Web site owner who feels no existing ring is suitable can apply to create a new ring. If the application is approved, WebRing, CrickRock, or World of WebRings will provide all the necessary code and instructions. New Web rings are listed in the directory once they contain at least five sites.

Web Ring Participation Costs

The cost to participate in these Web rings is absolutely nil. No application fees, no charge for the approval, no charge for the code to be inserted on your pages, no charge for the increased traffic a Web ring brings.

The Benefits of Web Rings

There are many benefits to both the users of Web rings and the participating Web sites. Benefits to the user include:

- Web rings provide a great navigation tool when looking for more information on a specific topic.

- Web rings are easy to use. They provide one of the most efficient ways to find specific content on the Internet.

- Web rings avoid the duplication found in search engines, where a site may appear several times in one search. Each site is linked only once in each Web ring.

- Web rings speed up search time.

- Web rings eliminate sifting through mounds of search engine results for appropriate sites.

Benefits to participating Web sites include:

- Web ring participation increases the number of targeted visitors to your Web site.

- The organizers of the Web rings make it easy to monitor how successful your ring is. Traffic reports and "top rings" statistics are made available to participants.

- Web rings drive traffic to your site.

Business Reluctance to Participate in Web Rings

One of the biggest hurdles Web rings face in being adopted by the business sector is that when you join a ring, you are linking to the competition. It is likely that this mentality explains why Web rings have been so popular for personal sites and special-interest groups, but have failed to catch on in today's business community. But, again, small businesses and retail-oriented sites have not shied away from rings. For example, rings and banner programs are hot marketing strategies for stores that sell collectibles. This is particularly true for hard-to-find collectibles. Take the Pez phenomenon: Not being on a Pez Web ring could be a crucial mistake for vendors. After all, if a customer hits a site and it doesn't have a specific Pez, the quest isn't over—it's on to the next site. What better way to get there than via a ring? Your site might just be the next one.

Lately we have seen growth in the commercial application of Web rings. There are a few reasons for this:

- A number of articles have appeared in Internet marketing magazines related to the high volume of traffic through these Web rings. Businesses have sometimes found that the bulk of the traffic to their site is coming through the Web ring.

- Other articles talk about the benefits of being conveniently located near your competition, bringing more traffic for everyone. Several have likened it to what happens in the real world in the fast-food industry. When a McDonald's opens, you quickly see a Burger King, Wendy's, Pizza Hut, KFC, and Taco Bell all open up close by. This means more business for everyone.

Other Marketing Opportunities Provided by Web Rings

When you have found a Web ring that attracts your target market, you can participate and enjoy the increase in visitors to your site. You can search through the list of participants in a Web ring to arrange reciprocal links. You can also search a Web ring for banner advertising purposes. You can either exchange banners or purchase advertising on these sites. You can find sites that may be appropriate for cooperative advertising purposes. You can exchange coupons with another site you are linked to, which works especially well when you sell noncompeting products to the same target market.

Internet Resources for Chapter 23

I have developed a great library of online resources for you to check out regarding Web rings in the Resources section of my Web site at *http://www.susansweeney.com/resources.html*. There you can find additional tips, tools, techniques, and resources.

I have also developed a seminar on this topic which can be taken at any time over the Internet, can be taken live over the Internet at a scheduled time, or can be purchased as a seminar on CD. See *http://www.susansweeney.com/store.html*.

24

Landing Pages

When you promote an offer online, whether it be a banner ad, newsletter promotion, or pay-to-play campaign, you want to maximize the results of your effort. You want to take the interested person directly to the information they are looking for—not to your home page where they may have to navigate to get to the specific information. When done properly, creating a targeted landing page for an ad can greatly increase conversions, or the number of customers who act on your offer. In this chapter, we cover:

- What is a landing page?

- Considerations for landing page content

- Landing page layout

- Testing your landing page.

What Is a Landing Page?

A landing page is a Web page that is created specifically to respond to a marketing campaign you are running. You can't provide all the details and the opportunity to make the purchase in the banner ad, so you develop a landing page to follow through from the banner ad. When your target market clicks on the banner ad, they are taken to the landing page that was developed specifically for that ad. The action you want the target market to take might be to make a purchase, join your e-club, view a live online demo, or participate in a survey. The key is that the landing page is usually geared toward a conversion or converting the browsers into buyers.

The way your landing page is developed depends entirely on your business objectives, your target market, and your offer itself. The landing page should focus on the one thing you want the visitor to do—keep it focused.

The presentation and the content, or copy, of your landing page have a huge impact on the ability of the landing page to close the offer. We begin with a look at content for your landing page. There are a number of points to make note of when preparing content for a landing page:

1. Your landing page should be a continuation of your ad—repeat and expand on the offer presented in your ad. The ad is designed to generate interest and the landing page is designed to close the sale.

2. Your landing page should emphasize the benefits of your offer—this is what justifies the purchase.

3. Your landing page content should flow from the advertisement. If your ad promotes your virtual tour, then when visitors click through to the landing page they should be given the opportunity to take that virtual tour. Take your target market where you want them to go. Tell them what you want them to do.

4. Your landing page should "speak" to your target market. Use their language, buzz words, or industry jargon. Use the appropriate tone for this particular target market.

5. Your landing page should have a dynamite headline. Grab their attention!

6. Your landing page should be written for scannability. Internet users don't read; they scan.

7. Your landing page should promote the "value-added" portion of the offer that will help with your objectives. Free shipping, free gift with purchase, a coupon or discount toward a future purchase, the number of reward points earned with purchase, etc., all add to the value of the offer.

8. Your landing page should create a sense of urgency—get your visitors to do what you want them to do NOW!. If they leave your site without making the purchase, it is often unlikely you'll get another opportunity. Using appropriate calls to action like "Order Today!," telling the target market that "there are limited quantities" or "limited space available," and techniques like time-stamping the offer with an expiration date create a sense of urgency that encourages the target market to take immediate advantage of the offer.

9. Your landing page content should minimize risk. If you have a money back guarantee, emphasize it! Anything that helps to close the deal should be prominently displayed.

10. Your landing page should ask for the sale—maybe multiple times and places. You don't get what you don't ask for.

11. Your landing page should include content that enhances your credibility. Things like client testimonials or product/service reviews. Content that helps establish credibility also helps build trust, which is key to doing business online.

12. Your landing page should be optimized for the search engines. If you are running a promotion for just a couple of days, then odds are you do not want your landing page indexed by the search engines. In this case you would use your robots exclusion protocol in your robots.txt file to tell the search engines not to index the page. See Chapter 6 for search engine optimization and Chapter 8 for pay-to-play considerations.

Once you have developed a dynamite landing page, you will want to do some testing to maximize your conversion; very few people get it perfect the first time. You will want to test different page content format and lengths, different jargon and tones, different layouts, different offers, and a number of other things to find the right balance to best sell your product or service.

Considerations for Landing Page Content

Your most important information on the landing page should be above the fold. The fold is where the bottom of the browser window sits and additional scrolling is required to view the remaining content. This is what your target market sees when they land on your landing page. It is usually this content that encourages them to keep going or to click away.

Your landing page should focus on the one thing you want them to do. You want to eliminate anything that might distract the target market from doing what you want them to do.

Be wary of "banner blindness." People tend to not even notice the information that is in the standard banner ad areas. Stay away from having any content that looks like an ad in shape, size, and color.

Leverage the elements on this landing page. You want to give your visitors the option to sign up for your permission-marketing-based newsletter or e-club. You want to make use of the viral marketing tell-a-friend function. You do not want these elements to take over the page and distract the user, but you want to encourage these actions—be subtle!

Give your target market access to anything needed to close the sale. What information do they need? Shipping information? Warranty/returns/exchanges information? Privacy information? Your contact information? Make sure that they have access to whatever they need.

Make sure the landing page looks great. Choose things like font types, styles, and color to your best advantage. Photography should be professionally done; you can always tell the difference.

Provide your target customer with options on how to make the purchase. Prominently display alternative purchase options. Your visitor might be extremely interested in your offer, but not so comfortable making the purchase online.

Simplify the actual purchase process with as few clicks as possible. People like things that are clear and easy to do. I remember hearing somewhere that for every additional step or question asked that does not pertain directly to the target market's initial intent, you lose 10 percent of your audience.

In line with keeping the buying/registration process as simple as possible, make sure you always downplay the effort involved to complete the transaction. For example, if you have a registration form that spans two pages, then offer visual cues such as "Step 1 of 2" so that the target market knows what to expect at all times.

All of the best practice techniques that go into building a Web site apply to your landing page as well. The landing page still has to be cross-browser-compatible, easy to use, quick to load, have clean code, effectively brand your business, etc. See Chapter 2 for best practices.

Testing Your Landing Page

There is always something you can do a bit better to maximize your landing page results. There are any number of things you can test and tweak to refine your landing pages. Even the smallest changes can have a big impact. When running a marketing campaign, employ A/B testing to see which landing page techniques generate the best responses from your target market.

When performing A/B testing, you might do a split-run campaign where you run a marketing campaign that directs 50 percent of your target market to landing page A and the other 50 percent to landing page B.

Here are some items to consider when testing your landing pages:

Landing Page Content

1. Is short or long copy more effective?

2. Is it better for you to use bulleted lists to emphasize key points as opposed to paragraphs of information?

3. Does separating content with tag lines or headers increase the number of responses?

4. What happens if you bold or emphasize key points in your copy?

5. What impact does changing the writing style, or tone of your copy, have on your landing page's ability to convert?

Landing Page Layout and Presentation

6. What impact does changing the presentation of the offer itself have on results? "Buy one, get one free," "50% off," "1/2 price," "Save $100 off the list price," showing the original $200 price tag with a strikethrough and the new price next to it emphasized in bold red font as $100, etc., are all different ways of presenting the same offer. Which method generates the best response from your target market?

7. Does your landing page perform better with vivid imagery, little imagery, or no imagery? Maybe showing different color shots of the same product if it is available in more than one color will boost sales. Try it.

8. What colors on the page elicit the most favorable responses from your target market? Does the contrast between the page copy and the background influence sales?

9. What font types, styles, and sizes are most effective?

10. How many navigation options work best on the landing page? Are you providing the target market with so many navigation options that they get distracted, or would the page be effective with more navigation options intact?

11. Where is the best position on the landing page to place the "buy" or "order" button? When the target market completes the order form or selects the product, the first thing you want them to do is add the item to their shopping cart or submit their request, not cancel the order. This means putting the "buy" button as the obvious next step, before the clear or cancel option. Do you even want the cancel option to be immediately visible? That might cause the target market to hesitate.

12. Does the "buy" button generate more of a response if it simply says "Submit," "Buy Now!," or "Order your Valentine's Day Gift Basket Now!"?

13. Have you tested different approaches for your ordering process? Does a short or a long order form work best? Does the same order form perform better if it is split across two steps on two different pages?

14. Have you tested variations of your offer to see what generates more results? It might be that the target market is willing to pay a slightly higher price if they know the shipping is free. In a similar note, maybe a free gift will help boost sales depending on what your offer is.

15. Have you tried cross-promoting different related products and services with your initial offer to maximize the purchase size? You have to be careful because you do not want to give the target market too many options that they simply become confused or disinterested in your original offer.

Capitalizing on any great campaign requires a great closing. Your closing is your landing page—a prime reason you never want to put all of your eggs in one basket. It is highly recommended that you test and refine your landing pages over time. This is by no means a complete list of items worth testing, but it is a good place for you to start.

It is best to test one element at a time so that you can measure results and determine the effectiveness of the new change. If you change too many items at once, it will be difficult to attribute how much of an impact the items you changed had on the effectiveness of that page. If you made three adjustments to your landing page at once, it might be that two of the three components have increased the response rate, but the third might have dragged it down a bit, so you are not quite reaching your potential. If you just change one element at a time, you can tell what impact your change has on the landing page's ability to convert.

This same testing logic applies to the online marketing campaigns you partake in as well. You want your marketing efforts and your landing pages to work together.

Internet Resources for Chapter 24

I have developed a great library of online resources for you to check out regarding landing pages in the Resources section of my Web site at *http:// www.susansweeney.com/resources.html*. There you can find additional tips, tools, techniques, and resources.

I have also developed a seminar on this topic which can be taken at any time over the Internet, can be taken live over the Internet at a scheduled time, or can be purchased as a seminar on CD. See *http://www.susansweeney.com/ store.html*.

25

Really Simple Syndication

RSS, or Really Simple Syndication, provides Webmasters and content providers a distribution vehicle for their content that is guaranteed to be delivered. This distribution channel makes it easy for individuals to access the most current information, but also for other site owners to publish the syndicated content on their sites as well.

In this chapter, we cover:

- What is RSS?

- How does RSS work?

- What to send via RSS

- Benefits of RSS

- How to promote your RSS content

- Getting the most out of your RSS.

What Is RSS?

RSS is an acronym for Really Simple Syndication. RSS is a format for syndicating news and other content that can be broken down into discrete items. RSS is really a delivery channel. It allows you to send content to subscribers and to other Web sites. Once information is in RSS format on a site, an RSS reader can check the feed for updates and react to the updates in a predefined way. RSS can deliver many different types of content—text, PDF files, audio, video, or PowerPoint files can quickly and easily be disseminated.

How Does RSS Work?

To publish your material and make it available to the masses for their review or publication on their Web site, you first need to create an RSS feed. You will develop an XML file structured in the proper format, upload it to your server, and then provide a link to that file on your Web site. There are many tools online that make this an easy process. There are RSS software programs that enable the user to quickly and easily create and publish syndicated content.

Once you have your RSS feed developed, you need to develop your content to be included in the RSS feed. Usually you will develop and provide the content on your Web site and will then develop a summary letting the subscribers to your feed know about the new content, with a link directly to it. Alternatively, you could provide the full content in your feed.

Your subscribers need an RSS news reader or news aggregator that will enable them to access and display the RSS content. There are many different RSS readers and news aggregators available for free. You might want to include some information on RSS and links to recommended RSS readers from your site to enable newer users easy access (see Figure 25.1). The news aggregator helps viewers keep up with all their favorite resources by checking their RSS feeds and displaying the new or recent items from each of them.

There are also Web-based RSS services that work with your browser. After you run through your initial setup, you subscribe to any RSS service you want to access on a regular basis.

The RSS readers automatically retrieve updates from sites that are subscribed to, providing the user with the latest content as it is published.

RSS Content Options

There are all kinds of content that can be sent through RSS:

- Coupons

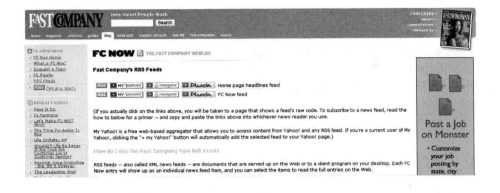

Figure 25.1. Fast Company provides everything a user needs to subscribe to its RSS feed—information, tools and instructions.

- Specials

- Reports

- Articles

- Newsletters

- Blogs

- News—company, industry, or general

- Product announcements

- Audio content (see Chapter 27 on podcasting)

- Audio interviews

- Video content (see Chapter 27 on videocasting)

- Video product demonstrations

- Marketing materials for your affiliates (see Chapter 17 on affiliate marketing)

- Press releases

- White papers and educational content

- Schedule feed for teams, corporate meetings, etc.

- Appcasting, or software application updates

- Specific material for employees, association members, or customers

- Specific types of requested information or subscribed content

- Real estate listings

- Job postings

- Dating matches.

What you're looking to do is get information in front of your target market on a regular basis. You'll provide the information directly to your target market or through sites that market to the same target market you do for more leverage.

We are seeing personalized or customized feeds where a subscriber might indicate that he or she woul like to receive the travel and investment articles but not the healthcare articles. There are all kinds of RSS feeds available online these days. We see travel agencies with their last-minute deals, magazines with their latest articles, software companies with their latest upgrades, online dating services with their latest matches—they can even send the content to your mobile phone!

Leverage your exposure by partnering with targeted sites that have significant traffic and that provide branded relevant, valuable, and interesting content for their visitors. For example, a golf course might have its golf pro develop golf tips to be provided to other golf-related sites; this provides a real win-win—the partner site has great new content that is updated on a regular basis without having to do any work, and the golf course providing the tips gets valuable exposure to the target market and hopefully increased traffic to its site and more business. Whenever you brand your content, make sure you provide a consistent resource box which includes your contact information and a link to your Web site.

There are many opportunities to use RSS feeds to gain exposure with your target market online.

Benefits of RSS

The benefits of RSS are many:

1. You are guaranteed 100 percent delivery. Spam filters are not an issue. This means that your marketing and other messages to customers and potential customers are getting through.

2. You can quickly and easily get exposure on other sites that have the same target market you do by having your content published on those sites through content syndication. You immediately increase your reach.

3. Through your RSS feed opportunity, you can build your targeted database.

4. You can improve your search engine ranking through providing keyword-rich content that is distributed to other sites with the link back to your site.

5. You will increase targeted traffic to your site.

6. You will increase your brand awareness.

7. Through distribution of great content, you can establishes yourself as an expert.

8. You have a great potential to increase revenue through your use of RSS with the delivery of coupons, specials, and promotions with the links back to your storefront.

9. You don't have to worry about compliance with legislation, privacy policies, spam, or age guidelines.

10. You will build trust, your reputation, and credibility.

11. RSS feeds are significantly less work than maintaining and promoting through private mail lists. You don't have to worry about cleaning lists, running your content through the spam checker, or removing bad e-mail addresses.

12. RSS content is seeing significant click-through rates.

How to Promote Your RSS Content

Once you have an RSS feed, you will want to maximize the number of subscribers who read your feed and you will want to develop a strategy to have as many sites as possible post your syndicated content on their sites. Of course, you will always look for sites that are selling to the same target market you are. Likely they will be providing noncompeting products or services.

You will want to create a page on your site specifically for your RSS information. On that page you will provide a little education on RSS—what it is, how it works, and how one would subscribe. You'll also provide links to some recommended RSS readers along with step-by-step instructions on how to subscribe. Provide your visitors with all the benefits of subscribing—sell the sizzle! Incorporate viral marketing (see Chapter 4) and make it easy for them to tell their friends about your RSS feed.

Provide the standard RSS button in a consistent location on every page of your site. Make it easy for anyone to subscribe.

Promote your RSS feeds in your signature file with a link to the page on your site with all the details. Signature files are discussed in Chapter 9.

There are many RSS directories online to which you can submit your RSS feed for inclusion. With some you ask to be included, and others allow you to add your feed information yourself. Many of these directories provide lists of feeds under a number of categories. You can search "RSS directories" in Google or Yahoo! Search to find these.

There are RSS submission tools that will submit your RSS feed to a variety of RSS directories. Again, searching Google or Yahoo! Search for "RSS submission tools" will provide you with everything you need.

Many Internet browsers provide easy access to RSS feeds for their users. These browsers provide information on their Web sites as to how to make this happen. Yahoo! provides a Publisher's Guide to RSS (see Figure 25.2). In the Publishers Guide (*http://publisher.yahoo.com/whatis.php*) is information on auto-discovery, which is a way to let applications know that you have an RSS feed and makes it easy for those browsers to let their users subscribe directly to your feed.

Getting the Most out of Your RSS

As with everything in Internet marketing, you need to develop content after giving consideration to:

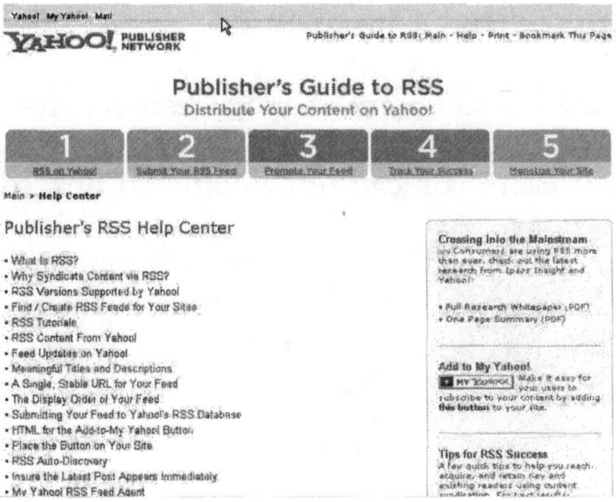

Figure 25.2. Yahoo! provides a Publisher's Guide to RSS.

- Your objectives with this Internet marketing technique

- Your target market(s) for this technique

- The specific products and services you want to promote with this technique

- You will want to give consideration to the terms of use for your content. Do you want to limit the content to noncommercial use on others' sites, or is it okay if they use it for commercial purposes?

Always make sure that you have mandatory source identification. When others use your content and want to publish or distribute it, you will want a resource box identifying you as the provider and, more importantly, a link to your Web site.

For the content that will bring you the most business, you want to publish it on a Tuesday, Wednesday, or Thursday. Tuesday is the most active day for RSS readership. The time of day is important as well. Morning scanners view the most content, whereas the midnight cowboys tend to have a higher click-through rate.

Internet Resources for Chapter 25

I have developed a great library of online resources for you to check out regarding RSS in the Resources section of my Web site at *http://www.susansweeney.com/ resources.html*. There you can find additional tips, tools, techniques, and resources.

I have also developed a seminar on this topic which can be taken at any time over the Internet, can be taken live over the Internet at a scheduled time, or can be purchased as a seminar on CD. See *http://www.susansweeney.com/ store.html*.

26

Blogs

Blogs are Web logs on a Web site that are updated on a regular basis, with the most recent posting appearing at the top of the blog. Sometimes they look like an ongoing diary or a journal on a site. Blogs are usually written in conversational style and can include text, images, and links to other content or to audio or video files.

In this chapter, we cover:

- What is a blog?

- How do I create my blog?

- To blog or not to blog?

- Benefits of having a blog

- Blog promotion.

What Is a Blog?

A blog is a chronological publication or online journal of postings to a Web site. The blog can include text, images, links to video files, links to audio files, or links to other Web sites.

Writing the content for your blog is referred to as blogging. Each article that you add to your blog is called a blog post, a post, or an entry in your blog. You are a blogger if you write and add entries or posts to your blog.

Blogs usually focus on one topic or area of interest. For example:

- A person might have a personal blog on his or her trip through South Africa.

- A market analyst might have a blog on his or her findings in a particular market niche—what's happening in the industry, news or articles on his or her latest research.

- A software company might have a blog on the latest version of its software product, update information, and upcoming enhancements.

How Do I Put a Blog on My Site?

When setting up your blog, you have several options:

1. There are a number of free blog hosting sites. An example of this type would be Blogger.com (see Figure 26.1), which was acquired by Google in 2003. Other popular blog hosts include LiveJournal, TypePad, and Xanga.

Figure 26.1. Blogger.com was acquired by Google in 2003.

2. You can set up your blog using blog software or a blog publishing system and host it yourself. Popular blog software packages include WordPress (*http://wordpress.org*) and Movable Type (*http://www.sixapart.com/movabletype*).

3. You can also create your own blog using HTML.

To Blog or Not to Blog?

As with everything related to your Web site content, you must go back to your objectives and your target markets. What are you hoping to accomplish with your Web site content? Whom are you hoping to interact with on your site? Is a blog the most effective technique to "speak to" your target market and get them to do what you want them to do? Is there a more effective mechanism? How much work is involved? Is this time well spent, or are there other techniques that would be more effective given the time commitment? You don't add Web site content just because it is the latest trend or because you can. Always go back to your objectives and your target market to see if this type of content is the most effective and most efficient way to accomplish what you want to online.

Pros and Cons of Blogging

Some pros are:

- Blogs are an easy way to add new content, thus keeping your Web site current.

- Blogs can be used to provide your potential and existing customers with the latest news on your products and services, industry news, updates, tips, or other relevant content.

- Using keyword-rich content can help your search engine placement.

- Blogs can be updated from anywhere. You can even send camera phone photos straight to your blog while you're on-the-go with Blogger Mobile.

- You can use your blog to establish yourself as an expert in your topic area.

- You can create an RSS feed to syndicate your blog, giving you instant access to your subscribers and the opportunity to have your blog content appear on relevant sites. See Chapter 25 for information on using RSS feeds to distribute your blog content.

Some of the cons are:

- Blogs need to be constantly updated. You need to have the discipline to keep it current.

- You have to have enough news or new content to make it worthwhile.

Promote Your Blog

Once you have a blog, you want to maximize its exposure; you want to have as many of your target market reviewing your blog on a regular basis as possible. Better still, you want to get as many of your target market as you can subscribing to your blog RSS feed.

There are blog directories where blogs are profiled by category. Often you can search the blog directory by keyword. Submit your blog to all of the popular blog directories. Great portals like BlogCatalog (*http://www.blogcatalog.com*) (see Figure 26.2), RSSTop55 Best Blog Directory and RSS Submission Sites (*http://www.masternewmedia.org/rss/top55*) would be great starting points.

Figure 26.2.   BlogCatalog is one of many great blog resources online.

Get your blog listed and high in the search results for your important keyword phrases in the Blog Search Engine (*http://www.blogsearchengine.com*), Bloogz (*http://www.bloogz.com*), and other popular blog search engines.

Promote your blog on your site and everywhere you can online. Generate links to your blog from related sites. Promote your blog in your e-mail signature file.

Resources for Chapter 26

I have developed a great library of online resources for you to check out regarding blogs in the Resources section of my Web site at *http://www.susansweeney.com/resources.html*. There you can find additional tips, tools, techniques, and resources.

I have also developed a seminar on this topic which can be taken at any time over the Internet, can be taken live over the Internet at a scheduled time, or can be purchased as a seminar on CD. See *http://www.susansweeney.com/store.html*.

27

Podcasting

Podcasting is a term that was coined a few years ago and comes from the terms *broadcasting* and *iPod*. Podcasting is the distribution of audio content for listening on personal computers, MP3 players, or other mobile devices.

Podcasting is all about creating content for a demanding audience that does not want to be marketed to, but rather wants to listen to what they want, when they want, and how they want.

In this chapter, we cover:

- What is podcasting?

- Podcast mechanics

- Podcast content

- Promoting your podcast.

What Is Podcasting?

The term *podcasting* is a little misleading, because although it comes from *broadcasting* and *iPod*, it has nothing directly to do with Apple iPods. Podcasting, in its simplest, relates to audio content that can be listened to on your personal computer, any MP3 player (not just the Apple iPod), and many mobile devices. The term has also been used to relate to video content that can be downloaded and viewed at your convenience as well; others use the term *videocasting* for such content.

Podcasts can be downloaded from the source Web site on an individual basis or can be subscribed to through an RSS feed. When a site makes audio or video content available through an RSS feed, you can subscribe to the content. As new audio or video files are made available, subscribers get notification in their RSS reader; the reader will download the content to a location the subscriber has specified on his or her hard drive. When a subscriber connects a mobile device or MP3 player to his or her computer, the files can be added to that device for future listening or viewing.

We are seeing podcasting take off because it enables listeners to enjoy the audio content when they want—they can listen to the 6 p.m. news while on a 10:30 p.m. flight, they can enjoy an Internet marketing podcast on search engine optimization while on the treadmill first thing in the morning, or they can listen to last night's sports podcast while tanning by the pool.

Podcast Mechanics

Podcasting is a relatively easy process. You need your content, a few pieces of equipment, and a Web site or host for distribution, and you're in business.

The equipment you need includes:

- A laptop or desktop computer with an Internet connection.

- A microphone. For good audio quality, you will usually want to purchase an external mic that plugs into your computer.

- Audio recording software. There are lots of downloadable free and paid audio software programs online.

- An MP3 encoder which will convert your audio into an MP3 file. iTunes can convert audio content to an MP3 file, or there are a number of popular free encoders online.

Once you have your content prepared, you will plug your microphone into your computer, start your audio recording software, and record your podcast. When you are finished, you can use the editing tools in your audio recording software to make any changes or enhancements to your content. You can remove that cough or the pause, add music as background, or add special sound effects.

Save your podcast as an MP3 file. When naming your file, consider including your important keyword phrase where appropriate for search engine optimization purposes.

Now you have to put your podcast online. If you already have a Web site, you will FTP the file to your Web site host. You will then make your podcast available through your Web site as an individual podcast or as a series of podcasts available to subscribers through your RSS feed. See Chapter 25 for details on how to develop your RSS feed.

Podcast Content

There are all kinds of content suitable for podcasts:

- Training

  - Tutorials

  - Training sessions

- Self-guided walking tours. Podcasts will be used extensively in the travel and tourism industry. We are already seeing many destination marketing organizations providing downloadable:

  - Audio walking tours of their area

  - Audio tours of museums

  - Parks tours

  - Art gallery tours

  - Driving directions

  - Tours of particular places of interest

- TV and radio shows

Figure 27.1. CNN.com provides podcasts through its RSS feed.

- Talk shows

- Sportscasts

- Newscasts (see Figure 27.1 for CNN podcasts)

• Music

- Introduction of new artists

- New CDs announced

- Band interviews

- Books.

Promoting Your Podcast

Once you have developed your audio or video content, you will usually want to get as wide a distribution as you can. Ways to promote your podcast include:

- Promote your podcasts in your e-mail signature file.

- Promote your podcasts on your Web site. On your podcast page, you should make it easy for people to subscribe to your RSS feed by providing them with information on your podcast content, the benefits received by the content (sell the sizzle!), and the tools to be able to subscribe and access the content.

- Promote your podcasts on popular podcast directories. There are many great podcast directories oline like Podcast.net (*http://www.podcast.net*), Podcast Alley (*http://www.podcastalley.com*), and Podcast.com (*http:// www.podcast.com*).

- Promote your podcast through popular podcast sites (e.g., iTunes—*http:// www.itunes.com*; and Yahoo!Podcasts—*http://podcasts.yahoo.com*) (see Figure 27.2).

- Submit your podcast to podcast search engines like Singing Fish (*http:// search.singingfish.com/sfw/home.jsp*) (see Figure 27.3).

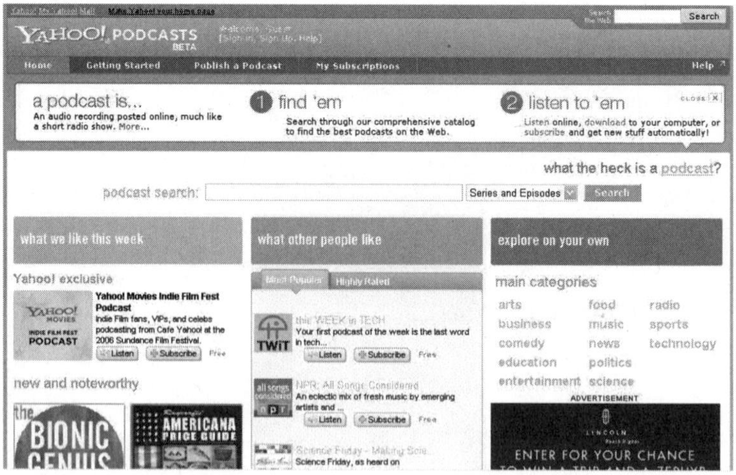

Figure 27.2. Promote your podcast through Yahoo!Podcasts.

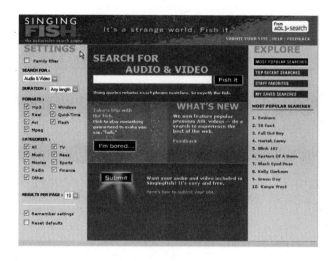

Figure 27.3. Singing Fish is an audio and video content search engine.

Internet Resources for Chapter 27

I have developed a great library of online resources for you to check out regarding podcasting in the Resources section of my Web site at *http://www.susansweeney.com/resources.html*. There you can find additional tips, tools, techniques, and resources.

I have also developed a seminar on this topic which can be taken at any time over the Internet, can be taken live over the Internet at a scheduled time, or can be purchased as a seminar on CD. See *http://www.susansweeney.com/store.html*.

28

Mobile Marketing

There are over 1.8 billion people with mobile devices capable of voice, text, image, and Internet communication. That's a huge market already, and one that will escalate in the coming years as we see less-developed countries go directly to wireless for their telephones. We are beginning to see location-based services (or LBS) really take hold. Every new advancement in Internet-based technology provides new marketing opportunities.

In this chapter, we cover:

- What is mobile marketing?

- Benefits of mobile marketing.

What Is Mobile Marketing?

Mobile marketing is using a mobile or a wireless device for marketing purposes. Mobile marketing is a marketer's dream come true—it enables a marketer to communicate directly, one-on-one, to the target market with the opportunity for a direct response in real time. There are a number of mobile marketing opportunities that are becoming commonplace:

- SMS (short messaging service). SMS allows text messages of up to 160 alpha-numeric characters to be sent and received on your mobile phone. Through SMS you can do things like vote for your favorite American Idol or enter "text to win" contests.

- MMS (multimedia messaging service). MMS is an enhanced transmission service that enables video clips, color pictures, and audio files to be sent and received by mobile phones. Through MMS you can view film clips of the movies you are choosing between while in the line at the theatre.

- Instant messaging. Microsoft, AOL, and Yahoo! all offer instant-messaging products that enable quick and easy access to over 200 million consumers with text, audio, and video content.

- LBS (location-based services). As the name would suggest, LBS uses location as a key element in providing relevant information to users. For example, you are in a strange city and want to find the closest Staples, along with directions on how to get from where you are to where they are, to get your print job done. LBS would help you out.

- Profile-specific advertising. Each mobile phone has a unique identifier in the telephone number. Once you know a unique identifier, you can build a profile of the owner. Once you have a profile, you can send very targeted offers.

- Mobile blogging. In a matter of seconds, color pictures, video, and audio files can be instantly added to a blog through a mobile device.

- Subscribed content. You can provide targeted content to subscribers through RSS from your site to a mobile device. You can send daily coupons or e-specials to subscribers.

Benefits of Mobile Marketing

The different mobile marketing applications provide a variety of benefits to the marketer:

- Mobile marketing allows direct, personal communication in real time with the opportunity for immediate, direct response.

- By building a customer profile, you can be very targeted with your campaigns or offerings.

- Brand awareness can be increased.

- Messages can be sent through this medium very cost-effectively.

- Traffic to Web sites can be increased.

- Customer loyalty can be enhanced.

- Sales can be increased when you provide the right offer at the right time to the right customer.

- Interactivity—the target customer is engaged using this technology.

- There are over 1.8 billion consumers with access to this technology.

- Two-way dialogue between marketer and target market allows one-on-one marketing.

- Immediate impact.

- Personalized messages get a much higher response rate than generic messages.

- Sponsored messages can be provided.

- Messages are delivered instantaneously.

- This medium makes it easy for people to spread the word quickly and easily.

We are in the very early stages of mobile marketing. We have seen a quick uptake on some mobile marketing opportunities, like the voting for your favorite American Idol. Other mobile marketing applications will take a little longer to see wide adaptation. With the significant increase in the number of 3G devices that are becoming mainstream and the number of marketers becoming more mobile marketing savvy, we are sure to see mobile marketing take off over the next 12 to 18 months.

Internet Resources for Chapter 28

I have developed a great library of online resources for you to check out regarding mobile marketing in the Resources section of my Web site at *http://www.susansweeney.com/resources.html*. There you can find additional tips, tools, techniques, and resources.

I have also developed a seminar on this topic which can be taken at any time over the Internet, can be taken live over the Internet at a scheduled time, or can be purchased as a seminar on CD. See *http://www.susansweeney.com/store.html*.

29

The Power of Partnering

We have talked about many different online marketing opportunities through the course of this book. Often there are great opportunities that are overlooked because of their simplicity. Partnering is one of those often-overlooked opportunities. There are many other sites that are selling to our target market. Quite often they are selling noncompeting products or services. Quite often they have significant traffic to their sites or significant databases that they communicate with on a regular basis. If you can find a win-win opportunity to partner with these sites, you can have significant results.

In this chapter, we cover:

- Ideal partner sites

- Partnering opportunities.

Ideal Partner Sites

When you look for sites to partner with, you are looking for:

- Sites that have your ideal target market as their site visitor

- Sites that have significant targeted traffic

- Sites that have a significant permission-based database

- Sites that have noncompeting products or services.

Once you identify the types of partners or the types of noncompeting products of potential partners, it will be easier to find and develop a list of potential partners. For example, if you sell pots and pans, you might identify appliance sites as potential partner sites. If you have a country inn, you might identify local attraction sites as potential partners—you are both selling to the same target market, but you are selling noncompeting products and services. If you sell skis, you might identify ski hills as potential partners. Once you have identified the types of partners you are looking for, you will be able to do research on-line to find specific potential partners.

Partnering Opportunities

Once you have found potential partners, next you need to look at win-win ways to partner with these sites. There are all kinds of ways to work together to do cross-promotion, leverage the exposure on each other's site, or provide exposure through each other's database.

> Cross-promotion through banner advertising. You can exchange banners on each other's site. If you have pots and pans and you are partnering with the appliance site, you can have a banner that indicates that any customer of yours can get a 10 percent discount on the appliance site, with a link to their site in the banner ad. The appliance site can provide the quid pro quo—your banner on their site can provide their customers with the same 10 percent discount for purchasing from your site.

> Co-operative banner advertising. Drop-down ads provide the viewer with the option to click on different parts of the banner ad and be taken to different sites. You could partner with four others who are all selling to the same target market to develop and place this type of drop-down menu ad. The result is either the same amount of advertising you did

previously at 20 percent of the cost, or spending the same and getting five times the exposure.

Partner with others on contests. Find sites that are selling to the same target market and offer your product as part of the prize for their contest as long as the other site provides some details on your product and a link to your site. Leverage the link by getting your most important keywords in the text around the link pointing to your site to increase your link relevancy score and your search engine placement. You can also partner with others on your contests. The greater the prize, the more exposure you'll see through the contest.

Partner with others' e-specials. Look for sites that provide e-specials to their target market and see if you can provide them with a great e-special. This works great for industry associations and also travel agencies. If you have a spa or resort, providing a great package at a great price to a travel agency that has a significant database could result in not only significant new business but also new visitors to your site and, if you develop the landing page properly, new members to your e-club.

Partner with directories or meta-indexes that provide links to your type of site. Look for a mutually beneficial opportunity. At the very least look for an opportunity to have your listing appear at the top of the page, have it stand out in some way, or have your banner ad appear on the most appropriate page of their directory.

Partner with your industry associations. If you have a listing, make sure that your description is as appealing as it can be. Provide a call to action in your description. Have the link go the most appropriate page of your site—it's not always the home page! Look for areas on their site where you can gain a little extra exposure. Do they have sections like:

– Top 10

– Featured

– Recommended

– Site of the day/week

– Suggested.

These all provide an opportunity for added exposure. Another example is that if you have a tourist attraction, look for all the destination marketing organizations in your geographic area for things like "Suggested Itineraries" to get your attraction included—even if you have to write it yourself. There are lots of these opportunities out there.

Partner with industry associations to get your press releases or story ideas in front of the media. Most industry associations have a media center. If you've got a press release or a story that would be of interest to the media, the industry association's media center would be a great place for exposure. Perhaps they'd be interested in a joint press release to their media list.

Be a contributing journalist to e-zines that have your target market as their subscribers. Make sure you have your contact information in the resource box, with a link back to your Web site.

There are all kinds of partnering opportunities available; you just have to do a little brainstorming. Think about who is selling noncompeting products or services to the same target market you are and figure out a win-win opportunity.

Internet Resources for Chapter 29

I have developed a great library of online resources for you to check out regarding partnering in the Resources section of my Web site at *http://www.susansweeney.com/resources.html*. There you can find additional tips, tools, techniques, and resources.

I have also developed a seminar on this topic which can be taken at any time over the Internet, can be taken live over the Internet at a scheduled time, or can be purchased as a seminar on CD. See *http://www.susansweeney.com/store.html*.

30

Grand Opening Tips for Your Web Site Virtual Launch

Just as you would have a book or software launch, you can have a Web site launch. In preparation, you must develop a launch strategy. In this chapter, we cover:

- Development of your Web site launch strategy

- Web site announcement mailing lists

- Direct e-mail postcards to your customers or prospective clients.

Launching and Announcing Your Web Site

A new Web site or your new location in **cyberspace** can be launched in many of the same ways that you would launch a new physical store location. This might involve both online and offline activities. Just as you would prepare a book launch strategy or a new software product launch strategy, you can develop an appropriate launch strategy for your new Web site. Sometimes a launch strategy could be more work than the benefit that would be gained. On the other hand, if you are opening the next Amazon, it is imperative.

Cyberspace
Virtual location where Web sites live.

Your Web Site Virtual Launch

Let's take a look at a traditional retail store grand opening. For the grand opening, which usually lasts for an evening or a day, there are invitations to the media, press releases distributed to the media, invited guests, opening ceremonies, advertising, and possibly gift giveaways.

A Web site virtual location launch occurs in cyberspace, and the "grand opening" can last for a day, a week, or a month. Many of the activities you would include in your traditional grand opening can also be included in your Internet grand opening. The effectiveness of your launch can be increased with the following tips:

- Media attention can be generated through the distribution of press releases online and offline. Make your press release interactive. (See Chapter 21 for press release distribution information.)

- Guests can be invited to your online opening through postings in newsgroups, newsletters, "What's New" sites, banner advertising, direct e-mail, and signature files, as well as through offline direct mail and advertising.

- Opening ceremonies can be just as exciting online as offline. They can last for a month rather than a day. The opening must be designed to appeal to your target market.

- You can feature special guests in chat areas for your grand opening or several special guests over the duration. Again, relate your guests and the topics to be discussed to the needs and wants of your target market.

- You can run contests that require visitors to visit various parts of your site to compete for prizes. Perhaps they have to complete a multiple-choice quiz whose answers are found throughout your site. This way you encourage your guests to visit all those pages you want them to. You can also ask if they would like to be notified via e-mail of the winner. This gives you an opportunity to send them e-mail with their permission.

- You can have audio and video greetings from your site.

- You can encourage your Web site visitors to spread the word through viral marketing opportunities.

- Special free gifts can be provided to the first 20 or 50 visitors to your site. You can also provide prizes to the first 100 to link to your site.

- Do some offline advertising for your new URL (see Chapter 31 for innovative offline opportunities), or take advantage of online advertising via announcement sites.

There are many other innovative "grand opening" attention grabbers that can be brainstormed with marketing and public relations individuals. Whatever you decide to do, make it memorable, make it appropriate for your target market, and provide reasons for them to return.

Internet Resources for Chapter 30

I have developed a great library of online resources for you to check out regarding Web site launch in the Resources section of my Web site at *http://www.susansweeney.com/resources.html*. There you can find additional tips, tools, techniques, and resources.

31

Effective Offline Promotion

There are many benefits to cross-promoting your Web site using traditional media and print materials. Your Web site can answer many questions and provide more information than you can print in a magazine or newspaper ad. Your site can be kept up to date with the latest information available. People can request additional information or order online. In this chapter, we cover:

- Tips for offline promotion of your Web site

- Offline promotion opportunities.

Offline Promotion Objectives

Because visitors can be directed from offline promotion to request additional information or order online, you should promote your URL on every piece of promotional material you produce! The more exposure your URL receives, the more likely it is that people will remember it when they go online.

Be creative with your offline promotion campaign. Brainstorm with innovative thinkers to come up with a number of good places to promote your URL; for example, try displaying your URL in your TV and radio commercials, magazine and newspaper ads, and billboards. The more places your URL appears, the more it will get noticed. Some businesses even incorporate their URL into their building and vehicle signage. Answer your telephone "YourCompanyName.com, Good Morning." This is quite effective in letting people know that you want them to visit your Web site and providing them with your URL at the same time. Next time they have a question or want to place an order, they can go directly to the Web site.

Displaying your URL in traditional media encourages people to visit your site for more information about your company. Another benefit is that people usually can order from your Web site. Naturally, your site should be up to date, with all of the latest information on products, prices, and sales promotions. If a six-month-old advertisement is seen in a magazine, as long as the URL is displayed in the ad, readers can go to your site and get current information. Your Web site is your most effective advertisement, but it is an advertisement that people have to know about before they can view it.

If you have a bricks-and-mortar location, you can consider having posters or promotional material on display letting people know about your Web site or encouraging them to join your e-club.

URL Exposure through Corporate Literature and Material

It is important that your corporate image be consistent in both your online and offline promotional campaigns. Businesses should use the same colors, style, fonts, logo, and tag lines on all of their marketing materials. As a rule of thumb, try to place your URL on everything you put your logo on—which means just about every piece of corporate literature. Make sure to include your URL on the following:

- Letterhead

- Business cards

- Corporate brochures

- Envelopes

- Checks

- Fax cover sheets

- Report covers

- Flyers

- Advertisements

- Direct-mail pieces

- Newsletters

- Press releases

- Media kits.

URL Exposure through Promotional Items

If your company uses promotional items as giveaways at trade shows and events, it is a good idea to incorporate your Web site marketing with these items. Figures 31.1 and 31.2 offer examples of the different promotional products that you can order on the Internet for your business. Promotional items that are

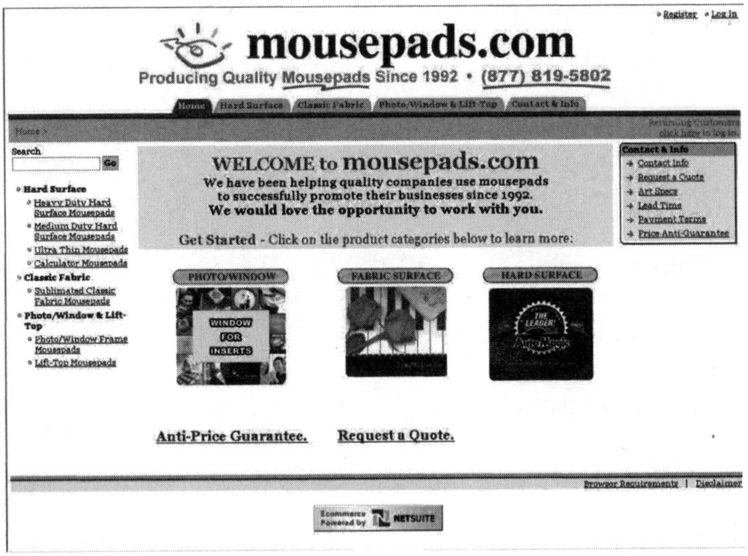

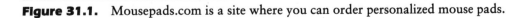

Figure 31.1. Mousepads.com is a site where you can order personalized mouse pads.

Figure 31.2. At epromos.com you can put your Web address on a multitude of different products.

used in and around computer workstations are ideal because your URL is visible when people are in a position to actually visit your site. Some examples are:

- Mouse pads

- CD holders

- Screen cleaning kits

- Software

- Screen savers

- Pens and pencils

- Scratch pads

- Coffee mugs

- Coasters

- Letter openers

- Stress balls

- Calendars

- Sticky notes.

URL Exposure through Clothing

Articles of clothing are another great promotional item. When people wear an article of clothing with your URL on it, they become a walking billboard for your site. I personally have a jacket that was provided by Webjacket.com (see Figure 31.3), and the quality is great. Your corporate jacket provides exposure for your company and your Web site. If you have a corporate uniform, your URL should be displayed. Put your URL and a catchy phrase or tag line on items such as:

- Golf shirts

- T-shirts

- Sweatshirts

- Hats

Figure 31.3. Webjacket.com allows you to customize your corporate jacket with your logo and your URL right on its site.

- Aprons

- Jackets.

URL Exposure on Novelty Items

Novelty items can be an effective place to print your URL. If your target market is a younger audience, then put your URL on items that appeal to them, such as:

- Frisbees

- Balls

- Beach towels

- Sunglasses

- Key chains

- Magnets

- Chocolate bars

- Bumper stickers.

Promotion with a Touch of Creativity

Be creative and come up with catchy slogans that have a connection with the promotional item. For example:

- Clocks: "Take some time to visit our Web site at . . ."

- Rulers: "For a measurable difference, visit us at . . ."

- Coffee mugs: "Take a break and visit our Web site at . . ."

- Tape measures: "Visit our Web site at *http://www.YourURL.com* and see how our site measures up."

- Magnifying glasses: "You don't need one of these to see that our site is the best. Come visit us online at . . ."

- Watches: "Isn't it about time you visited us at . . . ?"

- Bookmarks: "Take a break from reading and visit our Web site at . . ."

URL Exposure on Your Products

If possible, put your URL on your products themselves. This is an innovative idea that Joe Boxer has used. They stitch their URL into the waistband of their underwear.

Internet Resources for Chapter 31

I have developed a great library of online resources for you to check out regarding offline promotion in the Resources section of my Web site at *http://www.susansweeney.com/resources.html*. There you can find additional tips, tools, techniques, and resources.

32

Web Traffic Analysis

Today, technology not only allows us to generate interactive Web sites for our viewers, it allows us to learn about our viewers as well. All Web site administrators should be using Web traffic analysis software that enables them to analyze not only what page of the Web site their visitors came to first, but also where they came from, how long they were there, and what they did while they visited. Once you have this information, you can do some calculations to see what is working for you and what is not.

In this chapter, you will learn:

- What your Web server's log files can tell you

- How analyzing log files with Web traffic analysis software can benefit your Web site

- How to develop a profile of your visitors

- How to optimize your Web site to accommodate your visitors

- How to get the most for your marketing dollar

- How to generate leads for your business

- How analysis software can help you to manage your online advertising budget

- How to get Web traffic analysis software for your Web site

- The popular brands of Web traffic analysis software.

Do You Know Who Is Visiting Your Web Site?

Retailers have always spent endless hours trying to analyze the shoppers who visit their stores. They are constantly trying to collect data about their markets so that they can decide what the best forms of advertising are for their target market, what consumers really want in order to make wiser buying decisions, what services are important to them, what product features their target market is looking for, and so on. The same thing is happening today on the Internet. Companies are constantly collecting data on their target market—their needs, wants, preferences, and desires. Most people are unaware that they are even doing this.

Web traffic analysis software helps companies focus on their target market like never before. It helps them understand the traffic on their Web site and enables them to make the changes that are critical to producing the results that they desire from their Web site. "But how do they do it?" you ask.

Using Log Files to Your Advantage

All Web servers log a list of all the requests for individual files that people have requested from a Web site. These logs include the HTML files and their embedded graphic images and any other associated files that get transmitted through the server. These logs can be analyzed by Web traffic analysis tools to generate the following data:

- The number of visitors to your home page and every other page of your site

- Where the visitors came from in terms of their IP addresses

- How many times each page on your Web site was requested

- What time, day of the week, and season people access your site

- Which browser your visitor is using

- Which keywords or phrases your visitors are using to find your site using a search engine

- Which advertisements are viewed the most on your Web site

- Detailed information on visitors and demographics.

This might not sound like very important information; however, there are some very amazing things you can do with this data. Like any good experiment, you must collect the data first, complete the experiment, and then make the recommendations.

Analyzing Log Files with Web Traffic Analysis Software

By analyzing the data from your log files, you can determine the changes necessary to generate better results. By tracking the visitors on your Web site in terms of where they spend their time, how they came to your site, and if they do what you want them to do, you can fine-tune your Web site to fit the specific needs of your target market.

Developing a Profile of Your Visitors

Who is visiting your site? Are most of your visitors from the United States, Canada, or Australia? Are your visitors AOL users? Are they university students or government employees? Are your visitors primarily Mac or PC users? Which browser are they using? Which version of the browsers are they using?

By analyzing the log files, you can learn a great deal about your audience. You can see how the majority of your audience came to your site and what they like to do while they are there—meaning whether they request information or not, if they download products, or if they are interested in free giveaways. You can use this information to find out if your site needs to be changed to accommodate the needs of your visitors. For example, if you find that many of your visitors are spending a lot of time on your Specials page, maybe it would be in your best interest to start a weekly or bi-weekly e-special e-mail to inform your audience about new additions to this section of your Web site.

The log files can tell you when your audience is entering your site. For example, if the log files indicate that your traffic is mostly at night, you could predict that most people visit your site from home. Because many homes still do not have high-speed access, you might want to check your graphic sizes to make sure that it is not taking too long for your site to load. If your analysis tells you that not many people visit your site on Saturday, you could select this day as your maintenance day. You don't want to make changes to your site on days when you receive high traffic because it is very discouraging to your visitors to receive HTTP 404 errors because your site is temporarily down.

You can also see your visitor's IP address, which the software translates into his or her geographical location; some of the software is even capable of narrowing the data down to the city (see Figure 32.1). From a marketing perspective, this can benefit you in planning your marketing efforts in other media. If you are planning a television campaign for your business, you might want to start in a city that frequently visits your site, thus increasing the chance of a successful campaign.

Web traffic analysis software indicates which browser your visitors are using when visiting your Web site (see Figure 32.2). Although you want to have a Web site that is designed to be compatible with both older and newer browsers, this data can be used to your advantage. Older browsers that cannot read Java scripting properly and that do not have the proper plug-ins for a Flash introduction might still be in use by your viewers. However, if a majority of your viewers are using the latest browsers, you could incorporate more of the latest technology into your site. Remember that you should always offer a "Skip Flash" option on your site and the latest Java plug-ins for people with older browsers.

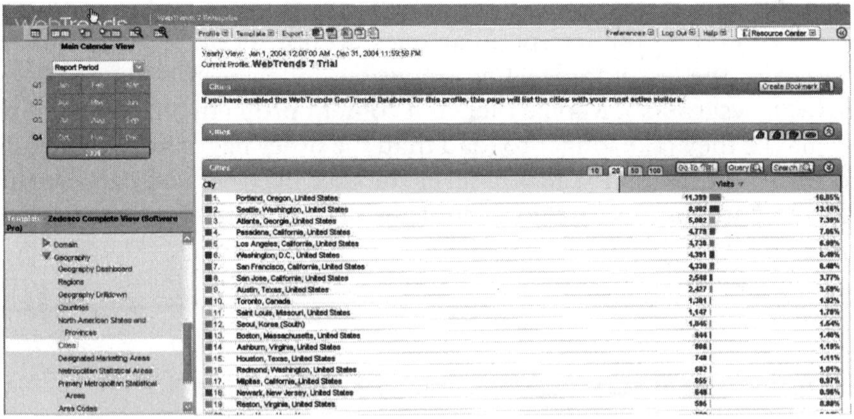

Figure 32.1. WebTrends can tell you what cities are bringing you the most traffic.

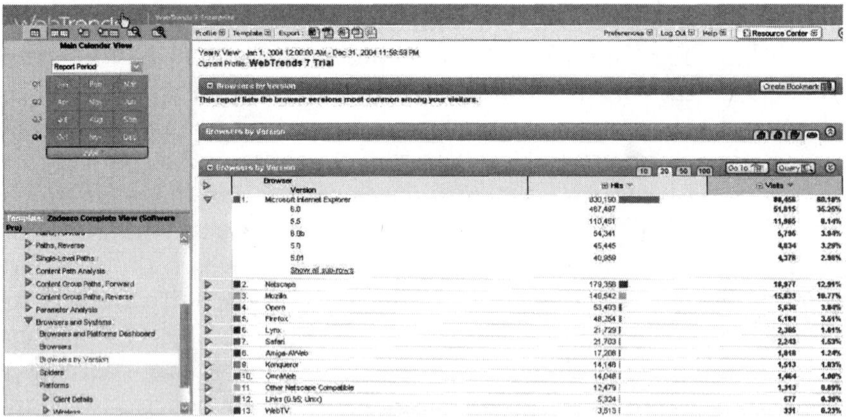

Figure 32.2. This WebTrends report lets you know which version of each browser your visitors are using.

Which Pages Are Popular and Which Pages Are Not?

What pages are most popular with your visitors? Do you see traffic spike when you have new content or release a newsletter or news release? Do you get more traffic on the weekend or during the week? Are your online marketing efforts having an impact? Are people clicking through?

When you look at the log files and see where your visitors are spending most of their time on your site, you can also tell where they are not. You can then use this information to determine what the popular pages on your site incorporate that the less popular ones do not. Perhaps the popular pages are similar to the less popular, but are visited by a specific source (i.e., search engines, newsgroups). Maybe there is a content problem on the less popular pages, or maybe they take longer to load than the other pages and visitors do not want to wait for them to load. Whatever the case may be, you can use this information and attempt to fix those problems that would keep visitors from spending time on all the pages of your site.

Find Out How Each Visitor Found Your Site

By finding out how each visitor came to your site, you can boost your traffic tremendously. You can determine which of your banner ads is producing the

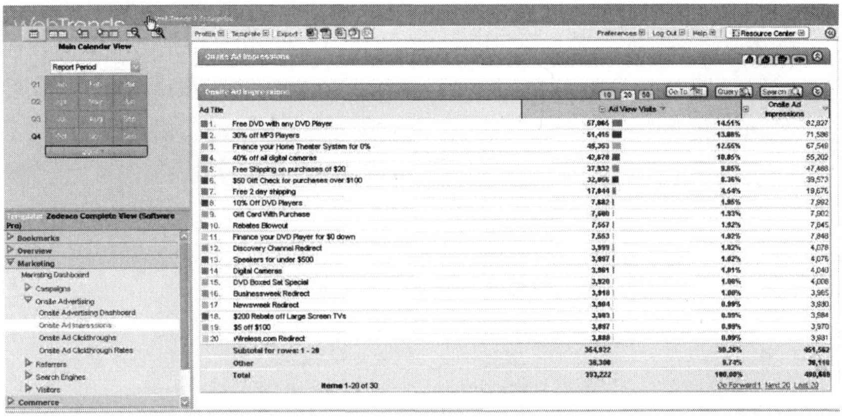

Figure 32.3. This WebTrends report identifies the number of views for each banner ad.

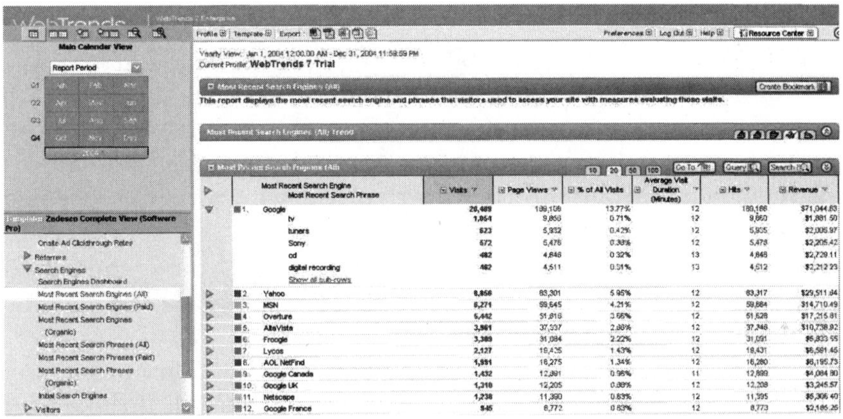

Figure 32.4. This WebTrends report illustrates the first-time visitor sessions initiated by searches from each search engine.

best results (see Figure 32.3). You can use this information to help you with the selection of banners you use and also the allocation of your online advertising budget. You can determine how many visitors found your site through search engines (see Figure 32.4). You can even determine which keyword led to the most visitors through the search engines (see Figure 32.5).

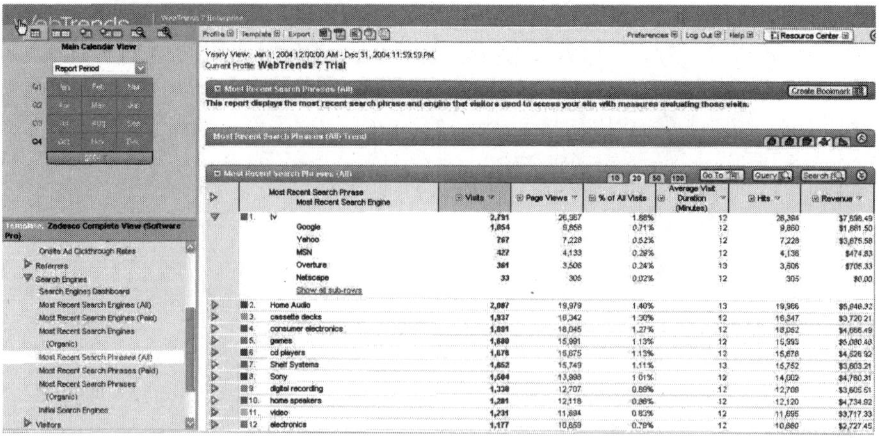

Figure 32.5. This WebTrends report identifies the specific keywords that led the most visitors to your site through the search engines.

You can also find out where your visitors go when they leave your Web site. You want your viewers to stay at your site as long as possible. If you notice that the majority of your viewers are not traveling through your entire site and are not viewing important information that you want them to see, you may want to manipulate the layout of your Web site to decrease the "flight effect." If you notice that your top exit page is your home page, you might even decide to try a whole new approach because people seem to be turned off from searching through your site right from the beginning.

Single-access pages are pages on your Web site that are accessed through a link or search engine and then are immediately exited. If these pages represent a high percentage of your Web site traffic, it is very important that you convey a strong message while you have the visitors' attention. If you have pages like this, you should reevaluate what is on those pages and try to come up with content that entices your visitor to search through the rest of your site.

Most of the Web traffic analysis software will tell you which keywords and phrases your visitors used to find your site using a search engine. This is extremely valuable information because you can use these keywords to increase your popularity in the search engines. By knowing the most popular keywords your visitors are using to visit your site, you can make sure you use them in your meta-tags, Alt tags, and page titles, and in the text of your page for higher placement in the search engines. Also, by seeing which search engines are being used more by your visitors, you can choose to bid on keyword-sponsored listings for that engine to achieve maximum visibility to your market.

Another benefit of observing who is viewing your site is that you can see when spiders and crawlers from search engines have crawled to your page. This means that your site most likely will be indexed on their corresponding search engine. This is good to know, not only because it reassures you that you are going to be indexed, but also because by knowing this, you will not resubmit your site to the search engine and risk spamming.

Identifying Your Target Market

After you have collected data from your log files and used the Web traffic analysis software to determine which demographic groups are actually visiting your site, you then must determine whether these are the groups that you want to target. If not, you must then determine how you are going to reach your target market. For example, you might find that you need to change your online advertising campaign. Or perhaps you should reevaluate your Internet marketing strategy, taking into consideration the new data that you have collected.

Find Out What Forms of Online Promotion Work for Your Site

When you first launch your Web site, you are going to aggressively implement your Internet marketing strategy by experimenting with all of the different forms of online marketing. However, when you analyze who is actually visiting your site and you find out where the majority of your traffic is coming from, you can then determine where to focus the majority of your marketing efforts. You might find that a link on a particular Web site is resulting in a high amount of traffic to your site; therefore, you might consider purchasing a banner advertisement on that site. The same goes for all of the other forms of Internet marketing. If, after a short period of time, your analysis software tells you that you are receiving low traffic from a banner ad that you have purchased, you should pull it off that site and allocate your investment to another site on the Internet. This is a good way to make sure you get the most for your investments in online marketing.

How Do You Get Web Traffic Analysis Software for Your Site?

One option is to use a tracking service like eXTReMe Tracking (*http://www.extreme-dm.com*), where the tracking software resides on the service provider's server. You place the tracker code on your Web site, which provides all the input to the tracking software, and then you have access to all the tracking reports.

You can purchase Web traffic analysis software if you wish, but for it to work it must be installed on the server where you host your Web site. If you are hosting your own Web site, you definitely have to purchase your own software; however, if you are paying an ISP to host your Web site, the host should already be able to provide some sort of analysis software. Most people don't take advantage of the tremendous marketing opportunities available from analyzing their traffic; therefore, they do not ask their ISP about the software. It should be available to you, for you are paying for their services. If it is not, simply ask them to purchase the Web traffic analysis software of your choice, for they would much rather have you as a client than say no. In some cases they might charge you an additional fee for this service.

Internet Resources for Chapter 32

I have developed a great library of online resources for you to check out regarding Web traffic analysis in the Resources section of my Web site at *http:// www.susansweeney.com/resources.html*. There you can find additional tips, tools, techniques, and resources.

I have also developed a seminar on this topic which can be taken at any time over the Internet, can be taken live over the Internet at a scheduled time, or can be purchased as a seminar on CD. See *http://www.susansweeney.com/ store.html*.

33

Web Metrics

Over the past few years, the Internet has come a long way toward being a sales and distribution channel for most businesses. As with any distribution channel, there are costs involved. Where business costs are involved, the owners want to see a return on their investment. To determine the return on investment, businesses need to measure and analyze a number of things.

Over the past year we have seen more and more companies allocate significantly more of their marketing budget to Internet marketing. Businesses are taking the Internet very seriously these days. Businesses are beginning to measure their Web site's effectiveness from both a marketing and a merchandising perspective. In this chapter, we cover:

- Measuring your online success

- What to measure

- Conversion ratio

- Sales per visitor

- Cost per visitor

- Cost per sale

- Net profit per sale

- Return on investment

- Web metrics tools.

Measuring Your Online Success

E-commerce is a numbers game. The trick is to focus on the right numbers so that you can make accurate decisions about how to improve your Web site, and ultimately, your customer conversion rate. Without e-metrics, the Web continues to be a grand experiment, a government research project that escaped the lab, mutated, and took over the world. But with e-metrics you have the opportunity to approach the Web from an objective, systematic perspective. You can move from trial and error to trial, measure and improve.

Bryan Eisenburg

CIO Future Now Inc.

http://futurenowinc.com

It is becoming imperative that companies track the effectiveness of their online marketing campaigns in real time and immediately make adjustments, if necessary. It is also imperative that companies track the effectiveness of the elements on their Web site and make adjustments over time.

From a marketing perspective, organizations want to measure and improve advertising effectiveness, click-throughs, cost of customer acquisitions, etc.

From a Web site perspective, organizations want to improve online sales, cross-sells, up-sells, customer retention rates, average order per customer, number of page views per visitor, customer loyalty, newsletter sign-ups, and so on. They want to determine the most popular areas of the site so the content can be improved. They want to identify popular "exit" pages so they can modify them and make their site more "sticky."

There are a few basic ways to improve your success online:

- Generate more traffic to your Web site—that's what this book is all about.

- Improve your conversion rate or convert more of your Web site visitors into paying customers.

- Your sales conversion rate is affected by:

  - How well you have targeted your audience

  - How good your offer is

  - How convincing your copy is

  - How well your audience knows you—loyalty and trust factors

  - Reducing the clicks to buy—the more clicks to the checkout, the more abandoned shopping carts

- Get your customers to buy more. Ways to do this include:

  - Cross-sell

  - Up-sell

  - Improve your sales copy

  - Offer value-added services, such as gift wrapping and expedited shipping.

If you don't track, you can't measure. If you don't measure, you don't improve. It is as simple as that.

What to Measure

The digital nature of the Web makes the medium inherently measurable. You need to know what to measure, how to measure it, and how to improve over time. Quite often industry benchmarks are irrelevant. What you are concerned with is measuring your own organization's results and ratios and improving them month after month. As long as you keep getting better at what you're doing and are improving your performance and bottom line, does it really matter that there is a benchmark out there that you're not beating? There are too many variables at play that can distort industry-wide or Internet-wide benchmarks.

Some of the key metrics that you want to measure include:

- Conversion ratio

- Sales per visitor

- Cost per visitor

- Net profit per sale

- Return on investment.

Conversion Ratio (CR)

A conversion ratio is the number of times a desired action is taken, presented as a percentage of the number of opportunities for the action to be taken. Although most people look at this ratio as the conversion of a site visitor into a paying customer, there are many other conversion ratios that are relevant. Conversion ratios of site visitors to sign-ups for any permission marketing opportunity (newsletters, coupons, e-specials) is a very important ratio.

By way of example, let's assume you have 300 visitors to your Web site in a day and you have 30 sales in the same time period. The sales conversion ratio would be:

The number of people who purchase divided by the number of people who visit the site: 30/300 = 10 percent.

If you had 3,000 visitors and 30 sales, your conversion ratio would be 1 percent: 30/3,000 = 1 percent.

If you can find a way to increase your conversion ratio from 1 percent to 2 percent, you will double your sales. Obviously, the higher the conversion ratio the better.

Sales per Visitor (SPV)

The sales per visitor is calculated by taking the gross sales or total dollar sales amount for a period of time divided by the number of visitors over the same period of time.

If you have $3,000 in sales for the day and 300 visitors, you have a $10 sales per visitor ratio: $3,000 sales/300 visitors = $10 SPV. You want to increase this number over time.

Cost per Visitor (CPV)

Your cost per visitor can be calculated two ways. You can look at your total cost per visitor over all marketing activities, or you can choose to measure your cost per visitor for a specific campaign. The specific-campaign measurement is more relevant because you want to know which Internet marketing activities are most cost-effective and yield a higher return on investment.

To calculate your overall cost per visitor, you simply take all your marketing expenses and divide by the number of unique visitors.

To calculate a campaign-specific cost per visitor, you take the cost of the campaign and divide it by the number of unique visitors provided by that campaign. Here's an example: Let's say you run a banner advertising campaign that costs you $20 CPM (cost per thousand impressions). And let's further assume you get a 1 percent click-through rate. Your 1 percent click-through yields you ten visitors (1,000 × 1 percent = 10 visitors). Your cost per visitor for this campaign is $2. You take the campaign cost (in this case, $20) and divide it by the number of visitors (in this case, 10): $20/10 visitors = $2 cost per visitor for this campaign.

Cost per Sale (CPS)

Your cost per sale is calculated as the cost of your campaign divided by the number of sales it produces.

Let's follow through on the previous example. Our campaign cost was $20 for 1,000 banner ad impressions. We had a 1 percent click-through rate, or 10 visitors. Let's assume that 10 percent of our visitors bought, so 10 percent is one sale. To calculate our cost per sale, we take our campaign cost and divide it by the number of sales: $20 campaign cost/1 sale = $20 CPS.

Net Profit per Sale (NPPS)

Let's continue with our example. Let's assume that each sale produces a $45 gross profit. Gross profit is calculated by taking the selling price and subtracting the cost of goods sold. Net profit per sale is calculated by taking the net profit and subtracting our cost per sale (which is the previous calculation we figured as $20). The net profit per sale for this campaign is: Gross profit per sale – cost per sale: $45 – $20 = $25 NPPS.

Return on Investment (ROI)

The return on investment before nonmarketing expenses is calculated by taking the net profit per sale and dividing it by the investment or the cost per sale. In this case, you had a $25 net profit per sale divided by $20 cost per sale: $25/$20 = 125 percent ROI.

This campaign was profitable. But you need to do these calculations for all of your campaigns so that you can compare them against each other to see where you want to focus your marketing dollars and also to improve your ratios over time on the same types of marketing activities—in other words, get better at the game.

Web Analytics—The Next Generation

We are seeing the next generation of Web metrics tools providing analysis on a whole additional level. At Verb Interactive, we have been using a product called Click Tracks (see Figure 33.1) to provide us with analysis of user behavior, A/B testing, and improving conversions. This product is a powerful tool to help you understand your Web site visitor behavior and to assist you in seeing what specifically is working and what is not in terms of your online marketing. Their navigation report shows you any of your Web pages exactly as they appear on your site with overlaid statistics on how many people clicked on each link (see

Figure 33.1.   Click Tracks is a great third-generation analytics tool.

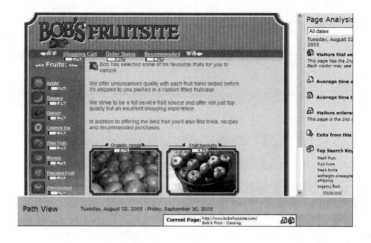

Figure 33.2. With Click Tracks page analyzer, you see each page of your site with an overlay of statistics.

Figure 33.2). You can also use their navigation report to do A/B testing. You can see how visitors reacted to a previous version of a specific page and compare that with the latest version of that page.

You can analyze your site page by page with the page analysis feature. This feature shows page popularity, entry and exit rates, and details of specific keywords that brought visitors to that specific page of your site. You can see where the page visitors came from (another page on your site, another site, or perhaps from your newsletter) and where they went after leaving the specific page.

Click Tracks provides great behavioral analysis as well. You can compare actions taken by returning visitors with visitors who spent a long time on your site or first-time visitors to your site. You can compare behaviors or actions taken by those who found you through a search engine versus those who received your newsletter. You can compare actions taken by visitors from various countries. The parameters, the types of reports, and the analysis you can do are amazing.

Internet Resources for Chapter 33

I have developed a great library of online resources for you to check out regarding Web metrics in the Resources section of my Web site at *http://*

www.susansweeney.com/resources.html. There you can find additional tips, tools, techniques, and resources.

I have also developed a seminar on this topic which can be taken at any time over the Internet, can be taken live over the Internet at a scheduled time, or can be purchased as a seminar on CD. See *http://www.susansweeney.com/store.html.*

About the Author

Susan Sweeney, CA, CSP

Susan Sweeney, CA, CSP, renowned industry expert, consultant, and speaker, tailors lively keynote speeches and full- and half-day seminars and workshops for companies, industries, and associations interested in improving their Internet presence and increasing their Web site traffic and sales. Susan is a partner of Verb Interactive (*www.verbinteractive.com*), an international Internet marketing and consulting firm. Susan holds both the Chartered Accountant and Certified Speaking Professional designations. She is an experienced Internet marketing professional with a background in computers, marketing, and the Internet. Susan is the author of several books on Internet marketing and e-business: *101 Ways To Promote Your Web Site, Internet Marketing for Your Tourism Business, 3G Marketing on the Internet, Going for Gold, 101 Internet Businesses You Can Start from Home,* and *The e-Business Formula for Success*. She is also the developer of a two-day intensive Internet Marketing Boot Camp. Susan offers many Web-based teleseminars, seminars on CD, and e-books related to Internet marketing.

Susan is a member of the Board of Directors of the Canadian Association of Professional Speakers, and is a member of the National Speakers Association and the International Federation for Professional Speakers. Susan holds her Certified Speakers Professional designation which is the only earned designation for professional speakers. Less than 10 percent of professional speakers hold this professional designation.

Verb Interactive is a marketing firm that provides Internet and international marketing consulting and training services to industry and government. Their clients range in size from single-person startup operations to multi-million-dollar international firms. Their primary services include Internet marketing workshops, Web site design and development, Internet marketing strategies, Web site report cards, Internet marketing consulting, market research, and competitive analysis. During their workshops and training sessions, they ensure that their clients have a complete understanding of the principles involved with developing a strong online presence. The team of Internet marketing analysts at Verb Interactive is highly trained in the area of Internet marketing, and all stay up-to-date with the latest technological advancements and industry trends in the online marketing world. Every person on the team has extensive practical hands-on experience and the necessary skills to use proven tips, tools, and techniques to generate high volumes of traffic to your site.

As a result of technological change and global competitiveness, a strong Internet presence is essential. Susan instructs individuals with her enthusiastic personality combined with her vast hands-on international marketing experience, which keeps her listeners informed and captivated. Let Susan help you increase your traffic and make your business prosper!

Susan Sweeney, CA, CSP
75 Brentwood Drive
Bedford, Nova Scotia, Canada B4A 3S2
Phone: 902/468-2578; Fax: 902/468-0380
www.susansweeney.com
www.verbinteractive.com
susan@susansweeney.com

Index

\<H1/H1\>, 93
\<HEAD/HEAD\>, 86–87
\<META-NAME="keywords/description/
robots" CONTENT="...">, 86,
90, 101
"101 Ways Insiders Club" Web site, vi–vii
"404-File Not Found," 27, 104–105,
226, 349

A
About.com, 115
About Contests, 37
above the fold, important information,
304
A/B testing, 306, 360, 361
acceptable practices of search engines,
97–98
ad copy in subject line (avoiding) e-mail,
151
"Add your URL," submissions to search
engines, 113
Ad Group (designing), PPC, 131
administrator's review of submissions to
directories, 122
Advanced Search, search engines,
238–239
advertisements
continued on landing pages, 303
popularity of, traffic analysis, 348
advertisers (contacting), e-zines, 289
advertising company for banner ads, 253,
257
advertising networks, 262–263
advertising online, 248–267. See also
banner ads; offline promotion;
promoting your Web site
advertising networks, 262–263
benefits of, 249–250

brand awareness building objective,
251
budget for, 251
call to action, 264
classified ads, 264
click-throughs, 252, 253, 257, 260–261
commercial links, 265–266
content sites for, 260
cost-effectiveness of, 249
cost per thousand (CPM), 252, 260,
262, 359
enticements for classified ads, 264
friendly classified ads, 264
geo-targeting, 253
headlines for classified ads, 264
hits, 252
impressions, 252, 260, 261
information delivered by, 249
keywords for, 252–253
leads generation objective, 251
location, importance of, 260
media relations vs., 269–270
newsgroups, tips, 174–175
objectives for campaign, 249, 251
objectives (planning your Web site)
and, 3–4
offline promotion and, 267
offline promotion vs., 13, 15, 249, 250
page views, 252
publishers, advertising networks, 263
records, keeping, 264
resources for, 267
response from, 249
sales generation objective, 251
search engines for, 260
seminar on, 267
sponsorships, 264–265, 266
success of, traffic analysis, 353

target market and, 262–263, 266
testing classified ads, 264
traffic generation objective, 251
advertising (rules about)
    newsgroups, 172, 174, 176
    publicly accessible mailing lists, 181,
        182, 183
advice columns for repeat traffic, 45
affiliate programs, 227–234
Amazon.com and, 227, 228, 232
Application Service Provider (ASP) for,
    232
    benefits of, 231–232
    brand awareness increased from, 232
    check payment (automatic), affiliate
        software, 234
    click-through programs, 230
    commission-based affiliate programs,
        228, 230
    contact systems, affiliate software, 233
    defined, 8
    e-mail to affiliates, 231
    finding appropriate program, 230
    flat-fee referral programs, 228–229, 230
    HTML for links, 231
    icons for links, 231
    keywords and, 231, 232
    link popularity and search engine
        ranking, 227, 232
    link strategy for, 225
    newsletters (generic) for, 231
    objectives (planning your Web site)
        and, 228, 230
    payments, prompt, 231
    placement of links, 231
    products and services and, 228
    purchasing affiliate software, 232–234
    real-time statistics, affiliate software,
        233–234
    reporting, prompt, 231
    reporting-period statistic distribution
        (automatic), affiliate software,
        234
    resources for, 234
    sales force expanded from, 232
    search engine rankings and, 227, 232

seminar on, 234
signup (automated), affiliate software,
    233
software for, 232–234
succeeding with your affiliate site,
    230–231
target market and, 228, 232
tracking system (automated), affiliate
    software, 233
two-tier commission program, 228
types of, 228–230
value-added services, 231
variable-payment options, affiliate
    software, 234
alliance partners, permission marketing,
    63
AlltheWeb, 68, 135
AltaVista
    competition analysis, 218
    consolidation in industry, 68
    link strategy and, 214
    meta-indexes, 238
    pay-per-click (PPC), 132, 135
alt category of newsgroups (alternative
    topics), 170
Alt tags
    banner ads, 256, 262
    graphics, Alt tags for, 7
    keywords in, 25–26, 69, 91, 102
Amazon.com
affiliate programs, 227, 228, 232
    brand awareness, 5
    uniform resource locator (URL),
        reducing complexity of, 103
    viral marketing on, 48–49
American Idol and mobile marketing, 330
America Online. See AOL
analyzing log files with software, 348,
    353–354
anchor text (hypertext links), keywords,
    69, 91–92, 115
animated banner ads, 253, 255, 256,
    257–258
Animation Online, 253–254
announcing your Web site. See launching
    your Web Site

answering telephone with URL, 340
anti-spam legislation, 60–61, 195–196,
    202–204
AOL (America Online)
  brand awareness, 5
  Google AdWords and, 132
  Google and, 67
  importance of, 68
  instant messaging, 329
  technology sharing, 114
Apple.com, 274
Apple iPods, 322
Application Service Provider. See ASP
approving sample message, direct mail
    lists, 208
archive of past issues, e-zines, 294
area of interest, databases organized by,
    207
"article banks," e-zines, 290
articles
  e-zines, providing articles to, 53, 290
  media relations and, 269
  pass-it-on viral marketing and, 53
AskJeeves, 67, 107, 132
ASP (Application Service Provider)
affiliate programs and, 232
  private mailing lists and, 192
assigning keywords to page. See place-
    ment of keywords
associate programs. See affiliate programs
attachments caution
  e-mail, 155–156, 159
  news releases, 278
  viral marketing, 51
audio content and podcasting, 322–323
audio greetings for launching your Web
    site, 337
audiozines for pass-it-on viral marketing,
    52, 53
autobots. See autoresponders
automailers. See autoresponders
automated submissions (avoiding),
    submissions to search engines, 98,
    117–118
autoplay sounds, minimizing, 22
autoresponders, 161–166. See also e-mail

  benefits of, 162–163
  brevity of, 165
  call to action, 165
  cost-effectiveness of, 162
  defined, 161–162
  fax-on-demand systems, similarities to,
    161
  features of, 164
  free autoresponders, 163
  grammar, importance of, 165
  HTML messaging, 164
  mail list administration of, 162, 163
  mail list software feature, 193
  marketing using, 165
  multiple messages at predetermined
    intervals, scheduling, 162, 163,
    164
  personalization, 162, 164, 165
  providers of autoresponder service, 163
  repeat traffic and, 46
  resources for, 165–166
  scannability, writing for, 165
  seminar on, 166
  size of message, 164
  spelling, importance of, 165
  subject line, importance of, 165
  target market and, 163, 165
  timeliness of, 149, 162
  tone of message, 165
  tracking reports, 164
  types of, 163
  Web host autoresponders, 163
  Web site vs., 163
awards, 242–247
  call-in offers, 244–245
  Cool Sites, 244, 245–246
  criteria for, 242, 243, 245–246, 247
  download free stuff, 244
  File Transfer Protocol (FTP), 244
  hosting awards, 246–247
  Hot Sites, 245–246
  icon for award, 247
  link strategy for, 244, 245, 246
  nomination for, 243–244
  permission marketing opportunities
    from, 246

preparation for traffic from, 242,
  244–245
resources for, 247
submissions for, 244–245
tag lines for announcing, 145
viral marketing opportunities from,
  246
Webby Awards, The, 243
What's New Web sites, 243

B
background colors
  programming your Web site, 23, 104
  spamming and, 200
background sounds, minimizing, 22
Bacon's, 274, 275
banner ads, 253–264. See also advertising
    online
  advertising company for, 253, 257
  advertising networks, 262–263
  Alt tags, 256, 262
  animated banner ads, 253, 255, 256,
    257–258
  brand awareness increased from, 251
  browsers and, 257
  call to action, 253, 257
  changeability ease of, 250
  changes in, 248
  click-throughs, 253, 257, 260–261
  content sites for, 260
  contest giveaways in, 254
  costs, 260–261
  defined, 251
  developing banner ads, 253–254,
    256–257
  DHTML, 259–260
  download speed and, 256, 258, 259
  drop-down menu banner ads contain-
    ing embedded HTML, 258, 259,
    333–334
  expanding banner ads, 257, 258
  Flash banner ads, 259
  floating banner ads, 259–260
  free offers in, 254
  geo-targeting, 253
  GIF format, 255

impressions and costs, 252, 260, 261
interstitial ads, 258–259
Java banner ads, 259
landing pages and, 257, 302–303
launching your Web site with, 337
leads generation from, 251
link strategy for, 256, 257
link trading, 226
location, importance of, 260
meta-indexes for, 237, 240
outsourcing, 253
partnering and, 333–334
permission marketing vs., 187
PR company for, 253, 257
purchasing consideration, 261–262
readability of, 256
repeat traffic from, 32
rich media in, 248
rotating banner ads, 255
scrolling banner ads, 255
search engines for, 251, 260
Shockwave banner ads, 259
simplicity for, 256
sizes of, 253, 254, 256
sponsorships and, 265, 266
static banner ads, 253, 254
target market and, 249, 251
testing banner ads, 257
time-efficiency of developing banner
    ads, 250
tips for, 256–257
trading banner ads, 263–264
traffic analysis for, 250, 350–351, 353
Unicast banner ads, 260
Web rings for, 301
Web sites for, 251
"banner blindness" caution, 305
BBC (blind carbon copy)
  e-mail, 151–152
  private mailing lists, 152
  spamming and, 152
Beaver Run, 63
bidding on keywords, PPC, 138
biz category of newsgroups (business
    topics), 170
BizLand Download Time Checker, 16

Blacklists, monitoring, 202
blind carbon copy. See BBC
BlogCatalog, 320
Blogger.com, 318
blogs, 317–318
   benefits of, 319–320
   cons of, 320
   current, keeping Web site, 319
   defined, 317–318
   directories of, 320
   hosting sites (free), 318
   HTML for creating, 319
   keywords and, 319, 321
   latest news, providing customers with, 319
   mobile marketing and, 329
   objectives (planning your Web site) and, 319
   promoting, 320–321
   Really Simple Syndication (RSS) and, 320
   reputation building from, 319
   resources for, 321
   search engines ranking and, 319, 321
   seminar on, 321
   setting up, 318–319
   signature files, 321
   software for, 319
   "speaking to" target market with, 319
   target market and, 319, 320
   updating blogs, 319, 320
   Web site and, 319, 321
Blog Search Engine, 321
Bloogz, 321
Blue Mountain, 54–55
body of news releases, 272
body text, keywords, 70, 92–94
bookmarks for repeat traffic, 40
bots, 66–67, 101, 116, 117
brainstorming
   objectives (planning your Web site), 5–6, 9
   offline promotion, 339
brand awareness
   affiliate programs for, 232
   banner ads for, 251

creating and establishing objective, 3, 5
   mobile marketing for, 330
   objectives (planning your Web site) and, 251
   pay-per-click (PPC) for, 129
   private mailing lists for, 188–189
   Really Simple Syndication (RSS) for, 313
   repeat traffic for, 29, 35
bridge (doorway) pages, 97, 99
brochure (electronic), e-mail, 158
brochureware, unacceptability of, 2
brokers for sign-ups, private mailing lists, 196
browsers
   banner ads and, 257
   landing pages and, 305
   programming your Web site and, 26
   Really Simple Syndication (RSS) and, 314
   use of browsers, traffic analysis, 347, 349, 350
BruceClay, 114
budget for
   advertising online, 251
   direct mail lists, 208–209
   pay-per-click (PPC), 138–139
bulk e-mail, 159, 180
bulk mail lists, direct mail, 207
bulletin boards for repeat traffic, 40
Business.com, 113, 115
business-oriented Web site, 11, 12
business reluctance to participate in Web rings, 300
button (attention-grabbing), viral marketing, 50, 51
buying process on landing pages, 305, 307

C
calendar of events for repeat traffic, 34, 58, 187
call-in offers, awards, 244–245
call to action in
   advertising online, 264
   autoresponders, 165

banner ads, 253, 257

descriptions, submissions to directories, 121

e-mail, 153–154

e-zines, 294

HTML, link strategy, 223

landing pages, 304

partnering, 334

pay-per-click (PPC), 138

permission marketing, 187

private mailing lists, 197, 198

publicly accessible mailing lists, 182, 184

signature files, 144

viral marketing, 49

Canadian

legislation, anti-spam, 60, 196, 202–204

U.S. spellings (keywords) vs., 81

CAN-SPAM (Controlling the Assault of Non-Solicited Pornography and Marketing Act), 60–61, 202

CAPS, avoiding

e-mail, 151, 159

newsgroups, 175, 176

programming your Web site, 23

spamming, 200

submissions to directories, 123

Carlson Wagonlit, 25

Cartoons4fun, 42

cartoons for repeat traffic, 42

cascading style sheets (CSS), 102

case sensitivity, keywords, 81

catch phrases. See tag lines

categories

newsgroups, 169–170

selecting for submissions to directories, 113, 118–119, 120, 121

Web rings, 296–297

changeability ease of banner ads, 250

changing listing in directories, 122

charter of

newsgroups, 171–172

publicly accessible mailing lists, 183

checklists for pass-it-on viral marketing, 53

check payment (automatic), affiliate software, 234

children-oriented Web site, 11

circulation of e-zines, 286

city and date, news releases, 271

classified ads, 264

Clay, Bruce, 114

"Click here" on signature files, 141

click-through programs, affiliate programs, 230

click-throughs

advertising online, 252, 253, 257, 260–261

banner ads, 253, 257, 260–261

Really Simple Syndication (RSS), 313

Click Tracks, 360–361

cloaking, spamming, 96, 98

close of news releases, 272

closing, landing pages, 307

clothing, URL exposure, 343–344

CNN, 67, 132, 135, 325

code (clean) for search engines, 102

colors

discrimination and spamming, 200

programming your Web site, 23, 104

commercial activity (rules about), newsgroups, 172, 174

commercial links, 265–266

commercial meta-indexes, 236, 240

commission-based affiliate programs, 228, 230

common objectives, 3–6

communication with private mailing lists, 197–199

communities. See newsgroups

company

company or product information (providing) objective, 3, 4–5

identity (creating and establishing) objective, 3, 5

literature, URL exposure, 340–341

repeat traffic and image, 45

signature files and image, 143

comp category of newsgroups (computer topics), 170

competition analysis
  keywords, 79, 119, 123
  link strategy, 216–219
  planning your Web site, 14–16
competition (linking to), Web rings, 300
competitions for repeat traffic, 34–37
competitor's name in keywords, 80
completing Web site before submitting to search engines and directories, 125
computer programs used for submissions to search engines, 98
comScore Networks, 105
consistency of Web site, 21, 23, 25
consolidation in industry, search engines, 68
contact information
  news releases, 271
  objective (planning your Web site), 4
  programming your Web site, 22
  signature files, 141, 143
contacts (conserving), private mailing lists, 188
contact systems, affiliate software, 233
content
  duplication, spamming, 96, 98
  e-zines, 292
  landing pages, 303–306
  podcasting, 323, 324–325
  private mailing lists and approval of, 195
  Really Simple Syndication (RSS), 310–312, 314–315
  updating of Web site, link strategy, 226
  Web page, developing content for each, 22
  Web site and target market, 11
content notes, 22
content sites for
  advertising online, 260
  banner ads, 260
Contest Hound, 36
contests
  banner ads for, 254
  launching your Web site with, 337
  partnering with, 334
  permission marketing and, 34–37, 58, 59–60
  repeat traffic from, 34–37, 58, 59–60, 187
  tag lines for announcing, 145
Contests and Sweepstakes Directory, 37
contextual advertising, PPC, 135–136
contract with outsource company, private mailing lists, 194–195
contribution (making), newsgroups, 174, 176
Controlling the Assault of Non-Solicited Pornography and Marketing Act (CAN-SPAM), 60–61, 202
control (none) over media relations, 269–270
convenience importance to customers, 13
conversion ratio (CR), 357, 358
conversions from landing pages, 302, 303, 304
CoolSavings.com, 32, 33
Cool Sites, 244, 245–246
co-operative banner ads, 333–334
cooperative permission marketing, 63
Costal Living, 284
cost-effectiveness of
  advertising online, 249
  autoresponders, 162
  e-mail, 148, 149
  e-zines, 288
  media relations, 269
  mobile marketing, 330
  permission marketing, 58, 61, 64
  viral marketing, 47
cost per click (CPC), PPC, 137, 138, 139
cost per sale (CPS), 359
cost per thousand (CPM), 252, 260, 262, 359
cost per visitor (CPV), 359
costs
  banner ads, 260–261
  direct mail lists, 209–210
  Web rings, 299
coupons

repeat traffic from, 31–33, 58, 187
Web rings, exchanging coupons, 301
courtesy in
    e-mail, 159
    newsgroups, 176
CPC (cost per click), PPC, 137, 138, 139
CPM (cost per thousand), 252, 260, 262,
    359
CPS (cost per sale), 359
CPV (cost per visitor), 359
CR (conversion ratio), 357, 358
creativity for URL exposure, 344–345
credibility, enhanced from landing pages,
    304
CrickRock WebRing System, 296, 298,
    299
criteria for awards, 242, 243, 245–246,
    247
cross-posting (avoiding), newsgroups,
    175, 176
cross-promotion, banner ads, 333. See
    also offline promotion; promoting
    your Web site
CSS (cascading style sheets), 102
current (keeping Web site) for blogs, 319
customer loyalty (encouraging) objective,
    6, 8–9. See also relationship
    building
customer profiles, mobile marketing, 330
customer relationship reinforced from
    media relations, 269
customer retention improved from
    permission marketing, 187
custom error pages, search engines,
    104–105
customers, staying current with e-zines,
    291
customer service and product support
    (providing) objective, 3, 4
cyberspace, 336
cyber-squatting, 97

D
daily newspapers for news releases, 277
data mining, 63, 207
dayparting, PPC, 136–137

deadlines, news releases, 277
dead links, avoiding, 27, 215, 226
default colors for links, 23
delivery guaranteed from RSS, 309, 313
demographic information, 36, 348
description meta-tags, keywords, 69, 88,
    90
descriptions and submissions to directo-
    ries, 121, 122–123
Destination Hotels & Resorts, 272
Destinations2Discover, 285
developing
    banner ads, 253–254, 256–257
    signature files, 141–142
DHTML, 66–68, 102, 259–260
differences among search engines submis-
    sions, 112–113, 115, 125
different groups, different signature files,
    142
different keywords for each Web page,
    71, 78, 126
digest form, publicly accessible mailing
    lists, 181, 182
direct mail lists, 206–211. See also e-mail
    approving sample message, 208
    area of interest, databases organized
        by, 207
    budget, working with, 208–209
    bulk mail lists, 207
    costs, 209–210
    data mining, 63, 207
    double opt-in lists, 207, 209
    finding appropriate company, 207–208
    fine-tuning list, 208
    grammar, importance of, 210
    hypertext links, 210
    hypertext links, unrestricted, 208
    launching your Web site with, 337
    message content, 208, 210
    opt-in lists, 207, 209
    per-name basis for costs, 209, 210
    personalization, 208, 210
    private mailing lists, converted from,
        210
    rental lists for sign-ups, private mailing
        lists, 196

renting lists, 180
reputable companies, 207–208, 209–210
resources for, 211
scannability, writing for, 210
seminar on, 211
spelling, importance of, 210
subject line, importance of, 210
surveys for building databases, 207
targeting appropriate, 207–208
target market and, 207
topic lists, 207–208
tracking services, 208, 210
tracking technology for building
     databases, 207
working with company, 208–209
directories. See also submissions to
     directories
  blogs, 320
  meta-indexes, finding with, 237
  partnering and, 334
  podcasting, 326
  Really Simple Syndication (RSS), 314
  search engines vs., 113, 115, 116, 119
  Web rings vs., 296
discounts for repeat traffic, 31–33
discussion groups. See newsgroups
discussion lists. See publicly accessible
     mailing lists
distribution service for news releases,
     273–276
Dogpile, 67
domain names, keywords, 7, 69, 92, 123
domain spam (mirror sites), 96
doorway pages, 97, 99
do's and dont's of signature files, 142–143
double opt-in lists, 207, 209
downloadable items, products and
     services, 14
download free stuff, awards, 244
downloading and attachments, e-mail,
     155
download speeds
  banner ads and, 256, 258, 259
  news releases and, 278
  planning your Web site and, 15–16,
     26, 27

Dr. Watson, 215
drop-down banner ads containing embed-
     ded HTML, 258, 259, 333–334
duplicating Web pages, spamming, 96, 98
dynamic pages and special characters,
     search engines, 103

E
ease of use, Web rings, 299
eBay, 5, 229
E-books for pass-it-on viral marketing, 52
e-business cards, 140–141. See also
     signature files
e-cards for viral marketing, 54–56
e-club, integrating with permission
     marketing, 58, 187, 195, 196
editing tools for podcasting, 323–324
editorial calendar for e-zines, 289
editors and news releases, 276–277
effective messages
  e-mail, 150–156
  publicly accessible mailing lists,
     181–183
effectiveness of permission marketing, 58,
     61, 64
Eisenburg, Bryan, 356
electronic business cards, 140–141. See
     also signature files
electronic magazines. See e-zines
e-mail, 148–160. See also autoresponders;
     direct mail lists; newsgroups;
     news releases; private mailing
     lists; publicly accessible mailing
     lists
  ad copy in subject line, avoiding, 151
  addresses (managing), private mailing
     lists, 191, 192, 193
  affiliates and, 231
  attachments caution, 155–156, 159
  benefits of, 148
  blind carbon copy (BBC), 151–152
  brevity of, 152, 159
  brochure (electronic), 158
  call to action, 153–154
  CAPS, avoiding, 151, 159
  cost-effectiveness of, 148, 149

courtesy in, 159
downloading and attachments, 155
effective messages, 150–156
emoticons, 156–157, 159
first impression, importance of, 149
formatting messages, 152–153
Frequently Asked Questions (FAQs), 159
"From" headings, personalization, 151
grammar, importance of, 152, 159
graphics caution, 153
growth of, 148
HTML vs. text e-mail, 154
http:// before www in, 152–153
hypertext links in, 152–153
interactivity of, 149
library of responses for, 159
lists, 8
marketing tips, 158–159
netiquette, 159–160
news releases, 277–278
original message, including in reply, 154, 176
paragraph length, 152
permanent record, 153
personalization, 151, 158, 159
personal quality of, 149
platform compatibility and, 155, 156
private mail list marketing vs., 149
prompt reply, 159–160
relationship building using, 149, 152
reply tips, 154, 159–160
resources for, 160
response rate, 154
responses (library of) for, 159
"selling the sizzle," 187
seminar on, 160
shorthand, 156, 157–158
signature files, 140–141, 154–155
snail mail vs., 149, 186
spelling, importance of, 152, 153, 159
subject line, importance of, 150–151
text vs. HTML e-mail, 154
time-efficiency of, 148, 149
"To" headings, personalization, 151
tone of, 152

uniform resource locator (URL) in, 152–153
unsolicited bulk e-mail, avoiding, 159
viruses, 155–156
e-mail-based e-zines, 284, 285–286
e-mail-on-demand. See autoresponders
e-mail program for managing private mailing lists, 191
emoticons, e-mail, 156–157, 159
employment opportunities for repeat traffic, 37
enticements for classified ads, 264
entry pages analysis for monitoring results of search engines, 108–109
epromos.com, 342
equipment needed for podcasting, 323
ESPN, 135
event announced in tag lines, 145
Excite, 135, 218
existing customers
    newsgroups for communicating with, 169
    potential customers vs., 10
"exit" pages, identifying, 356
expanding banner ads, 257, 258
expectations of target market, determining, 10, 11, 13
expedited reviews, submissions to directories, 115–116
exposure (maximizing your), PPC, 137–138
eXTReMe Tracking, 353–354
e-zines, 283–294
    advertisers, contacting, 289
    archive of past issues, 294
    "article banks," 290
    articles, providing to, 53, 290
    benefits of, 287–288
    call to action, 294
    circulation of, 286
    content for, 292
    cost-effectiveness of, 288
    customers, staying current with, 291
    defined, 283, 284
    editorial calendar for, 289
    e-mail-based e-zines, 284, 285–286

fees, 284, 285, 286
finding appropriate e-zines, 286–287
geographic reach of, 288
growth of, 284
guidelines for advertising, 288–290
hypertext links in, 289
length of, 292
lifespan of ads in, 287
line length for, 292
link strategy for, 288, 289
loyalty building from, 291
marketing options using, 286
newsgroups for promoting, 293–294
news releases, providing to, 290
offline magazines and e-zines, 284
opt out (unsubscribe) instructions, 292, 293
partnering and, 335
policies of, 290
privacy policy, 293
private mailing lists built from, 292, 293, 294
promoting e-zines, 293–294
publisher, contacting, 289
relationship marketing from, 291
repetition of advertising, success of advertising, 289
reputation building from, 290, 291
resources for, 294
response rates, 288
seminar on, 294
sharing of e-zines, 288, 292–293
spamming caution, 293, 294
starting your own e-zine, 291–294
subscribers to, 284, 285, 286, 289
subscribing instructions, 292, 293, 294
target market and, 285, 286, 287, 288, 290
testing e-zines, 293
timeliness of ads, 287–288
tracking information availability from, 289
tracking responses, 290
trust, established from, 291
viral marketing opportunities from, 288, 292–293, 294
Web-based e-zines, 284, 285
Web site for promoting, 294
eZINESearch.com, 287

F
FAQs (Frequently Asked Questions)
e-mail, 159
newsgroups, 167, 171–172, 174, 175
objectives (planning your Web site), 4, 5, 106, 159
publicly accessible mailing lists, 181, 183
Fast Company, 311
fax-on-demand systems, similarities to autoresponders, 161
featured section for repeat traffic, 39
fees
e-zines, 284, 285, 286
meta-indexes, 240
submissions to directories, 115–116
file names, keywords, 69, 92
File Transfer Protocol (FTP), 244
filtering, mail list software, 193
filter words, keywords, 81
FindGift.com, 44
finding appropriate
affiliate programs, 230
direct mail lists, 207–208
e-zines, 286–287
link sites, 215–216, 216–220
meta-indexes, 237–239, 240
newsgroups, 171
partnering sites, 332–333
publicly accessible mailing lists, 179–181
search engines, important, 68
search engines or directories for submissions, 126
Web rings, 298
Findwhat.com, 107
fine-tuning direct mail lists, 208
fine-tuning keywords, 78–85. See also keywords; monitoring results of search engines; placement of keywords
Canadian vs. U.S. spellings, 81

case sensitivity, 81
competition analysis, 79, 119, 123
competitor's name in keywords, 80
different keywords for each Web page, 71, 78, 126
filter words, 81
misspellings in keywords, 80–81
modifiers, 85
multiple-word keyword phrases, 85
objectives (planning your Web site) and, 79
organizing keywords, 79–80
plural keywords, 80
popularity of keywords, 79
prioritizing keywords, 79–80
rankings, checking, 109–110
singular keywords, 80
stop words, 81–84
traffic analysis for, 72, 75, 107–108
U.S. vs. Canadian spellings, 81
first impression (importance of) e-mail, 149
five W's (who, what, where, when, and why), 272
flames, publicly accessible mailing lists, 178
Flash banner ads, 259
Flash intros caution, search engines, 26, 68
flat-fee referral (affiliate) programs, 228–229, 230
"flight effect," 214, 352
floating banner ads, 259–260
focus of landing pages, 303, 305
FOLLOW/NOFOLLOW, 101
follow up for news releases, 277
font colors, programming your Web site, 23
fonts (large) and spamming, 200
format of
    e-mail messages, 152–153
    new releases, 270–272
    private mailing lists correspondence, 198
forms (filling out all fields), submissions to directories, 113, 119–120, 121–122

forums for repeat traffic, 40
frames and search engines, 100, 113
Franchise Solutions, 265, 266
free-for-all links, avoiding, 224–225
free stuff
    autoresponders, 163
    gifts for launching your Web site, 338
    meta-indexes, 236, 240
    offers in banner ads, 254
    repeat traffic and, 30–31, 32
    submissions to search engines, 117
    tag lines and, 145
Frequently Asked Questions. See FAQs
friendly classified ads, 264
"From"
    e-mail, personalization, 151
    private mailing lists, 195, 199
FTP (File Transfer Protocol), 244
Future Now Inc., 356

G
games for
    pass-it-on viral marketing, 53
    repeat traffic, 43
"gatekeeper," publicly accessible mailing lists, 178
gateway (doorway) pages, 97, 99
geographical location of visitors, 349
geographic modifiers, PPC, 107
geographic reach of e-zines, 288
geo-targeting
    banner ads, 253
    pay-per-click (PPC) campaigns, 131, 136
GIF format, banner ads, 255
gift registry for repeat traffic, 45
goals (setting), publicly accessible mailing lists, 182–183
Google
    acceptable practices, 98, 99
    "Add your URL," 112–113
    competition analysis, 74–75, 218
    importance of, 68, 115
    indexed Web sites, number of, 116
    link popularity and ranking, 214
    localization of search, 106, 107
    Open Directory database used by, 70

partnering with, 67
ranking criteria of, 70
RSS submission tools, 314
Search Options, 238–239
spider, 67
submission to, 116, 117
technology sharing, 114
title tags, 87, 88
title tags of competition, checking, 74–75
verifying inclusion, 118
Google AdSense, 230
Google AdWords, 130–132. See also PPC (pay-per-click) strategy
account, setting up, 131
budget, setting, 131
contextual advertising, 136
cost per click (CPC), 130, 131
geo-targeting campaigns, 131, 136
keywords for, 131
maximum cost per click (CPC), 131
multiple ads, 131
partners (network), 132
success of, 129, 130
traffic-estimation tool, 131
Google Groups, 171
GPS coordinates, 107
grammar, importance of
autoresponders, 165
direct mail lists, 210
e-mail, 152, 159
newsgroups, 176
grand opening (traditional) and launching your Web site, 337
graphic links, link strategy, 222, 223, 224
graphics. See also icons
e-mail caution, 153
keywords caution, 93
meta-indexes and link, 236
programming your Web site, 22, 25–26
signature files caution, 142–143, 145–146
target market and, 11, 12
viral marketing and, 54
gratuitous responses (avoiding), newsgroups, 174, 176
gross profit, 359

growth of
e-mail, 148
e-zines, 284
mobile marketing, 328, 330, 331
Web rings, 298, 300
guidelines for advertising, e-zines, 288–290

H
<H1/H1>, 93
<HEAD/HEAD>, 86–87
headers
keywords and, 70
news releases, 271
headlines
classified ads, 264
landing pages, 303
news releases, 271
Help page, search engines, 238
hidden text and links, spamming, 95, 98
hierarchical organization of publicly accessible mailing lists, 178
hits, 252
home page
keywords and, 94
programming your Web site, 27
submissions to search engines, 117
hosting awards, 246–247
hosting sites (free) for blogs, 318
HotBot, 214, 218
Hotmail.com, 54
Hot Sites, 245–246
"hot spots," 26, 105
how visitors find your Web site, 350–351
HTML
autoresponders, messaging, 164
blogs, creating, 319
issues, spamming, 200
mail list software capability, 191, 192
submissions to search engines/directories and validating, 125
text e-mail vs., 154
HTML for links
affiliate programs, 231
link strategy, 221, 222, 223, 231
meta-indexes, 236, 240
http:// before www in e-mail, 152–153

signature files, 141
humanities category of newsgroups, 170
humor for repeat traffic, 42
hypertext links
     direct mail lists, 210
     direct mail lists and unrestricted, 208
     e-mail, 152–153
     e-zines, 289
     keywords, 69, 91–92, 115
     meta-indexes, 236, 240
     news releases, 273
     signature files, 141
     spamming, 200

I
icons. See also graphics
     affiliate programs links, 231
     award, 247
     link strategy, 222, 223, 231
     meta-indexes links, 240
image conveyed from Web site, 22–23
image maps and search engines, 26, 105,
          113
importing existing database, private
          mailing lists, 195–196
impressions, 252, 260, 261
improving success, methods for, 356–357
Inbox360.com, 194
incentive-based permission marketing, 64
incentives for
     links, 223
     viral marketing, 51
inclusion request e-mail, meta-indexes,
          236, 240
industry associations for partnering,
          334–335
infobots. See autoresponders
information delivered by advertising
          online, 249
Inktomi, 68, 214
"Insiders Club" Web site, vi–vii
instant messaging, mobile marketing, 329
instructions on how to participate in viral
          marketing, 51
Intel, 25
Interactive Advertising Bureau, The, 254

interactive news releases, 273, 274
interactivity of
     e-mail, 149
     mobile marketing, 330
internal search tool, 24–25
international search engines, 118
Internet Explorer (Microsoft), meta-tags
          of competition, checking, 74
Internet marketers for programming your
          Web site, 21
Internet marketing. See promoting your
          Web site
Internet News Bureau, 276
interstitial ads, 258–259
IP addresses of visitors, 347, 349
ISPs and traffic analysis, 354
iTunes, 326

J
jamming keywords ("tiny text"), 95
Java banner ads, 259
jokes for repeat traffic, 42
journaling. See blogs
journalists and media relations, 270, 274,
          277–278, 281
Juno, 135

K
Kanoodle, 130
keywords. See also fine-tuning keywords;
          monitoring results of search
          engines; placement of keywords
     address of Web site and, 72
     advertising online and, 252–253
     affiliate programs and, 231, 232
     Alt tags and, 25–26, 69, 91, 102
     blogs and, 319, 321
     brainstorming for, 72–73
     buying, 129, 133, 138–139
     competition analysis, 14–15, 72,
          73–75, 79, 119
     different keywords for each Web page,
          71, 78, 126
     directories and, 121
     domain names and, 7, 69, 92, 123
     evaluation tools, 72, 75–78

focus of Web site and, 72
geographical considerations, 73
geographic keywords, 106
Google AdWords: Key Suggestions, 77–78
industry and, 72
link strategy and, 216, 219, 221, 222, 223, 231
master keyword list, building, 71–78, 79
naming files (podcasting) and, 324
Overture's Search Term Suggestion Tool, 76–77
page description and, 7
pay-per-click (PPC), 137
products and services and, 73
ranking of search engines and, 7, 66, 114–115
regional considerations, 73
search engine query for suggested related keywords, 78, 79
suggestion tools, 72, 75–78
target market and selection of, 66, 71, 72
tools for, 72, 75–78, 94
traffic analysis, 72, 75, 107–108, 348, 351–352
Wordtracker, 75, 76, 77
keyword search for newsgroups, 171
keyword stacking, 95, 98
keyword stuffing, 95, 98

L
landing pages, 302–308. See also programming your Web site
above the fold, importance information, 304
A/B testing, 306, 360, 361
ad continued on, 303
banner ads and, 257, 302–303
"banner blindness" caution, 305
benefits of offer, emphasized on, 303
browsers and, 305
buying process on, 305, 307
call to action, 304
closing, importance of, 307
content of, 303–306
conversions from, 302, 303, 304
credibility, enhanced from, 304
cross-promotion on, 307
defined, 302–303
focus of landing pages, 303, 305
headline, importance of, 303
layout of, 306–307
pay-per-click (PPC), 137–138
permission marketing opportunities from, 305
presentation of, 306–307
resources for, 308
risk minimizing, 304
sale, closing the, 304, 305
scannability, writing for, 303
search engines and, 304
seminar on, 308
"speaking to" target market, 303
target market and, 303, 305
testing landing pages, 304, 305–308
trust, established from, 304
urgency, creating sense of, 304
"value-added," promoting, 303
viral marketing opportunities from, 305
latest news (providing customers with), blogs, 319
LA Times, 24
launching your Web site, 336–338. See also media relations
audio greetings for, 337
banner ads for, 337
contests for, 337
cyberspace, 336
direct mail for, 337
free gifts for, 338
grand opening (traditional) and, 337
newsgroups for, 337
newsletters for, 337
offline promotion for, 337, 338
opening ceremonies, 337
permission marketing opportunities from, 337
press releases for, 337
resources for, 338

signature files for, 337
special guests for, 337
target market and, 337
uniform resource locator (URL) for, 338
video greetings for, 337
viral marketing opportunities from, 337
"What's New" sites for, 337
layout of landing pages, 306–307
LBS (location-based services), mobile marketing, 328, 329
leads generation
  banner ads for, 251
  objective, advertising online, 251
legal issues and contests, 36
legislation regarding permission marketing, 60–61, 195–196, 202–204
leveraging viral marketing, 51
library of responses for e-mail, 159
lifespan of
  ads in e-zines, 287
  links, 213–214
Link Popularity, 218, 219
link popularity and search engine ranking. See also link strategy
  affiliate programs, 227, 232
  link strategy, 213, 214, 217
  submissions to search engines, 70–71, 115
Link Popularity Check, 218
link request letters, 217, 220–221
link schemes, 98
links farms, 97
link strategy, 212–226. See also link popularity and search engine ranking; meta-indexes; Web rings
  affiliate programs, 225
  awards, 244, 245, 246
  banner ads, 256, 257
  call to action in HTML, 223
  competition analysis, 216–219
  content of Web site, updating, 226
  dead links, avoiding, 215, 226
  defined, 212
  e-zines, 288, 289

finding appropriate link sites, 215–216, 216–220
"flight effect" of links, 214, 352
free-for-all links, avoiding, 224–225
graphic links, 222, 223, 224
HTML for links, 221, 222, 223, 231
icons for links, 222, 223, 231
importance of, 213
incentives for links, 223
keywords and, 216, 219, 221, 222, 223, 231
lifespan of, 213–214
link request letters, 217, 220–221
marketing log, maintaining, 225
media relations, 281
meta-indexes, 223, 240
news releases, 273
outbound links, 214–215, 226
partnering, 334
permission marketing, 59
placement of links, 214, 222, 223–224, 226, 231
programming your Web site, 24, 26, 27, 115
Really Simple Syndication (RSS), 312, 313
reciprocal links, 216, 217, 221, 301
repeat traffic, 30, 32, 33, 34, 35, 37–38, 39
resources for, 226
search engine ranking and, 217
search engines and, 67, 115, 219–220
seminar on, 226
tag lines in HTML, 223, 224
testing links, 215, 226
thumbnail icon for link, 222, 223, 224
tools for, 215, 216–217, 218–219
trading links, 225–226, 296
uniform resource locator (URL) for, 216–217, 218
updating Web sites and, 226
viral marketing, link button placement, 49, 50, 51
Web rings, 223, 296, 301
Web site, asking for links on, 222
LiveJournal, 318

localization, optimization for search engines, 105–107, 123
location-based services (LBS), mobile marketing, 328, 329
location (importance of) banner ads, 260
log files for traffic analysis, 347–348, 348–349, 350, 353
LookSmart, 115, 119
loyalty
   customer loyalty (encouraging) objective, 6, 8–9
   e-zines for building, 291
   loyalty programs (creating) objective, 6, 8–9
   mobile marketing for building, 330
lurking, 167, 168, 172, 175, 181
Lycos, 78

M
magazines, online. See e-zines
Mahone Bay, 56
mailbots. See autoresponders
mailing lists. See bulk mail lists; direct mail lists; private mailing lists; publicly accessible mailing lists
mail list administration of autoresponders, 162, 163
mail list software for managing private mailing lists, 191–194
management of private mailing lists, 190–194
managing effective public relations, 269
marketing. See promoting your Web site
marketing log (maintaining), link strategy, 225
market research from newsgroups, 169
mass-marketing e-mails. See private mailing lists
masternewmedia.org/rss, 320
Maximum Press Web site, vi–vii
measuring success, Web metrics, 356–358
Media Builder, 254
media center, 5, 18, 280–281
Mediafinder, 274, 275
media kit, 268
media relations, 268–282. See also news

releases; offline promotion
   advertising vs., 269–270
   articles for, 269
   benefits of, 269–270
   control (none) over, 269–270
   cost-effectiveness of, 269
   customer relationship reinforced from, 269
   journalists and, 270, 274, 277–278, 281
   link strategy for, 281
   managing effective public relations, 269
   media center for, 5, 18, 280–281
   media kit for, 268
   newsworthiness, 270, 272, 278–280
   partnering and, 335
   permission marketing opportunities from, 281
   resources for, 282
   seminar on, 282
   Tag Image File Format (TIFF), 281
   timing of release, control (none) over, 270
   viral marketing opportunities from, 281
"Members Only" Web site, vi–vii
message editor, mail list software, 193
messages. See also posting messages to
   direct mail lists, 208, 210
   spam words in, 200–201
<META-NAME="keywords/description/robots" CONTENT="...">, 86, 90, 101
Metacrawler, 135
meta-indexes, 235–241
   banner ads on, 237, 240
   commercial meta-indexes, 236, 240
   defined, 235–237
   directories for finding, 237
   fees, 240
   finding appropriate meta-indexes, 237–239, 240
   free meta-indexes, 236, 240
   graphics for link, 236
   HTML for link, 236, 240

hypertext links, 236, 240
icon for link, 240
inclusion request e-mail, 236, 240
link strategy for, 223, 240
partnering and, 334
publicly accessible mailing lists, finding
    with, 180
resources for, 241
search engines for finding, 237–238,
    240
search engines vs., 237
specific topics of, 236–237
sponsoring opportunities, 240
submission to, 236
tag line for link, 236, 240
target market and, 240
meta-search engines, 67
meta-tags and keywords, 69, 70, 74,
    88–90, 115
metrics. See Web metrics
Microsoft
    instant messaging, 329
    Internet Explorer, 74
    Outlook, 151
    signature files, 141–142
    Visio, 18
mirror sites (domain spam), 96
misc category of newsgroups, 170
misleading title changes, spamming, 95
misspellings in keywords, 80–81
MMS (multimedia messaging service),
    mobile marketing, 329
mobile devices and podcasting, 322, 323
mobile marketing, 328–331
    American Idol and, 330
    benefits of, 329–331
    blogging, 329
    brand awareness increased from, 330
    cost-effectiveness of, 330
    customer profiles, 330
    defined, 328–329
    growth of, 328, 330, 331
    instant messaging, 329
    interactivity of, 330
    location-based services (LBS), 328, 329
    loyalty building from, 330

multimedia messaging service (MMS),
    329
personal communication, immediate
    response, 330
personalization, 330
profile-specific advertising, 329
resources for, 330
sales increased from, 330
seminar on, 330
short messaging service (SMS), 329
sponsored messages, 330
subscribed content, 329
target market and, 330
timeliness of, 330
two-way dialogue from, 330
moderated discussion lists, 178
modifiers, keywords, 85
monitoring results of search engines,
    107–110. See also fine-tuning
    keywords; keywords; search
    engines
    entry pages analysis for, 108–109
    paid inclusion account reports for, 110
    paths through Web site analysis for,
        109
    pay-to-play (PPC) account tracking for,
        110, 111
    rankings, checking, 109–110
    return of investment (ROI) as measure
        of success, 107–108, 355, 360
    traffic analysis for, 72, 75, 107–108
monthly magazines for news releases, 277
Mousepads.com, 341
Movable Type, 319
MP3 files
    podcasting, 322, 323, 324
    repeat traffic from, 45–46
    viral marketing, 53
MSN, 54, 132, 135, 214
MSN adCenter, 129, 130
MSN/Microsoft Search Engine, 113
MSN Search, 68, 115
multimedia effects and target market, 12
multimedia messaging service (MMS),
    mobile marketing, 329
multiple listings, submissions to search

engines, 126
multiple messages at predetermined
    intervals, scheduling with
    autoresponders, 162, 163, 164
multiple-word keyword phrases, 85
multi-threading sending, mail list soft-
    ware, 193
music and podcasting, 325
MyLeisureTravel.com, 62

N
navigation
    ease of, programming your Web site,
        23–24, 26
    search engines caution, 102
    Web rings, 297, 298, 299
needs of target market, determining, 10,
    11
netiquette
    e-mail, 159–160
    newsgroups, 175–176
    signature files, 143, 145
    submissions to search engines, 126
NetMechanic, 125, 215
net profit per sale (NPPS), 359
Netscape, 67, 114, 132
networking from private mailing lists,
    188
Network Solutions, 220
Netzero, 135
news category of newsgroups, 170
newsgroups, 167–176. See also e-mail
    advertising, rules about, 172, 174, 176
    advertising tips, 174–175
    benefits of, 169
    brevity of postings, 173, 176
    CAPS, avoiding, 175, 176
    categories of, 169–170
    changes in, 168–169
    charter of, 171–172
    commercial activity, rules about, 172,
        174
    contribution, making, 174, 176
    courtesy in, 176
    cross-posting, avoiding, 175, 176
    defined, 168

existing customers, communicating
    with, 169
e-zines promoting with, 293–294
finding appropriate newsgroups, 171
Frequently Asked Questions (FAQs),
    167, 171–172, 174, 175
grammar, importance of, 176
gratuitous responses, avoiding, 174,
    176
keyword search for, 171
launching your Web site with, 337
lurking, 167, 168, 172, 175
market research from, 169
netiquette, 175–176
original message, including in reply,
    154, 176
posting messages, 167, 168, 172–174
potential customers and, 169, 172
private responses, 173, 174
publicly accessible mailing lists pro-
    moting with, 183
publicly accessible mailing lists vs., 178
Reply option, using, 174
reputation building from, 169
resources for, 176
rules, abiding by, 171–172
scannability, writing for, 173
seminar on, 176
shorthand (e-mail), 156, 157–158
signature files, 175, 176
spamming, avoiding, 175, 176
spelling, importance of, 176
subject line, importance of, 173, 175
symbols, avoiding, 175
targeting appropriate, 171
target market and, 169, 175
testing posting, 172
thread, staying on the, 174
topic, keeping on, 173, 176
Usenet newsgroups, 168, 171
newsletters
    affiliate programs and generic newslet-
        ters, 231
    launching your Web site with, 337
    permission marketing with, 59, 60
    viral marketing and, 49, 50

news releases, 270–277. See also e-mail;
        media relations
    attachments caution, 278
    benefits of, 273
    body of, 272
    city and date, 271
    close of, 272
    contact information in, 271
    daily newspapers for, 277
    deadlines, 277
    defined, 270
    distribution service for, 273–276
    download speeds and, 278
    editors and, 276–277
    e-mail news releases, 277–278
    e-zines for, 290
    follow up for, 277
    format of new release, 270–272
    header, 271
    headline, 271
    hypertext links in, 273
    interactive news releases, 273, 274
    journalists and, 270, 274, 277–278,
        281
    link strategy for, 273
    monthly magazines for, 277
    newsworthiness, 270, 272, 278–280
    Notice of Release, 270–271
    platform compatibility and, 278
    quotes from key individuals in, 272
    radio for, 277
    samples, 272, 274
    sending news releases, 273–276
    statistics in, 272
    subject line, importance of, 278
    timing guidelines, 277
    tips for, 276–277
    TV for, 277
    who, what, where, when, and why
        (five W's), 272
    writing a news release, 270–272
newsworthiness, media relations, 270,
        272, 278–280
new users and RSS, 310, 311, 314
New York Times, 132
next generation of Web metrics, 360–361

Nielsen Net Ratings, 250
"NOFRAMES" tags (between) keywords,
        70, 100–101
nomination for awards, 243–244
noncompeting sites for partnering, 333
Notice of Release, news releases,
        270–271
novelty items, URL exposure, 344
NPPS (net profit per sale), 359
number of visitors to site, 347

O
objectives, 3–10. See also planning your
        Web site
    advertising online, 3–4
    advertising online campaign, 249, 251
    affiliate programs and, 228, 230
    blogs and, 319
    brainstorming for, 5–6, 9
    brand awareness, creating and estab-
        lishing, 3, 5
    brochureware, unacceptability of, 2
    common objectives, 3–6
    company identity, creating and estab-
        lishing, 3, 5
    company or product information,
        providing, 3, 4–5
    contact information, providing, 4
    customer loyalty, encouraging, 6, 8–9
    customer service and product support,
        providing, 3, 4
    Frequently Asked Questions (FAQs), 4,
        5, 106, 159
    importance of, 1, 9
    keywords and, 79
    loyalty programs, creating, 6, 8–9
    offline promotion, 339–340
    permission marketing, 6, 8, 9, 18
    primary objectives, 3–6
    Really Simple Syndication (RSS) and,
        315
    repeat traffic and, 29, 36, 42
    repeat traffic generators, 6, 7
    sales force, leveraging, 6, 8
    search engine friendly design, 6–7
    secondary objectives, 6–9

selling products or services, 3, 4
stickiness elements, 6, 9, 36, 356
storyboarding and, 18
viral marketing elements, 4, 6, 7, 18
Office of the Privacy Commissioner of Canada, 60
offline magazines and e-zines, 284
offline promotion, 339–345. See also promoting your Web site
   advertising online and, 267
   advertising online vs., 13, 15, 249, 250
   answering telephone with URL, 340
   brainstorming, 339
   clothing, URL exposure, 343–344
   company literature, URL exposure, 340–341
   creativity for URL exposure, 344–345
   launching your Web site with, 337, 338
   novelty items, URL exposure, 344
   objectives of, 339–340
   private mailing lists and, 196
   products, URL exposure, 345
   promotional items, URL exposure, 341–343
   repeat traffic and, 31, 32
   resources for, 345
   traffic analysis and, 349
   uniform resource locator (URL) exposure for, 339–344
"101 Ways Insiders Club" Web site, vi–vii
OneStat.com, 85
online advertising. See advertising online
online copywriters for programming your Web site, 21
online promotion. See promoting your Web site
online publications. See e-zines
Open Directory, 113, 115, 119
opening ceremonies, launching your Web site, 337
optimization for search localization, 105–107, 123
opting-out
   e-zines, 292, 293
   permission marketing, 61, 202

opt-in lists, direct mail lists, 207, 209
opt-in marketing. See permission marketing
organic listings, search engines, 68
organizing keywords, 79–80
original message (including in reply), 154, 176
outbound links, 214–215, 226
Outlook (Microsoft), 141–142, 151
outsourcing
   banner ads, 253
   mail list management, 194–195
Overture, 107
ownership of e-mail addresses, maintaining, 194

P
page copy, keywords, 93–94, 106
pages of Web site
popularity of, traffic analysis, 347, 350
   submitting to search engines, 113–114, 126
page swapping, spamming, 95–96
page views, 252
paid inclusion, submissions to search engines, 117–118
paid inclusion account reports for monitoring results of search engines, 110
paragraph length
   e-mail, 152
   private mailing lists, 198
participating in Web rings, 298–299
partnering, 332–335
   banner ads for, 333–334
   call to action, 334
   contests for, 334
   co-operative banner ads, 333–334
   cross-promotion through banner ads, 333
   directories for, 334
   drop-down banner ads for, 333–334
   e-zines for, 335
   finding appropriate sites for, 332–333
   industry associations for, 334–335
   link strategy for, 334
   media relations for, 335

meta-indexes for, 334
noncompeting sites for, 333
permission marketing and, 333
resources for, 335
seminar on, 335
specials for, 334
targeted sites, RSS, 312, 313
target market and, 332–333
partnership programs. See affiliate
    programs
pass-it-on viral marketing, 48, 51–54
paths through Web site analysis for
    monitoring results of search
    engines, 109
patlive.com, 4
payments, prompt for affiliate programs,
    231
pay-per-click. See PPC
pay-to-play. See PPC
People, 284
permanent record, e-mail as, 153
permission marketing, 57–64. See also
    private mailing lists
  alliance partners, 63
  anti-spam legislation, 60–61, 195–196,
    202–204
  awards for, 246
  banner advertising vs., 187
  benefit in participating in, 57–58
  benefits of, selling, 62, 64
  call to action, 187
  Canadian legislation, 60, 196, 202–204
  contests for, 34–37, 58, 59–60
  Controlling the Assault of Non-
    Solicited Pornography and
    Marketing Act (CAN-SPAM),
    60–61, 202
  cooperative permission marketing, 63
  cost-effectiveness of, 58, 61, 64
  customer retention improved from, 187
  data mining, 63, 207
  e-club, integrating with, 58, 187, 195,
    196
  effectiveness of, 58, 61, 64
  incentive-based permission marketing,
    64

landing pages for, 305
launching your Web site for, 337
legislation regarding, 60–61, 195–196,
    202–204
link strategy for, 59
media relations for, 281
newsletters for, 59, 60
objective (planning your Web site), 6,
    8, 9, 18
opting-out, 61, 202
partnering and, 333
Personal Information Protection and
    Electronics Document Act
    (PIPEDA), 60, 202–204
personalization, 61–62, 188
privacy policy, displaying on Web site,
    22, 61, 188, 189
private mailing lists, 186–188
repeat traffic for, 29, 30, 31, 33, 36,
    38, 46
resources for, 64
response rate, 187
sales increased from, 185, 186–189
security policy, displaying on Web site,
    22, 61
selling the benefits, 62, 64
seminar on, 64
spamming and, 186
target market and, 57–58, 61, 62, 64
U.S. legislation, 60–61, 202
use of, 59–60
warranty registrations for, 59
Web site and, 187
per-name basis for costs, direct mail lists,
    209, 210
personal communication, immediate
    response from mobile marketing,
    330
Personal Information Protection and
    Electronics Document Act
    (PIPEDA), 60, 202–204
personalization
  autoresponders, 162, 164, 165
  direct mail lists, 208, 210
  e-mail, 151, 158, 159
  mobile marketing, 330

permission marketing, 61–62, 188
private mailing lists, 191, 192, 198, 199
    Really Simple Syndication (RSS), 312
personal quality of e-mail, 149
PIPEDA (Personal Information Protection and Electronics Document Act), 60, 202–204
placement of keywords, 85–94. See also fine-tuning keywords; keywords
    Alt tags, 69, 91, 102
    body text, 70, 92–94
    description meta-tags, 69, 88, 90
    domain names, 7, 69, 92, 123
    file names, 69, 92
    graphics caution, 93
    <H1/H1>, 93
    <HEAD/HEAD>, 86–87
    headers, 70
    home page, 94
    hypertext links (anchor text), 69, 91–92, 115
    <META-NAME="keywords/description/robots" CONTENT="...">, 86, 90, 101
    meta-tags and keywords, 69, 70, 74, 88–90, 115
    "NOFRAMES" tags (between) placement, 70, 100–101
    page copy, 93–94, 106
    ranking criteria of search engines and, 66, 114–115
    repeating keywords, avoiding, 86, 95
    same keywords for each page, mistake of using, 86
    title tags, 7, 69, 70, 74–75, 86–88, 106
placement of links, 214, 222, 223–224, 226, 231
planning your Web site, 1–19. See also objectives; products and services; programming your Web site; promoting your Web site; target markets
    competition analysis, 14–16
    download speeds, 15–16, 26, 27
    online vs. offline, 13, 15

resources for, 19
    reverse engineering competitor's Web site, 15–16
    seminar on, 19
    storyboarding, 16–18, 21
platforms (Mac, PC) and programming your Web site, 26
plural keywords, 80
Podcast Alley, 326
Podcast.com, 326
podcasting, 322–327
    audio content and, 322–323
    content for, 323, 324–325
    defined, 322–323
    directories of, 326
    editing tools, 323–324
    equipment needed for, 323
    keywords and naming files, 324
    mobile devices and, 322, 323
    MP3 files, 322, 323, 324
    music and, 325
    pass-it-on viral marketing, 53
    podcast sites, 326
    promoting, 325–327
    radio and, 324–325
    Really Simple Syndication (RSS) and, 323, 324, 326
    repeat traffic and, 45–46
    resources for, 327
    search engines and, 326–327
    "selling the sizzle," 326
    seminar on, 327
    signature files, 326
    submissions to search engines, 326–327
    training content, 324
    TV and, 324–325
    videocasting and, 323
    walking tours, self-guided, 324
    Web site and, 326
Podcast.net, 46, 326
point of contact (collecting information at), private mailing lists, 196
policies of e-zines, 290
popularity of keywords, 79
Position Pro, 124

postcards (virtual) for viral marketing, 7, 55–56
posting messages to
  newsgroups, 167, 168, 172–174
  publicly accessible mailing lists, 178
Postmaster Direct, 209
Post Master Direct Response, 180
potential vs. existing customers, 10
PPC (pay-per-click) strategy, 128–139.
    See also Google AdWords; search engines; Yahoo! Search Marketing
  Ad Group, designing, 131
  benefits of, 129
  bidding on keywords, 138
  brand awareness from, 129
  budget, maximizing, 138–139
  call to action, 138
  changes to programs, 130
  contextual advertising, 135–136
  cost per click (CPC), 137, 138, 139
  dayparting, 136–137
  defined, 128
  exposure, maximizing your, 137–138
  geographic modifiers, 107
  geo-targeting campaigns, 131, 136
  keywords, buying, 129, 133, 138–139
  keywords for, 137
  landing pages, 137–138
  resources for, 139
  seminar on, 139
  targeted leads from, 129–130, 131, 137
  tracking for monitoring search engine results, 110, 111
PR company for banner ads, 253, 257
preparation for traffic from awards, 242, 244–245
preparing directory submission, 119–120
presentation of landing pages, 306–307
press releases for launching your Web site, 337
preview capability, mail list software, 193
primary objectives, 3–6
prioritizing keywords, 79–80
privacy issue, private mailing lists, 189–190
privacy policy
  displaying on Web site, 22, 61, 188, 189

e-zines, 293
viral marketing, 51
private mailing lists, 185–205. See also e-mail; permission marketing
  anti-spam legislation, 60–61, 195–196, 202–204
  Application Service Provider (ASP) for, 192
  autoresponders, mail list software, 193
  benefits of, 185–186, 188–189
  Blacklists, monitoring, 202
  blind carbon copy (BBC) and, 152
  brand awareness from, 188–189
  brokers for sign-ups, 196
  call to action, 197, 198
  Canadian legislation, 60, 196, 202–204
  communication with, 197–199
  contacts, conserving, 188
  content, approval of, 195
  contract with outsource company, 194–195
  Controlling the Assault of Non-Solicited Pornography and Marketing Act (CAN-SPAM), 60–61, 202
  direct mail lists converted to, 210
  direct mail rental lists for sign-ups, 196
  e-club, integrating with, 58, 187, 195, 196
  e-mail addresses, managing, 191, 192, 193
  e-mail vs., 149
  e-zines for building, 292, 293, 294
  filtering, mail list software, 193
  formatting correspondence, 198
  "From" field, 195, 199
  HTML capability, mail list software, 191, 192
  importing existing database, 195–196
  legislation regarding, 60–61, 195–196, 202–204
  mail list software for managing, 191–194
  management of, 190–194
  message, size of, 201
  message editor, mail list software, 193

multi-threading sending, mail list software, 193
networking from, 188
offline promotion and, 196
opting-out, 61, 202
outsourcing mail list management, 194–195
ownership of e-mail addresses, maintaining, 194
paragraph length, 198
permission marketing, 186–188
Personal Information Protection and Electronics Document Act (PIPEDA), 60, 202–204
personalization, 191, 192, 198, 199
point of contact, collecting information at, 196
preview capability, mail list software, 193
privacy issue, 189–190
products and services promotion from, 189
promoting, 197
Really Simple Syndication (RSS) vs., 313
registering with publicly accessible mailing lists, 197
reporting, mail list software, 193–194
reputation building from, 188
resources for, 204–2051
response rate, 204
revenue from, 189
scannability, writing for, 198
scheduling, mail list software, 193
seminar on, 205
signature files, 196, 197, 201
spam checker, mail list software, 193
spam rating, 199–202
starting your own, 183, 195–197
subject line, importance of, 199
subscribes, 191, 192, 193, 196–197
technology (right) for, 190–194
tele-sales for sign-ups, 197
test accounts, 202
timing of communications, 195, 198
tracking, 191, 192, 193–194, 204

undeliverables, managing, 192, 194, 201
unsubscribes, 191, 192, 193, 198, 201
U.S. legislation, 60–61, 202
viral marketing for, 196–197, 198
Web site and, 196, 197
Web site integration, mail list software, 193
where we need to be, 190
private responses, newsgroups, 173, 174
product-or service-based viral marketing, 48, 54–56
products and services, 13–14. See also planning your Web site
affiliate programs and, 228
children-oriented Web site, 13
convenience importance to customers, 13
downloadable items, 14
importance of, 2, 13
online vs. offline, 13, 15
private mailing lists for promoting, 189
profiles of customers, 14
Really Simple Syndication (RSS) and, 315
service Web site, 14
software Web site, 13–14
storyboarding and, 18
testimonials, 14
travel agency Web site, 14
uniform resource locator (URL) exposure, 345
wish list service, 13
profile of visitors, developing, 348–350
profiles of customers, 14
profile-specific advertising, mobile marketing, 329
programming your Web site, 20–27. See also landing pages; planning your Web site; promoting your Web site
"404-File Not Found," 27, 104–105, 226, 349
Alt attributes, 25–26
autoplay sounds, minimizing, 22
background colors, 23, 104

background sounds, minimizing, 22
browsers and, 26
CAPS, avoiding, 23
colors, 23, 104
consistency of Web site, 21, 23, 25
contact information, including, 22
content, developing for each page, 22
content notes, 22
dead links, avoiding, 27
default colors for links, 23
download speeds, 15–16, 26, 27
font colors, 23
GPS coordinates, 107
graphics, 22, 25–26
home page, 27
"hot spots," 26, 105
image conveyed from Web site, 22–23
image maps, 26, 105, 113
internal search tool, 24–25
Internet marketers for, 21
link strategy for, 24, 26, 27, 115
navigation, ease of, 23–24, 26
online copywriters for, 21
platforms (Mac, PC) and, 26
privacy policy, including, 22, 61, 188, 189
readability of Web site, 23
resources for, 27
reviewing Web site, 27
scannability, writing for, 23
screen widths and resolutions of visitors, 26
scrolling marquee text, avoiding, 27
search engine friendly design, 21, 24, 26
search tool, internal, 24–25
security information, including, 22, 61
seminar on, 27
site maps, 24, 25, 27
size of text and readability, 23
sounds, minimizing, 22
storyboarding and, 16–18, 21
text, developing for each page, 21, 22–23
text notes, 22–23
thumbnail graphics, 26, 222, 223, 224

"Under Construction," avoiding, 22, 94, 122
visual notes, 26–27
widths of screens of visitors, 26
promoting
blogs, 320–321
e-zines, 293–294
podcasting, 325–327
private mailing lists, 197
Really Simple Syndication (RSS) content, 314
promoting your Web site, vi–vii. See also advertising online; affiliate programs; autoresponders; awards; blogs; direct mail lists; e-mail; e-zines; landing pages; launching your Web site; link strategy; media relations; meta-indexes; mobile marketing; newsgroups; offline promotion; partnering; permission marketing; planning your Web site; podcasting; PPC (pay-per-click); private mailing lists; programming your Web site; publicly accessible mailing lists; repeat traffic; RSS (Really Simple Syndication); search engines; signature files; submissions to search engines; traffic analysis; viral marketing ("word-of-mouse"); Web metrics; Web rings
promotional items, URL exposure, 341–343
promotions for repeat traffic, 33
prompt reply, e-mail, 159–160
proofreading directory submission, 122, 123
PRWeb, 276
publications, online. See e-zines
publicity. See media relations

publicly accessible mailing lists, 177–184. See also direct mail lists; e-mail
  advertising, rules about, 181, 182, 183
  advertising list, 183
  brevity of messages, 182
  bulk e-mail lists, avoiding, 159, 180
  call to action, 182, 184
  charter of, 183
  digest form, 181, 182
  effective messages, 181–183
  finding appropriate publicly accessible mailing lists, 179–181
  flames, 178
  Frequently Asked Questions (FAQs), 181, 183
  "gatekeeper," 178
  goals, setting, 182–183
  hierarchical organization of, 178
  lurking, 181
  meta-indexes for finding, 180
  moderated discussion lists, 178
  newsgroups for promoting, 183
  newsgroups vs., 178
  posting messages to, 178
  private mailing lists, registering with, 197
  renting lists, 180
  repeating postings, avoiding, 182
  resources for, 184
  response rate, tracking, 182–183
  rules, abiding by, 181
  seminar on, 184
  signature files, 181, 182, 183
  spamming, 180
  sponsorships, 183, 266
  starting your own, 183–184
  subject line, importance of, 181, 182
  subscribing to, 178, 181
  tag lines, 181, 182, 183
  targeting appropriate, 179–181
  target market and, 177–178
  testing posting, 182
  topic, keeping on, 182
  tracking response rate, 182–183
  types of, 178–179
  unmoderated discussion lists, 178–179
  viral marketing for, 184
  Web site and, 183, 184
public relations. See media relations
publisher (contacting), e-zines, 289
publishers, advertising networks, 263
purchasing
  affiliate software, 232–234
  banner ads, 261–262
  keywords, 129, 133, 138–139
software for traffic analysis, 353–354

Q
quotes from key individuals in news releases, 272

R
radio
  news releases and, 277
  podcasting and, 324–325
rankings of directories, 119
rankings of search engines. See also link popularity and search engine ranking
  affiliate programs and, 227, 232
  blogs, 319, 321
  checking keywords, 109–110
  criteria of search engines, 66, 69–71
  keywords and, 7, 66, 114–115
  monitoring results of search engines, 109–110
  Really Simple Syndication (RSS) and, 313
  submissions to search engines, 114–115, 117
rationale for encouraging repeat visits repeat traffic, 29
readability of
  banner ads, 256
  Web site, 23
Really Simple Syndication. See RSS
real-time statistics, affiliate software, 233–234

rec category of newsgroups (recreation topics), 170

reciprocal links, 216, 217, 221, 301

record keeping of
advertising online, 264
submissions to search engines, 123–124

referrals. See affiliate programs; viral marketing ("word-of-mouse")

refining searches, search engines, 238–239, 240

refresh meta-tags, 96, 104

registering private mailing lists, 197

registering with search engines, 116–117. See also submissions to search engines

relationship building
e-mail for, 149, 152
e-zines for, 291
media relations for, 269

remedies for spamming, 99

reminder services for repeat traffic, 43–45

renting direct mail lists, publicly accessible mailing lists, 180

repeating keywords, spamming, 86, 95

repeating postings (avoiding), publicly accessible mailing lists, 182

repeat traffic, 28–46. See also promoting your Web site
advice columns for, 45
autoresponders for, 46
banner ads for, 32
bookmarks for, 40
brand awareness from, 29, 35
bulletin boards for, 40
calendar of events for, 34, 58, 187
cartoons for, 42
company image and, 45
competitions for, 34–37
contests for, 34–37, 58, 59–60, 187
coupons for, 31–33, 58, 187
demographic information, 36, 348

discounts for, 31–33
discussion groups for, 40
employment opportunities for, 37
featured section for, 39
forums for, 40
free stuff for, 30–31, 32
games for, 43
gift registry for, 45
humor for, 42
jokes for, 42
legal issues and contests, 36
link strategy for, 30, 32, 33, 34, 35, 37–38, 39
MP3/podcasting for, 45–46
newsgroups for, 40
objectives (planning your Web site) and, 29, 36, 42
offline and online marketing, 31, 32
permission marketing opportunities from, 29, 30, 31, 33, 36, 38, 46
promotions for, 33
rationale for encouraging repeat visits, 29
reminder services for, 43–45
resources for, 46
RSS feeds for, 39, 46
sample giveaways, 31, 32
seminar on, 46
signature files, 31, 36, 41, 144–145
Site of the Day/Week (award) for, 41
specials for, 33, 58, 187
stickiness from, 6, 9, 36, 356
surveys for, 41
target market and, 29, 30, 34, 37, 38, 41, 42, 45
Thought of the Day for, 42
Tip of the Day/Week for, 38–39, 58, 187
trivia for, 42
uniform resource locator (URL) for, 31
update reminders for, 43
viral marketing opportunities from, 29, 31, 32, 33, 36, 42, 43
What's New page for, 30
winner of contest, announcing, 37

repeat traffic generators objective, 6, 7

repetition of advertising, success of advertising (e-zines), 289
Reply option, newsgroups, 174
reply tips, e-mail, 154, 159–160
reporting
    mail list software for, 193–194
    promptly for affiliate programs, 231
reporting-period statistic distribution (automatic), affiliate software, 234
reputable companies for direct mail lists, 207–208, 209–210
reputation building from
    blogs, 319
    e-zines, 290, 291
    newsgroups, 169
    private mailing lists, 188
    Really Simple Syndication (RSS), 313
research tool, search engines as, 65, 67, 215
reseller programs. See affiliate programs
responders. See autoresponders
response rate
    advertising online, 249
    e-mail, 154
    e-zines, 288
    permission marketing, 187
    private mailing lists, 204
    publicly accessible mailing lists, 182–183
    responses (library of) for e-mail, 159
    resubmitting to search engines and directories, 69, 126
return on investment (ROI), 107–108, 355, 360
revenue from
    private mailing lists, 189
    Really Simple Syndication (RSS), 313
reverse engineering of competitor's Web site, 15–16
reviewing Web site, 27
Revisit Meta-tags, 102
rich media

banner ads, rich media in, 248
    search engines and, 103–104
risk minimizing, landing pages, 304
robots meta-tag, 100
ROI (return on investment), 107–108, 355, 360
rotating banner ads, 255
RSS (Really Simple Syndication), 309–316
    benefits of, 313
    blogs, 320
    brand awareness increased from, 313
    browsers and, 314
    click-throughs, 313
    content for, 310–312, 314–315
    defined, 309–310
    delivery guaranteed from, 309, 313
    directories of, 314
    feeds for repeat traffic, 39, 46
    link strategy for, 312, 313
    new users and, 310, 311, 314
    objectives (planning your Web site) and, 315
    page on Web site for, 314
    partnering with targeted sites, 312, 313
    personalization, 312
    podcasting, 323, 324, 326
    private mailing list built from, 313
    products and services and, 315
    promoting RSS content, 314
    reputation building from, 313
    resources for, 316
    revenue increased from, 313
    RSS readers, 310
    search engines ranking and, 313
    "selling the sizzle," 314
    seminar on, 316
    signature files, 314
    subscribing instructions, 314
    target market and, 312, 315
    terms of use of content, 315
    timing of, 315
    tools for, 314
    trust, established from, 313
    viral marketing opportunities from, 314

XML file for, 310
RSSTop55 Best Blog Directory, 320
rules (abiding by)
    newsgroups, 171–172
    publicly accessible mailing lists, 181

S
sale (closing the), landing pages, 304,
    305
sales conversions, 357
sales force
    affiliate programs for expanding, 232
    leveraging sales force objective, 6, 8
sales generation objective, advertising
    online, 251
sales increased from
    mobile marketing, 330
    permission marketing, 185, 186–189
sales per visitor (SPV), 358
same keywords for each page, mistake
    of using, 86
sample giveaways for repeat traffic, 31,
    32
scannability, writing for
    autoresponders, 165
    direct mail lists, 210
    landing pages, 303
    newsgroups, 173
    private mailing lists, 198
    programming your Web site, 23
scheduling, mail list software, 193
sci category of newsgroups (science
    topics), 170
screen widths and resolutions of visi-
    tors, 26
scrolling banner ads, 255
scrolling marquee text, avoiding, 27
search engine friendly design
    objective (planning your Web site), 6–7
    programming your Web site, 21, 24,
    26
search engines, 65–111. See also fine-
    tuning keywords; keywords; link

popularity and search engine
    ranking; link strategy; meta-
    indexes; monitoring results of
    search engines; placement of
    keywords; PPC (pay-per-click);
    rankings of search engines;
    spamming; submissions to
    directories; submissions to
    search engines
    Advanced Search, 238–239
    advertising online with, 260
    banner ads on, 251, 260
    bots, 66–67, 101, 116, 117
    cascading style sheets (CSS), 102
    code (clean), importance of, 102
    consolidation in industry, 68
    custom error pages, 104–105
    DHTML drop-down menu caution,
    66–68, 102
    directories vs., 113, 115, 116, 119
    dynamic pages and special characters,
    103
    finding important search engines, 68
    Flash intros caution, 26, 68
    FOLLOW/NOFOLLOW, 101
    frames, 100, 113
    Help page, 238
    image maps, 26, 105, 113
    landing pages and, 304
    link strategy for, 67, 115, 219–220
    localization, optimization for, 105–107,
    123
    meta-indexes finding with, 237–238,
    240
    meta-indexes vs., 237
    meta-search engines, 67
    navigation techniques caution, 102
    optimization for search localization,
    105–107, 123
    organic listings, 68
    podcasting and, 326–327
    ranking criteria of, 66, 69–71
    refining searches, 238–239, 240
    research tool, search engines as, 65,
    67, 215

resources for, 110–111
Revisit Meta-tags, 102
rich media, 103–104
robots meta-tag, 100
searches, refining, 238–239, 240
Search Options, 238–239
seminar on, 111
special characters and dynamic pages, 103
spiders, 101, 113, 213, 353
splash pages, 103–104
tables, use of, 104
target market and, 68
technology sharing among, 67, 114
traffic analysis for search engines used, 351, 352, 353
"Under Construction," avoiding, 22, 94, 122
understanding search engines, 66–68
updating Web site and, 94
Web rings vs., 296, 298, 299
Search Engine Watch, 68, 115, 219
Search Engine World, 81, 125
Search Options, 238–239
search time, speeded up by Web rings, 299
search tool, internal, 24–25
secondary objectives, 6–9
security policy, displaying on Web site, 22, 61
segmenting your target market, 10–11
selling products or services objective, 3, 4
selling the benefits of permission marketing, 62, 64
"selling the sizzle," 187, 314, 326
seminars on
  advertising online, 267
  affiliate programs, 234
  autoresponders, 166
  blogs, 321
  direct mail lists, 211
  e-mail, 160
  e-zines, 294
landing pages, 308
link strategy, 226
media relations, 282
mobile marketing, 330
newsgroups, 176
partnering, 335
pay-per-click (PPC), 139
permission marketing, 64
planning your Web site, 19
podcasting, 327
private mailing lists, 205
programming your Web site, 27
publicly accessible mailing lists, 184
Really Simple Syndication (RSS), 316
repeat traffic, 46
search engines, 111
signature files, 147
submissions to search engines and directories, 127
traffic analysis, 354
viral marketing, 56
Web metrics, 362
Web rings, 301
sending news releases, 273–276
service Web site, 14
setting up blogs, 318–319
sharing of e-zines, 288, 292–293
Shockwave banner ads, 259
shorthand, e-mail, 156, 157–158
short messaging service (SMS), mobile marketing, 329
signature files, 140–147
  award announced in tag lines, 145
  benefits of, 143
  blogs, 321
  call to action, 144
  "Click here" on, 141
  company image from, 143
  company's exposure increased from, 143
  contact information in, 141, 143
  contest announced in tag lines, 145
  defined, 140
  developing your, 141–142

different groups, different signature files, 142
do's and dont's of, 142–143
electronic business card, 140–141
e-mail, 140–141, 154–155
event announced in tag lines, 145
examples of, 145–146
free stuff in tag lines, 145
graphics caution, 142–143, 145–146
http:// before www in, 141
hypertext links in, 141
launching your Web site with, 337
length of, 142, 143
line length, 142
Microsoft Outlook and, 141–142
netiquette and, 143, 145
newsgroups, 175, 176
podcasting, 326
private mailing lists, 196, 197, 201
publicly accessible mailing lists, 181, 182, 183
Really Simple Syndication (RSS), 314
repeat traffic, 31, 36, 41
reputation of company enhanced from, 143
resources for, 147
seminar on, 147
sigvertising, 144
special offers in tag lines, 144
tag lines in, 141, 143, 144–145
testing signature files, 143
text file (.txt), 141
uniform resource locator (URL) in, 141
word processor for developing, 141
signup (automated), affiliate software, 233
sigvertising, 144
Singing Fish, 326–327
single-access pages, traffic analysis, 352
singular keywords, 80
site maps, 24, 25, 27
Site of the Day/Week (award) for repeat traffic, 41
size considerations
autoresponders, message, 164, 165
banner ads, 253, 254, 256
e-mail, message, 152, 159
e-zines, 292
newsgroups, message, 173, 176
private mailing lists, message, 198, 201
publicly accessible mailing lists, message, 182
text and readability, Web site, 23
small utility programs for pass-it-on viral marketing, 52
SMS (short messaging service), mobile marketing, 329
snail mail vs. e-mail, 149, 186
soc category of newsgroups (social issues topics), 170
software for
affiliate programs, 232–234
blogs, 319
traffic analysis, 348, 353–354
software Web site, 13–14
sounds (minimizing), programming your Web site, 22
Southern Living, 284
spam checker, mail list software, 193
spamlaws.com, 61
spamming, 94–99. See also search engines
acceptable practices of search engines, 97–98
automated submissions, 98, 117–118
avoiding, guidelines, 94–97
background color and, 200
Blacklists, monitoring, 202
blind carbon copy (BBC) and, 152
CAPS, 200
cloaking, 96, 98
color discrimination and, 200
computer programs used for submissions, 98
content duplication, 96, 98
cyber-squatting, 97
defined, 8
domain spam (mirror sites), 96
doorway pages, 97, 99

duplicating Web pages, 96, 98
e-zines, 293, 294
fonts (large) and, 200
hidden text and links, 95, 98
HTML issues, 200
hypertext links in, 200
jamming keywords ("tiny text"), 95
keyword stacking, 95, 98
keyword stuffing, 95, 98
link schemes, 98
links farms, 97
message, spam words in, 200–201
misleading title changes, 95
newsgroups, 175, 176
page swapping, 95–96
permission marketing and, 186
publicly accessible mailing lists, 180
quality guidelines, 98–99
refresh meta-tags, 96, 104
remedies for, 99
repeating keywords, 86, 95
subject line, spam words in, 199–200
title changes (misleading), 95
spam rating, private mailing lists,
        199–202
"speaking to" target market
    blogs for, 319
    landing pages for, 303
special characters and dynamic pages,
        search engines, 103
special guests for launching your Web
        site, 337
special offers in tag lines, 144
specials for
    partnering, 334
    repeat traffic, 33, 58, 187
specific topics of meta-indexes, 236–237
spelling, importance of
    autoresponders, 165
    direct mail lists, 210
    e-mail, 152, 153, 159
    newsgroups, 176
spiders, 101, 113, 213, 353
splash pages and search engines, 103–104

sponsoring opportunities, meta-indexes,
        240
sponsorships
    advertising online, 264–265, 266
    banner ads, 265, 266
    mobile marketing messages, 330
    publicly accessible mailing lists, 183,
        266
Sports Illustrated, 284
SPV (sales per visitor), 358
Squaw Valley, 280
starting your own
    e-zine, 291–294
    private mailing lists, 183, 195–197
    publicly accessible mailing lists, 183–184
static banner ads, 253, 254
Station.com, 43
statistics in news releases, 272
stickiness, 6, 9, 36, 356
stop words, keywords, 81–84
storyboarding
    objectives, 18
    planning your Web site, 16–18, 21
    products and services, 18
    programming your Web site, 16–18, 21
    target market and, 18
subcategories
    submissions to directories, 119, 120
    Web rings, 297
subject line, importance of
    autoresponders, 165
    direct mail lists, 210
    e-mail, 150–151
    newsgroups, 173, 175
    news releases, 278
    private mailing lists, 199
    publicly accessible mailing lists, 181,
        182
    spam words in, 199–200
submissions for awards, 244–245
submissions to directories, 118–123. See
        also search engines; submissions
        to search engines

administrator's review of, 122
call to action in descriptions, 121
CAPS, avoiding, 123
categories, selecting, 113, 118–119, 120, 121
changing listing, 122
completing Web site before submitting, 125
descriptions, importance of, 121, 122–123
directories vs. search engines, 113, 115, 116, 119
expedited reviews, 115–116
fees for, 115–116
finding directories for, 126
forms, filling out all fields, 113, 119–120, 121–122
guidelines for, 119, 121–122, 123, 126
HTML, validating, 125
preparing directory submission, 119–120
proofreading submission, 122, 123
ranking and, 119
resources for, 127
resubmitting to, 126
seminar on, 127
subcategories, selecting, 119, 120
titles, importance of, 121, 123
validating Web site before submitting, 125
submissions to search engines, 112–127. See also search engines; submissions to directories
"Add your URL," 113
automated submissions, avoiding, 98, 117–118
completing Web site before submitting, 125
differences among search engines, 112–113, 115, 125
finding search engines for, 126
free submissions, 117
guidelines for, 117, 126
home page, importance of, 117
HTML, validating, 125
international search engines, 118

link popularity and ranking, 70–71, 115
multiple listings, 126
netiquette, abiding by, 126
pages of Web site, submitting, 113–114, 126
paid inclusion, 117–118
podcasts, 326–327
ranking criteria and, 114–115, 117
record keeping of, 123–124
registering with search engines, 116–117
resources for, 127
resubmitting to, 69, 126
search engines vs. directories, 113, 115, 116, 119
seminar on, 127
technology sharing among search engines, 67, 114
tools for, effective use of, 124–125
uniform resource locator (URL) for, 67, 113, 116, 126
validating Web site before submitting, 125
verifying inclusion, 118
submission to meta-indexes, 236
SubmitPlus, 125
subscribed content, mobile marketing, 329
subscribers to
e-zines, 284, 285, 286, 289
private mailing lists, 191, 192, 193, 196–197
publicly accessible mailing lists, 178, 181
subscribing instructions
e-zines, 292, 293, 294
Really Simple Syndication (RSS), 314
success, measuring with Web metrics, 356–358
SuperPages.com, 107
surveys for
building direct mail lists, 207
repeat traffic, 41
SusanSweeney.com, vii, 364

Susan Sweeney's Internet Marketing Mail List, vii, 50
Sweeney, Susan, vii, 363–364
Sweepstakes Wire, The, 36
symbols (avoiding), newsgroups, 175
Sympatico.ca, 135
syndicating content. See RSS (Really Simple Syndication)

T

tables and search engines, 104
Tag Image File Format (TIFF), 281
tag lines
    HTML, link strategy, 223, 224
    meta-indexes, 236, 240
    publicly accessible mailing lists, 181, 182, 183
    signature files, 141, 143, 144–145
talk category of newsgroups (conversation), 170
targeted leads from PPC, 129–130, 131, 137
targeting appropriate
    direct mail lists, 207–208
    newsgroups, 171
    publicly accessible mailing lists, 179–181
target markets, 10–12. See also planning your Web site
    advertising online, 262–263, 266
    affiliate programs, 228, 232
    autoresponders, 163, 165
    banner ads, 249, 251
    blogs, 319, 320
    business-oriented Web site, 11, 12
    children-oriented Web site, 11
    content of Web site and, 11
    direct mail lists, 207
    existing vs. potential customers, 10
    expectations of target market, determining, 10, 11, 13
    e-zines, 285, 286, 287, 288, 290
    graphics and, 11, 12
    importance of, 2, 10

landing pages, 303, 305
launching your Web site, 337
meta-indexes, 240
mobile marketing, 330
multimedia effects and, 12
needs of target market, determining, 10, 11
newsgroups, 169, 175
partnering, 332–333
permission marketing, 57–58, 61, 62, 64
potential vs. existing customers, 10
publicly accessible mailing lists, 177–178
Really Simple Syndication (RSS), 312, 315
repeat traffic, 29, 30, 34, 37, 38, 41, 42, 45
search engines, 68
segmenting your target market, 10–11
storyboarding and, 18
technology of, 11–12
tone of Web site and, 11
traffic analysis, 347, 348, 353
viral marketing, 52, 53
wants of target market, determining, 10, 11
Web rings, 298, 301
"WOW" factor, 10, 18
technology of target market, 11–12
technology (right) for private mailing lists, 190–194
technology sharing among search engines, 67, 114
tele-sales for sign-ups, private mailing lists, 197
"Tell a Friend" button, 7, 31, 33, 36, 43, 48, 49, 51
Teoma, 67, 78, 79, 112–113
terms of use of content, RSS, 315
test accounts, private mailing lists, 202
testimonials, 14
testing
    banner ads, 257

classified ads, 264
e-zines, 293
landing pages, 304, 305–308
links, 215, 226
newsgroups postings, 172
publicly accessible mailing lists
        postings, 182
signature files, 143
text, developing for each Web page, 21,
        22–23
text file (.txt), signature files, 141
text notes, 22–23
text vs. HTML e-mail, 154
Thought of the Day for repeat traffic,
        42
thread (staying on the), newsgroups, 174
thumbnail graphics, 26, 222, 223, 224
TIFF (Tag Image File Format), 281
Tile.net, 179, 181
Time, 284
timeliness of
        autoresponders, 149, 162
        banner ads, developing, 250
        e-mail, 148, 149
        e-zines ads, 287–288
        mobile marketing, 330
timing of
        news releases, 277
        private mailing lists communication,
                195, 198
        Really Simple Syndication (RSS), 315
        release, control (none) over, media
                relations, 270
        Web site access, 347, 348–349
"tiny text" (jamming keywords), 95
Tip of the Day/Week for repeat traffic,
        38–39, 58, 187
title changes (misleading), spamming,
        95
titles and submissions to directories,
        121, 123
title tags, keywords, 7, 69, 70, 74–75,
        86–88, 106

"To" headings (personalization) e-mail,
        151
tone of
        autoresponders message, 165
        e-mail, 152
        Web site, 11
tools for
        link strategy, 215, 216–217, 218–219
        Really Simple Syndication (RSS), 314
        submissions to search engines, 124–125
Topica, 179, 181
topic (keeping on)
        newsgroups, 173, 176
        publicly accessible mailing lists, 182
topic lists, direct mail lists, 207–208
tracking. See also traffic analysis
        affiliate software software, automated
                tracking, 233
        autoresponders reports, 164
        direct mail lists, 207, 208, 210
        e-zines, 289, 290
        pay-per-click (PPC), search engine
                results, 110, 111
        private mailing lists, 191, 192,
                193–194, 204
        publicly accessible mailing lists, re-
                sponses, 182–183
trading
        banner ads, 263–264
        links, 225–226, 296
traffic analysis, 346–354. See also
                tracking
        advertisements, popularity of, 348
        advertising online, success of, 353
        analyzing log files with software, 348,
                353–354
        banner ads, 250, 350–351, 353
        browsers used, 347, 349, 350
        demographic information, 63, 348
        "flight effect," 214, 352
        geographical location of visitors, 349
        how visitors find your Web site,
                350–351
        IP addresses of visitors, 347, 349
        ISPs and, 354

keywords, 72, 75, 107–108, 348, 351–352

log files for, 347–348, 348–349, 350, 353

number of visitors to site, 347

offline advertising and, 349

pages of Web site, popularity of, 347, 350

profile of visitors, developing, 348–350

purchasing software for, 353–354

resources for, 354

search engines results, 72, 75, 107–108

search engines used, 351, 352, 353

seminar on, 354

single-access pages, 352

software for, 348, 353–354

spiders, when viewing site, 353

target market and, 347, 348, 353

timing of Web site access, 347, 348–349

updating site and, 349

viral marketing, 54

Web rings, 299, 300

where visitors go when they leave your Web site, 352

traffic generation objective, advertising online, 251

training content, podcasting, 324

travel agency Web site, 14

Travel Industry Association of America, 38

Travelocity, 5

Trip.com, 266

trivia for repeat traffic, 42

trust, established from
e-zines, 291
landing pages, 304
Really Simple Syndication (RSS), 313

TV
news releases and, 277
podcasting and, 324–325

two-tier commission (affiliate) program, 228

two-way dialogue from mobile marketing, 330

TypePad, 318

U

undeliverables (managing), private mailing lists, 192, 194, 201

"Under Construction," avoiding, 22, 94, 122

Unicast banner ads, 260

uniform resource locators. See URLs

unmoderated discussion lists, 178–179

unsolicited e-mail. See spamming

unsubscribes, private mailing lists, 191, 192, 193, 198, 201

update reminders for repeat traffic, 43

updating
blogs, 319, 320
Web site and link strategy, 226
Web site and search engines, 94
Web site and traffic analysis, 349

urgency, creating sense of, landing pages, 304

URLs (uniform resource locators)
e-mail, 152–153
launching your Web site, 338
link strategy, 216–217, 218
offline promotion, 339–344
repeat traffic, 31
signature files, 141
submissions to search engines, 67, 113, 116, 126

U.S.
Canadian spellings (keywords) vs., 81
legislation, anti-spam, 60–61, 202

Usenet newsgroups, 168, 171

V

validating Web site before submitting to search engines and directories, 125

"value-added," landing pages, 303

value-added services, affiliate programs, 231

ValueClick, 262, 263

variable-payment options, affiliate software, 234

Verb Interactive, 153–154, 360, 363–364

verifying inclusion in search engines, 118

videocasting and podcasting, 323

video greetings for launching your Web site, 337

videos (fun) for pass-it-on viral marketing, 53

viral marketing ("word-of-mouse"), 47–56
   articles for pass-it-on viral marketing, 53
   attachments, avoiding, 51
   audiozines for pass-it-on viral marketing, 52, 53
   awards for, 246
   Blue Mountain, 54–55
   button, attention-grabbing, 50, 51
   call to action, 49
   checklists for pass-it-on viral marketing, 53
   cost-effectiveness of, 47
   E-books for pass-it-on viral marketing, 52
   e-cards for, 54–56
   e-zines for, 288, 292–293, 294
   games for pass-it-on viral marketing, 53
   graphics included in, 54
   Hotmail.com, 54
   incentives for, 51
   instructions on how to participate in, 51
   landing pages for, 305
   launching your Web site for, 337
   leveraging, 51
   link button placement, importance of, 49, 50, 51
   media relations for, 281
   MP3/podcasts for pass-it-on viral marketing, 53
   newsletters and, 49, 50
   objective (planning your Web site), 4, 6, 7, 18
   pass-it-on viral marketing, 48, 51–54
   postcards (virtual) for, 7, 55–56
   privacy policy importance, 51
   private mailing lists, 196–197, 198
   product-or service-based viral marketing, 48, 54–56
   publicly accessible mailing lists, 184
   Really Simple Syndication (RSS) for, 314
   repeat traffic for, 29, 31, 32, 33, 36, 42, 43
   resources for, 56
   seminar on, 56
   small utility programs for pass-it-on viral marketing, 52
   target market and, 52, 53
   "Tell a Friend" button, 7, 31, 33, 36, 43, 48, 49, 51
   traffic analysis of, 54
   videos (fun) for pass-it-on viral marketing, 53
   word-of-mouth viral marketing, 48–51

virtual communities. See newsgroups

virtual launch of Web site. See launching your Web site

viruses, e-mail, 155–156

Visio (Microsoft), 18

VisitNC.com, 236

visual notes, 26–27

W

W3C HTML Validation Service, 125

walking tours (self-guided), podcasting, 324

wants of target market, determining, 10, 11

warranty registrations for permission marketing, 59

WCI, 38–39

WDG HTML Validator, 125

Web address. See URLs (uniform resource locators)

Web-based e-zines, 284, 285

Webby Awards, The, 243
Web Developer's Virtual Library, 89
Web host autoresponders, 163
Webjacket.com, 343
Web metrics, 355–362
  A/B testing, 306, 360, 361
  Click Tracks, 360–361
  conversion ratio (CR), 357, 358
  cost per sale (CPS), 359
  cost per visitor (CPV), 359
  "exit" pages, identifying, 356
  gross profit, 359
  improving success, methods for, 356–357
  measuring success, 356–358
  net profit per sale (NPPS), 359
  next generation, 360–361
  resources for, 361–362
  return on investment (ROI), 107–108, 355, 360
  sales conversions, 357
  sales per visitor (SPV), 358
  seminar on, 362
  stickiness, 356
  success, measuring, 356–358
Web Position, 94, 109, 124
WebPositionGold, 98, 227, 228, 229
WebRing, 296, 298, 299
Web rings, 295–301
  banner ads on, 301
  benefits of, 299–300
  business reluctance to participate in, 300
  categories of, 296–297
  competition, linking to, 300
  costs, 299
  coupons, exchanging, 301
  defined, 223, 295, 296–298
  directories vs., 296
  ease of use, 299
  finding appropriate Web rings, 298
  growth of, 298, 300
  link strategy for, 223, 301
  link trading, 296
  navigating, 297, 298, 299

  participating in Web rings, 298–299
  reciprocal links, 301
  resources for, 301
  search engines vs., 296, 298, 299
  search time, speeded up by, 299
  seminar on, 301
  subcategories, 297
  target market and, 298, 301
  traffic analysis, 299, 300
Web sites and, 299–300
Web site integration, mail list software, 193
Web sites. See also promoting your Web site
  asking for links on, 222
  autoresponders vs., 163
  banner ads on, 251
  blogs and, 319, 321
  e-zines promoting on, 294
  permission marketing from, 187
  podcasting and, 326
  private mailing lists and, 196, 197
  publicly accessible mailing lists and, 183, 184
  Web rings and, 299–300
WebTrends, 108, 349, 351, 352
What's New page for repeat traffic, 30
"What's New" sites for launching your Web site, 337
What's New Web sites, 243
where visitors go when they leave your Web site, 352
where we need to be, private mailing lists, 190
who, what, where, when, and why (five W's), 272
widths of screens of visitors, 26
winner of contest, announcing, 37
Winning Ways Online Sweeps, 37
wish list service, 13
"word-of-mouse." See viral marketing
word-of-mouth viral marketing, 48–51
WordPress, 319

word processor for developing signature files, 141
working with company, direct mail lists, 208–209
World of WebRings, 296, 298, 299
"WOW" factor, 10, 18
writing a news release, 270–272
writing for scannability. See scannability, writing for

X
Xanga, 318
XML file for RSS, 310

Y
Yahoo!
Advanced Search, 238–239
brand awareness, 5
fee for expedited review, 116
importance of, 68
instant messaging, 329
Podcasts, 326

Publisher's Guide to RSS, 314, 315
Search, 112–113, 214
submissions to, 113, 122–123
title tags and, 87
"Under Construction," avoiding, 122
Yahoo! Search Marketing, 132–135. See also PPC (pay-per-click) strategy
ads, developing, 133–134
budget importance, 133
contextual advertising, 136
cost per click (CPC), 134
description, creating, 134
headline, creating, 134
keywords for, 133, 134
partners (network), 134–135
pay-per-click (PPC), 129
pay-to-play, 110, 111
sponsored listings, 132–133
"squatters," 133
success of, 129, 132
Support Center, 134

Reader Feedback Sheet

Your comments and suggestions are very important in shaping future publications. Please e-mail us at *moreinfo@maxpress.com* or photocopy this page, jot down your thoughts, and fax it to (850) 934-9981 or mail it to:

Maximum Press
Attn: Jim Hoskins
605 Silverthorn Road
Gulf Breeze, FL 32561

**IBM Software for
e-business on demand**
by Douglas Spencer
384 pages
$49.95
ISBN: 1-931644-17-9

**Building an On
Demand Computing
Environment with IBM**
by Jim Hoskins
152 pages
$39.95
ISBN: 1-931644-11-X

**IBM On Demand
Technology for the
Growing Business**
by Jim Hoskins
96 pages
$29.95
ISBN: 1-931644-32-2

**Exploring IBM Server
& Storage Technology,
Sixth Edition**
by Jim Hoskins
288 pages
$54.95
ISBN: 1-885068-28-4

**Building on Your
OS/400 Investment**
by Jim Hoskins
120 pages
$29.95
ISBN: 1-931644-09-8

**Building on Your AIX
Investment**
by Jim Hoskins
104 pages
$29.95
ISBN: 1-931644-08-X

**Conquering Information
Chaos in the Growing
Business**
by Jim Hoskins
68 pages
$29.95
ISBN: 1-931644-33-0

**Exploring IBM
@server pSeries,
Twelfth Edition**
by Jim Hoskins
and Robert Bluethman
352 pages
$54.95
ISBN: 1-931644-04-7

To purchase a Maximum Press book, visit your local bookstore
or call 1-800-989-6733 (US/Canada) or 1-850-934-4583 (International)
online ordering available at *www.maxpress.com*

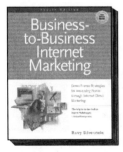